AMERICAN MONSTER

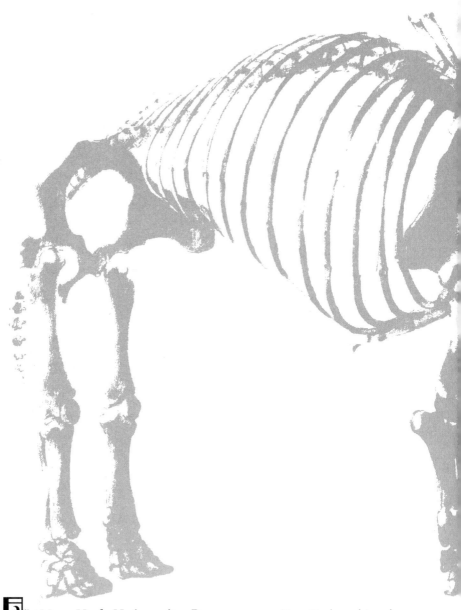

New York University Press • *New York and London*

AMERICAN MONSTER

HOW · THE · NATION'S · FIRST
PREHISTORIC · CREATURE
BECAME · A · SYMBOL · OF
NATIONAL · IDENTITY

PAUL SEMONIN

NEW YORK UNIVERSITY PRESS
New York and London

© 2000 by New York University
All rights reserved

Library of Congress Cataloging-in-Publication Data
Semonin, Paul, 1936–
American monster : how the nation's first prehistoric creature
became a symbol of national identity / Paul Semonin.
p.   cm.
Includes bibliographical references and index.
ISBN 0-8147-8120-9 (cloth : alk. paper)
1. Mastodon—United States. 2. Paleontology—Social aspects—United
States—History—18th century. 3. National characteristics, American.
I. Title.
QE882.U7 .S35 2000
306.4'5—dc21   00-009020

New York University Press books are printed on acid-free paper,
and their binding materials are chosen for strength and durability.

Manufactured in the United States of America

10 9 8 7 6 5 4 3 2 1

For Anuncia and Tavi

Contents

Illustrations

Preface

Over the years, I have had the opportunity to describe this project many times to friends and acquaintances. Nearly always I began with the discovery of an enormous tooth on the banks of the Hudson River in the early eighteenth century, which Puritan clergymen believed was scientific proof of the existence of human giants mentioned in the Bible. As I elaborated on the cultural world that gave birth to the American monster, people would inevitably ask, "Is this a novel? Is this fiction or nonfiction?" At first, I was quick to assure everyone the mastodon story was real history, not a fictional account of the discovery of prehistoric creatures in the early American republic. But because people kept asking, I realized the question touched on something that was at the heart of my book—the existence of myth and metaphor in the language of natural history.

In effect, people saw immediately that natural history did not function as a transparent medium for the discovery of scientific truth but instead contained many elements of fiction, despite being in the system of thought that we call science. Indeed, even before they had read a page of my book, I had achieved my purpose, because they saw the way that naturalism functioned as an invisible refracting lens in American culture. When I realized this, I drew a certain satisfaction in answering this question differently, pointing up instead the thin line between fact and fiction and calling attention to the important role of myth and metaphor in framing our ideas of naturalistic knowledge.

Every scientific theory has its metaphorical meaning, from the "survival of the fittest" to the "big bang theory," and we need to be more aware of how these metaphors are constructed, rather than deciphering the difference between fact and fiction—of rooting out the mythology from pure scientific thought. Myths and metaphors are—essential thought patterns expressing our most basic values and beliefs. In fact, naturalism is a kind of myth itself, and as such, it helps channel our thoughts toward a belief in literal truth—a value-free mind-set that is a dangerous illusion when it comes to understanding our use of knowledge and the motives for our actions.

Above all, history and science provide us with key elements of our identity as individuals and a society. Like other forms of storytelling, they use myth and metaphor to make events intelligible and to give meaning to our lives, often going far beyond the modern-day notion of an objective account of what happened to become a part of the literary and visual arts like any other creative cultural expression. For this reason, I encourage you to read this book not to find the factual truth of the mastodon story but, rather, to experience the cultural complexity of the symbols we use every day to define our relationship to the natural world and to other inhabitants on the planet. In the end, our most challenging task will be to create a new symbolic language that transforms our view of prehistoric nature as a violent place dominated by ferocious carnivores into something that celebrates the dignity and interdependence of all forms of life in the universe.

In the modern world, history itself has become a problematic medium, since the tradition of the new tends to devalue the old, encouraging us to think of our ancestors as inferior beings who lived their lives without flush toilets and television, not to mention numerous other conveniences of industrial society. As a result, we must overcome certain prejudices to understand their experiences and the importance of their values and beliefs today. As David Lowenthal observed, "The past is a foreign country," a view that reflects our alienation from the past as well as the cultural changes that have taken place over time. In such time travel, the historian serves as a kind of translator and guide helping readers understand the language of our ancestors, who often seem to be speaking to us in a foreign dialect instead of an easily intelligible modern language.

Accordingly, I have chosen to leave all quotations in their original form with regard to spelling and syntax. Reading eighteenth-century English may prove challenging at times, but I think it helps give authenticity to the principal actors' ideas and to remind us of the root meanings of the words we use every day. In addition, these original figures of speech give us valuable clues to the hidden assumptions associated with similar cultural expressions in our own language and culture. In an effort to reduce academic clutter, I have eliminated repeated footnote references from the same document when these are short texts like letters or brief articles and the location of the cited material is clearly indicated in my narrative.

This book has its own history, which may help many readers understand its interdisciplinary character and emphasis on the fusion of natural history and nationalism in early American culture. I first encountered the tooth of the American *incognitum* in a late-eighteenth-century broadside advertising the contents of the American Museum in New York City, an institution that fifty years later became famous as Barnum's American Museum. At the time, I was interested in understanding the role of natural history in the early career of the legendary showman P. T. Barnum, who made his first million as the proprietor of this museum of curiosities. I thought the tooth of the American *incognitum* would make an excellent case study of a museum curiosity and offer insights into the cultural world that contributed to Barnum's success. However, in a few weeks, the mastodon story mushroomed into something far more elaborate than the chapter I had envisioned in my doctoral dissertation on the prehistory of Barnum's American Museum.

Thanks to the indulgence of my dissertation committee, who allowed me to divert my energies into sketching out the tale of the tooth, I was able to write an early draft of the mastodon's story. I am especially thankful to the members of my dissertation committee in the Department of History at the University of Oregon—Daniel Pope, Matt Dennis, Howard Brick, and Ken Calhoon—for allowing me to digress from the already crooked path of my doctoral research to pursue the American monster through the cultural thickets of the early republic. Without their initial encouragement and subsequent support, I would never have discovered the link between patriotism and prehistoric nature in the new American nation.

Near the end of his life, after publishing many volumes of his famous *Histoire naturelle*, the French naturalist Buffon told an interviewer, "I learn to write every day." This has been very true for me when writing this book, and my readers have been an essential part of the learning process, enabling the book to be much better than I ever imagined at the beginning. I owe a special debt of gratitude to Kay Kruger-Hickman, whose inspired editing provided a rare combination of talents—everything from an uncanny ability to spot misplaced modifiers to the worldly knowledge of an intellectually engaged scholar deeply concerned with the cultural issues at the heart of the book. Near its completion, Allen Carey-Webb read the entire manuscript and gave me the benefit of a postmodern professor's critique of the text, greatly adding to the depth of analysis and the clarity of my ideas. From its inception, George Gessert quietly nurtured the cutting-edge ideas in the manuscript, encouraging me to look more closely at the shifting boundary between nature and culture. David Peterson del Mar, who witnessed the birth of this project in the office we shared as graduate students at the University of Oregon, offered invaluable emotional support and intellectual companionship as we both looked at different manifestations of violence in American culture.

Numerous other people read portions of the manuscript and gave encouragement along the way, ranging from helpful hints about my writing quirks to cutting the grass at crunch time, when I could no longer see the forest for the trees. Among those friends who endured many hours of mastodon talk and gave me valuable feedback on the project were John and Catherine Smith, Don Cooke, Judy and Tim Volem, Martha Walters, Stephen Vonder Haar, Donna Lesh, Stephanie Wood, Bob Haskett, Don Janzen, Bill Christian, Gary Carson, and Milly Henry. My special thanks go to Jim and Mary Ottaway whose hospitality and insightful comments made my visits to mastodon country in the Hudson River valley memorable experiences. I am also grateful to Lisa Livelybrooks for spotting the mammoth tooth and Catherine Smith for delivering the goods at a critical juncture near the end of the writing process when I was a bit delirious and had begun to doubt that such bones actually existed.

Every author should have the privilege of working with a sympathetic and responsive editor like Niko Pfund. From the moment the proposal first crossed his desk, he enthusiastically supported this project, then patiently nursed the manuscript through its long gestation, and served as midwife at the monster's birth. The scholars and authors whose work has supplied essential nutrients for the great beast's appetite are too numerous to name, but I hope they have received adequate credit in the footnotes and bibliography accompanying this text. I also would like to pay my respects to the late Barbara Tuchman whose book of essays *Practicing History* was a constant companion throughout the writing of this book and provided many valuable tips on techniques for writing historical narrative.

No one has provided more substantive support on all levels for this project than Anuncia Escala, whose candor and passion kept the whole family on an even keel during our long voyage through the antediluvian world. Her advice early on was "Don't ramble—get to the point," and that remark proved to be a beacon in the night for this inveterate rambler. I wish to express my gratitude and love by dedicating this book to her and to our son Tavi, whose generation will have the difficult task of creating a new cosmology for the industrial world in an era when the myth of wild nature itself is threatened with extinction.

Introduction

Patriotism and Prehistoric Nature

Mild is my behemoth, though large his frame;
Smooth is his temper, and repress'd his flame,
While unprovoked. This native of the flood
Lifts his broad foot, and puts ashore for food;
Earth sinks beneath him, as he moves along
To seek the herds, and mingle with the throng.

—Edward Young, 1719

IMAGINE THE MASSIVE jaws of the mastodon, a herbivorous, elephant-like creature, crushing deer and elk in its mouth and gnashing
their flesh and bones between monstrous grinders (figure 1). You may
find it difficult to envision this extinct, leaf-eating animal as a terrifying prehistoric monster, as elephants today are regarded with affection.
They are lovable animals with Disneyesque names, and mastodons
have become harmless relics in natural history museums ruled by ferocious *Jurassic Park* dinosaurs. But more than two hundred years ago
when the American nation was founded, the mastodon was an unknown creature whose awesome appetite was the subject of serious debate. For the founding fathers, the mastodon was the dinosaur of the
early American republic, the first large mammal to be officially declared
extinct and, in effect, the nation's first prehistoric monster. Even
though this image of the mastodon as a carnivore defies our present
knowledge of its diet and demeanor, many citizens of the new republic
viewed the majestic Ice Age creature in this way when its skeleton was
finally dug up at the beginning of the nineteenth century.

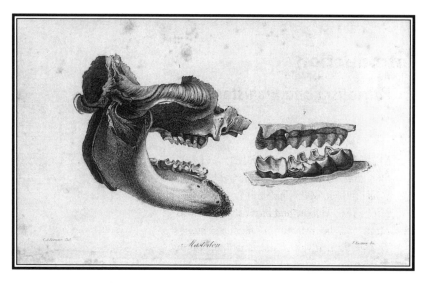

FIGURE 1. Jaws of the mastodon in Peale's Philadelphia Museum from John Godman's *American Natural History*, 1826. Courtesy Bancroft Library, University of California at Berkeley.

In the eighteenth century, when dinosaurs had not yet been discovered and few people were even aware of the existence of prehistoric nature, the fossil remains of the mastodon were an unsolved mystery. No one knew the identity of the animal to whom the gigantic bones belonged, so they called the mysterious creature the American *incognitum*, employing the Latin term for the unknown. While this Latin name seems an enigmatic anachronism to the modern eye, the term was nearly a household word in the early republic, at least among the American gentry who collected the mastodon's bones and speculated about its identity. In their eyes, the American *incognitum* had become a symbol of national identity and the central character in a great natural mystery involving the disappearance of one of God's creatures.

The fist-size teeth and gigantic jawbones of the American *incognitum* were specimens prized by the founding fathers even while they fought the Revolutionary War. Indeed, both General George Washington and Thomas Jefferson took time out from their wartime duties to collect these bones from the battlefields and to speculate on the mysterious beast's identity. In the first years of the republic, American national consciousness was linked to early images of prehistoric nature, and the birth of the nation itself coincided with the creation of its first prehistoric monster, an imaginary creature whose ferocity matched the new nation's desire to conquer the natural world. By the time American naturalists unearthed the first complete mastodon skeleton in 1801, many citizens, urged on by a combination of natural history and nationalism, viewed the American *incognitum*, or the mastodon, as a symbol of both the violence of the newly discovered prehistoric world and the emerging nation's own dreams of an empire in the western wilderness.

The mystery of the mastodon began in 1705 with the discovery of a giant tooth along the banks of the Hudson River, not far from where American naturalists dug up the first complete mastodon skeleton nearly a century later. The enormous tooth initially led Puritan clergymen to speculate about the existence of human giants in ancient America. Within a few decades, however, most educated colonists came to believe the bones belonged to an elephant-like animal that they called a *mammoth*, employing the popular term used to describe a similar creature whose frozen carcass had been found in Siberia. At this time, the American animal's identity was not known because few people were even aware that creatures had once existed that were now extinct, to say nothing of the millions of years whose history had never been recorded.

During the ensuing century of debate over the strange bones, everyone from the Puritan preacher Cotton Mather to the Kentucky pioneer Daniel Boone became involved in identifying the monster. By the end of the Revolutionary War, the search for the American *incognitum's* identity had become a national quest, spurred by new discoveries of its bones and the emblematic character the strange beast had acquired in the early days of the republic. Infused with a kind of apocalyptic spirit, the quest for the bones was undertaken eagerly by many citizens with widely differing opinions. Thomas Jefferson, the nation's foremost authority on the bones, believed the living animal would still be discovered in the remote Northwest Territories, and other patriots maintained that the bones belonged to an extinct carnivore whose skeleton would prove that the ferocious beast's disappearance was God's blessing on the promised land.

The earliest images of this prehistoric monster were fashioned from a strange mixture of Indian myth, evangelical beliefs, natural history, and nationalism. Because the birth of the nation occurred simultaneously with the discovery of prehistoric nature, early American national rhetoric was filled with images drawn from biblical accounts of the earth's natural history, creating an American antiquity that many of the nation's inhabitants saw largely in terms of Noah's Ark and the Flood. In this respect, Genesis and geology walked hand in hand in the new nation's own creation narrative, in which the laws of nature and nature's God were indistinguishable.

The significance of the mastodon's story, however, lies not only in what it tells us about the myths permeating the founding fathers' views of the natural world but also in how it illuminates our own assumptions about prehistoric nature. Many people today find it difficult to imagine an era with no awareness of extinct animals, much less the millions of years of geological time before human life on earth. Upon hearing the tall tales told about the American *incognitum*, we are likely to wonder how it could have taken our forefathers a hundred years to discover that these bones belonged to an extinct, prehistoric animal. In fact, many of us still do not realize today that the American *incognitum*, or mastodon, was one of the first animals to be definitively declared an extinct species.

Until now, the mastodon's story has been told largely as part of the history of vertebrate paleontology, with relatively little attention to the way American nationalism helped shape the first images of prehistoric nature long before the dinosaurs were discovered. In addition to throwing new light on the scientific story, my account of the mastodon's discovery reveals much about the early development of American national consciousness and its relationship to ideas about the earth's natural history. In effect, with the rejection of America's native civilizations, the gigantic bones became symbols of the new nation's natural antiquity, the equivalent, in the eyes of the founding fathers, of the Greek and Roman ruins. To investigate the creation of this prehistoric monster, therefore, is to examine the wellsprings of our own national culture, especially the curious relation of our national ego to natural history. The mystery of the mastodon in early America presents a unique opportunity to view the genesis of our own obsession with violence and domination in the prehistoric world, an obsession rooted in the same subconscious needs that drove many early American patriots to imagine the mastodon as a bloodthirsty carnivore.

～

In the summer of 1801, the Philadelphia painter and museum owner Charles Willson Peale and his son Rembrandt excavated the first complete skeleton of the American *incognitum,* or mastodon. By then, the gigantic creature's bones had mystified naturalists in Europe and America for nearly a century, but the Peales were not convinced by arguments that the mysterious animal was a herbivorous, elephant-like animal that fed on shrubs and leaves. Instead, they believed the bones belonged to a carnivore, although they, like most Americans, had little inkling then of the monstrous predators that would dominate prehistoric nature in the age of Darwin and the dinosaurs.

Two years after the animal's bones were exhumed, while the younger Peale was touring England with the mounted skeleton, he published a pamphlet describing the ferocity of the American *incognitum.* According to his description of its unearthing, the discovery of the animal's huge jawbone on a farm in the Hudson River valley had been greeted with awe: "'Gracious God, what a jaw! how many animals have been crushed by it!' was the exclamation of all," Peale later recounted.[1] The Peales' broadside advertising the Philadelphia Museum's exhibition of the "Skeleton of the Mammoth" quoted an Indian legend, with Anglo-American embellishments, that highlighted the creature's alleged devastation of the ancient world: "Forests were laid waste at a meal, the groans of expiring animals were every where heard; and whole villages, inhabited by men, were destroyed in a moment."[2]

The mounting of the great beast's "horns," as the tusks were then called, reveals the dilemma created by the Peales' belief that the American *incognitum* was a carnivore. When they initially mounted its skeleton, the majestic curved tusks were inserted correctly, pointing upward like an elephant's tusks. But because they believed that the animal was carnivorous, when the mounted skeleton was placed in their Philadelphia Museum for public viewing, the Peales inserted the tusks pointing downward, arguing that they were walrus-like teeth used to grub along lake shores for shellfish, turtles, and fish.

Shortly after their discovery, the French anatomist Georges Cuvier, who was among the first to offer a scientific theory of extinction, formally named the American mastodon and declared it an extinct, herbivorous animal whose tusks pointed gracefully upward in his renderings of its skeleton. Nevertheless, the tusks of the Peales' mounted skeleton remained downturned for at least another decade. In November 1816, when the French traveler Édouard de Montulé visited the

Peales' museum, he left an embarrassing testimony to their mistaken beliefs in the carnivore in his sketch of the reconstructed skeleton with its tusks pointing downward.[3]

Like many American citizens, the Peales' fascination with this massive creature stemmed at least partly from its apparent rebuttal of a peculiar European theory that had made the beast an emblem of national honor in the eyes of the founding fathers. Before the Revolutionary War, the famous French naturalist George Louis Leclerc de Buffon presented his influential theory of American degeneracy, which gained considerable support among naturalists on the Continent. Buffon argued that owing to the New World's inferior soil and climate, the life-forms there, including the humans, had degenerated into smaller and less prolific creatures. "Even those which, from the kindly influences of another climate, have acquired their complete form and expansion shrink and diminish under a niggardly sky and an unprolific land, thinly peopled with wandering savages, who, instead of using this territory as a master, had no property or empire."[4]

In effect, Buffon's theory was an attack on the manhood of the American patriots and was particularly galling to those republicans who saw themselves as the Anglo-Saxon masters of a future empire extending across the continent to the Pacific Ocean. For the founding fathers, the discovery of the fossil remains of the American *incognitum* enabled them to refute Buffon's theory and to demonstrate the grandeur of the new republic's own natural antiquity. The campaign to repudiate Buffon's humiliating theory actually began during the American Revolution itself with the first efforts by the founding fathers to celebrate the new nation's natural history.

During the winter of 1780, following Benedict Arnold's betrayal, General George Washington's Continental Army lay huddled in the Hudson River valley, waiting for French emissaries to arrive with news of their support for the American revolutionaries. Shortly before Christmas, General Washington took time off to journey to the nearby farm of Rev. Robert Annan to view the enormous teeth of a mysterious unidentified creature dug up there a few months earlier. Rev. Annan was a country parson in New Windsor, a township about seventy miles north of New York City, a seaport then occupied by British troops. Located close to the site where the Peales excavated the first mastodon skeleton two decades later, the diggings at Rev. Annan's farm began an era when patriotic rhetoric was mingled with visions of a savage pre-historic nature ruled by the American monster.

When General Washington visited Rev. Annan's farm to see the mysterious bones, Thomas Jefferson was just starting to write his book *Notes on the State of Virginia*. Its publication in Paris five years later marked a milestone in American awareness of the unidentified creature and helped make the American *incognitum* a symbol of national pride. An ardent collector of fossils himself, Jefferson used precise measurements of American animals, including the huge bones of the "mammoth," as the creature was popularly called, to disprove Buffon's theory that the New World's wetness and humidity had produced biologically inferior life-forms in America, where only the insects, frogs, and reptiles were larger than those in Europe.

Why were the founding fathers so concerned with the fossil elephants during the American Revolution? And what did this prehistoric creature have to do with the formation of early American national consciousness? The answers to these questions lie in the century-long gestation of the monster and the symbolic character its bones acquired in American consciousness. In 1793, shortly after the Tammany Society's American Museum opened in New York, a broadside listed its collection as containing a giant tooth weighing more than four pounds, recently acquired from the salt licks near the Ohio River in Kentucky: "A Tooth of the American non-described animal, called the Mammoth, supposed to be four or five times as large as the modern Elephant."[5]

The Kentucky salt lick was designated as "Big Bone Lick" on maps of the western territories. In fact, the paths beaten through the wilderness to the lick by a variety of large animals had led early frontier scouts to this landmark along the Ohio River. Beginning with the discovery there in 1739 of the gigantic bones of the unknown creature by a French expedition to the Ohio valley, the Kentucky salt lick became the second major source of the bones of the American *incognitum*. These relics became the center of a controversy over the mysterious animal's identity soon after the first specimens from the Ohio valley were brought back to Paris, where they were examined personally by Buffon, the newly appointed director of King Louis XV's botanical garden and cabinet of curiosities.

Before the Revolutionary War, both Jefferson and Washington had obtained bones from the Kentucky salt lick, and many other fossil remains from this site were sent by frontier scouts and Indian traders to anatomists in London and Philadelphia. There they were compared with similar specimens of Siberian mammoths and African elephants, to determine whether the American *incognitum* was actually an unknown, extinct species. From the earliest speculation about the huge teeth, a central point of dispute was what kind of food the monstrous grinders consumed—in other words, whether the great beast was carnivorous or herbivorous. During his years as an American emissary in London, Benjamin Franklin received tusks and grinders from the Ohio valley and, in his correspondence, fueled speculation about the diet of the American "elephants."

Even though Franklin himself withheld judgment on this matter, his letters to naturalists in the colonies helped publicize the controversial views of Dr. William Hunter, the physician of Britain's Queen Charlotte. Hunter was the first to argue in a scientific paper, based on anatomical studies of its jaws and teeth, that the American *incognitum* was a unknown species that was probably extinct. What made his scientific views influential among the American colonists was his linking the beast's extinction to the idea that it had been a monstrous carnivore whose disappearance was God's blessing on the human race. This controversial theory marked a crucial turning point in the century-long debate over the American *incognitum*, as the idea of extinction found a receptive audience once the notion was linked to the animal's savagery. Casting the extinct creature in the role of a fearsome carnivore somehow made it easier to accept the mutability of God's nature while at the same time confirming the long-held Christian view of man's dominion over the natural world.

Besides their prominent mention in the journals and letters of Indian traders and frontier scouts, the bones from the Kentucky salt lick also became part of the popular genre of early American literature called *captivity narrative*. In 1755, Mary Ingles, the wife of a frontier settler, escaped from her Indian captors during a salting party at Big Bone Lick, and the tale of her daring escape made the site a landmark for early settlers. Nearly thirty years later, a young schoolteacher named John Filson published his famous guide for travelers to Kentucky, *The Discovery, Settlement and Present State of Kentucke*, whose colorful account, "The Adventures of Col. Daniel Boon," coupled his exploits with London's latest theories of the American *incognitum*: "How formidable an enemy to the human species, an animal as large as the elephant, the tyrant of the forests, perhaps the devourer of man!" Filson wrote of the fossil remains found at Big Bone Lick.[6]

Although Filson's Boone myth was highly romanticized, Boone actually had served as an intermediary in the quest for the bones of the American *incognitum* during the Revolutionary War. In 1781, while finishing his *Notes on the State of Virginia*, Thomas Jefferson gave Colonel Boone a letter to deliver to the Kentucky militia man General George Rogers Clark, asking him "to procure for me some teeth of the great animal whose remains are found on the Ohio."[7] By then, the American *incognitum* was well on its way to becoming a monster in the eyes of many citizens, for Filson's frontier fable contained striking images of the beast that had roamed the wilderness in ancient times—an animal whose ferocity, in Filson's eyes, matched the wild beauty of the wilderness. In many ways, Filson's mythic view of the American *incognitum* as the "tyrant of the forest" was symptomatic of the merging of American nationalism with early visions of prehistoric nature in the founding fathers' rhetoric.

In fact, the genealogy of this early American monster can be traced back to the earliest stirrings of national consciousness among Puritan preachers in colonial New England. The debate about the American *incognitum* initially revolved around the question of whether the enormous bones were animal or human, with many educated colonists believing that they belonged to human giants. In western Massachusetts, Edward Taylor, a Calvinist minister from England who had settled in the village of Westfield, copied into his diary the news account of the first tooth's discovery. A year later, after examining another tooth shown to him by a Dutch traveler from the Hudson River valley, Taylor composed a long poem to the "Gyant of Claverack."[8] Full of lyrical images of the fossil remains, his poem used Indian legends about a race of men taller than the tallest pine trees to give an authentic aura of Americanness to these human giants. What made Taylor's giant of Claverack singularly American was his blending of natural history and Indian lore with an apocalyptic vision of God's chosen people in the New World. In Taylor's poem, the American *incognitum* took its first steps toward becoming the terror of the antediluvian world celebrated by the founding fathers and the Peale family nearly a century later.

In 1706, after Taylor's colleague Cotton Mather, a scientifically minded Puritan clergyman from Boston (figure 2), examined several of these giant teeth from Claverack, he wrote the first learned account of

FIGURE 2. Mezzotint portrait of Cotton Mather at age sixty-five by Peter Pelham, 1727. Courtesy American Antiquarian Society.

the bones, which he sent to the Royal Society in London six years later. Agreeing with his fellow clergyman Edward Taylor, Mather maintained that the fossil teeth were scientific proof of the existence of the human giants mentioned in the Bible. His assertion that the monster of Claverack was the largest giant ever known was filled with a nationalistic spirit foreshadowing Jefferson's use of the monster to refute Buffon's theory of American degeneracy during the Revolutionary War.

Even though Taylor's and Mather's ideas quickly lost credibility among Anglo-American naturalists, the evangelical spirit they injected into the debate over the mysterious bones marked the beginning of their symbolic association with American nationalism, sentiments that eventually overshadowed their scientific significance. The hyperbole of these Puritan clergymen, which so many contemporary historians have ridiculed, in fact holds the key to understanding how the American *incognitum* later became a "carnivore" and an icon of national identity in revolutionary America. During the eighteenth century, the fossil remains of the American *incognitum* acquired an almost mythical character in the eyes of many colonists, especially those defining the national consciousness of the new republic.

In many respects, the bones' symbolic significance went much deeper than the question of national pride underlying Jefferson's quarrel with Buffon. For nearly a century, since the earliest speculations of Edward Taylor and Cotton Mather about the fossil teeth, the primary vehicle shaping both the learned and popular awareness of the giant bones was the creation narrative of Christianity and the story of Noah's Ark and the Flood. In the eyes of many clergymen and their congregations, the sense of wonder inspired by the bones of the American *incognitum* did not issue from their vision of the beast in the prehistoric landscape, for they were only beginning to entertain the idea of extinction and the "primitive" world of the prehuman earth. Instead, to many American Protestants, both evangelical and enlightened, the bones conjured up visions of the destruction of the earth by the Great Deluge and, finally, the inevitability of the Day of Doom. When they looked at the American landscape from which the bones were being dug up, learned and lay alike often saw the Apocalypse, the end of the world for which many were waiting and which the most calculating minds among them predicted would come within two hundred years.

From its earliest manifestations, the republic's new national identity was linked through evangelical religious beliefs and natural rights doctrine to a millennial vision of its natural history, fashioned equally by scientifically minded Puritan clergymen and natural philosophers. While the secular scientific view of the Darwinian era later created a fantastic prehistoric landscape full of exotic carnivores, the American enlightenment gave the prehistoric world religious meaning and millenarian expectations and the mysterious bones, an emblematic character.

For most educated Anglo-Americans, the immutable laws of nature would always remain the laws of God's nature, whether or not the Bible was interpreted literally. Learned Anglo-American clergymen saw no conflict between the Scriptures and the scientific method they promoted to celebrate the glory of God's nature. They tried to use fossil evidence to verify the creation myth of Christianity and the story of Noah's Ark and the Deluge. Influenced by the neoclassicism of Augustan England, they made the fossil remains of the American *incognitum* part of the Manifest Destiny of a chosen people, creating the first awareness of a nation that eventually saw its antiquity in the natural history of the earth rather than in the ruins of Greece and Rome.

This metaphorical view of fossils as the monuments of the new nation's antiquity was advanced by England's natural philosophers during Cotton Mather's lifetime. In 1668, the British mechanical genius Robert Hooke, a rival of Isaac Newton, was among the first to evoke the metaphor of fossils as the coins and monuments of the unwritten natural history of the antediluvian world. "These are the greatest and most lasting Monuments of Antiquity, which in all probability will far antidate [sic] the most ancient Monuments of the World, even the very Pyramids, Obelisks, Mummys, Hieroglyphicks, and Coins," Hooke declared of the fossilized cockleshells and oysters found in England far from the oceans. In 1709, a reviewer of the Swiss naturalist Johann Jacob Scheuchzer's *Herbarium of the Deluge* showed how such views of fossils had taken root in natural history thought: "Here are new kinds of coins, the dates of which are incomparably more ancient, more important and more reliable than those of all the coins of Greece and Rome."[9]

In 1684, Hooke's contemporary, the Anglican clergyman Thomas Burnet, offered a new theory of the natural causes of the Great Deluge in his *Sacred Theory of the Earth*, which amplified Hooke's metaphor by viewing the entire earth's crust as a natural ruins shaped by the receding waters of the Flood. Burnet's theory combined in a novel way the faded glory of classical antiquity with the creation narrative of Christianity to create an archaeological view of the earth's landscape. His view of wild nature as a ruin enabled American patriots, along with generations of Romantic authors and painters, to link national consciousness, religious destiny, and natural history in their search for the identity of the American *incognitum*.

During the century-long saga of the American *incognitum*, many people became embroiled in the controversy over the mysterious creature's identity. For our purposes, the person who best illustrates the overarching themes of the American *incognitum*'s story is the learned New England scholar Ezra Stiles, who was the poet Edward Taylor's grandson and a founding father involved during the Revolutionary War in the debate over the creature's identity. Stiles first heard stories as a child of the great bones of Claverack from his Uncle Eldad, who remembered his own father talking with Dutch traders about the bones from the Hudson River valley. In the last years of the Revolutionary War, Stiles, as did so many of the founding fathers, became an avid collector of these mysterious relics. Then president of Yale College, he still believed the bones of the American *incognitum* were the remains of human giants, as his grandfather had at the beginning of the century.

In 1784, following a visit from Thomas Jefferson, who was on his way to Paris to become the American ambassador to France, Stiles began a remarkable correspondence with him, eventually leading Stiles to abandon his belief in human giants. Two years later, after accepting Jefferson's view that the bones belonged to an elephant-like creature, Stiles made the first of two pilgrimages to the Hudson River valley site where the first giant tooth had been found in 1705. By the time the Peales dug up its skeleton, the American *incognitum* had become a symbol of American antiquity. In the eyes of the founding fathers, natural rights doctrine had joined the millenarian beliefs of the early Puritan settlers to create a nation that they believed was destined to extend the dominion of Christian civilization over all of God's nature.

Despite their desire to create a universal society and to repudiate Buffon's view of American degeneracy, the founding fathers continued to see themselves as the dominant race, bringing civilization to the "savages," both Native Americans and African slaves. The savagery of prehistoric nature, symbolized by the jaws of the American *incognitum*, was linked to their own aspirations of empire over the natural world, which, for them, included the heathen nations and races. In this perspective, the bones of the American *incognitum* help explain the tragic consequences of their racial views of the natural world.

The interpretations of the American *incognitum* were many, from the Indian myths and tall tales of frontiersmen to the pious scientific theories of learned Calvinist clergymen and Enlightenment philosophers. The unwavering naturalism of our own scientific civilization makes it difficult to imagine a time when there was no idea of extinction, except perhaps the specter of the Apocalypse. Nonetheless, the mastodon's fate is an appropriate metaphor for our own predicament today, when everyone can see the day of doom approaching for industrial society, whether from the anger of God's judgment on our Sodom and Gomorrah or simply the exhaustion of our fossil fuels. In the nuclear age, when extinction has become an instantaneous technological event, the mystery of the American *incognitum* sheds new light on the cultural world that created the modern American nation. It also offers a fresh perspective of our own vision of a violent prehistoric nature, which, after Darwin, has slowly reshaped our view of the natural world with the strength and pulverizing effect of a glacier. Our own eagerness to view prehistoric nature as a violent place ruled by ferocious beasts underscores the importance of understanding how the American *incognitum* became a terrifying monster in the eyes of many citizens of the early republic.

Belief in the savagery of prehistoric nature, as we shall see, had its roots in the master metaphor of early American national culture—the myth of wild nature, the idea that the New World was a wilderness inhabited by savages. Accordingly, during the nineteenth century, this concept served to justify the dominance of an industrial society in the name of piety and progress. This paradigm, which reached its full fruition in the ensuing age of Darwin and the dinosaurs, was first articulated by "civilized" Anglo-Americans, who transformed a herbivorous, elephant-like creature into the terror of the antediluvian world.

I

The Giant of Claverack in Puritan America

His nose like an Hanging Pillar wide
And Eyes like shining Suns, Each on Each side,
His Arms like limbs of trees twenty foot long,
Fingers with bones like horse shanks and as strong,
His Thighs do stand like two Vast Millposts stout.

       —Edward Taylor, 1706

THE SEARCH FOR the identity of the American *incognitum* began inauspiciously in the summer of 1705, near the lower boundary of Claverack manor in the Hudson River valley, not far from the frontier outpost of Albany. In this sparsely settled region, a Dutch tenant farmer found a fist-size tooth weighing nearly five pounds along the eastern bank of the river. The root of the giant tooth was badly decayed, but the top was pearly white like the eyetooth of a man, and its inner recess reputedly held a glassful of liquor. Despite the tooth's peculiarity, Peter Van Bruggen, a member of the assembly from Albany, purchased the strange specimen from the farmer for a half-pint of rum.

In July, when Van Bruggen came down to New York for an assembly meeting, he brought the tooth with him and showed it to several people, including Edward Hyde, viscount of Cornbury and the English governor of New York Province. "I was told of it, and sent for it to see, and ask'd if he would dispose of it," Lord Cornbury later wrote. "He said it was worth nothing, but if I had a mind to it, 'twas at my service."[1] The governor promptly sent it off to the secretary of the Royal Society in London in a box marked "tooth of a Giant."

In an era when Isaac Newton's celestial mechanics were asserting their authority over England's educated classes, the Royal Society emerged as Britain's foremost authority on scientific matters, especially those concerning the collection and cataloging of natural history specimens. In an effort to enhance the institution's prestige, Lord Cornbury's cousin Queen Anne issued instructions to all ministers and governors who went abroad to support the Royal Society's mission by providing answers to its inquiries. In 1703, Newton himself became president of the Royal Society, thus testifying to the rising prestige of the new science among a wide spectrum of English society, from the learned dons at Cambridge to Puritan clergymen in the colonies.

Lord Cornbury's readiness to believe that the enormous tooth belonged to a human giant reflected English Protestants' widespread reliance on the Scriptures to explain the earth's history. Nearly everyone, including Newton, believed the age of the earth extended no further back in time than the date of God's creation. In 1650, Irish Archbishop James Ussher calculated this event to have occurred on the night preceding Sunday, October 23, of the year 4004 before Christ's birth. English theologians and natural philosophers alike argued that if properly understood, the Bible stories could be corroborated by scientific evidence and offered the best explanation for the discovery of the strange fossils.

Such catastrophic events as the Great Deluge played a prominent role in the emerging theories about the earth's natural history and the disposition of fossil remains. Chronologists took very seriously the statement in the book of Genesis that "there were giants on the earth in those Dayes." Beyond these literal interpretations of the Bible, there was not yet any awareness of the existence of extinct creatures or the vast realm of prehistoric nature extending back millions of years in geological time. Although a lively debate was taking shape over whether similar gigantic bones uncovered at sites in England and Europe belonged to human giants or elephant-like land animals, virtually no one, including the most enlightened scientific minds, challenged the biblical time frame.

The tooth did, however, lead to conflicting opinions in New York about the identity of the monstrous creature. "Some said it 'twas the tooth of a human creature; others, of some beast or fish," Lord Cornbury wrote to the secretary of the Royal Society, "but nobody could tell what beast or fish had such a tooth."[2] The governor himself was convinced that the tooth belonged to a human giant, and he immediately instructed Johannis Abeel, the recorder of Albany, to send someone to Claverack to dig further near the place where the tooth had been found.

Within a few weeks, Lord Cornbury received more bone fragments unearthed by Abeel's agents and a brief note from the recorder describing their excavations along the top of the steep riverbank where the tooth had rolled down: "They found, fifteen feet underground, the bones of a corpse that was thirty feet long, but was almost all decayed, so soon as they handled them they broke in pieces."[3] The few whole pieces that the recorder sent to the governor did little to assuage the curiosity of Lord Cornbury's colleagues. So, "when I go up to Albany next," Lord Cornbury told his correspondent at the Royal Society, "I intend to go to the place myself, to see if I can discover any thing more concerning the monstrous creature."[4]

The eldest son of an English nobleman beset by financial problems, Lord Cornbury had arrived in New York three years earlier, the emissary of his first cousin Queen Anne. Lord Cornbury's official barge moving up the Hudson River was a familiar sight to colonists, who resented the extravagance of his administration and his edicts favoring the wealthy merchants and landowners who ruled New York Province. His tenure as governor ended disgracefully three years later when formal charges were brought against him of embezzlement and graft, along with accusations that he was a "drunken, vain fool," who allegedly appeared in the streets of New York dressed in woman's attire, apparently impersonating his cousin Queen Anne.

Lord Cornbury's frequent trips to Albany and his provocative speeches before the assembly were often reported in the first colonial newspaper, the *Boston News-Letter*, a weekly founded in 1704 by the Boston postmaster John Campbell. No doubt the eminence of Lord Cornbury's opinion in these official circles quickly brought news of the tooth's discovery to the editor's attention. An anonymous correspondent in New York sent the newspaper a short firsthand account of the event which was published at the end of July, only a few weeks after the tooth was found. Domestic news items like this were rare among the shipping news, official proclamations, and reports about the War of the Spanish Succession, which had broken out two years earlier. In the upper Hudson River valley, where the tenuous British foothold on the frontier of French Canada depended on an alliance with the five nations of the Iroquois Confederacy, news of the discovery of a giant tooth was thus a welcome digression.

Having examined the tooth himself and witnessed the concern it created among the New York gentry, the *Boston News-Letter*'s correspondent reported that it was "lookt upon as a mighty wonder, whither the Tooth of Man or Beast."[5] The correspondent's report also offered the first precise measurements of the fossil remains. The tooth weighed exactly four and three quarter pounds, and another bone "thought to be a Thigh-bone was 17 Foot long," although the latter had crumbled away when dug up.

The correspondent was evidently well informed, for many of his details concerning the "great prodigious Tooth" matched Lord Cornbury's account, including information about subsequent digging at the site and a second batch of bones presumably sent by Johannis Abeel. "There is since another Tooth taken up in the same place, which is a Fore Tooth, flat and broad, and is as broad as a mans Four Fingers, which I have not yet seen," the correspondent reported.[6] In fact, these specimens were only the first of many fossils dug up from the Hudson River site during the next few years. Soon other bones were circulating throughout New England, and in the coming months, the teeth from Claverack created a sensation among the learned gentry, conjuring up in their minds the first visions of mythical beasts and human giants in the wilds of the Hudson River valley.

The teeth and bones found along the upper Hudson River were exposed initially by the spring floods eroding the steep bluffs rising some sixty feet above the riverbank. Located about thirty miles south of the fur trading outpost of Albany, Claverack was part of a large manor, or patroonship, originally granted to the wealthy Amsterdam merchant Kiliaen Van Rensselaer when the upper Hudson River valley was under Dutch rule. In 1649, shortly before the Dutch lost the colony, the dense forests along the Hudson River to the south were inhabited largely by Mahican Indians, who were vying with their northern Iroquois rivals the Mohawks to retain their strategic role as middlemen in the fur trade with the Dutch merchants. After the British took over from the Dutch in 1664, the upper Hudson River continued to be a sparsely settled Dutch enclave clustered around the fur trading outpost, which contained only a few hundred households at the century's end.

A few new tenant farmers came into the area in 1686 when the Albany-based English merchant Robert Livingston acquired an enormous

tract of land measuring some 160,000 acres immediately below Claverack manor.[7] In 1692 Livingston built a manor house on the east bank
of the Hudson River, about six miles below the site where the fossil remains acquired by Lord Cornbury were later discovered. Livingston's
fraudulent dealings with previous English governors embroiled him in
many legal troubles with political enemies who challenged his title to
Livingston manor. In 1704, while Livingston was in London seeking
restitution from Queen Anne's ministers, Kiliaen Van Rensselaer gave
his brother Henry the southern section of his estate, known as Claverack, which bordered on the northern boundary of Livingston manor.
At this time, only a few tenant families—mostly of Dutch descent—
lived at Claverack, and the giant tooth seems to have been found when
interest in the area was rising.

By the time Livingston returned to his Hudson River manor in
1706, news of the discovery of the giant tooth and other fossil remains found at nearby Claverack was already spreading into nearby
New England. Dutch travelers from Albany brought specimens to
Boston and Hartford, where they attracted the interest of clergymen
and physicians puzzled by the unknown creature. News of the "great
prodigious Tooth" also spread quickly to the towns in western Massachusetts located along the primitive paths and wagon trails connecting Claverack manor with the settlements in the upper Connecticut
River valley near Springfield. In 1694, Rev. Benjamin Wadsworth of
Boston traveled this route from Boston to Albany with a party of
colonial officials sent to negotiate with the five nations of the Iroquois Confederacy. Their trip took nearly a week, and Wadsworth's
journal entry vividly describes the region between Claverack and the
frontier settlement of Westfield, in western Massachusetts, "as a
hideous, howling wilderness."[8]

When the *Boston News-Letter* reached the village of Westfield in
1705, the Congregationalist minister Edward Taylor copied the newspaper account into his diary. "Taylor, like many of his contemporaries,
was greatly interested in abnormalities of all kinds in the physical and
animal world," notes historian Donald E. Stanford.[9] In 1684, Increase
Mather, a Boston clergyman and the father of Cotton Mather, published his *Essay for the Recording of Illustrious Providences,* a collection
of strange occurrences aimed at drawing people back into the church
by advertising God's wonders in New England. Edward Taylor himself
had sent to Boston descriptions of unusual hailstorms, supernatural

occurrences, and monstrous births, which were among the natural wonders that Mather believed testified to God's glory.

In Taylor's eyes, the true heralds of the Claverack monster were the
bones themselves, brought to Westfield by Dutch traders from the Hudson River the year following the tooth's discovery. On June 14, 1706, a
Dutchman named Koon brought to his house a fist-size "Tooth of the
Monster buried at Claverack," weighing two pounds and one ounce,
along with other bone fragments the size of a man's calf.[10] Using an ar-
chaic form of *elephant* to signify *ivory*, Taylor described the bones as
"looking like dull Olivant." "The place were the Bone lay was 25 paces,
according to which the Monster was judged above 60 or 70 foot high,"
he noted in his diary, greatly augmenting Johannis Abeel's original estimate of a "corpse" thirty feet long. In the year since New York Governor Cornbury's letter to the Royal Society, Dutch settlers had noticed
the interest that these rarities were attracting among New Englanders,
and three days after Koon's visit, two other Dutchmen brought yet another tooth to Taylor's house.

At the age of twenty-three, Taylor had emigrated from England
to the Massachusetts Bay Colony in 1668 following the restoration of
Charles II to escape persecution for his Puritan beliefs.[11] After graduating from Harvard College in 1671, Taylor became the minister of
the newly organized Congregational Church in Westfield, a trapper's
settlement located on the colony's western frontier in the Berkshire
foothills of the upper Connecticut River valley. In addition to his
clerical duties, Taylor served as physician to the frontier village, although he never acquired a professional knowledge of medicine, as
Cotton Mather did. His ordination as the town's minister was delayed for eight years by King Philip's war, the Indian uprising led by
the young Wampanoag chieftain Metacomet, whose daring attacks
on frontier settlements in 1675 devastated the entire Connecticut
River valley.

Taylor's vision of "the Monster buried at Claverack" drew heavily
on the Indian legends of a giant race of men. In his study *Spirit of the
New England Tribes*, William S. Simmons noted the widespread belief
in a giant human named Wétucks or Manshop, who figured prominently in New England Indian myths and legends.[12] But by the time
Taylor saw the giant tooth and bones from Claverack, the Indians had
been driven out of the region, and settlers were already beginning to
move through western Massachusetts into the Hudson River valley.

When the Claverack monster captured his imagination, Taylor was already composing the lyrical poems that later made him the premier poet of the American colonies, even though none of his verses were published in his lifetime. It was not surprising, then, that after examining the tooth, Taylor composed a long poem extolling the Claverack giant as one of the New World's natural wonders. His flights of fancy unleashed by the mysterious bones clearly reveal how these natural curiosities were woven into his Puritan religious beliefs.

Written in the baroque style of an earlier generation of English nature poetry, Taylor's rhyming couplets are filled with reverence for natural history, although the latter was clearly God's nature in the New World, where everything in nature was a symbol of the Bible Commonwealth in America. The prologue to his poem hails the famous European cabinets of curiosities as "Magazeens of Miracles," collections of God's wonders, ranging from the huge oyster shell in the anatomical museum at Leyden to the giant Theco Tree of literary renown, whose branches reputedly shaded a thousand men. Awed by the unprecedented stature of the Claverack monster, Taylor compares its dimensions with those of legendary giants culled from the Bible, Virgil's *Aeneid*, the medieval romance of Guy of Warwick, and travelers' tales from Patrick Gordon's *Geography Anatomiz'd*. Taylor measures the giant of Claverack against the dragon of Northumberland, the Dun Cow of Dunsmore, and the boar of Lovain, all of whom figure prominently in the popular romance about Guy of Warwick, which Taylor probably read as a child growing up in England.[13]

After describing these legendary figures, Taylor turns to the giants mentioned in the Bible, like Goliath and King Og, who seemed like mere pygmies compared with the giant of Claverack:

> So in the limb of Rationalls youst see
> Nature exceeds itselfe. Where some twigs be
> That bring forth Pigmies (oh! poore Cricklings),
> Some, mo[n]strous Gyants, Emims, Anakims,
> As Og nine Cubits: six Goliah high![14]

His reference to Og had special significance in the wilderness setting, since several Puritan ministers had already compared him with the Indian tribes in New England. In the Bible, Og is a pagan giant and the king of Bashan, near Galilee, whose bedstead measured nine cubits and who was slain with all his people by Moses. In his account of King Philip's war, published in 1702, Cotton Mather equated the conquest of Bashan with the colonists' recent defeat of the Indian insurgent Metacomet, whom Mather compared with a pagan deity.

Like many New England preachers, Mather believed the Indian myths were the devil's work, a pernicious form of expression whose grotesque images he sought to suppress with the rationalism of Puritan discourse. "We have by a true and plain history secured the story of our successes against all the *Ogs* in this *woody* country from falling under the disguises of *mythology*."[15] Shortly before Edward Taylor wrote his elegant eulogy for the giant of Claverack, Mather made Og's downfall a metaphor for the destruction of various monstrous creatures, who, he felt, symbolized the false prophets of the pagans, from the Greeks of antiquity to the Wampanoag Indians.

In contrast to Mather's demonization of Indian myths, Taylor used the bones from Claverack to confirm the existence of these legendary giants and to legitimize the rhetoric of Indian folktales: "But yet we do conclude that by such Stories / Something there did appeare of Natures glory / In those large instances, and have just ground / From th' Gyants bones at Claverack lately found."[16] What brings the monster of Claverack to life in Taylor's poem are his own vivid metaphors, analogies drawn from everyday experience, which give the giant of Claverack a kind of folkloric stature:

> His nose like to an Hanging Pillar wide
> And Eyes like shining suns, Each on Each side,
> His Arms like limbs of trees twenty foot long,
> fingers with bones like horse shanks and as strong
> His Thighs do stand like two Vast Millposts stout.[17]

These homespun metaphors contrast sharply with the rhetoric of Cotton Mather's moralistic sermons. Rather than demonizing the monster of Claverack, Taylor's imagery uses the exaggeration later associated with the tall tales of American folklore, from Paul Bunyan to Big Foot.

In place of Mather's contempt for pagan mythology, Taylor ingeniously employs Indian myths to buttress his claim that the enormous bones of Claverack belonged to the largest of human giants. In a remarkably sympathetic fashion, which foreshadowed the fusion of the frontiersman with the noble savage in the Daniel Boone myth, Taylor introduces the testimony of the Indians at Claverack to support his argument. He recalls hearing tales from Indians about a giant "upon the Yorke River" some forty years earlier when he first arrived in the colonies. At that time, he considered the stories to be lies associated with Hobbamocco, the principal Indian deity that many colonists equated with the devil.

But after examining the bones from Claverack, Taylor's views changed, and he recorded in his diary the details of this Indian myth about "a monstrous person as high as the Tops of the Pine Trees, that would hunt Bears till they took to the Trees, & then would catch them with his Hands."[18] From the Dutchmen who showed him the bones, Taylor heard skeptical accounts of the Indian legends, which he also noted in his diary: "The Indians flocking to see the monstrous Bones upbraided the Dutch with Unbelief in that they would not believe the Report of a monstrous person w[hich] they had told them from the Fathers."[19]

In his poem, Taylor cleverly uses this anecdote and the rational evidence of the bones to prove the truth of these stories while deriding the Dutchmen who had dismissed the Indian legends about the giant humans:

> And Sopos Indians flocking them to See,
> Upbraiding th' Dutch incredulitee,
> Who, tho' they told them of this Mighty Don,
> They n're believ'd there ere was Such an One.
> But lest our Indians Credit's counted Crackt
> I'le strengthen it with matters true of Fact.[20]

The eyewitness accounts by the Dutchmen and the giant teeth and bones that Taylor had held in his own hands became empirical proof of the giant's existence as well as the veracity of the Indian myths.

Taylor's invocation of Indian myths to confirm that the Claverack bones belonged to human giants created a dilemma that may help explain why he did not finish his poem. By validating these folktales, he was embracing the pagan mythology that Cotton Mather had condemned only a few years earlier in his account of King Philip's war. Full of aspersions on the "savages," Mather's Indian war narrative equated them with the evil giant King Og, an embodiment of the devil to be hunted down like the monsters depicted in classical mythology. Even though Taylor shared Mather's Puritan belief that the pagan frontier was a fallen world and spoke of converting "the Wilderness to the promised land," his praise of the Indian myths brought him dangerously close to views that would have been considered heretical had he completed his poem in the same sympathetic spirit. Nonetheless, his wayward verse is a good example of the hybrid frontier mythology being fashioned by learned Puritans in the Massachusetts Bay Colony long before the founding fathers used Indian legends to describe the American *incognitum*.

While Edward Taylor could not take the final step toward honoring the dignity of Indian life, his blending of natural history and Indian lore with the apocalyptic vision of God's chosen people in America made his celebration of the Claverack giant a forerunner of future events. In his poem, the giant of Claverack surpassed all the monsters of antiquity, thereby confirming the doomsday rhetoric of the Puritans who saw their destiny in terms of a New Jerusalem in the wilderness. According to Karl Keller,

> Taylor's real importance as an *American* poet is in his defense of the New England way of theology. Therefore, in almost everything he wrote—sermons arguing against Stoddardean liberalism, historical verses tracing the evolution of religion toward New England purity, poetry dramatizing the personal value of preparing oneself for membership in church and community—he was, it would appear, a kind of nationalist.[21]

Literary historians Richard Ruland and Malcolm Bradbury highlight the protonationalistic spirit of Taylor's poetry, with its dramatic intensity and daring sense of language, which they link to the literary spirit of Emerson, Hawthorne, and Melville: "This is a markedly American world, for in the Puritan way America is made the special ground for the contest of grace, part of the sacred landscape of revelation in which historical and personal event enact providential meaning."[22] Yet these same authors neglect the most remarkable aspect of Taylor's private vision of the "Gyant of Claverack," his merging of Protestant myth with early scientific methodology and Indian lore, which foreshadowed the linking of natural history and nationalism in the founding fathers' view of the American *incognitum* nearly a century later.

Edward Taylor's homage to the giant of Claverack echoed the thoughts of his colleague Cotton Mather, Boston's foremost preacher and theologian. In the summer of 1706, shortly after Taylor first saw the fossil remains from Claverack, two Dutchmen from Albany showed similar bone fragments and teeth to Joseph Dudley, the governor of Massachusetts. In early July, Dudley wrote to Cotton Mather about the remarkable bones, comparing their dimensions with those of the specimens found the previous year at Claverack: "I could make nothing of them, but the tooth was of the perfect form of the eye tooth of a man, with four prongs or roots, and six distinct faces or flats on top, a little worn, all perfectly smoothed with grinding. I suppose all the surgeons in town have seen it, and I am perfectly of the opinion it was a human tooth."[23]

Dudley's letter gave Mather an estimate of the monstrous creature's size that corresponded exactly to the dimensions cited in Edward Taylor's poem. The two Dutchmen explained that just below the spot along the riverbank where the remains were found, "there is a plain discoloration of the ground, for seventy-five foot long at least, different from the earth in colour and substance, which is judged by every body that see it, to be the ruins and dust of the body that bore those teeth and bones." In other respects, the details of his account matched the story told to Taylor, a coincidence suggesting that the two Dutchmen from Albany had passed through Westfield on their way to Boston.

For Mather's benefit, Dudley repeated his belief that the remains belonged to a human giant rather than a whale or an elephant, and he referred to biblical accounts of the Great Deluge to explain the monster's death: "I am perfectly of the opinion, that the tooth will agree only to a human body, for whom the flood only could prepare a funeral." In the same spirit, he alluded to the giants mentioned by the Jewish scholars of the Old Testament with whom Mather was already familiar. In Dudley's opinion, these giants from the Old Testament, like Goliath, were not half so large as the monster of Claverack.

Governor Dudley deferred final judgment on the origin of the bones to learned English authors like Thomas Burnet, the Anglican clergyman whose 1684 book *The Sacred Theory of the Earth* had stirred up a debate in England about the earth's natural history. The governor also mentioned one of Burnet's critics, William Whiston, an English vicar whose *New Theory of the Earth*, published in 1695, explained the

Great Deluge as the earth's collision with a comet, a theory praised by Isaac Newton. "There is nothing left but to repair to those antique doctors for his origin, and to allow Dr. Burnet and Dr. Whiston to bury him at the deluge," Dudley wrote to Mather. "And, if he were what he shows, he will be seen again at or after the conflagration, further to be examined," Dudley added, referring to the Apocalypse.

Dudley's allusion to the Apocalypse reflected the resurgence of millenarian ideas among English Protestants, many of whom viewed unexplained natural wonders like the bones from Claverack as signs of Christ's return to earth before God's final judgment. Indeed, the restoration of the Protestant monarchs William and Mary to the English throne in 1689 had been accompanied by a revival of belief in the millennium. This doctrine, a medieval idea based on the prophecies in the Book of Revelation, claimed that Christ would return to the earth to rule for a thousand years before the Last Judgment at the end of the world. The restoration in England, the "Glorious Revolution," also revived the influence of the Anglican Church, which had little sympathy for the creation of a Bible commonwealth in the Massachusetts Bay Colony.

With the accession of Queen Anne to the throne, Dudley lobbied successfully from London to be appointed governor of Massachusetts, aided by the support of Cotton Mather, who had been friendly with him for several years and was related to him through marriage.[24] But by the time Dudley wrote to Mather about the Claverack bones, the Puritan clergyman's feelings about the governor had changed, and he now referred privately to him as "a *fop* in *boots*." Indeed, since arriving in Boston, Dudley had alienated many of the colonists through his encroachments on the prerogatives of elected officials and his edicts favoring restoration of the Anglican Church's influence. Behind the scenes, Mather was actively seeking Dudley's removal through his own lobbying with politicians in London. Despite these machinations, Mather sent Dudley portions of his "Biblia Americana," a massive manuscript he had begun in the aftermath of the Salem witch trials in 1692. This lengthy treatise sought to reconcile biblical revelations with the new science by providing scholarly commentary for nearly every verse of the Scriptures. In hopes that Dudley would use his influence to have the manuscript published in London, Mather had swallowed his pride and tried to curry the governor's favor.

Dudley's letter concerning the mysterious bones came at a time when Cotton Mather's political influence with the colonial authorities was declining, although he was still considered the most prominent Puritan minister in the colonies. In 1701, his father Increase was ousted from the presidency at Harvard College, and two years later, when the colonial assembly nominated his son for the post, Cotton himself was denied the privilege of succeeding his father. Ever since his ordination as a minister in 1685, Cotton Mather had served as copastor with his father of Boston's influential Second Church, whose congregation numbered some fifteen hundred persons, the largest in New England. His father had been instrumental in urging the English governor Sir William Phips to institute the Salem witch trials in 1692, and the young Mather's book *Memorable Providences Relating to Witchcraft and Possessions,* published in 1685 when he was twenty-two, helped fan the hysteria that led to the trials.

Fearful that a severe stammer would prevent him from becoming a clergyman, Cotton Mather had studied medicine at Harvard College and for several years thought about becoming a physician. His lifelong interest in the natural sciences, particularly those concerned with physical and spiritual sickness, were the product of a protoscientific sensibility. He saw the empiricism of the natural sciences as a new weapon to combat Catholic superstition and pagan folk beliefs while shoring up the authority of Protestant doctrine against the skepticism of the atheists. The Mathers' concern with witchcraft itself was symptomatic of the Puritans' interest in natural curiosities and their active involvement in the popularization of early scientific inquiry. In fact, witchcraft and diabolical possession were prominent among the strange occurrences described in Increase Mather's *Essay for the Recording of Illustrious Providences* published the previous year.

The elder Mather's fascination with natural curiosities led him to organize a Boston philosophical society in 1683, the first American scientific society. Although the organization lasted only a few years, it clearly demonstrated the merging of natural history thought with the spectral world of Puritan belief in occult phenomena.[25] In his early-seventeenth-century writings on natural philosophy, Francis Bacon advocated the formation of such philosophical societies to supervise the worldwide collection of specimens and the scientific study of natural history. Bacon's ideas took root among scholars and clergymen, who saw the scientific spirit as part of England's divine destiny, giving the learned classes an almost mystic sense of English nationalism that greatly influenced early American views of natural history.

Founded in 1660, London's Royal Society gave Bacon's new philosophy an organizational structure and led its first apologist, Thomas Sprat, to declare that the society epitomized "the present prevailing Genius of the English nation."[26] Published in 1667, Sprat's history of the young philosophical society gave expression to the nationalistic spirit of Protestant reformers and Anglican prelates, who believed Bacon's utilitarian natural philosophy had a religious purpose: "The universal Disposition of this Age is bent upon a rational Religion."[27] Puritan preachers like Cotton Mather and Edward Taylor incorporated this amalgam of millenarian science and English nationalism into their musings about the natural wonders in America, including the giant of Claverack.

The revocation of the Massachusetts colony's charter in 1684 led to the abandonment of the Boston philosophical society's activities during the political turmoil preceding the restoration of the Protestant monarchy five years later. In the aftermath of this event, the pursuit of Baconian science quickly became the primary weapon of theologians and clergymen in England against the spread of atheistic beliefs and radical religious sects hostile to Anglicanism. The publication of Isaac Newton's Principia Mathematica in 1687 revitalized the English Protestants' natural theology and millenarian beliefs, which had become popular before the political crisis.[28] Natural philosophers who believed in a literal interpretation of the biblical revelations predicting the millennium revived an apocalyptic tradition first begun by the English Reformation and later popularized by radical sects during Oliver Cromwell's rule.

In the age of Newton, scientifically minded clergymen and physicians devoted themselves to proving the biblical prophecies promising a millennium of peace and prosperity upon the imminent return of Jesus Christ. By the end of the seventeenth century, Bacon's new natural philosophy, along with Newton's revolutionary theories, had been incorporated into Protestant religious thought by England's leading clergymen naturalists. John Ray's The Wisdom of God Manifested in the Works of Creation, published in 1691, made the study of natural history virtually a form of worship. Accordingly, everyone from Governor Dudley to Cotton Mather greeted the discovery of the giant bones of Claverack in the spirit of the millennial ideas being promoted by both the natural philosophers at the Royal Society and the evangelical preachers in the American colonies.

In the summer of 1706, when Governor Dudley wrote to Cotton Mather, the resurgence of High Church Anglicanism under the reign of Queen Anne had eroded the Mathers' previous influence over the colony's government. With the ebbing of Puritan power in Boston's official circles, the younger Mather became known for his outbursts of angry criticism, and many had come to view him as a spokesman for outdated traditions. But Cotton Mather saw himself as the Homer of early America, comparing his vivid account of the Indian wars, *Decennium Luctuosum*, published in 1699, with Homer's *Iliad*. Unfortunately, his hot temper and pompous personality gave his classical learning and doctrinaire Puritan beliefs an overbearing quality that aggravated many colonists. Typical was a Quaker visitor to Boston who accused him of doing all the talking: *"Thou art a Monster, all Mouth and no Ears."*[29]

When news of the prodigious tooth and bones discovered at Claverack reached Mather, he was working on his manuscript "Biblia Americana," which he feared might remain unfinished owing to his ill health. From its inception, the manuscript was conceived as a comprehensive compilation of glosses on nearly every verse of the Scriptures, organized into six volumes divided according to the books of the Old and New Testaments. Mather's desire to use the latest scientific theories to prove the veracity of the biblical narrative led to lengthy commentaries filled with references to eminent English scientists, from Robert Boyle to Isaac Newton. In the opinion of Mather's biographer, the manuscript contributed "to Mather's becoming probably the most influential spokesman in New England for a rationalized, scientized Christianity."[30]

Encouraged by Governor Dudley's letter, Mather drafted an eloquent eleven-page gloss on the biblical passage in Genesis 6:4 referring to the existence of human giants in antediluvian times. "Concerning the Days before the FLOOD, the Glorious Historian has told us, *There were giants on the Earth, in those Dayes,"* Mather asserted before turning his attention to the newly encountered empirical proof of these giants' existence: "Could any undoubted Ruines and Remains of those GIANTS be found under the *Earth,* among the other *Subterraneous Curiosities* in o[u]r *Dayes,* it would be an Illustrious Confirmation of the *Mosaic History,* and an admirable obturation on the mouth of Atheism!"[31]

The empirical evidence inspiring Cotton Mather's commentary came from not only the *Boston News-Letter* and Governor Dudley's letter but also his conversations with the Dutchmen and the specimens he had seen himself: "Very many gentlemen, and I myself also, have had the Satisfaction, of Seeing and Handling, and Weighing one of these Teeth, dug up, with other proportionable Bones at the place aforesaid."[32] Mather's commentary barely mentioned any conflicting opinions about the creature's identity: "All that I have ever yett conversed withal, are compelled to Beleeve, That it must be an HUMANE TOOTH. It has the perfect form of the *Ey-Tooth* of a MAN."[33]

In his physical description of the Claverack site and the tooth and bones found there, Mather recited Dudley's letter and the *Boston News-Letter* article almost verbatim. But despite his dismissal of any controversy over the creature's identity, he was clearly aware that other opinions already figured in discussions of the bones. "The *Distance* from the *Sea*, takes away all pretension of its being a *Whale*, or any other Animal of the *Sea*, as well as the *Figure* of the *Teeth*," Mather explained. "Nor will the *Figure* of the *Teeth*, or the admeasurement of the Body, in the Ground, allow it to be the Remains of an *Elephant*."[34]

Like that of his fellow clergyman Edward Taylor, Mather's chief concern was to refute those who argued that the "*Antediluvian Giants* were but *Metaphorical* ones," that is, mythical giants rather than historical figures whose bones verified the literal truth of the biblical narrative. Yet Mather's own exaltation of the Claverack giant proves what fertile ground the scientific imagination could be for creating such fanciful images of the American monster, especially when they served to confirm biblical truths. Briefly, with erudition reminiscent of Taylor's inventory of mythical giants, Mather surveyed the human giants mentioned in the Bible by the prophets. In addition, he introduced those described by classical scholars like Pliny and Plutarch, as well as the giants mentioned by St. Augustine and later European travelers, including the Patagonian giant seen near the Straits of Magellan by the Italian seaman Antonio Pigafetta in the sixteenth century.

Mather dismissed the attempts by skeptics who tried to disprove the existence of the giants mentioned in the Bible. "But I have a greater authority than all of this, Namely, That of the *Giants* themselves. The *Giants* that once *Groaned under the waters*, are now *found under the Earth*, and their *Dead Bones* are *Lively Proofs* of the *Mosaic History*." Echoing Taylor's poem, Mather celebrated the Giant of

Claverack's unprecedented size, which he claimed dwarfed anything else seen on earth previously.

> Below the *Strata* of *Earth*, which the *Flood* left on the Surface of it, in the other *Hemisphere*, such Enormous *Bones* have been found, as all Skill in anatomy, must pronounce to belong to *Humane Bodies*, and could belong to none but GIANTS, in Comparison of whom, Og and GOLIATH, and all the Sons of *Anak*, must be hardly so much as *Pygmies*.[35]

Mather also referred to the works of the early historians of the New World, from Peter Martyr's *De Novo Orbe* to the Spanish Jesuit José de Acosta's *Historia natural y moral de las Indias*, which described the discovery of an enormous tooth in Mexico sixty years after Cortez's conquest of the Aztecs: "When I was in Mexico in the year 1586, they found one of those Giants buried in one of our Farms, of whom they brought a Tooth to be seen which without augmenting was as big as the *Fist of a man*."[36] Excerpts from the Spanish chronicles had appeared in Richard Hakluyt's *Purchas his Pilgrimes*, the encyclopedic collection of travel writing published in 1625 by the London clergyman Samuel Purchas, which deeply influenced the English colonists' early views of the New World.[37]

In the opening sentences of his gloss on Genesis 6:4, Mather opposed the idea that the fossils from Claverack were "Petrifying Sports of Nature," or *Lusus Naturae*, a theory then popular with many learned naturalists reluctant to believe that such bones were the remains of once living creatures. However, speculating later on the "generation," or reproduction, of these giants, Mather turned to the doctrine of "plastick virtue." His vacillation on this point is significant because the idea of "plastick virtue" was still widely used by many English naturalists to explain the anomaly of fossil remains found beneath the earth's surface. This notion was derived originally from Aristotle's theory of *vis plastica*, which maintained that fossils were the product of a mysterious force within the earth's crust that produced likenesses of organic organisms out of nonliving matter. Pliny the Elder, the Roman author whose writings about natural history influenced medieval Christian scholars and popular culture, helped popularize this belief that fossils were "bones" growing in the earth rather than the organic remains of living creatures. This confusion of organic fossils with the growth of crystals was partly responsible for the acceptance of the idea of *vis plastica*. But the underlying reason for its popularity was the reluctance of many sophisticated clergymen and physicians to accept the idea of extinction, since it implied that the earth's history extended beyond the time frame suggested by the Christian creation narrative.

The continuing influence of the Aristotle's *vis plastica* in Cotton Mather's lifetime stemmed also from the influence of the German Jesuit scholar Athanasius Kircher, whose encyclopedic work *Mundus Subterraneus*, published in 1664, attributed the form of many fossils to a *spiritus plasticus*. Kircher's ideas appealed to Mather because they sustained his belief that some of the large fossils belonged to human giants. In particular, Kircher argued that several enormous fossil skulls dug up in Sicily were very likely the bones of human giants, and among his book's illustrations were drawings of several different types of giants, including Homer's Polyphemus, which had been first identified with the Sicilian fossils by the Greek philosopher Empedocles (figure 3).

In the fourteenth century, Giovanni Boccacio, the author of the *Decameron*, claimed that these Sicilian skulls were the remains of the Homeric giant, which, he estimated, was nearly three hundred feet tall. Kircher himself traveled to Sicily to view the gigantic skulls unearthed there and afterward concluded that this human giant had been only thirty feet tall. In Kircher's drawing, Boccaccio's fanciful figure towers over several other historic giants, including a Mauritanian giant sixty cubits tall which dwarfed the tiny *Homo ordinarius* and the biblical giant Goliath. Kircher's study of the subterranean world attempted to put into perspective many centuries of speculation about the existence of human giants, usually based on the discovery of enormous fossils. Both Cotton Mather and Edward Taylor returned to this learned tradition to link large fossils with legendary human giants, and Mather explicitly praised Kircher's works in his own *Curiosa Americana*.

In contrast to his fellow clergyman Edward Taylor, Mather himself put little stock in Indian legends, but his description of the enthusiastic commentary of the Hudson River Indians on the specimens suggests that he had heard their legends from either Taylor or the Dutchmen from Albany: "Upon the Discovery of this horrible *Giant*, the *Indians* within an Hundred Miles of the place, agreed in pretending a Tradition, which they Said, they had among them, from Father to Son, for some hundreds of years concerning him; and that his Name was, *Maughkompos*." Then without hesitation, he dis-

FIGURE 3. Drawing of antediluvian giants from Athanasius Kircher's *Mundus subterraneus*, 1664. Cotton Mather cited this work to support his claim that the enormous tooth and bones found at Claverack belonged to human giants. Courtesy Bancroft Library, University of California at Berkeley.

missed the Indian accounts: "But there is very Little in any Tradition of our Salvages [sic] to be relied upon."[38]

Instead, Mather used the unprecedented size of the Claverack giant to establish its supremacy among his pantheon of legendary giants: "Of all those *Curiosities*, I know none that exceeds what has lately been found in an *American* plantation, adjoining to New England, and its being found in *America* makes it yett the more curious and marvellous."[39] In Mather's eyes, the giants mentioned in the Scriptures and elsewhere were puny compared with the seventy-foot Claverack creature, whose proportions he extrapolated from the measurements of the fossil remains and the Dutchmen's description of the dusty ruins they saw at the monster's burial site.

Procreation was a topic that fascinated Mather, from the cross-pollination of plants to the creation of Eve, whose birth inspired a lengthy discussion in his "Biblia Americana" of the anatomical growth of human embryos. His interest in monstrosities and abnormalities, from two-headed snakes and animal hybrids to giants and idiots, derived partly from the light they shed on the reproductive process. In another letter to the Royal Society concerning "A Monstrous Calf" whose head strongly resembled a human face, he later noted that "an attentive Consideration of these Curiosities might very much assist our Enquiries into that obscure work of Nature, Generation."[40]

Mather's speculation about reproduction, or "generation" as he called it, also colored his discussion of the giant of Claverack, whose genetic origins and divine purpose were the focus of his concluding remarks. At this time, he still believed in the theory of preformation, the popular notion that the whole body of every animal existed in miniature in the tiny "Stamina" visible under the microscope. Struggling to arrive at both a divine purpose and a scientific process for the giants' appearance, Mather put forward an explanation for their extinction that combined millenarian beliefs with a moralistic view.

> GOD, for punishment of a Wicked World, might order some of these Giganteous *Stamina*, to Enter the *Bodies* of the Children of Men, perhaps in their *Food*. The *Giants* thus brought forth, by *Parents* not exceeding the common Stature, were such a plague unto the world, that if a *Flood* had not Exterminated *them*, they would in a while, have Exterminated all the rest, without a *Flood*.[41]

No sooner had Mather added his gloss on the giant bones of Claverack to his "Biblia Americana" than his hopes for its publication were dashed by Governor Dudley's cavalier remarks about the clergyman's rambling discourse. Although he called Mather's manuscript "an Elaborate work, which I should be glad to see made public," he insulted the author by offering a few corrections with the excuse "If I should not offer at these two or three [trifles], you would not believe I had read it."[42] In late 1707, with the anonymous publication in London of a pamphlet attacking the governor, Mather definitively broke with Dudley, whom he condemned for his handling of Queen Anne's war against the French and their Indian allies. Having lost his political power in Massachusetts and ridiculed by the literati in London, Mather abandoned his efforts to influence colonial policy in New England and looked abroad to promote the publication of his scientific writings and the establishment of a worldwide reform movement.

Three years later, Mather sent an advertisement to London seeking subscribers who would help publish his immense manuscript "Biblia Americana," which he claimed offered the most recent scientific knowledge concerning the Creation, the Flood, and the Conflagration. Despite the failure of these efforts, the following year he added more than a thousand new illustrations to the manuscript and considered devoting more of his energies to collecting American natural curiosities, which he planned to send to the Royal Society in London. "The Improvement of Knowledge in the Works of nature is a Thing whereby God, and his Christ is glorified," Mather wrote in his diary in July 1711. "I may make a valuable Collection of many Curiosities, which this Countrey has afforded; and present it unto the Royal Society."[43]

Mather made the religious purpose for his scientific study of God's nature even more explicit two months later when he copied into his diary sentiments from an unidentified author that later were identified with the Enlightenment philosophy of many American patriots: "The Light of *Reason* is the work of God; the Law of *Reason* is the Voice of God."[44] These remarks remind us how deeply the "Laws of Nature and Nature's God" of the Declaration of Independence in Jefferson's era were imbued with the Protestant spirit pioneered by evangelical clergymen like Cotton Mather.

Despite his pompous behavior, Mather acquired a scholarly reputation among the members of London's prestigious Royal Society, many of whom corresponded with him. In 1712, Richard Waller, secretary of the Royal Society, invited Mather to communicate with the society, and the Massachusetts minister responded by sending the first of a series of thirteen letters that he later entitled *Curiosa Americana*. During the next twelve years, Mather sent eighty-two scientific letters to the Royal Society, each dealing with a separate American natural curiosity, from the woolen snow that had fallen in Connecticut to "A Monstrous Dragon" dug up in Virginia.

For the first of these letters to the Royal Society, Mather chose the gloss on the giant of Claverack, from his unpublished "Biblia Americana," no doubt to promote his own literary ambitions, although he was also aware of the debate in England over fossil remains and the earth's natural history. He prefaced the eleven pages of commentary on giants from his "Biblia Americana" with an introduction of himself and his manuscript that served to enlist sponsors for its publication and also to glorify the uniqueness of these American curiosities.

Mather's first letter was addressed to Dr. John Woodward, provincial secretary of the Royal Society and professor of physic at Gresham College. Woodward's celebrated *Essay toward a Natural History of the Earth*, published in 1695, claimed that fossils buried in the earth's crust were the "real spoils of once living animals" which had been dispersed among the various strata by the Great Deluge. Written in response to Thomas Burnet's controversial theory of the Great Deluge, the essay was based on a meticulous comparison of fossils with living animal specimens. Its principal effect was to revive the popularity of the Deluge as an explanation of how the fossil remains of marine animals came to be found so far from the oceans.

The essay was written during a time greatly influenced by the prophecies of universal doom associated with the resurgence of millenarian ideas in Newtonian England. In this sense, Woodward shared with Mather a desire to prove the historical truth of the biblical narrative through empirical evidence and deductive reasoning. But unlike Mather, Woodward compared the fossil remains with the bones of living animals. He believed the enormous bones often identified as giants might instead be the remains of unknown sea monsters living in the depths of the ocean. Neither Woodward nor Mather believed that the bones belonged to extinct creatures, although Mather suggested that the giants of Claverack had drowned during the Great Deluge.

Throughout Mather's letter is a triumphant tone in his description of the spectacular size of the giant of Claverack. His celebration of the monster's dimensions foreshadowed Thomas Jefferson's response decades later to European naturalists who maintained that the species of the New World were inferior in size. Mather's opening remarks to Dr. Woodward criticized European ignorance of the New World's "Subterraneous Curiosities," which he hoped to rectify with his commentary on the bones of Claverack. More important to the colonists, Mather's millenarian outlook injected an evangelical and protonationalistic spirit into the scientific debate about the American *incognitum*.

In his preliminary remarks, Mather evoked a sense of the American nation long before it was actually born. By associating the New Jerusalem in America with the ancient Israelite nation, he united the biblical narrative and natural history in a landscape metaphor: "The Sacred *Geography* is here survey'd; *Paradise* and *Palestine* are particularly laid out, and many Notable & Enlightening things are contributed unto this work, from the Modern Travellers."[45] His commentary on the bones of Claverack thus colored the story of their discovery with a mixture of scientific discourse, classical mythology, and millenarian beliefs that became the trademark of American national consciousness in the new republic. "The *Teeth*, which are a very durable sort of *Bones*, found beneath the Surface of the Earth, may serve as well as any *Tongues*, to tell us What *men* were once upon it."[46]

Early historians of vertebrate paleontology in America have emphasized the medieval character of Mather's belief that the bones of Claverack were those of the antediluvian giants mentioned in the Bible. While his ideas may look folkloric by scientific standards today, Mather's fanciful view of these curiosities demonstrates the difficulty in a prescientific era of trying to separate early scientific inquiry from religious beliefs, especially when so many of his contemporaries believed that the collection of such curiosities was sanctioned by the Christian faith. In his study of Mather's *Curiosa Americana*, David Levin points out:

> Just as Mather's subsequent letters will move easily from descriptions of American plants, birds, and rattlesnakes to apparitions, monstrous births, and medical prescriptions revealed in dreams, so his American Bible and his first letter to the Royal Society combine the occult, Biblical scholarship, and precise measurements of natural phenomena in the study of a remarkable discovery.[47]

Throughout the century-long controversy concerning the identity and extinction of the American *incognitum*, the biblical narrative of God's creation and the story of the Flood continued to inform even the most secularized scientific views. During the American Revolution, when the "Doctrine of Monsters" embraced by Cotton Mather and

Edward Taylor had run its course, the founding fathers still clung to many evangelical assumptions in their conception of the laws of nature and nature's God. In the end, Mather's strange concoction of science, religion, and myth offers a better insight into the cultural meaning of the American *incognitum* than all the learned papers of Enlightenment philosophers and anatomists, whose own views were often predicated on unacknowledged Christian beliefs and Bible stories.

In many ways, modern historians of science have tried to exorcise the demons of religious belief from their revered Newtonian natural philosophers, even though the basic assumptions of Christianity were integral to the development of Newton's scientific thinking. In Mather's case, his use of the term *Enlightening things* to describe his own *Curiosa Americana* highlights the religious character of the American Enlightenment, which many people today still assume was a largely secular movement. "Armed with his piety and his rationalism, between 1702 and 1712, Cotton Mather had crossed the threshold into the early Enlightenment."[48]

By 1715, Mather's hymn to natural religion had reached its fullest expression in the manuscript of his book *The Christian Philosopher,* which he sent to England with the proviso that if the work did not find a publisher, it was to be given to Dr. Woodward for deposit in the archives of the Royal Society. Published in 1720, the book was a compendium of ideas culled from the foremost natural philosophers. In contrast to the cumbersome erudition of his letters to the Royal Society, this collection of short essays was "adapted unto the general Capacity of Readers" and was recommended as reading for young candidates for the ministry, who, Mather felt, should devote more time to the study of natural philosophy.

Benjamin Franklin, who was born in Boston in 1706, the same year that Mather first saw the giant bones of Claverack, gained his early appreciation of natural history from Mather's later works. In Franklin's lifetime, despite the secularization of his own Enlightenment ideas, the controversy over the American *incognitum* always retained elements of the millenarian expectations associated with early Puritan science. More important, in the writings of Mather and Edward Taylor, speculation about the identity of the American *incognitum* first entered American consciousness not in the iconoclastic writings of Enlightenment philosophers like Thomas Jefferson and Benjamin Franklin but, rather, through the literary efforts of the evangelical Puritan divines to whom natural history was a confirmation of the literal truth of the Bible.

The intellectual world that gave birth to these early commentaries on the American *incognitum* was exceedingly complex, owing to the era's transitional character. In the early eighteenth century, during Queen Anne's reign, the missionary zeal of the Bible commonwealth in Massachusetts was being undermined by a resurgence of Anglicanism and the expansion of England's mercantile interests in the colonies. Restoration of the Protestant monarchy under William and Mary in 1689 had strengthened the Anglican Church, which now looked to Newtonian physics and natural theology to fortify the Protestant faith while preserving the church's authority over dissenting sects.

Edward Taylor and Cotton Mather were both Protestant reformers educated in the Greek, Latin, and Hebrew classics who saw themselves as missionaries in the American wilderness. They belonged to the socially prominent class of university-trained professionals who were carving a new niche in colonial society through the reform of religious life and the pursuit of scientific studies of the earth's natural history. Disturbed by the erosion of their evangelical mission in the American colonies and the cultural crudeness of frontier life, these Puritan clergymen turned to literary endeavors and scientific studies to express the intensity of their religious convictions and to compensate for their isolation and insecure social status.

In the aftermath of England's Glorious Revolution, when Puritan ministers became concerned about their waning influence over the colony's religious life, the American *incognitum* took its first steps toward becoming a mythical creature identified with the antiquity of the unborn American nation. In Edward Taylor's private poetry and Cotton Mather's scholarly commentary, the first images of an antediluvian monster worthy of the emerging republic began to take shape in the minds of American colonists. Devout Puritan beliefs obviously helped create their common vision of this creature whose significance extended far beyond the realm of scientific discovery. Symbolically speaking, the giant bones of Claverack became a banner of missionary zeal for these clergymen because the fossils had come from the inland frontier whose conquest gave a deeper spiritual meaning to their errand in the wilderness.

Phenomena like the mysterious bones discovered at Claverack offered Taylor and Mather an opportunity to incorporate the natural wonders of the New World into their visions of the promised land, to blend the antiquity of their classical learning and millenarian biblical prophecies with the authority of Newtonian science. In the American colonies, where evangelical beliefs had taken root alongside the pragmatism of an expanding commercial society, Protestant clergymen and physicians were more likely to consider the fossil remains as a sign of God's blessing on the New Israel in America than as evidence of monstrous creatures that then were found only in allegory and myth.

As their literary efforts reveal, these Puritan divines shared with other English and European Protestants an overwhelming belief in the Great Deluge as the decisive event explaining the earth's natural history and the anomaly of the fossil remains like those found at Claverack. Beyond its usefulness to clergymen, the fabulous story of Noah's Ark and the Deluge had become an effective medium for the popularization of scientific thought, particularly the burgeoning literature about the natural history of the earth. To appreciate the way that scientific views were reshaping the apocalyptic landscape with which the American *incognitum* was identified, we must look more closely at the influential new theories of the earth's natural history being propounded by English Protestants, namely, Thomas Burnet and Dr. John Woodward, whose ideas helped popularize the metaphor of the earth's landscape as a natural ruin shaped by the receding waters of the Great Deluge.

2

The Antediluvian World as a "New Found Land"

And yet these Mountains we are speaking of,
to confess the truth, are nothing but great ruines;
but such as show a certain magnificence in Nature;
as from old Temples and broken Amphitheaters of
the Romans we collect the greatness of that people.

—Thomas Burnet, 1684

TOWARD THE END of Queen Anne's reign, when Cotton Mather sent his account of the Claverack monster to the Royal Society, contemporary views of the antediluvian world and fossils were in a state of flux. In Mather's lifetime, theologians and physicians in England had put forward several new theories of the earth's natural history in an effort to fortify Protestant doctrine with the natural philosophy of the Newtonian era. Like Mather's own views of the Claverack bones, many of these "scientific" theories combined religious beliefs about the earth's history with the latest empirical evidence concerning fossils. Even though some of England's natural philosophers still believed that human giants had once inhabited the world, few naturalists thought that the enormous fossilized teeth were human remains.

Instead, the central debate now revolved around whether such fossils were from once living animals, and supporters of this idea disagreed as to what kind of creatures they represented. The most prominent clergymen and physicians, however, rejected the organic origin of fossil remains because this theory raised the issue of extinction, a heresy to those who believed in the perfection of God's creation. Their position was summed up by the era's most brilliant clergyman naturalist, John

41

Ray, whose book *The Wisdom of God Manifested in the Works of Creation* became the classic statement of the Christian doctrine of plenitude: "The number of true species in nature is fixed and limited and, as we may reasonably believe, constant and unchangeable from the first creation to the present day."[1]

During the 1690s, Thomas Burnet and Dr. John Woodward, to whom Mather addressed his own account of the Claverack bones, were the chief spokesmen for an influential new group of natural philosophers known as the "diluvialists." They sought to prove scientifically that the Great Deluge was the principal agency responsible for the earth's natural history and the perplexing disposition of fossil remains found below the earth's surface. Many geologists today believe that these men's fanciful theories delayed the discovery of prehistoric nature and geological time. The revival of the Deluge theory, however, actually helped popularize many new ideas about the earth's stratification and the organic origin of fossils, thereby opening the way for the acceptance of extinct species and discovering geological time a century later.

More important, by placing the creation narrative of Christianity and the story of Noah's Flood at the center of the debate over the antediluvian world, the diluvialists turned the earth's terrain into a sacred landscape that could be viewed as a natural ruin shaped by the Deluge's receding waters. The lasting influence of these theories was in the realm of metaphor and myth, since the diluvialists' millenarian beliefs about the apocalyptic destruction of the "first earth" by the universal deluge helped crystallize a Gothic view of the earth's landscape in the minds of succeeding generations of Romantic poets and painters. The circumstances surrounding this new metaphorical view and its implications for the giant bones of Claverack are essential to understanding the symbolism later attached to the American *incognitum*.

When the giant tooth from Claverack reached London in 1705, the Royal Society already had in its collection of natural curiosities several large grinders, identified as the fossil teeth of either large land animals or sea creatures. In 1681, at the request of the Royal Society, the London physician and botanist Nehemiah Grew published the 386-page *Catalogue and Description of the Natural and Artificial Rarities* preserved in the society's repository. Among the twenty-two plates illustrating the volume was a drawing of an enormous tooth identified by Grew as the "Petrify'd Tooth of a Sea Animal," a specimen known today to have been the lower right molar of a mastodon.[2] In addition, the Royal Society had in its possession two similar specimens identified as the "Petrify'd Tooth of a Land Animal" which had been donated several years earlier by the archbishop of Canterbury. These two specimens were among the earliest grinders collected by the society and had been found in September 1668, seventeen feet below the earth's surface, by John Somner, who had been sinking a well at Chartham, a village about three miles from Canterbury.

In 1669, Somner's brother William, a learned Canterbury antiquary well known for his historical survey *The Antiquities of Canterbury*, published a pamphlet entitled *Chartham News* describing these fossil remains, illustrated with elegant drawings of the enormous teeth. "Cheek-teeth, or Grinders, as to the form, they are all, not much unlike, but for the bigness, the Grinders of a Man," Somner observed of the "strange and monstrous bones," which he said were almost as big "as a Man's fist."[3] Like Cotton Mather, Somner alluded briefly to several historical accounts of such fist-size teeth found elsewhere, including the Spanish Jesuit José de Acosta's report of the bones of human giants found in New Spain.

Somner himself was skeptical that the bones belonged to human giants, for he was inclined to believe they were the remains of some kind of animal. "Some that have seen them, by the Teeth, and some other circumstances, are of opinion, that they are the Bones of an *Hippopotamus*, or *Equus Fluvialis*; that is, a *River-horse*," he explained.[4] He cautiously theorized that the bones belonged to some "Marine, or Sea-bred Creature" whose presence in the valley so remote from the ocean might be explained by the possibility the region was formerly an estuary submerged under the sea. Somner's speculations were the first tentative efforts of English antiquaries to get beyond the apocryphal attribution of such fossil remains to human giants. In 1703, shortly before Lord Cornbury sent the Claverack tooth to London, Somner's remarks received renewed public notice when the English vicar Nicolas Battely published a new edition of Somner's *Antiquities,* including his pamphlet and the handsome drawings of the fossil teeth found near Canterbury.

For several decades, English naturalists had carefully cataloged each new discovery of fossil remains, in both England and around the world. Battely's comments on Somner's pamphlet *Chartham News* referred to several other accounts of similar bones that had recently appeared in the Royal Society's journal *Philosophical Transactions*. In 1697,

Robert Hooke, the society's foremost authority on fossils, mentioned in a lecture to the society several reports of large bones discovered in England, including the "Head of an *Hippopotamus* at Chartham in *Kent.*" Even before the Claverack tooth reached the Royal Society, the fellows had cast their fossil net far afield, for Hooke's lecture also alluded to "the Bones of the *Mammatoroykost,* or of a strange Subterraneous Animal, as the *Siberians* fancy, which is commonly dug up in *Siberia,* which Mr. *Ludolphus* judges to be the Teeth and Bones of Elephants."[5]

In July 1701, Somner's *Chartham News* itself was reprinted in the Royal Society's journal. Two months later, John Luffkin, an English antiquary, responded with a letter about some "Bones of extraordinary Bigness" found in an Essex gravel pit, which he maintained were the bones of an elephant, not of a hippopotamus, or sea animal, as Somner had conjectured. In Luffkin's opinion, these bones were likely the remains of elephants brought to England by the Roman emperor Claudius during his wars with the Britains, since the sites of Roman encampments and routes by which they traveled were nearby.[6] Interestingly enough, many of these early accounts of such bones mentioned remnants of Roman ruins, usually pavement and mosaic work, encountered by persons digging wells and cellars, revealing the wide acceptance at this time of the popular analogy between the ruins of nature and the monuments of antiquity.

Ironically, the originator of this modern metaphor of fossil relics was not a diluvialist himself but, rather, an advocate for what later came to be known as "vulcanism," the theory that the earth's history had been shaped largely by cataclysmic earthquakes and volcanic eruptions instead of the Great Deluge. In 1705, when Lord Cornbury's "tooth of a Giant" reached the Royal Society, Richard Waller, the secretary, had just published *The Posthumous Works of Robert Hooke,* a comprehensive collection of essays by the British natural philosopher who had served for many years as the Royal Society's curator of experiments. The publication in 1665 of Hooke's treatise *Micrographia, or Some Physiological Descriptions of Minute Bodies Made by Magnifying Glasses* had established his reputation for brilliant theoretical formulations based on mechanical experiments and empirical evidence. Hooke was the first to use a compound microscope to study fossils, and his comparison of the microstructure of charcoal and fossilized wood marked the beginning of his lifelong fascination with fossils, whose organic origin he had first extrapolated from the two specimens' similar anatomical structure.

In 1668, Hooke delivered to the Royal Society the first of many lectures on earthquakes challenging the pivotal role of the Great Deluge in the earth's history. In Hooke's opinion, Noah's Flood had not lasted long enough to alter the earth's surface. Instead, he felt that the catastrophic effects of earthquakes on the earth's landscape were a more plausible explanation for how fossils came to be found on mountaintops and embedded in stone deep beneath the soil.

> That a great part of the Surface of the Earth hath been since the Creation transformed and made of another Nature, namely, many Parts which have been Sea are now Land; and divers other Parts are now Sea which were once a firm land; Mountains have been turned into Plains and Plains into Mountains and the like.[7]

For his contemporaries, the most controversial aspect of Hooke's theory of the earth's instability was his parallel assertion that living organisms may have undergone similar changes, with new species being created while others had become extinct. "There have been many other species of creatures in former ages, of which we can find none at present, and 'tis not unlikely also but that there may be divers new kinds now, which have not been from the beginning."[8] In this case, his argument was based on the well-known fact that varying climatic conditions and food sources produced alterations in existing species, from dogs, sheep, goats, and deer to hawks and pigeons. "And to me it seems very absurd to conclude, that from the beginning things have continued in the same state that we now find them, since we find everything to change and vary in our own remembrance."[9] These remarkably modern views of the earth's history had little resonance among Hooke's contemporaries, who regarded them as idiosyncratic speculations of an eccentric scholar unable to prove them empirically.

In any case, despite his powerful argument embracing extinction and the organic origin of fossils, Hooke's novel theory of catastrophic change never challenged the conventional Christian chronology of the earth's history nor the conformity of the Scriptures with rational inquiries into natural history. The principal obstacle to the acceptance of his idea of extinction continued to be the unwillingness of most Protestant natural philosophers and clergymen to believe that God's creation had any imperfections, that any living beings had disappeared from the earth. To them, the underlying problem lay in the short time span that

Hooke and his contemporaries presented and, more important, their assumption that the earth's history had coincided with human history. In other words, the concept of prehistoric life was impossible, since the earth had no history before God's creation of Adam.

Even though Hooke's ideas were largely rejected by his colleagues, the posthumous edition of his *Discourse on Earthquakes* left an indelible imprint on generations of Anglo-American and European naturalists, owing to his metaphorical view of fossils as the coins and monuments of the earth's unwritten natural history. More than anyone else, Hooke was responsible for launching among the antiquarians and natural philosophers of the Newtonian era this view of fossils as relics of the natural world. As a classically educated scholar, Hooke spoke to an audience familiar with ecclesiastical literature and also the Greek and Latin classics. Like other university-trained natural philosophers of the Newtonian era, Hooke's writings about natural history combined religious doctrine, classical literature, and scientific thought, held together by the millenarian spirit of the Protestant Reformation, which spurred England's colonization of America and its emergence as an imperial power.

Behind Hooke's natural philosophy lay the metaphors of a modern mythology of conquest, the doctrine of natural history itself, which in the Baconian tradition had become the means of dominating the universal realm of nature in the name of evangelization and enlightenment. For Francis Bacon, the early-seventeenth-century architect of this new doctrine, the master metaphor for obtaining the secrets of nature was the mining of the earth's surface, an analogy that he often used to illustrate the process by which knowledge of natural history was obtained. In Bacon's words, "the truth of nature lies hid in certain deep mines and caves," and only by "digging further and further into the mine of natural knowledge" could humankind recover its lost dominion over the natural world.[10]

In order to convince his learned audience of the significance of fossils, Hooke artfully employed this Baconian premise, linking Bacon's aspirations for empire to the relics of the earth's natural history:

> If in digging a Mine, or the like, an artificial Coin or Urne, or the like Substance be found, no one scruples to affirm it to be of this or that Metal or Earth he finds them by trial to be of: Nor that they are *Roman, Saxon, Norman,* or the like, according to the Relievo, Impressions, Characters, or Form they find them of.

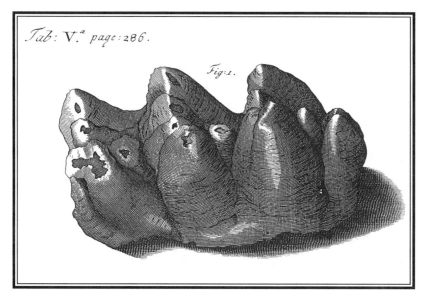

Tab: V.ᵃ page:286.

Fig:1.

FIGURE 4. Drawing of a fossil grinder in the Royal Society's collection from Robert Hooke's *Posthumous Works*, 1705. This tooth was earlier identified by Nehemiah Grew as the "Petrify'd Tooth of a Sea Animal."

Then, referring to the anomaly of the oyster and cockle shells found buried in England's countryside far from the sea, Hooke eloquently linked Bacon's view of natural history with images of ancient empires:

> Now, these Shells and other Bodies are the Medals, Urnes or Monu-
> ments of Nature. These are the greatest and most lasting Monuments
> of Antiquity, which, in all probability will far antidate [*sic*] all the most
> ancient Monuments of the World, even the very Pyramids, Obelisks,
> Mummys, Hieroglyphicks, and Coins, and will afford more informa-
> tion in Natural History than those other put altogether will in Civil.[11]

This remarkable passage is from an undated lecture by Hooke, published in 1705 by Richard Waller in *The Posthumous Works of Robert
Hooke*, but a similar passage appeared in his earliest lecture on earthquakes dated 1668. Among the numerous renderings of fossils in
Hooke's *Posthumous Works* is an elegant drawing of the grinder from the
Royal Society's collection that had been identified by Nehemiah Grew
as the "Petrify'd Tooth of a Sea Animal" (figure 4).

In keeping with his metaphorical view of these relics from the antediluvian world, Hooke's lectures frequently alluded to the "Mythlogic History of the Poets" to support his own theories about the earth's history and the significance of the fossil record. From Plato's legend of the lost island of Atlantis, which he used to bolster his theory of catastrophic earthquakes, to the war of the giants described in Ovid's *Metamorphosis*, classical mythology for Hooke often contained a disguised account of the earth's history, making his own metaphorical view of fossils all the more appealing to learned naturalists of the Newtonian era. By the time the giant bones of Claverack were discovered, Hooke's ingenious metaphor had become a commonplace in the works of many antiquarians and naturalists writing about the antediluvian world. By then, the diluvialists had captured the metaphor, largely through the literary efforts of the Anglican prelate Thomas Burnet and his critics, who came to view the earth's entire landscape as a ruins created by the receding waters of the Great Deluge.

In Robert Hooke's *Discourse on Earthquakes*, the natural causes of the Flood remained obscure, and its overall significance was reduced by his contention that its short duration had diminished its role in shaping the earth's landscape. During the turbulent restoration of England's Protestant monarchy, an event that many Protestants regarded as a providential act auguring the millennium of Christ's rule on earth, the diluvialists extended Hooke's metaphor to envision all the earth's landscape as a natural ruin, a powerful poetic analogy that influenced generations of literary discourse.

The chief architect of the revival of diluvialism and the originator of this influential new metaphor was the Anglican bishop Thomas Burnet, whose *Sacred Theory of the Earth* appeared in 1684, three years after the original Latin edition led to an intense debate among learned scholars about the natural history of the Great Deluge. An eminent prose stylist and clergyman educated at Cambridge University, Burnet became the master of Charterhouse in 1685, shortly after the first volumes of his *Sacred Theory* appeared. Four years later, he was appointed royal chaplain to William of Orange following the latter's ascension to the English throne. Unlike Hooke, Burnet was not trained in the experimental sciences, nor was he a Newtonian natural philosopher, although he was extremely sympathetic to the new science. Instead, he saw himself primarily as a theologian who used natural philosophy to provide rational explanations for the Scriptures, whose authority was being challenged by the new mechanistic principles of the celestial sciences articulated by Descartes and Newton.

Fossils were not what inspired Burnet's vision of the earth's crust as a natural ruins. In fact, his *Sacred Theory of the Earth* never mentions them, although this work eventually exerted great influence on the debate over fossils. Instead, the physical evidence that engendered this metaphor in Burnet's mind was the earth's mountains, specifically the Swiss Alps, which he had seen a decade earlier during his grand tour of the Continent. In 1671, Burnet had crossed the Alps while traveling with the earl of Wiltshire, to whom he dedicated his *Sacred Theory*. According to his own account, he had begun writing his book in an effort to explain the disturbing impact on him of "those wild, vast, and indigested Heaps of Stones and Earth." In the process, he compared the rugged mountains to the monumental ruins of classical antiquity, extending Hooke's metaphor to the earth's entire surface: "And yet these Mountains we are speaking of, to confess the truth, are nothing but great ruines, but such as show a certain magnificence in Nature; as from old Temples and broken Amphitheaters of the *Romans* we collect the greatness of that people."[12]

Throughout *Sacred Theory*, Burnet uses this metaphor of the earth's landscape as a ruin to create a picturesque image of the mountains that he found both terrifying and majestic. But ultimately for him, the Alps were images of disorder and confusion rather than harmonious beauty. "I fancy, if we had seen the Mountains when they were born and raw, when the Earth was fresh and broken, and the Waters of the Deluge newly retir'd, the Fractions and Confusions of them would have appear'd very ghastly and frightful."[13] In fact, Burnet's opinion of this mountainous terrain was deeply ambiguous, for the jagged peaks also inspired a religious awe in him, which decades later became a distinctive feature of the Gothic landscape admired by Romantic painters and authors:

> There is something august and Stately in the Air of these things that inspired the mind with great thoughts and passions. We do naturally upon such occasions think of God and his greatness, and whatsoever hath but the shadow and appearance of INFINITE, as all things have that are too big for our comprehension, they fill and over-bear the mind with their Excess, and cast it into a pleasing kind of stupor and admiration.[14]

Born in 1635 of Scottish ancestry, Burnet had spent his formative years at Cambridge University during the 1650s, when the influence of the poet and philosopher Henry More was reaching its peak. Deeply influenced by René Descartes' *Principles of Philosophy*, which envisioned an infinity of worlds in the universe, Cambridge Platonists like More tried to reconcile the rationality of the French philosopher's mechanistic cosmology with conventional Christian chronology. In his *Principles of Philosophy*, published in 1644, Descartes depicted the earth's original starlike form as a smooth outer surface that had eventually solidified as crust and later collapsed into an underlying fluid layer. While it cooled, the irregular shape of the earth's existing landscape was created. In the latter half of the seventeenth century, the precise mechanism of the Great Deluge became a cause célèbre among English Protestants trying to reconcile Cartesian reason with revelation, especially after the Glorious Revolution when millenarian beliefs in the Apocalypse joined with the experimental sciences to invent new theories of the earth's natural history.

In his *Sacred Theory*, Burnet created a grandiose natural history of the Great Deluge that provided physical explanations of the biblical narrative while conforming to the Cartesian philosophy of nature. In the end, Burnet saw the earth's landscape as a ruin not in Hooke's archaeological sense but, rather, as a manifestation of God's power. In his opinion, the antediluvian world, Adam and Eve's Garden of Eden, had been a paradise, a perfectly smooth sphere without mountains or seas, whose upright axis of rotation had produced a perpetual springlike climate.

> In this smooth Earth were the first Scenes of the World, and the first Generations of Mankind. It had the Beauty of Youth and blooming Nature, fresh and fruitful, not a Wrinkle, Scar or Fracture in all its Body; no Rocks nor Mountains, no hollow Caves, nor gaping Channels, but even and uniform all over.[15]

Burnet's elegant prose gave his readers what purported to be a physical description of the antediluvian world, a literary exercise whose audacity he acknowledged. "This is a bold Step; such a supposition carries us into another World, which we have never seen, nor even yet heard relation of."[16] Burnet named this primeval world the "first Earth," and in keeping with the millennial zeal nurturing his view of the earth's natural history, he offered this newly discovered antiquity of the antediluvian world to his king like a conquered territory: "New-found Lands and Countries accrew to the Prince, whose Subject makes the first Discovery," Burnet wrote in his dedication to King Charles. "And having retriev'd a World that has been lost, for some thousands of years, out of the Memory of Man, and the Records of Time, I thought it my Duty to lay it at your Majesties Feet."[17]

Burnet borrowed his theory of crustal collapse from Descartes and the Danish naturalist Nicholas Steno, both early pioneers of the concepts of sedimentation and stratification. But Burnet's naturalistic description of the cataclysmic events surrounding the Great Deluge incorporated other scientific evidence. For a rational explanation of its physical causes, he attempted to calculate the exact amount of water necessary for the universal deluge. After concluding that forty days and nights of rain would be insufficient to cover the entire globe, he claimed the floodwaters had come from an underlying layer of water beneath the earth's surface, released when the earth's original crust cracked and collapsed. "We have now proved our Explication of the Deluge to be more than an Idea, or to be a true piece of Natural History."[18]

Though fanciful by modern standards, Burnet's arguments were highly praised by his contemporaries, including his friend Isaac Newton, who corresponded enthusiastically with him about the theory. Eventually, what created the most controversy was Burnet's Gothic view of the earth's landscape, the "Ruins of a broken World" that Noah saw emerging from the receding waters of the Deluge. "What a rude Lump our World is that we are so apt to dote upon," he wrote of the earth's misshapen terrain, which he compared to the moon's "rude and ragged" surface as recently viewed through telescopes. "They are both in my judgment the image or picture of a great Ruine, and have the true aspect of a World lying in its rubbish."[19]

The symmetry of Burnet's cosmic theory of the earth's history encompassed not only the Creation and the Great Deluge but also the Conflagration and the future Millennium, which he conceived as a cycle of seven symmetrical phases. The latter were illustrated in his book's frontispiece, picturing Jesus standing atop a circle of seven spheres depicting the earth's cycle of transformations, from the birth of

Paradise as a perfect sphere to its anticipated return to an ideal spherical shape after the fiery cataclysm of God's final judgment (figure 5). In many respects, the key to the popularity of Burnet's theory was his vivid description of the final Conflagration, or the Apocalypse.

During the political crisis accompanying the restoration of the Protestant monarchy, there was wide interest in Burnet's description of exactly how, in physical terms, the Conflagration and the Millennium would occur. Burnet published the final two books of his *Sacred Theory* shortly after the ascension of William of Orange to the English throne in 1689, an event capping a strong revival of millenarian beliefs in England.[20] In his effort to combine scientific methodology with millennial prophecy, Burnet made natural history an ally in the struggle against the Antichrist, who haunted his apocalyptic landscape: "Now the fateful time presses, Nature inclines towards its end, and any dangers like rocks in the sea, are the more to be feared, the nearer we come to them."[21] The powerful appeal of his Gothic vision of the earth's landscape stemmed from his romantic blending of images drawn from classical antiquity, millenarian doctrine, and natural philosophy.

Burnet's natural history of the earth used the biblical prophets' apocalyptic vision to create a universal history of the natural world that transcended the rise and fall of Greek and Roman civilization, a blending of Christianity and the pagan philosophy typical of the English Renaissance culture: "In the mean time, what subject can be more worthy [of] the thoughts of a serious person, than to view and consider the Rise and Fall, and all the Revolutions, not of a Monarchy or an Empire, or the *Grecian* or *Roman* State, but of an intire [sic] World.[22] Ironically, when he compared the irregularity and disorder of the earth's surface to the ruins of antiquity, Burnet created an image of the landscape that led to a new appreciation of wild nature in the next generation by natural philosophers, who opposed the formal gardens and idealized aesthetic of the neoclassical Renaissance order.

For the emerging views of the American landscape, Burnet's elegiac view of the wild nature as a ruin wrought by natural forces during the Great Deluge combined in a novel way the earth's natural history with the ruins of classical antiquity and the millennial destiny of the New World in America. In his *Sacred Theory*, illustrations of the existing earth's surface, the product of the crustal collapse during the Deluge, showed the American continents dotted with mountains, an image joining the "New Worlds" of Noah and Columbus. In this new vision

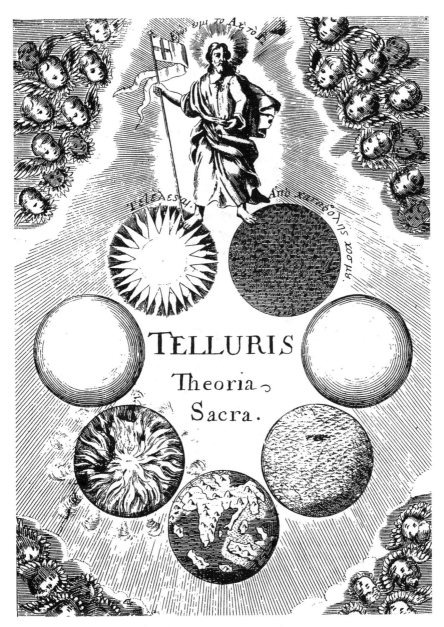

FIGURE 5. The frontispiece from the first edition of Thomas Burnet's *Telluris theoria sacra*, or *Sacred Theory of the Earth*. Burnet maintained the earth was created as a perfect sphere and subsequently became "a wreck of a world" following Noah's Flood before returning to a perfect sphere at the Apocalypse.

of the earth's antiquity, fossils became the archaeological evidence of Mosaic history, "the Beginnings and Progress of a RISING WORLD," as Burnet called the ruins of the earth after the Deluge. In his picturesque view of the earth's existing landscape, the faded glory of the classical world was blended together with the creation narrative of Christianity to produce a sublime view of the American wilderness, a vision that set the stage for the substitution of natural history for the new nation's antiquity a century later.

In the 1690s, Burnet's *Sacred Theory* became the subject of debate during a period of speculation about the earth's natural history and the nature of fossils. Surprisingly, the ambivalent aesthetics of Burnet's Gothic landscape, rather than his scientific theory of the Great Deluge, generated the most commentary and criticism. John Keill, an eminent mathematician, easily demonstrated Burnet's errors in mathematical computation, and he dismissed his theory as poetic fantasy, full of rhetoric and revelation rather than reason. Nonetheless, despite his flimsy scientific methodology, Burnet's poetic vision of the earth's natural history garnered high praise from many contemporary writers, who saw in his landscape inspiration for a new aesthetic of the beauty of wild nature.

By the time Cotton Mather wrote to the Royal Society, England's literary journalists and poets had been captivated by Burnet's elegant prose. Joseph Addison had already celebrated Burnet's *Sacred Theory* with a Latin ode, and Richard Steele had devoted an issue of *The Spectator* to it.[23] Burnet's graphic description of the burning of the earth during the Conflagration inspired generations of geology-conscious poets who, like Steele, saw the majesty of his "funeral oration over this Globe," in which the "Mountains and Rocks of the Earth are melted as Wax before the Sun, and their place is no where found."[24] In *The Complete English Gentleman*, Daniel Defoe quoted Burnet's *Sacred Theory*, and the earl of Shaftbury's descriptions of Europe's mountains in his influential essay "The Moralists," published in 1709, introduced the new aesthetic of wild nature which was the paradoxical product of Burnet's own disgust with and awe before the Alps.

Burnet's vivid imagery was etched in the minds of many American naturalists, from Benjamin Franklin to Thomas Jefferson. But in Cotton Mather's lifetime, the immediate impact of his *Sacred Theory* was to spur new visions of the Great Deluge as the principal agency explaining the anomaly of the fossil remains being unearthed around the world. Burnet himself had ignored the issue of the fossils, preferring instead to embrace a theory of the earth's natural history whose basic premises were largely incompatible with the growing evidence the fossils' organic origin.

In rectifying this inconsistency, the most influential diluvialist to emerge in Burnet's wake was the British naturalist to whom Mather addressed his *Curiosa Americana*. A leading critic of Burnet's theory, Dr. John Woodward had published a book-length countertheory entitled *An Essay toward a Natural History of the Earth* in 1695.[25] Elected to the Royal Society in 1702, Woodward was well known among English naturalists not only for this volume but also for his early experiments in plant physiology. In contrast to Burnet's neoclassical interest in Cartesian physics, Woodward's training as a physician at Cambridge led him to look at the world in Lockean terms, placing more emphasis on empirical evidence than on aesthetic theory. "From a long train of Experience," he argued, "the World is at length convinc'd that Observations are the only sure Grounds whereon to build a lasting and substantial Philosophy. All Parties are so far agreed upon this matter, that it seems now the common sense of Mankind."[26]

With this empirical philosophy in mind, Woodward brought the fossil evidence back to center stage in the debate over the earth's natural history and the physical causes of the Great Deluge. Published in the year he received his degree at Cambridge, Woodward's essay reflected a firsthand knowledge of fossils gathered during his travels and observation of excavation sites throughout England. His treatise is filled with descriptions of the fossils he had observed in caves, mines, and quarries, together with corroborating evidence from literary accounts of other sites around the world. Although he shared with Burnet the desire to explain the natural causes of the Great Deluge and Moses' account of the earth's history, he accused Burnet of setting forth "an imaginary and fictitious Earth."[27]

In many ways, the central issue dividing these two diluvialists was the nature of the antediluvian earth. Relying on empirical evidence, Woodward sought to show how Burnet's theory of the perfect sphere differed from both the Mosaic account in the Bible and the "Matter of Fact." The similarity between the fossil remains of animal and plant life found in the earth and the living specimens examined by Woodward led him to conclude that the antediluvian forms of life did not differ greatly from those now found: "That these Productions of the *Original*

Earth, differ not from those of the *Present*, either in figure, in Magnitude, in Texture, or any other respect, is easily learn'd by comparing them."[28] For England's naturalists, the argument revolved around how the fossil remains of marine life came to be embedded in rocks at the bottom of mines and quarries or on the tops of high mountains. Woodward acknowledged that many naturalists still viewed this anomalous displacement of marine life as "a kind of Lusus of Nature," or "Jest of Nature," although he himself argued that "they are the real Spoils of once living Animals: and not Stones, or natural Fossils, as some late learned men have thought." "'Tis a *Phenomenon* so surprizing and extraordinary, that 'tis not strange a man should scarcely credit his very Senses in the case," he observed.[29]

Woodward's assertion that fossil remains were organic was made more palatable by his static view of the earth's history and the prominent role of the Great Deluge. Although he seemed to accept the notion that the earth's surface was composed of various strata, he rejected the idea that the landmasses were created by either slow sedimentation or violent earthquakes. Instead, he created his own fanciful theory, arguing that Noah's Flood had led to the complete dissolution of the earth's surface. Its crust, including the fossils, had been reconstituted when its components resettled in layers, according to the "Laws of Gravity." In his words,

> the whole Terrestrial Globe was taken all to pieces and dissolved at the Deluge, the Particles of Stone, Marble, and all other solid Fossils dissevered, taken upon into the Water, and there sustained together with Sea-shells and other Animal and Vegetable bodies: and that the present Earth consists, and was formed out of that promiscuous Mass of Sand, Earth, Shells and the rest falling down again, and subsiding from the Water.[30]

Woodward rejected Burnet's theory that the Great Deluge was a cataclysmic natural event without providential causes. He maintained that this catastrophe was a supernatural act undertaken with a design and purpose, albeit an act that had left its record in natural history.

By using fossil evidence to demonstrate the unity of God's creation, Woodward made the natural history of the Flood an indispensable element of Christian doctrine, and the popularity of his theories made him, in the words of his critic Antonio Vallisneri, "the Grand Protector of the Universal Deluge." In contrast to Burnet, who saw the earth as a "disorderly Pile of Ruines and Rubbish," Woodward viewed everything in nature—from the antediluvian world to the new landscape created by the Deluge—as divinely designed by God, "the most consummate and absolute Order and Beauty, out of the highest Confusion and Deformity: acting with the most exquisite Contrivance and Wisdom."[31] Instead of Burnet's "dirty little planet," Woodward's natural world was ordered by the laws of gravity, which were themselves a reflection of the divine wisdom of God's design. "I am indeed well aware that the author of the *Theory of the Earth* differs very much from me in opinion as to this matter," Woodward remarked of Burnet's view. "He will not allow that there are any such Signs of Art and Skill in the Make of the Perfect Globe as are here mentioned."[32]

For Woodward, the Deluge had wiped out the "first earth," the paradise that Christians called the Garden of Eden, where humankind existed without deprivation and sin. In his opinion, Noah's Flood created a wilderness desert in which science and industry were necessary for human survival. This description of the fallen world encountered by Noah after the Deluge set up Woodward's theory of the progress of society from the days of pagan barbarism to Christian civilization, an idea that later became fundamental to the founding fathers' secularized Enlightenment doctrine. While Woodward mocked the philosophers who searched for the "Primitive Earth" of Paradise, both the Bible and empirical evidence proved to him that the antediluvian world differed from the current natural world mainly in the degree of its fertility. "From those Remains we may judge what sort of Earth *that* was," he declared of the fossilized animal and vegetable remains, "and see that it was not much different from *this* we now inhabit."[33]

In Woodward's account of the antediluvian world, fossils became the remnants of Paradise, a pastoral world whose luxuriant life-forms contrasted with the barren world Noah saw emerging from the receding floodwaters of the Great Deluge. Unlike Burnet, Woodward claimed the earth's terrain had undergone virtually no changes since Noah's Flood, an assertion that preserved the conventional Christian chronology and the plenitude of God's creation: "The *Terraqueous Globe* is to *this Day* nearly in the same *condition* that the *Universal Deluge* left it; being also likely to *continue* so till the Time of its final *Ruin* and *Dissolution*, preserved to the *same End* for which 'twas first *formed.*"[34]

In effect, Woodward's Great Deluge created the circumstance out of which a new hierarchy of nations and races arose with the advent of Christian civilization:

> Those first Ages of the new World were simple, and illiterate to Admiration, and 'twas a long time e're the Cloud was withdrawn: e're the least spark of Learning (I had almost said of Humanity) broke forth, or any Man betook himself to the promotion of Science. Nay the Effects of it are visible to this hour: a general Darkness yet prevails, and hangs over whole Nations, yea the far greater part of the World is still barbarous and savage.[35]

With this simple logic, Woodward united the main elements of the creation narrative of Christianity with the natural history of the New World, bringing a subtle but effective religious force to the empirical evidence pertaining to the history of the antediluvian world. In this perspective, America was not simply the "New World" discovered by Columbus in 1492 but also the ruined world revealed to Noah when the waters of the Great Deluge subsided.

The creation of this new archaeological image of the landscape was a significant aspect of these early theories of the earth's natural history. Through the metaphor of the earth as a natural ruins, American patriots were later able to join together national identity, religious destiny, and natural history. In his *Essay toward a Natural History of the Earth*, Woodward brought together the critical elements of God, nature, and empire in a turn of phrase demonstrating why the fossil remains at Claverack were called the "ruins" of the giant: "Amongst the rest there were indeed some who believed these to be Remains of the General Deluge, and so many Monuments of that calamitous and fatal irruption."[36]

By the beginning of the eighteenth century, English naturalists had already appropriated this term, *monuments*, from the antiquarians, who used it to describe everything from ancient coins to architectural ruins.[37] Ironically, through their theories of the Great Deluge, the diluvialists encouraged the acceptance of the organic interpretation of fossils even while they gave them a religious significance. Thus the organic interpretation of fossils itself became a powerful argument supporting the historical nature of the Deluge, which explains why so many Protestant clergymen eagerly embraced this scientific doctrine.[38]

In the early eighteenth century, the chief popularizer of this apocalyptic view of fossils was the Swiss naturalist and physician Johann
Jacob Scheuchzer, who published his *Herbarium of the Deluge* in 1709,
only a few years before Cotton Mather's letter to the Royal Society. Illustrated with drawings of fossil plants, Scheuchzer's work figured
prominently in discussions of the Great Deluge and echoed Robert
Hooke's archaeological metaphor in its defense of John Woodward's
view of fossils' organic origin. "Here are the new kinds of coins, the
dates of which are incomparably more ancient, more important and
more reliable than those of all the coins of Greece and Rome," stated a
reviewer from Paris's Academy of Sciences, regarding Scheuchzer's influential treatise.[39] In this way, evangelism and enlightenment together
formed a new metaphorical view of the earth's natural antiquity.

Scheuchzer was Woodward's translator on the Continent, and he
became the best-known advocate of Woodward's Deluge theory with
the publication in 1731 of his *Physica Sacra,* which contained 745 full-
page copper engravings. Fossils were a prominent feature of the engravings, documenting episodes from biblical history with the latest scientific evidence. "Scheuchzer and most of his contemporaries saw no
difficulty in assuming that the Creation and the Deluge had taken place
just as and when a literal reading of the texts suggested," observed historian Martin J. S. Rudwick in his *Scenes from Deep Time*.[40]

In Scheuchzer's scenes depicting the creation narrative, living
animals and fossils often intermingled, setting an important pictorial
precedent. In the panel showing Noah's Ark and the Flood, a variety
of fossils were placed in the decorative border as relics of the Deluge.
"In the frame of the scene are specimens of fossils that, Scheuchzer
believed, confirmed the exact season of the event."[41] Even though
Scheuchzer believed that all fossils had originated at the Deluge, this
iconographic tradition helped incorporate the archaeological views
of the antediluvian landscape into the millenarian spirit of Protestant science.

In Newtonian natural philosophy, the impetus for these new theories about the nature of fossils stemmed from the desire to establish the
literal truth of the Bible's account of the earth's history, particularly
the story of Noah's Ark and the Flood. Diluvialists like Thomas Burnet
and Dr. John Woodward were products of the revival of millenarian beliefs emphasizing the linear movement of time from the Creation and
the Flood through the New Covenant to the Conflagration and the

Millennium. "The idea that the Earth had a *history*—using the word in its modern sense not in the earlier sense that is preserved in the term 'natural' history—first entered 'scientific' debate not from the realm of natural philosophy but from that of evidential theology."[42] In an era permeated with millenarian prophecies of Christ's return to earth, the Bible emerged as the authoritative source on which the new "universal" chronology of the Newtonian era was based.

Isaac Newton himself was closely involved in the construction of this chronology, which derived from the apocalyptic prophecies popular among English Protestants. In his *Chronology of the Ancient Kingdoms Amended*, Newton synchronized the histories of the great pagan civilizations with biblical history through the logic and empirical evidence of natural philosophy. In effect, Newton shared Cotton Mather's desire to expel from Protestant thought any lingering respect for pagan mythology, whether it be Greek or Roman or East Indian or Chinese. "The Book of Daniel and the Apocalypse of St. John, Newton showed, were prophetic historical statements which had proved to be factually true down to the minutest detail." noted historian Frank E. Manuel. "In his *Observations Upon the Prophecies*, Newton demonstrated that they had been abundantly fulfilled in East European history, by spelling out specific events, complete with geographic locations, names of kings, dates of battles, and revolutions of empires, to which they correspond."[43]

By the time Cotton Mather's *Curiosa Americana* reached London, fossils had become physical relics of this new "universal" history of nature even while the natural philosophers themselves puzzled over their identity and the anomalies they created for the earth's natural history. The diluvialists' wide influence on these early views came from their reinforcement of Christian doctrine and the way that the Great Deluge enabled Anglo-Americans to substitute the natural history of the earth for the rise and fall of ancient kingdoms and empires. For them, the earth's natural history itself became an instrument of evangelization, eradicating the heresies of classical civilization and pagan societies with the authority of the empirical sciences sacrosanct to Protestant religious doctrine.

As historian Ernest Lee Tuveson demonstrates in his book *The Redeemer Nation*, the idea of history as progress, which underlay the redemptive mission of the American nation, had its roots in these millenarian prophecies predicting the Kingdom of God on earth. "The

Protestant eschatology was substantially new, and by the end of the seventeenth century the novel idea that history is moving toward a millennial regeneration of mankind became not only respectable but almost canonical."[44] In other words, the idea that the progress of societies from barbarism to civilization was the law of this universal history was first expressed in this new apocalyptic tradition, the yearning for an earthly utopia or millennium, which led many late-seventeenth-century Protestants to create a history of nature consistent with the biblical prophecies. The fossilized bones of the Claverack monster were testimony to the "New Found Land" of the antediluvian world which would soon be transformed from a Garden of Eden into a terrifying prehistoric world ruled by savage carnivores.

Far from being the proponents of anachronistic beliefs, diluvialists like Thomas Burnet and Dr. John Woodward introduced a new mythology of the earth's natural history. Through their popularization of the analogy between fossils and the relics of ancient civilizations, this metaphorical view became even more powerful because it was anchored equally in the experimental sciences and evangelical Christianity. The interchangeability of these symbols drawn from millenarian prophecy, classical antiquity, and the natural sciences helps explain the mythical character of the giant bones of Claverack. For the American *incognitum*'s story, the survival and significance of such myths and metaphors in Protestant doctrine far outweighed the scientific errors.

3

The Mystery of the Siberian Mammoth

In such Manner, not only the holy Scripture may serve to prove natural History, but the Truth of the Scripture, which says that Noah's
Flood was universal, a thing which is doubted by many, may be
proved again by natural History.

—Dr. John Breyne, 1737

IN EARLY 1714, when the Royal Society published a brief summary of
Cotton Mather's letter concerning the giant of Claverack, England's
leading naturalists were already turning away from the "Doctrine of
Monsters." With the aid of the developing field of comparative
anatomy, they were beginning to mount a campaign against the idea
that such fossils were the remains of human giants. Their refutation of
this idea was made possible by the discovery of another unknown
species, the Siberian mammoth, whose bones and teeth were used to establish that such large fossils belonged to elephant-like animals rather
than human giants.

In the early eighteenth century, Dutch diplomats and Swedish prisoners of war in Siberia employed by the Russian czar, Peter the Great,
sent back accounts of the frozen carcasses of a mysterious beast that
Mongolian tribesmen called the *mammut*. In addition to these reports,
the discovery of these remains on the remote Siberian frontier was recounted in legends carried back to Europe by ivory traders and foreign
emissaries who traveled to this recently conquered territory. Like the
giant of Claverack, the mammoth was an unknown creature whose discovery greatly puzzled European naturalists.

The word *mammoth* soon became the popular term applied to fossil
elephants in both Siberia and North America, introducing an element

62

of confusion into the debate over the identity of the American *incogni-tum*. The strange tales associated with the Siberian creature soon be-came intertwined in North America with Indian legends about mythi-cal beasts that once roamed the American wilderness. Despite the new emphasis on scientific study of the fossil remains, the debate over the identity of the American *incognitum* continued to incorporate many el-ements of myth and legend, since the beast's shadowy existence con-jured up fantastic images even in the minds of the anatomists.

Many people believed that Noah's Flood was the historical agent responsible for the dispersion of the bones of these elephant-like crea-tures to Siberia and North America. In many ways, therefore, the dis-covery of the Siberian mammoth only deepened the belief in the per-fection of God's nature. The exhumation of its carcass from the tundra, with flesh and skin still on the bones, seemed to prove that such fossil remains belonged to living animals rather than an extinct species. Thus the emergence of comparative anatomy as a field of study marked a turning point in the search for the identity of the American *incognitum*, yet the Siberian mammoth's legacy also gave new life to many legends and myths about the antediluvian world.

In the decades before Cotton Mather's *Curiosa Americana*, the Royal Society's journal *Philosophical Transactions* published numerous letters from correspondents concerning the discovery of large fossils in England and around the world. These correspondents ranged from physicians with medical training in anatomical description to clergy-men naturalists concerned mainly with the religious and philosophical implications of these curiosities. The growing volume of commentary on the meaning of the fossils generated a debate over whether the large bones belonged to elephant-like creatures or human giants. The pres-ence of enormous fossil remains far from the elephant's tropical habitat inevitably engendered speculation about the earth's history and the cir-cumstances that led to their interment in the North. While many nat-uralists were moving away from the notion that such fossils were human remains, virtually everyone still relied on the Great Deluge to explain their discovery so far from the tropics.

Surprisingly, Cotton Mather's theories about the existence of human giants received only mild criticism from the journal's editors. Indeed, the most damning aspect was their decision not to publish Mather's letter, an act of omission whose implicit criticism was all the more obvious to readers, given the journal's common practice of publishing such communications in their entirety. To Mather's satisfaction, however, the summary of his letter did mention his "Biblia Americana," the manuscript he hoped to publish. But the editors cast doubt on his opinions by questioning his assertion "of there having been, in the *Antediluvian* World, Men of very large and prodigious Statures, by the Bones and Teeth of some large Animals, found lately in *Albany* in *New England*, which for some Reasons, he judges to be Human."[1]

The editors reserved their sharpest criticism for Mather's failure to provide an adequate anatomical description of the bones, something the London physicians were coming to realize was essential to identifying the mysterious creature. The editors briefly summarized the few details in Mather's letter, the weight and dimensions of several large teeth and the seventy-foot-long discoloration of the soil attributed to the rotting monster's body. But they expressed disappointment at the paucity of physical description: "It were to be wish'd the Writer had given an exact Figure of these Teeth and Bones."[2]

Their skepticism was made more explicit the following year with the publication of a commentary by the eminent Dublin physician Thomas Molyneux on an elephant's jaw dug up in the northern Ireland. Workmen sinking the foundation for a mill alongside a stream on Bishop Killmore's land in the County Cavan had found four large teeth. They came into the possession of the clergyman Francis Nevile, who promptly passed them on to the bishop of Clogher, along with a crude drawing and speculation on their identity.

> It will be well worth consideration what sort of Creature this might be, whether Human or Animal. If Human, it must be larger than any Giant we read of; if Animal, it could be no other than an Elephant, and we do not find those Creatures were ever the Product of this Climate.[3]

Like Cotton Mather, Nevile offered no clinical description of the teeth, preferring instead merely to speculate about the identity of the monstrous creature, which, he implied, could be either human or animal.

Nevile's letter and drawing of the tooth were passed on to the archbishop of Dublin, who sent them to the city's foremost surgeon, Thomas Molyneux, for his professional opinion. Not satisfied with the accuracy of Nevile's drawings of the teeth, Molyneux sought out the actual specimens themselves before submitting his own anatomically precise analysis to the archbishop. "This I take to be one of the greatest Rarities that has been yet discovered in this Country," Molyneux wrote. From the outset, he was "pretty well convinced they must have been the Grinding Teeth of an Elephant."[4] But to prove his point, he introduced empirical evidence based on his comparison of the fossil teeth with those of several elephants recently dissected in England. When the Royal Society published Nevile's letter along with Molyneux's commentary, the latter's rejection of the Doctrine of Monsters was stated so baldly as to be impolite: "As for the Hint of their being *human* or *gigantick*, 'tis so groundless a Thought, and so contradictory to *comparative Anatomy* and all *Natural History*, it does not deserve our consideration."[5]

Comparative anatomy had easily solved the problem of identifying the teeth found at Cavan, since they matched with clinical exactness the structure of the recently dissected specimens from living elephants. But the surgeon could not resolve the question of

> how this large Body'd *Animal*, a *Native* of the remote warm climates of the *world*, should be deposited in this wild *Northern Island*, (where *Greeks* or *Romans* never had a footing) so many *Miles* from sea, and so distant from those Places of the Ilse where People might most probably resort.[6]

Echoing earlier commentaries on such puzzling fossils, Molyneux ruled out the possibility that the creatures had been brought to England by Roman emperors, opting instead, like his predecessor Robert Hooke, to explain the anomaly through geographical change in the region:

> The surface of this Terraqueous Globe might, in the earliest Ages of the *World*, after the *Deluge*, but before all Records of our oldest *Histories*, differ widely from its present *Geography*, as to the Distribution of the *Ocean* and *Dry-land*, its *Islands*, *Continents* and *Shores*, so as to allow this Beast, and others of its Kind, for ought I know, that may by some such Accident hereafter be luckily discovered, a free and open Passage into this Country from the Continent.[7]

Although Molyneux was familiar with earlier accounts of such fossils unearthed in England, from Somner's *Chartham News* to John Luffkin's letter about the elephants of Emperor Claudius, he felt that the answer to this deeper question about how the fossils came to England lay in comparing their remains with the bones of other elephant-like creatures being discovered elsewhere around the world, from North America to the Siberian steppes. "For I am inclined to think, (even from these Imperfect Hints) that if we had more correct Histories and Observations of this kind, made in distant Countries, and skillfully registered, with all their instructive Circumstances," he informed the archbishop, "they might lead us into great and momentous *Truths* relating to the *Deluge*, to the wise Methods of Providence, in replenishing all Regions of the *World* with *Animal Beings* soon after the *Flood*."[8]

Molyneux was among the first to introduce into the debate over the fossil remains the idea of rigorously applying the principles of comparative anatomy to determine their identity. The casual observations of clergymen naturalists would no longer suffice, and the hyperbole of antiquarians like Cotton Mather served no other purpose than to cloud the issue of their true identity. Coming on the heels of Mather's theories, Molyneux's plea for scientific rigor in analyzing the fossil remains marked the beginning of the formal refutation of the "Doctrine of Monsters" by England's anatomists and surgeons, who were becoming the protagonists in the search for the identity of the American *incognitum*.

Unlike the antiquarian correspondents, Molyneux spoke with considerable authority, since his professional training was buttressed by high social status, which gave him access to everyone from Sir Isaac Newton to England's royal family. In 1700, he published "An Essay concerning Giants," about the large forehead bone kept in the school of medicine at Leyden. This Dutch specimen offered him his first opportunity to argue that most of "the pretended Giants remains" in museum collections "were Bones belonging to some of the largest Quadrupeds, as *elephants*, or some of the largest sort of fishes of the *Whale-kind*."[9]

Molyneux's plea for comparative anatomy was welcomed by the fellows of the Royal Society, many of whom shared his skepticism about the existence of antediluvian giants. In response to his paper, they ordered that all the specimens of this sort in their own collection be examined carefully, with an eye to applying the methodology that Molyneux recommended. In addition, several other specimens from the outside were brought together for viewing, including several teeth from the private collection of the London surgeon Hans Sloane, who in recent years had been personally responsible for reviving the society's journal. Several fellows even went to Westminster to examine the skull of a large elephant with all its teeth intact which, when compared with Molyneux's drawings, confirmed his claims that the teeth from Cavan belonged to an elephant. With Molyneux's letter, the Royal Society for the first time published accurate anatomical drawings of the various teeth in question, so the journal's readers could judge for themselves how the teeth found at Cavan compared with those of the Westminster skull and the fossil elephant's grinder in the Royal Society's own collection.

The new field of comparative anatomy now provided the principal methodology for naturalists seeking the identity of American *incognitum*. To emphasize the importance of accurate anatomical descriptions of such fossil remains, Molyneux himself surveyed several recently published accounts of large grinders and teeth, largely to demonstrate that the bones of elephants, like the specimens from northern Ireland, were being found in other places distant from the animal's normal habitat in warm climates.

Among these reports was one that marked the opening of a new frontier in the search for the identity of the fossil elephants. Without placing undue emphasis on its significance, Molyneux referred to one of the earliest accounts of the gigantic bones recently encountered in Siberia, namely, the book *Travels from Muscovy to China over Land* by Evert Isbrand Ides, a Dutch envoy in the diplomatic service of Peter the Great:

> And I am well persuaded, by the best Construction I can make of those imperfect and obscure Accounts, we have in *Evert Isbrand Iddes*, which he confesses he only gathered from the barbarous *Ostiacks* Inhabitants of that Country, concerning the vast *Teeth* and *Bones* and Limbs of "Mammuths" as he calls them, frequently found and diligently sought after to make profit of them, in the Hills, and Banks of several Rivers in *Siberia*, the *Keta, Jenize, Trugan, Mongamsea* and *Lena*.[10]

This was one of the earliest appearances in English of the term *mammoth*, and by a curious coincidence this name became the popular term used during the late eighteenth century by the founding fathers for the American *incognitum*. Even though Molyneux cast aspersions on the Ostiack tribesmen from whom Ides heard these accounts, the

Dutch envoy's opinion confirmed his own belief "that they are nothing else but the Remains and *Skeletons* of *Elephants* buried there, and accidentally discovered by the *Earth's* opening, and falling down on the sudden Thaws, after severe long Frosts."[11]

Fossil ivory had been exported from Siberia since antiquity, although its main destination was China rather than Europe. For thousands of years, Chinese merchants had imported Siberian ivory that they believed came not from elephants but from giant underground rats living beneath the tundra. According to the "Ben zao gan mu," a sixteenth-century Chinese natural history treatise, the first mention of these creatures appeared in ancient Chinese ceremonial books of the fourth century B.C., in which the beast was called *fen shu*, or "the self-concealing mouse."[12] The late-seventeenth-century Chinese emperor Kang-xi himself wrote a book on animals in which he alluded to descriptions of the *fen-shu* in the ancient books: "There is in the north in the country of Olosses near the sea, a kind of rat as big as an elephant which lives underground and dies as soon as it comes into the air or is reached by the sunlight."[13] Even though the emperor gave credence to ancient tales about the underground rat from Siberia, he compared the "teeth," or tusks, with those of elephants and noted that the Russian inhabitants of the remote territory made bowls, combs, and knife handles from the ivory.

The term *mammoth* first entered the English vocabulary in the 1690s, in the Dutch emissaries' accounts of their travels to Siberia. In 1694, Nicholas Cornelius Witzen, burgomaster of Amsterdam, who had been the Dutch ambassador to Moscow in 1666, published his memoir of Russia. It contained an early account of the Siberian travels of Evert Ysbrant Ides, the Dutch diplomat sent by the czar to the court of Emperor Kang-xi. Besides being the first European book to print the word *mammoth*, Witzen's account describes how the teeth of "elephants" were found by Russian settlers along the banks of Siberian rivers: "By the Inlanders, these teeth are called Mammouttekoos, while the animal itself is called Mammount."[14]

English naturalists also seem to have learned of the word *mammoth* about the same time from Hiob Ludolph, a German orientalist whose *Grammatica Russica* was published two years later in 1696. In the appendix, he describes in detail the teeth of the "Mammotovoikost" and recounts the Siberian folktales about the underground rat to whom they allegedly belonged. Ludolph's reference caught the eye of Robert

Hooke, then curator of experiments at the Royal Society. In 1697, while lecturing the Royal Society on the teeth and bones of elephants being unearthed around the world, Hooke made one of the earliest references in English to the Siberian creatures:

> We have lately had several Accounts of Animal Substances of various kinds, that have been found buried in the superficial Parts of the Earth, that is not very far below the present Surface, as particularly the parts of the Head of an *Hippopotamus* at *Chartham* in *Kent,* that of the Bones of the *Mammatovoykost,* or of a strange Subterraneous Animals, as the *Siberians* fancy, which is commonly dug up in *Siberia,* which Mr. *Ludolphus* judges to be the Teeth and Bones of Elephants.[15]

In Hooke's commentary, the Siberian mammoth entered the English vocabulary alongside descriptions of other fossil elephants, not only helping stimulate debate over the identity of the American *incognitum,* but also supplying the term that became the popular name for this creature.

In the years immediately after the discovery of the giant tooth at Claverack, the travel writings about Siberia that had the widest popularity among English readers were those by Evert Ysbrant Ides himself.[16] On his way to China, Ides had traveled with a collector of fossil ivory who claimed to have seen the head of a mammoth protruding from the tundra. In the spring, when the ice broke up, the swollen Siberian rivers eroded the riverbanks, exposing the frozen carcasses of the Siberian mammoths, whose tusks were then collected by annual expeditions of ivory hunters. Ides's party passed through areas of Siberia inhabited by several Mongol tribes, notably the Yakuts, Ostiacks, and Tunguses, who for centuries had been the source of folktales about the earth moles of the tundra. In a more systematic fashion, Ides publicized the stories of the Mongol tribes about the creature they called the *mammut,* which, according to them, "continually, or at least, by reason of the very hard frosts, mostly lives underground, where it goes backwards and forwards."[17] Ides brought to his European audience apocryphal accounts of the Siberian beast, claiming that "if this animal comes near the surface of the frozen earth so as to smell or discern the air, he immediately dies, whence the reason that several of them are found dead on the high banks of the river, where they unawares come out of the ground."[18]

Like his predecessors Ludolph and Witzen, Ides doubted the Siberian folktales, preferring instead the sensible views of Russian settlers and ivory traders, who maintained that the *mammut* was an elephant-like beast, an antediluvian creature that had lived in Siberia when the climate was warm enough to sustain its existence. No one could explain why the climate had changed so drastically, and many Russian settlers believed the bones may have been carried to Siberia by the Great Deluge.

Peter the Great was the person responsible for expanding the European naturalists' awareness of the Siberian mammoth during the first decades of the eighteenth century. In 1700, shortly before England became embroiled in the War of the Spanish Succession, Russia joined its neighbors Saxony and Denmark in declaring war on Sweden, whose power had been growing in that area. In 1707, the Swedish army led by King Charles invaded Russia, marching some forty thousand troops deep into the interior, only to be routed two years later by the czar's forces. Following their defeat, many of the captured Swedish officers were sent into exile in Siberia where the czar put them to work surveying the vast mineral resources of this recently conquered but relatively unknown territory.

Under the czar's auspices, a Swedish captain named Johann Bernhard Müller began studying the Ostiacks, one of the Mongol tribes mentioned earlier by European travelers to the remote Russian frontier. In December 1716, after an arduous trip to the region only recently converted to Christianity, Müller sent the czar his report, "The Manners and Customs of the Ostiacks." Six years later, when Müller's report was translated into English, it brought to British readers the first widely circulated eyewitness account of the Siberian mammoths.

Having an eye for clinical details, Müller made only a fleeting reference to the folktales about the earth moles of Siberia. Instead, he summarized the opinions of educated Swedish prisoners and the Russian settlers whose own views echoed the "scientific" theories then emerging in Europe about the fossil elephants. "The common Opinion of the Inhabitants is, that they are real Elephants Teeth, and have lain buried ever since the universal Deluge."[19] But surprisingly, Müller dismissed this notion as an absurd hypothesis, since no one had ever found this tropical animal in the Siberian tundra: "Be that as it will, the Notion that these Bones are real Elephants Teeth, cannot be supported by any probable Argument, considering that Elephants are utterly un-known in those Parts, nor could they subsist in that cold Climate, if they were carried thither."[20]

Müller was equally skeptical of his Swedish colleagues who sub-scribed to the old theory of *lusus naturae*, "sports of nature," to ex-plain the growth of the fossils in the earth: "Some of our Country-men think it to be the *Ebur fossile*, and consequently a Product of the Earth, which was likewise my Opinion for a good while."[21] The fact that the tusks of these mysterious animals were often found together with pieces of the animal's bloody flesh at the broken end was enough to convince Müller this conjecture was wrong: "Besides, they often find Skulls and Jaw-bones with Molar Teeth or Grinders in them of a prodigious Size, the Substance of which one cannot deter-mine, whether it is Stone or Bone."[22]

Like the London surgeons who soon applied the rigorous new cri-teria of comparative anatomy to the question of the beast's identity, Müller placed greater emphasis on empirical evidence and the configu-ration of the grinders, which he himself had examined. "I myself, and several of my Fellow-Prisoners, have often seen such Teeth, one of which weighed twenty or twenty four Pounds or better."[23] References to the "teeth" in such accounts generally mean the tusks, since anat-omists were only just beginning to make clinical studies of the large mo-lars and grinders whose precise configurations eventually supplied the decisive evidence that both the mammoth and the American *incogni-tum* were extinct species.

Finally, Müller considered a third opinion suggesting that the re-mains belonged to a living animal whose description was similar to the accounts of the fabled earth mole of Siberian folktales: "Others again maintain, that they are the Horns of a live huge Beast, which lives in Morasses and subterraneous Caves, subsisting by the Mud, and working itself by the Help of its Horns through the Mire and Earth."[24] Even though he had spoken with many persons who claimed to have seen such beasts in the high mountain caves, Müller rejected these accounts for the same reason that the Royal Society was skeptical of Cotton Mather's theory—they lacked empirical evidence and anatomical ac-curacy: "Notwithstanding these Accounts, one does not know how far to rely upon them, for that Nation do not trouble themselves about exact Enquiries of that Nature, and care but little for Curiosities, any further than it is for their own Profit."[25]

In this description of the Siberian mammoth, the mythical beast of the popular imagination battled for credibility with the clinical creature that European anatomists were convinced belonged to the elephant family. In many ways, the Siberian mammoth brought into the debate over the American *incognitum* new facts and fantasies, although its initial effect on the English naturalists was to dispel any lingering belief that such large bones were the remains of human giants. Its lasting effect was also to keep alive many fanciful notions about the fossil elephants, whose true identity still remained a mystery even to learned anatomists.

Before receiving Müller's report, the czar sent yet another Dutch diplomat to the Chinese emperor's court. The journal of this envoy, Laurence Lange, who traveled from St. Petersburg to Beijing by way of Siberia, fed the speculation at the czar's palace and in European capitals about the mammoth's true identity. Lange was obviously familiar with earlier Dutch travel writings like Witzen's *Noord en oost Tartary*, which offered the first descriptions of the Siberian mammoth. Almost immediately, Lange introduced into his speculation about this beast references to the legendary biblical creature the "behemoth": "Some speculative Searchers into Natural Philosophy will have this *Maman* to be the *Behemoth* mentioned in the 40th Chapter of *Job*, the Descriptions of which most exactly fits the Nature of this Beast."[26] Bible scholars identified this animal with the hippopotamus, or river horse, which Ludolph pictured in his *New History of Ethiopia*, published in 1682, as a ferocious beast with monstrous teeth (figure 6).

Lange twisted the details of the Siberian folktales to conform to the Bible's description of the behemoth, even though a hippopotamus basking among the rushes of an African river had little in common with the mammoth's bones found on the banks of the ice-clogged Siberian rivers. His willingness to make such parallels was rooted in his belief that the mammoth was a living creature, a notion that appealed to many European naturalists reluctant to accept the idea of extinction:

> But what most persuades me that they are Bones of Beast which is to this Day subsisting, is that many credible Persons averred to me, that they themselves had seen Horns, Jaw bones and Ribs of it, with fresh Blood and Flesh sticking to it, assuring me at the same Time, that any body who would be at the Pains, might, easily gather a whole Skeleton.[27]

FIGURE 6. Engraving of the "Behemoth," or hippopotamus, from Hiob Ludolf's *New History of Ethiopia*, 1682. The bones of the Siberian mammoth and the American *incognitum* were often identified with the behemoth, the largest of God's creatures described in the Book of Job, 40:10. Courtesy of Bancroft Library, University of California at Berkeley.

While European anatomists were seeking naturalistic descriptions of the "mammoth," the great beast's identity still evoked elements of myth and folklore, both Christian and pagan. Prehistoric nature was still an unknown, enigmatic realm just beginning to emerge from the Christian unconscious, and its lack of definition made it an imaginary place often shaped as much by fantasy as fact. Baron Philipp Johann Tabbert von Strahlenberg, a Swedish prisoner commissioned by Peter the Great to survey vast tracts of Siberia, heard the same folktales about the *mammut* that other travelers had disputed. While surveying Siberia, he met a Russian settler who drew a picture of the elusive *mammut*, whose remains he claimed to have seen himself. In 1722, Strahlenberg sent the settler's drawing back to Sweden where it became one of the earliest renderings of a Siberian mammoth to be seen in Europe. The drawing bore little resemblance to the elephant-like creature described by either the Mongolian folktales or the ivory hunters and travelers to Siberia. Instead, the beast looked more like a unicorn with two horns or an ox with sharp, curved claws instead of hooves and coiled tusks protruding from the forehead.

During the early Enlightenment, the belief in unicorns remained a European myth, influencing early images of the fossil creatures even among the Continent's most renowned natural philosophers. In 1663, when workers in a gypsum quarry in Germany found some enormous bones and tusks, Otto von Guericke, the mayor of Magdeburg and a famous physicist who had invented the vacuum pump, attempted to reconstruct the skeleton from the bone fragments. Of course, no one then had any inkling of the Siberian mammoth's existence, although there had been speculation since antiquity that such bones belonged to an elephant-like creature. In his drawing based on von Guernicke's reconstruction, the late-seventeenth-century German philosopher Gottfried Wilhelm Leibniz depicted a fantastic unicorn-like animal with a horn protruding from its forehead and large molar teeth in each jaw, a drawing that paleontologists claim was one of the earliest attempts to reconstruct an animal from fossil remains (figure 7). Leibniz's drawing did not receive wide attention in Europe until 1749 when it was published posthumously in his book *Protogaea*, along with a description of the imaginary creature.

In the next decades, the bones and tusks of the Siberian mammoths, along with those of living elephants, became the principal specimens that comparative anatomists used to solve the riddle of the American *incognitum*'s identity. Because many early travelers' accounts of the mammoth were first published in Dutch or Swedish, news of the mysterious Siberian beast filtered slowly into British consciousness and the minds of the American colonists. In 1722, with the rising interest in the expansion of czar's Russian empire, stories of the Siberian mammoth became available to a wider audience in England with the publication of *The Present State of Russia*, an English translation of a book by Friedrich Christian Weber, who had been the German ambassador to the czar's court from 1714 to 1720. The ambassador's lengthy description of Russia's government and Far Eastern diplomacy also contained the first English translations of

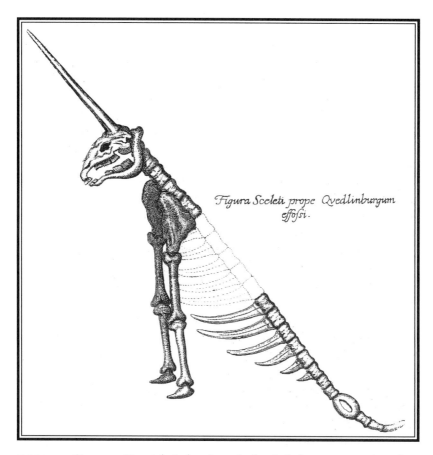

FIGURE 7. Otto von Guericke's drawing of a fossil skeleton reconstructed from bones found in 1663 in a gypsum quarry in Germany. One of the earliest attempts to picture a prehistoric animal, the drawing gained wide attention when it was later reproduced in Gottfried Wilhelm Leibniz's *Protogaea* in 1749.

Laurence Lange's journal "Travels to China" and John Bernard Müller's "The Manners and Customs of the Ostiacks."

Not long after the publication of Weber's *Present State of Russia*, London's most eminent surgeon and naturalist, Sir Hans Sloane, received the first of several Siberian tusks for his renowned collection of curiosities. By then, Sloane had been made a baronet and later became president of the Royal Society upon Isaac Newton's death five years later. In 1722, John Bell of Antermony, a Scottish physician employed by the czar, returned to Moscow after seven years in China. While traveling with a caravan through Siberia en route to China, the governor's wife there gave him, as payment for curing her of an illness, the tusk of a mammoth found in the Ob River north of Tobolsk. Upon his return to Moscow, Bell made a trip back to England where he personally delivered to Sloane the fine Siberian tusk, which was nearly six feet long: "I brought a large tooth or mammon's horn with me to England, and presented it to my worthy friend, Sir Hans Sloane, who gave it a place in his famous museum, and was of opinion also that it was the tooth of an elephant," Bell later recounted.[28] His gift to Sloane gave the London physician the anatomical evidence that he needed to discredit the lingering belief that such large fossils belonged to human giants.

For nearly two decades, Sloane spent much of his time gathering the bones of fossil elephants from Siberia to North America until he was finally able to make a comprehensive argument disproving the "Doctrine of Monsters." In 1728, shortly after he succeeded Newton as president of the Royal Society, Sloane published two articles in the society's journal that definitively laid to rest the notion that such bones belonged to human giants. His articles inaugurated a new era of comparative anatomy, when the debate among naturalists about the identity of the American *incognitum* revolved around clinically exact comparisons of its bones and teeth with those of living elephants and the Siberian mammoth.

Published in two parts by the Royal Society's journal *Philosophical Transactions*, the first installment of Sloane's article, "An Account of Elephants Teeth and Bones found under Ground," confined itself chiefly to the fossil remains of this particular species. In many cases, however, the actual identity of the animals in question remained a mystery, since their bones did not conform exactly to those of any living elephant. Sloane's topics ranged from Thomas Bartholin's treatise on unicorns, *De Unicornu,* to the remarkable six-foot-long Siberian tusk brought to London by John Bell of Antermony. Bell's tusk was compared with local specimens like the "elephants' teeth" found in a gravel pit outside London in 1715 by the pharmacist John Conyers and the six-foot-long tusk described by Rev. Morton in his *History of Northamptonshire*. By juxtaposing the accounts of such bones with the fossil teeth in his own collection, Sloane was able to demonstrate with a kind of clinical exactness that these tusks and bones belonged to elephant-like animals rather than freaks of nature, mythical creatures, or human giants.

Because Sloane's own collection of fossils was one of the largest in Europe, he greatly extended the horizons of comparative anatomy by including in his survey a detailed commentary on the Siberian specimens. His article featured glosses on the best-known Siberian accounts, beginning with Ludolph's *Grammatica Russica* and Isbrant Ides's *Travels*, along with the reports by the Swedish prisoners of war and Dutch diplomats in the service of the czar.

In Sloane's eyes, the physical description of the Siberian specimens was convincing proof that they belonged to an elephant-like creature. But to explain why these remains had been found near the Arctic Circle, he relied on the opinions of Russian settlers who agreed with him that climate change and the universal Deluge were responsible for the curious displacement of these fossil elephants far from their usual tropical habitats. "They also are of Opinion, that there were Elephants in this Country before the Deluge, when this Climate was warmer, and that their drowned Bodies floating on the Surface of the Water of that Flood, were at last washed and forced into subterranean Cavities."[29] Thus, even as he brought new clinical exactness to comparative anatomy, Sloane gave a kind of scientific credence to the story of Noah's Flood, which still served as the principal explanation for many learned accounts of the earth's natural history.

In the second installment of his article, Sloane addressed directly the issue of whether these fossil bones were, as many ancient and modern authors argued, the "undeniable Monuments of the Existence of Giants." His survey included the well-known accounts from classical times to the present and produced the most comprehensive inventory of stories about the bones of human giants since the encyclopedic works of Anthanasius Kircher, the seventeenth-century Jesuit cosmographer whose theories influenced Cotton Mather. Sloane's compilation included the weights and measurements of the different specimens mentioned by various scholars who had claimed that the enormous bones unearthed over the centuries belonged to human giants. In each case, Sloane highlighted the details suggesting that these bones were actually those of elephants.[30]

Unlike Cotton Mather, who had used such literary accounts of human giants to corroborate his theory of the Claverack monster, Sloane focused mainly on those descriptions using comparative anatomy to discredit the theory of human giants. His survey was remarkably comprehensive, as it was drawn not only from the classical and ecclesiastical literature but also from contemporary European accounts of bones. But while Sloane's articles marked a major turning point in the story of the American *incognitum*, he made no direct mention of the giant bones of Claverack or Cotton Mather's letters to the Royal Society. And even though several fossils in the Royal Society's collection figured in his account, Sloane did not refer to the original specimen from Claverack sent to London by Lord Cornbury in the package labeled "tooth of the giant." This omission is all the more curious, since Sloane's papers contain copies not only of Cotton Mather's *Curiosa Americana* but also of the letters of Lord Cornbury and James Abeel, who were responsible for the initial commentaries on the Claverack monster.[31]

In England, such specimens were now usually compared with the bones of living elephants, often with the aid of anatomically exact drawings of the specimens. In his *Natural History of Staffordshire*, Dr. Robert Plot described "the lower Jaw of some Animal, with large Teeth sticking in it, dug up in a Marle-pit in his Ground, which upon Comparison he found exactly agreeable to the lower Jaw of the Elephant's Skull in Mr. Ashmole's Museum at Oxford."[32] In case after case, Sloane demonstrated that upon closer inspection, the bones and teeth exhibited as those of giants had been found to be only the remains of elephants or whales. "Thus the Fore-fin of a Whale, stripp'd of its Webb and Skin, was not long ago publickly shewn for the Bones of a Giant's Hand."[33]

Sloane was well aware that the mystery of the fossil elephants in Siberia and North America was not solved by this clinical evidence. Indeed, his own examination of their teeth and bones revealed that many of these specimens were not exactly the same species as living elephants but, rather, were unknown animals for which there was no living match. Speaking with the authority of England's leading surgeon and naturalist, he made an eloquent plea for a more rigorous approach to the investigation of these anomalies:

> I cannot forbear on this Occasion to observe, that it would be an Object well worthy the Inquiries of Ingenious Anatomists, to make a Sort of comparative Anatomy of Bones. I mean to examine, with more Accuracy than hath been hitherto done, what Proportions the Skeletons and Parts of Skeletons of Men and Animals bear to each other, with Regard either to the Size, or Figure, or Structure, or any other Quality.[34]

Indeed, Sloane seemed to sense the shifting paradigm of scientific inquiry that would eventually lead to the discovery of the American *incognitum*'s identity and extinction, not to mention the existence of prehistoric nature and geological time.

The London anatomists were not alone in their growing skepticism about the "Doctrine of Monsters." Their counterparts on the Continent were moving toward the same reliance on comparative anatomy to determine the identity of Siberian mammoth and the fossil elephants in America. In March 1728, shortly before Sir Hans Sloane's article was published, John Breyne, a German physician and fellow of the Royal Society, presented a lecture on the fossil elephants to a learned society in Danzig. He used new evidence from Siberia to argue that the mammoth's teeth and bones belonged to antediluvian elephants whose remains had been brought to the tundra by the Deluge. Six years earlier, Dr. Breyne had received two very large teeth from the Siberian mammoth sent by Dr. Daniel Messerschmidt, a German physician employed by the Russian czar.

The specimens brought back by Messerschmidt included an enormous fossilized tooth, a grinder weighing more than eight pounds, and a fragment of a tusk. These remains prompted Breyne to deride the folkloric accounts of the Siberian creature. In particular, he dismissed outright the apocryphal stories about the mammoth in Isbrant Ides's *Travels*, along with those in the two influential accounts by the Dutch diplomat Laurence Lange and the Swedish Captain John Bernard Müller, published in Weber's *Present State of Russia* in 1722.

> It would not be worth your while, nor our Pains, to detain you with the Refutation of some merely fabulous Opinions, quoted by the said Authors, about the Origin of those Teeth and Bones. Therefore I deign only to pick out of the Testimonies of Matters of Fact of the foresaid Authors.[35]

Like Sir Hans Sloane, Dr. Breyne was turning away from the fantastic toward the factual, even though he continued to reserve a special place for Noah's Flood in his own theory about the mammoth's identity. For him, the facts that mattered most were the descriptions and drawings of the tusks and grinders themselves, details that enabled him to conclude that these curiosities were definitely the teeth and bones of elephant-like animals. "To be convinced hereof, one needs but to compare these Teeth with the Figures of those which some Years ago were digged up in *Ireland,* and those which represent the very natural Teeth of *Elephants,*" Breyne declared, referring to the remarks and drawings published in 1715 by the Dublin physician Dr. Thomas Molyneux.[36]

To explain how the remains of these fossil elephants got to Siberia, Dr. Breyne relied on the biblical narrative rather than factual evidence. "That those Teeth and Bones of *Elephants* were brought thither by no other Means but those of a Deluge, by Waves and Winds, and left behind after the Waters returned into their Reservoirs, and were buried in the Earth, even near to the Tops of high Mountains."[37] In Breyne's approach to biblical history, we are reminded again of how many learned naturalists in the scientific community took literally the Christian creation narrative in regard to the earth's natural history. Early scientific theories about fossils were colored by religious doctrine as people in England and Europe first became aware of geological phenomena and extinction. "And because we know nothing of any particular extraordinary Deluge in those Countries, but of the universal Deluge of *Noah,* which we find described by *Moses,*" Dr. Breyne pointed out, "I think it more than probable, that we ought to refer this strange *Phenomenon* to said Deluge."[38]

Enlightened scholars from Isaac Newton to Hans Sloane had tried to demonstrate the significance of the fossil remains by using them to verify the Bible's account of creation. In this enterprise, Dr. Breyne merely followed suit. "In such Manner, not only the holy Scripture may serve to prove natural History, but the Truth of the Scripture, which says that *Noah's* Flood was universal, a thing which is doubted by many, may be proved again by natural History."[39] Many learned critics of the "Doctrine of Monsters" shared the same assumptions about the Bible's authority as those underlying the much maligned belief of Cotton Mather that the Claverack bones belonged to human giants.

In 1730, when the German naturalist Daniel Messerschmidt returned to Danzig after leaving the czar's service, he gave Dr. Breyne detailed drawings of parts of a mammoth's skeleton unearthed during his travels to Siberia. While in Siberia, Messerschmidt obtained a signed statement for the czar from an educated Russian settler named Michael Wolochowicz, an eyewitness to the excavation of a mammoth's skeleton whose hairy head had been found protruding from the eastern bank of the Indigirka River in Siberia. Wolochowicz confirmed not only the

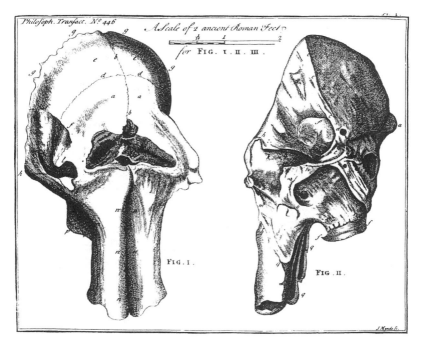

FIGURE 8. Daniel Messerschmidt's drawing of the Siberian mammoth's skull was reproduced in an article by Dr. John Breyne in the Royal Society's journal *Philosophical Transactions*, 1738. This illustration later proved useful in determining that the Siberian mammoth and American mastodon were separate species.

circumstances surrounding the excavation of the mammoth's bones but also the idea that they belonged to a living creature, by noting that he had found pieces of the beast's skin and flesh still intact:

> I saw a piece of skin putrefied, appearing out of the side of a sand-hill, which was pretty large, thick-set, and brown, somewhat resembling that of *Goat's* hair, which skin I could not take for that of a *Goat*, but of the *Behemoth*, inasmuch as I could not appropriate it to any animal I knew.[40]

This testimony added authenticity to Messerschmidt's drawings, which included three views of the mammoth's skull, together with renderings of a grinder, a curved tusk, and a thighbone (figure 8).

Five years later, Dr. Breyne sent copies of Messerschmidt's drawings to Hans Sloane, along with English translations of his original lecture about the Siberian mammoth and Wolochowicz's testimonial. The anatomically accurate renderings of the Siberian mammoth's bones were the type of drawings that the editors at *Philosophical Transactions* had complained were missing from Cotton Mather's *Curiosa Americana*. In contrast to the short shrift given to Mather's correspondence about the Claverack giant, when the Royal Society published Dr. Breyne's communication in 1737 it included his entire letter and lecture, along with the text of Wolochowicz's testimonial and reproductions of Messerschmidt's drawings.

For Dr. Breyne, the mammoth's skull was decisive proof "that this Skeleton belongs to an *Elephant,* and not to the chimerical *Behemoth* of the Rabbins," as claimed by other scholars. Yet in his Danzig lecture, he turned to Sloane's rival Dr. John Woodward to explain how the bones were brought to Siberia by the universal Deluge: "Wherefore the best Judges follow the Opinion of the learned Dr. *Woodward,* the *Scheuchzers,* and others . . . in taking them for the Bones of antediluvian Animals, or of such as were convey'd thither in the universal Deluge."[41] While the anatomists were moving toward clinical studies of the fossil elephants, they still associated them with myths and metaphors from Christian culture, transforming the earth's landscape into a sacred terrain where the bones of extinct creatures became testimony to the truth of religious doctrine. Clearly, neither Dr. Breyne nor his colleagues at the Royal Society had scrutinized these specimens sufficiently. They were still unaware that the bones and teeth of the mammoth belonged to a separate species, a discrepancy that they probably overlooked because it raised the issue of extinction and the existence of unknown creatures in God's nature.

Shortly after the publication of Dr. Breyne's communiqué to the Royal Society, the discovery of fossil elephants by a French expedition to the Ohio River valley suddenly shifted the center of attention away from Siberia to a remote salt lick on the Kentucky frontier which soon became the central focus of the debate about the American *incognitum*. George Washington and Thomas Jefferson later collected specimens from this new site, located in an inland territory acquired by the England during the French and Indian Wars in 1763. Known to frontier scouts as "Big Bone Lick," this graveyard of the fossil elephants yielded an enormous number of gigantic bones throughout the eighteenth century. Many of them came under the scrutiny of France's leading naturalist George Louis Leclerc de Buffon, the Parisian anatomist whose theories of American degeneracy played a key role in the creation by the founding fathers of the new nation's first prehistoric monster.

4

Big Bone Lick

"The Place Where the Elephant Bones Are Found"

At a Distance of about Six Hundred Miles S.W. of *Fort Pitt,* near the Banks of *Ohio,* is a Salt-Lick, in a clear open Plain, having a Road leading to it beat by Buffaloes, and other wild Game, spacious enough for Three Coaches to go a-breast. Here we found the Remains of those huge Animals called *Elephants,* and by holy Job named *Behemoth,* in such Quantities that several Waggons might be soon laden with excellent Ivory.

—Anonymous, 1767

THE HUDSON RIVER valley was not the only place in the American colonies where mysterious bones were unearthed during the early eighteenth century. Fossil remains were found elsewhere, from Virginia to South Carolina, but generally these were only scattered specimens whose discovery was reported without the fanfare attached to the Claverack monster. When the discovery of the Siberian mammoths provided convincing evidence that such fossils belonged to elephant-like animals rather than human giants, the American *incognitum* still was a shadowy creature in the minds of the colonists, largely because so few of its bones had been found.

Not until a French military expedition to the Ohio valley in 1739 discovered "elephant" bones at a salt lick there did the American *incognitum* begin to gain its true stature in the eyes of the colonists and European anatomists. From this moment, "Big Bone Lick"—as it was later called by English-speaking settlers in the region—became a repository of enormous bones, whose size and abundance made the salt lick a landmark for travelers to the Ohio valley. The sulfurous springs were not hard to find in the wilderness, since buffalo, deer, and elk had created wide paths to the site for thousands of years, making the lick a hunting ground for the Indians and their ancestors. During the French and Indian Wars, the bones from the Ohio salt lick first became known to many of the founding fathers, especially Benjamin Franklin and a young militia officer named George Washington, who went to the Ohio valley with the British army during the campaigns against the French.

Before the London physician Sir Hans Sloane repudiated the "Doctrine of Monsters," he had begun to expand his knowledge of American curiosities beyond the dispatches sent by Cotton Mather to the Royal Society. In 1725, Benjamin Franklin, a nineteen-year-old printer's apprentice who had come to England to learn the trade, visited Sloane and sold him some American curiosities. Two years earlier, Sloane was one of the British naturalists who sponsored the voyage to South Carolina of the young English botanist Mark Catesby, whose book *The Natural History of Carolina, Florida and the Bahama Islands*, published in 1731, became the first illustrated study of American flora and fauna. Catesby was already well known in London, largely as a result of the seeds and plant specimens he had sent back to England during an earlier trip to Virginia. In preparing Catesby's second trip to America, Sloane made sure he had the support of both the Royal Society and the governor of South Carolina, who agreed to give Catesby an annual pension so that he might "observe the rarities of that country."

During his four years in South Carolina, Georgia, and the Bahamas, Catesby continued to send live plants, dried leaves, seeds, skins, and dead birds to the English collectors who had sponsored his voyage. His trip also marked a turning point in American natural history because he devoted most of his time to painting hundreds of watercolors of wildlife unknown to Europeans. His pictures of American flora and fauna were published in a two-volume set of hand-colored engravings that created a sensation in 1729 when they began to appear in twenty-plate installments.

Catesby's drawings were the first renderings to depict the birds and reptiles of North America in their natural habitat, and in the early eighteenth century, his engravings helped create a vogue for handsomely illustrated natural history books. In an era when anatomical drawings held the key to the mystery of unknown species, Catesby's exquisite watercolor renderings of living wildlife in America were further evidence of how important visual culture was to the scientific imagination. "The Illuminating Natural History is so particularly essential to the perfect understanding of it that I may aver a clearer Idea may be conceiv'd from the Figures of Animals and Plants in their proper colours, than from the most exact Description without them."[1]

Upon his return to England in 1726, Catesby also brought news of some large teeth and a tusk dug up by African slaves from the Biggin Swamp near Charleston. Unfortunately, he did not make drawings of these specimens, and the only mention of them is in the second volume of his *Natural History*, published seventeen years later. Catesby was obviously familiar with earlier reports of fossil remains found in Virginia, but his own comments on them were influenced by the emerging geological view of the American landscape:

> All parts of *Virginia*, at the Distance of Sixty Miles, or more [from the sea], abound in Fossil shells of various Kinds, which in *Stratums* lie embedded a great Depth in the Earth, in the Banks of Rivers and other Places, among which are frequently found the *Vertebras*, and other Bones of Sea Animals.[2]

The most startling fossil remains that Catesby encountered were the large teeth and a tusk found by African slaves in the swamps near Charleston. Aware of the controversy over the identity of the fossil elephants in America, Catesby compared these teeth with the grinders of African elephants:

> At a place in *Carolina* called *Stono*, was dug out of the Earth three or four Teeth of a large Animal, which by concurring Opinion of all the *Negroes*, native *Africans*, that saw them, were the Grinders of an Elephant, and in my Opinion they could be no other; I having seen some of the like that were brought from *Africa*.[3]

Although this cryptic remark was all Catesby had to say publicly about the role of African slaves, Sir Hans Sloane no doubt got a firsthand account of these bones shortly after the artist returned to London in 1726. Sloane was then preparing his own influential articles on the fossil elephants, but without any actual specimens or anatomical drawings of the bones, he did not mention them in his articles.

In the late summer of 1739, while Catesby was preparing the second volume of his *Natural History*, Charles Le Moyne, baron de Longueuil and a major in the French colonial army, led an expedition from Canada down the Ohio River in a campaign against the Chickasaw Indians. Composed of 440 French troops and Indians, Longueuil's forces traveled down the Ohio River in canoes from the mouth of the Allegheny, where Pittsburgh now stands, entering a region uncharted by earlier French explorers. To map the area, Longueuil took along an eighteen-year-old cadet named Gaspard Chaussegros de Lery, who was responsible for surveying the expedition's route.

About halfway down the Ohio River, Longueuil's party camped on the river's eastern bank, near a small creek. Shortly afterward, an Indian hunting party brought several enormous bones into his camp, including a femur and some tusks, which they had found along the edge of a nearby marshland. Longueuil's Indian guides led the French soldiers several miles up a buffalo path from the Ohio River to the large muddy pond. There they were met with the strange sight of a multitude of enormous bones bleaching in the sun around fetid marsh waters smelling of sulfur.

Baron Longueuil left no official record of his discovery of the salt lick, but the site quickly became a landmark featured on French maps of the region, thanks to the compass surveys by Chaussegros de Lery, who had carefully charted the meandering course of the Ohio River. In 1744, when the famous French cartographer Jacques Nicholas Bellin published his official map of the Louisiana Territory, the Ohio salt lick was featured prominently, identified as "the place where the elephant bones were found in 1729" (figure 9). Bellin's map of the Ohio River valley was part of a much larger map of Louisiana and the Mississippi River, summarizing a vast amount of cartographic knowledge, which may account for his erroneous dating of Longueuil's discovery of the salt lick. In any case, English colonists remained unaware of the fossil elephants in the Ohio valley, since the first Indian traders and surveyors from Pennsylvania and Virginia did not reach the salt lick for several more years.

In September 1748, the Swedish botanist Peter Kalm arrived in Philadelphia to begin nearly three years of travel and study of American flora and fauna. A pupil of the Swedish physician Carolus Linnaeus, whose new system for classifying plants, animals, and minerals

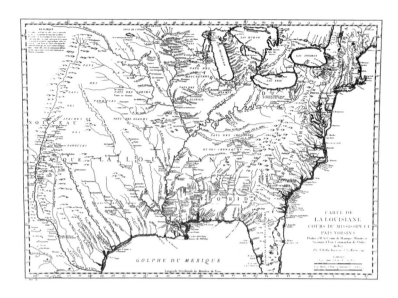

FIGURE 9. Map of Louisiana, with detail, by the French geographer
Jacques Nicholas Bellin showing the location of the Ohio valley salt
lick where a French expedition found "elephant bones" in 1739.
Designated as "the place where the elephant bones are found," the
site later became known as Big Bone Lick. Courtesy Map Division,
New York Public Library, Astor, Lenox, and Tilden Foundations.

had revolutionized the field of natural history fifteen years earlier, Kalm had been sent to the British colonies by the Swedish Academy of Sciences to study American plants. In his memoir *Travels into North America,* Kalm recounts how shortly after his arrival in Philadelphia, he went out to visit the botanical garden of John Bartram, a Quaker farmer whose occasional medical practice among his neighbors had made him a self-taught authority on plants. By the 1740s, Bartram's garden had become well known in Europe, largely through the efforts of Peter Collinson, a London Quaker and wool merchant who had organized an extensive network of European collectors to whom Bartram supplied seeds and plant specimens of exotic American species.[4]

In Bartram's garden, the two botanists discussed a variety of topics pertaining to American plant life, everything from the use by English ladies of the dry, shining, silvery leaves of the "life everlasting" for year-round decoration, to the application of compresses made from the same plants to treat bruises. When Kalm asked his host whether the American landscape had ever been covered by water, the conversation turned to Noah's Flood and its relation to some elephant bones found in Siberia and other places where elephants no longer existed. In response to Kalm's inquiry, Bartram cited a long list of evidence for the Deluge in America, ranging from the oyster shells dug up in the "Blue Mountains," three hundred miles from the sea, to the petrified shells found embedded in the limestone, flint, and sandstone there.

Then, to explain the existence of the great bones found in Siberia, which some had said were elephant bones and tusks, Bartram recited a theory of climate change based on Thomas Burnet's idea that the earth had shifted its axis at the time of the Flood: "Mr. *Bartram* from hence took occasion to defend Dr. *Thomas Burnet*'s opinion that the earth, before the deluge, was in a different position towards the sun."[5] Like that of his good friend Benjamin Franklin, whose religious beliefs were less enthusiastic, Bartram's vision of the earth's history was deeply influenced by the diluvialists, who had transformed the landscape into a sacred terrain, a romantic ruin of God's creation governed by both natural laws and evangelical beliefs.

For a self-educated Pennsylvania botanist, Bartram's ideas about the earth's history were quite sophisticated for his time, especially given his lack of scientific training in mineralogy, the field that until then had produced the most meticulous commentary on such anomalies. In 1751, shortly after Kalm's departure, Peter Collinson wrote to Bartram about the fossil remains of an unknown species of mollusk often found with these seashells. Bartram responded with a remarkably farsighted vision of mountain chains beneath the ocean's surface, which he believed proved that the mountaintops had once been covered by water. "I cannot agree with Dr. Woodward, that the rocks and mountains were so dissolved at the deluge as he represents; nor with Burnet, that there were no rocks before the flood. Moses expressly says, that *all the hills were covered*."[6]

In Bartram's opinion, the seashells and petrified marine fossils embedded in rocks in the "Blue Mountains" had been deposited *before* the flood, during the Creation itself, when the terrestrial particles of matter first began to subside and coalesce, "after the spirit of God had moved on the face of the waters, and light was separate from darkness; before beasts lived on dry lands, or fowls flew in the air."[7] To explain the anomaly of finding seashells so far from the ocean, Bartram again alluded to Burnet's theory "that the earth's axis was in a different position to the sun before the flood," an event that he felt may have altered the region's climate.

Although he was familiar with the early English theories of the earth's history, Bartram's view of the mountains and the fossils demonstrated how religious beliefs and scientific ideas became intertwined when they were applied to the American landscape, especially when they incorporated naturalistic truths about the earth's history. For many American naturalists, such anomalies, along with the cosmological questions they raised, injected a peculiar reverence for the wonder of God's nature into the geological features of the American landscape, where the landforms themselves were viewed with religious awe. For Bartram, Genesis and geology went hand in hand, and geology, which did not yet exist as an area of secular, scientific endeavor, was a sacred science.

Bartram's views of the earth's history were fairly typical of Philadelphia's natural philosophers, led by Benjamin Franklin, the editor of the *Pennsylvania Gazette*. By then, his homespun aphorisms in *Poor Richard's Almanac* were selling ten thousand copies a year and had made him a wealthy man. In 1748, when Peter Kalm came to Philadelphia, Franklin was about to retire from his printing business, at age forty-two, to devote his time to his scientific studies. Two years earlier, Peter Collinson had sent him an account of some German experiments with electricity, together with a glass tube and directions for repeating the

experiment. Franklin immediately set about creating ingenious electrical devices, including a makeshift lightning rod and an electrified portrait of the English king with a gilt crown that gave the viewer a shock
when touched.

Franklin had already given serious thought to the anomalies of the
American landscape that John Bartram discussed with his esteemed
Swedish visitor. In July 1747, before Kalm visited Philadelphia,
Franklin wrote to Jared Eliot, a Connecticut clergyman naturalist,
about the seashells found in the Appalachian Mountains, pointing out
that there were found "in many Places near the highest Parts of them,
Strata of Seashells, in some Places the Marks of them are in solid
Rocks."[8] How these mountains were formed posed the most perplexing
question for Franklin, who was just beginning to perceive the disloca-
tion of strata characteristic of exposed rock surfaces and to contemplate
the reality of cataclysmic changes in the earth's history. "When I was
once riding in your Country, Mr. Walker show'd me at a Distance the
Bluff Side or End of a Mountain, which appeared striped from top to
Bottom, and [he] told me the Stone or Rock of that Mountain was divided by Nature into Pillars."[9] Like his friend Bartram, who also was
collecting petrified plant and animal remains, Franklin's language reflected the influence of Thomas Burnet's writings on the American
colonists: "'Tis certainly the *Wreck* of a World we live on! We have
Specimens of those Seashell Rocks broken off near the Tops of those
Mountains, brought and deposited in our Library as Curiosities."

During the 1750s, after Kalm left America, the bones from the
Ohio valley salt lick gradually became a widely known curiosity sought
by Indian traders and frontier scouts. While French naturalists in Paris
were undertaking the first scientific studies of the fossil remains from
Longueuil's expedition, eyewitness accounts of the salt lick, along with
a few bones, began to trickle back to the English colonies from the
Ohio valley territory. Indian traders and peddlers from the British
colony of Pennsylvania had moved across the Allegheny Mountains
into the upper Ohio River valley, following the migrating Indians—
mostly Senecas, Delawares, and Shawnees—who were moving into
Ohio country from the Great Lakes region and the Susquehanna valley
in Pennsylvania. With the spread of Pennsylvania-based peddlers, trading towns sprang up in the upper Ohio valley, from Log's Town near the
forks of the Ohio, where present-day Pittsburgh now stands, to Pickawillany, farther west on the headwaters of the Great Miami River.

The most successful of these early Indian traders was George Croghan, a newly arrived Irish immigrant who created a network of trading houses in the principal Indian towns throughout the upper Ohio valley during the 1740s. Born in Dublin of Protestant parents, Croghan had come to western Pennsylvania in 1741 during a potato famine, and with the assistance of the colony's ruling circles, he quickly became the most experienced Indian trader and diplomat in the Ohio valley. In 1747, the Pennsylvania government officially appointed him their Indian agent to deliver presents to the Ohio Indians, including powder, lead, vermilion, knives, and tobacco, along with promises of more favorable terms of trade. Like many successful Indian traders, Croghan learned the Delaware and Iroquois languages and was familiar with the habits and customs of the Indian peoples throughout the region.

The inroads made by Pennsylvania peddlers in the Ohio valley alarmed French colonial officials, whose knowledge of the region remained limited, since nearly a half-century of warfare with the Iroquois five nations had denied the French direct access to the region. In the spring of 1749, a new threat to France's authority appeared when King George of England granted 200,000 acres in the region to the Ohio Company of Virginia, an enterprise founded by a group of Virginia planters who planned to profit from land speculation and settlement in the Ohio valley. During the summer, the French sent a military expedition to the upper Ohio valley, commanded by Pierre-Joseph Céloron de Blainville, whose mission was to reassert France's power in the region. Rumors of the French expedition prompted the governor of Pennsylvania to send George Croghan to Ohio country in August 1749, to reinforce England's alliances with the Indian communities and to curtail illegal settlement on unpurchased Indian lands in the region by white settlers.

The first Anglo-American to explore the Kentucky side of the Ohio River, where the curious salt lick was located, was Christopher Gist, the son of a surveyor from Maryland, hired in 1750 by the Ohio Company of Virginia to survey lands in the upper Ohio valley as far south as the Ohio River falls. In November, Gist set out from the upper Potomac River valley in Virginia and traveled north along an old buffalo trace, crossing the Allegheny Mountains to the tributaries leading to the forks of the Ohio River and the trading outpost of Log's Town. But instead of following the Ohio downriver, he headed inland on a well-traveled Indian path toward several Delaware trading towns located near the headwaters of the Muskingum River. There he encountered George Croghan, Pennsylvania's deputy agent of Indian affairs, who was busy shoring up Pennsylvania's ties with Indians in Ohio country. Traveling with Croghan, Gist went to Pickawillany, the newest trading town, located to the west on the upper reaches of the Great Miami River.

Before heading south toward the falls, Gist stayed overnight with Robert Smith, a Pennsylvania trader who lived on the east bank of the Great Miami River, opposite the town of Pickawillany. According to Gist, Smith claimed to have gathered several teeth and bones from the salt lick in the 1740s after Longueuil's expedition had passed through the Ohio valley. In convincing detail, Smith described the skeletons of three large beasts that he had seen at the lick several years earlier. "He assured Me that the Rib Bones of the largest of these Beasts were eleven Feet long, and the Skull Bone six feet wide, across the Forehead, & the other Bones in Proportion."[10]

Beyond these gargantuan dimensions, Smith offered little else in the way of identifying features, except to note that "there were several Teeth there, some of which he called Horns, and [he] said they were upwards of five Feet long, and as much as a Man coud well carry." Smith's vivid memory of the tusks undoubtedly stemmed from the fact that "he had hid one in a Branch at some Distance from the Place, lest the French Indians shoud carry it away."[11] The existence of these bones was not widely publicized at the time, owing to the remoteness of Smith's trading activities and his failure to send any specimens to interested parties. During his overnight visit with Smith, Gist apparently asked the trader to obtain some bones before he set out the next morning for the falls of the Ohio.

Upon his arrival at the lower Shawnee town located near the mouth of the Scioto River, a Mingo chief warned Gist not to venture farther south because there was a party of hostile Indians hunting downriver. But because the Virginia planters had instructed him to go to the falls, Gist nonetheless crossed over the Ohio River and traveled downriver about eighteen miles before heading inland across the countryside toward the falls. About a half-day's ride from the Shawnee town, he met two men working for Robert Smith, who were bringing to him two large teeth from the salt lick.[12]

Gist may never have reached Big Bone Lick, as his diary does not have a clear description of the salt lick and the route he took, traveling on horseback rather than by canoe, went through the countryside rather than down the Ohio River. In any case, upon hearing rifle shots of Indians loyal to the French farther south, Gist turned back without reaching the falls and instead returned several months later to Virginia. There he made a gift of a large tooth to his employers at the Ohio Company: "The Tooth which I brought in for the Ohio Company, was a Jaw Tooth of better than four Pounds Weight," Gist noted in his journal. "It appeared to be the farthest Tooth in the Jaw, and looked like fine Ivory when the outside was scraped off."[13]

No record of this tooth's fate has survived, although it may have been one of the early specimens that found their way back to London during this period without clear documentation of their origins. The wealthy London merchant Peter Collinson, who later published an article on the Ohio bones, claimed to have received two monstrous teeth from the Ohio salt lick that were sent to him by the governor of Virginia. But little else was said about these specimens, since Gist's journal itself was not made public and the Virginia planters seem to have taken less interest in the tooth than did the clergymen and physicians in New England and Pennsylvania.[14]

In June 1750, before Gist set out on his journey, the twenty-three-year-old Connecticut scholar Ezra Stiles (figure 10), a newly ordained minister working as a tutor at Yale, examined a giant tooth weighing four pounds. "A curious Gentleman brot from N. York one of these Teeth and shewed it at N. Haven to the scholars in his Way to Boston, from whence he intended to carry it to the Royal Society in London," Stiles later recalled.[15] Even though we do not know the exact provenance of this specimen, it led Stiles to look through his grandfather Edward Taylor's unpublished manuscripts for his unfinished poem about the Claverack monster. From New England to the Kentucky frontier, curiosity about the fossil elephants was beginning to attract the attention of a new generation of American colonists to whom the bones was soon associated with their struggle for independence.

In the spring of 1753, the newly appointed French governor of Canada ordered the construction of several forts from Lake Erie to the forks of the Ohio River, opening a new phase of the military campaign against British land agents, settlers, and traders in the region. To protest the French intrusion on Virginia's land claims, Robert Dinwiddie, the lieutenant governor of Virginia, sent Major George Washington, who

FIGURE 10. Portrait of Ezra Stiles, age twenty-nine, by Nathaniel Smibert, 1756. Courtesy of Yale University Art Gallery, gift of graduates to the university.

was then only twenty-one years old, to Fort Le Boeuf, near Lake Erie, with an ultimatum demanding that the French cease building forts. Traveling through the upper Ohio valley by canoe and raft on icy winter waters, Washington's guide on the trip was Christopher Gist, the Virginia surveyor who had firsthand knowledge of the Ohio salt lick.

FIGURE 11. Portrait of George Washington, age
twenty-one, from *The Journal of Major George
Washington*, an account of his first journey into
Ohio country published in 1754.

The French commander at Fort Le Boeuf politely refused Governor
Dinwiddie's demands, but Washington's visit to Ohio country is significant because it may have been the first time the future commander of
the Continental Army heard eyewitness accounts of the fossil elephants at Big Bone Lick.

Upon Washington's return to Virginia, Governor Dinwiddie had
the young major's journal published in Williamsburg in early 1754,
hoping that his account of French intrusion into the Ohio valley would
stir the Virginia assembly to action. Although the journal did not refer
to the Ohio salt lick, Governor Dinwiddie nevertheless sent it to London, where it was immediately reprinted by Thomas Jeffrey, the royal
geographer, along with an engraving of the young major (figure 11) and
a detailed "Map of the Western parts of the colony of Virginia, as far as
the Mississippi." This map, though containing a more accurate depiction of the course of the Ohio River, made no mention of the place
where the elephant bones had been found.

English cartographic knowledge of the region was changing rapidly, for the following year Lewis Evans, a Philadelphia mapmaker, published his "Map of the Middle British Colonies in America." It designated the site of the salt lick on the Ohio River simply with the phrase "Elephant Bones found here," the term first used by French mapmakers a decade earlier (figure 12). A Welshman who had come to Philadelphia in 1736, Evans was a member of Benjamin Franklin's circle and had traveled with John Bartram on several occasions while collecting data on the topography of the middle colonies. His knowledge of Ohio country was based largely on accounts by travelers to the region, although his map showed many of the Indian paths used by early explorers like Christopher Gist. The publication of Evans's map in 1755 was the first time the salt lick appeared on English maps of Ohio country, an important cartographic event indicating the colonists' increased interest in the site as settlement spread beyond the Alleghenies.

During the early years of the French and Indian Wars, English colonists were cut off from Big Bone Lick, the important new source of

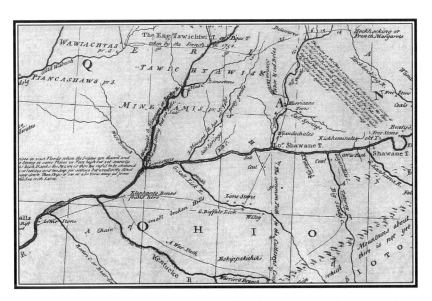

FIGURE 12. Detail from *Map of the Middle British Colonies in America*, by the Pennsylvania map maker Lewis Evans, 1755. The site of the Ohio salt lick visited by frontier scouts and Indian traders is indicated by the phrase "Elephant Bones found here."

bones belonging to the fossil elephants in America. Nonetheless, through a surprising turn of events in 1756, stories about these curiosities continued to filter back from the frontier, not as reports from Indian traders and frontier scouts, but instead as exotic details in the tale told by a white woman who had escaped her Indian captors while visiting the salt lick. The resurgence of France's influence in the Ohio valley led many Indians loyal to the French to harass British traders and land agents and to attack English settlers on the western frontier in Pennsylvania and Virginia.

In the early summer of 1756, Shawnee Indians from Ohio country raided a frontier settlement at Draper's Meadows along the ridge of the Allegheny Mountains, near the headwaters of the Roanoke River in western Virginia. Recently established by Scotch-Irish settlers from Pennsylvania, the small settlement included the family of William and Mary Ingles, who had purchased property from Colonel James Patton, a well-known Virginia land speculator. During the Shawnee raid, Colonel Patton and several other settlers were killed, and Mary Ingles, her sister-in-law, and Mary's two children, aged two and four, were taken prisoner. Later, on the Ohio River, the family was separated, and Mary Ingles was taken by her captors to the lower Shawnee town at the mouth of Scioto River, a few days' travel from Big Bone Lick.

A few months later, Mary Ingles was taken down the Ohio River to Big Bone Lick with a salt-boiling party, along with an old Dutch woman who had been a captive for many years. Sent into the surrounding woods to gather black walnuts and grapes, the two women plotted their escape, each taking with them a blanket and a tomahawk, which, as Mary Ingles often recounted afterward, she had acquired from a French trader seated on an enormous bone from the salt lick. "I have frequantly [sic] Heard my mother say when she left the lick that she exchanged her tomehock [sic] with one of three frenchmen who was sitting on One of the large Bones that was there and cracking walnuts," her son wrote years later.[16] Following the old buffalo trace to the Ohio River, the two women began a five-hundred-mile trek through the wilderness that eventually led to their escape from the Shawnees.

Evidently, Mary Ingles told the story of her escape from captivity many times until her death in 1815 at the age of eighty-three. Her tale became part of the new genre of frontier tales known as *captivity narratives*, stories of daring escapes by white women from their Indian captors, which served, in the eyes of many colonists, to justify the brutal conquest of Ohio country and the acquisition of Indian lands. In this case, because her story included a fascinating glimpse of Big Bone Lick during the French occupation of the Ohio valley, Mary Ingles's anecdote about the elephant bones also circulated among European naturalists.

English colonists increasingly saw the conquest of Indian lands in Ohio country as their manifest destiny, despite the efforts of British colonial authorities to curb settlement beyond the Allegheny Mountains. In 1758, Colonel George Washington made his fourth trip to the region, accompanying the British forces that captured Fort Duquesne and renamed it Fort Pitt after the new British prime minister, William Pitt, whose leadership finally turned the war in England's favor.

The following summer, George Croghan, who had been appointed deputy to the Crown's first superintendent of Indian affairs, was back at the fort, giving Indians extravagant gifts aimed at easing their fears of English settlement. English settlers from Pennsylvania and Virginia were already reappearing in isolated river valleys beyond the Alleghenies, only this time they came with a virulent racial hatred of the Indians, whose loyalty to the French and attacks on frontier settlements had led settlers to view them as dehumanized savages. In this new atmosphere of Indian hating, captivity narratives had wide currency, and Mary Ingles's story may well have provided the first news of the fossil elephants at Big Bone Lick to many American colonists not privy to the reports of Indian traders and frontier scouts.

The recapture of Fort Pitt by the British army immediately rekindled hopes among land speculators and backcountry settlers that the Ohio valley would be reopened to settlement by the colonists. But Britain's Indian policy had shifted radically during the war. Colonial authorities tried to win the Indians' allegiance by promising to limit English settlement beyond the Alleghenies. In 1761, Colonel Henry Bouquet, the new British commander at Fort Pitt, issued a proclamation banning any settlement or hunting on Indian lands.

The Swiss-born Colonel Bouquet had studied mathematics in Holland and had become friends with several Dutch scientists before coming to America in 1754 with Britain's colonial army. In September 1761, he welcomed an esteemed American visitor to Fort Pitt, John Bartram, the Philadelphia botanist, who had come to Ohio country in hopes of finding exotic new specimens for his customers in England. Undeterred by the threat of Indian attacks, Bartram had made the three-hundred-mile trek across the Alleghenies on horseback over the newly opened Forbes Road, admiring the coal, slate, limestone, and whetstone beds laid bare in quarries and strip mines along the way. Traveling with James Kenny, a Quaker friend who had a small trading store at Fort Pitt, Bartram's party was outfitted at Fort Pitt for a trip down the Ohio River by their gracious host Colonel Bouquet, who provided them with an Indian interpreter and a boat with four oarsmen, along with several soldiers for protection against hostile Indians.

With Colonel Bouquet's escort, Bartram's party traveled a short distance down the Ohio, just beyond Log's Town, to the abandoned site of an old trading outpost. There they camped near the residence of Colonel William Johnson, Britain's superintendent of Indian affairs. After spending six nights camping along the banks of the Ohio River, Bartram later expressed disappointment at having seen so few wild animals on his trip, only two or three deer, several snakes, and a tame bear at Fort Pitt. Surprisingly, in his brief travels through the upper Ohio valley, Bartram encountered no news of the fossil elephants, not even any Indians or English traders hawking bones from the salt lick, which lay hundreds of miles farther downriver.

This situation, however, changed dramatically the following summer while Bartram was completing the journal of his trip to Ohio country for Peter Collinson, his chief correspondent in London. Delegations of Indians frequently came to Fort Pitt seeking trade goods and favors. Among them, during the summer of 1762, were several Shawnee Indians who brought a large tooth and tusk to Colonel Bouquet, probably as gifts to cement ties with the newly established British colonial authorities. Excited by his marvelous new acquisition, Bouquet wrote immediately to John Bartram:

> I got, a few days ago, a very great curiosity, from about six hundred miles down the Ohio, an elephant's tooth, weighing six pounds and three quarters, and a large piece of one of the tusks, which puts it beyond doubt, that those animals have formerly existed on this continent.[17]

Upon receiving Colonel Bouquet's letter, Bartram immediately contacted his friend James Wright, a Quaker naturalist living in western Pennsylvania, and asked him to obtain information about the tooth and tusk at Fort Pitt. With the assistance of an interpreter, Wright talked to two Shawnee Indians who gave him a colorful description of several skeletons buried at the Ohio salt lick, about four days' journey below the lower Shawnee town. The Shawnees told him there were five "entire Sceletons" at the lick, all lying with their heads pointing toward one another. When asked about the animal's size, the Indians compared the great beast to a small stable nearby, adding that a shoulder bone, with a socket the size of a large bowl, reached their own shoulders in height and a small boy could crawl into the cavity when the bone was broken. The skulls of the animals were so large "a Man Could but Just Grasp [them] in Both his Arms, with a long Nose, And the Mouth on the under side," and the "horns," or tusks, measured some ten to twelve feet in length.[18] In their testimony, the Indians revealed the unique character of the salt lick as a landmark in Ohio country, for according to them, "there were many roads thro this Extent of land, larger & more beaten by Buffalas [sic] and other Creatures, that had made them to go to it, than any Roads they saw in this Part of the Country."

For Anglo-American naturalists, Wright's letter marked an important milestone in the association of Indian legends with the American *incognitum*, stories that later helped make the mysterious creature a national symbol in the eyes of the founding fathers. The Shawnees' tale was the earliest documented version of an Indian myth later popularized by Thomas Jefferson in his commentary on the mysterious bones during the Revolutionary War. When asked whether they had ever seen any such animals alive, the Shawnees told Wright that "they had never heard them spoken of, other then as in the Condition they are at present, nor ever heard of any such creature having been seen by the oldest Man, or his father." But they did have a tradition about some mighty animals that had once lived on the savanna and had been hunted by giant men of the same stature, who threw these great beasts on their backs as an Indian now does a deer.

The Shawnee story echoed Indian legends about human giants in New England, like those mentioned by Edward Taylor, which had talked about "Great & Strong Men" who made marks in the surrounding rocks when they sat down with these beasts on their backs, "such as a Man makes by sitting down on the Snow." Eventually, when none of these human giants were alive any longer, the Shawnees explained, "God Kil[l]ed these Mighty Creatures, that they should not hurt the Present race of Indians," by striking them all dead with lightning bolts, including, apparently, the five skeletons at the salt lick.[19]

Shortly before Bouquet's letter to Bartram, Peter Collinson had written to the Philadelphia botanist from London, requesting "some more particular Observations on the Great Buffalo, Their Bones or skeletons are now standing in a Licking place not far from the Ohio of which I have Two of their Teeth."[20] Evidently, Collinson had received reports about the same locale, and possibly some bone specimens, from George Croghan and J. Greenwood, two veteran Indian traders: "Both [of these traders] saw them & gave Mee relation of them, but they omitted to Take Notice what Hoofs they had, & what Horns." These anatomical features were essential to determining the animal's "Genus or Species," and Collinson implored Bartram, "Prethee inquire after them, for they are wonderful beyond description if what is related of them may be depended on."

In late July, still unaware of Wright's report from Fort Pitt, Collinson again wrote to Bartram, somewhat urgently, asking for information about the Ohio salt lick. "I forgett if I ever Mention'd two Monstrous Teeth I had sent Mee by the Govr of Virginia—one tooth Weighs 3 3/4 pds, 15 Inches round, the other 1 3/4 pounds—13 1/2 inches round."[21] By then, Collinson had received a similar report from the Indian trader named Greenwood, who apparently had gone to London about this time. Certain details in Collinson's letter are strikingly similar to the news Bartram received from his friend James Wright. "One Greenwood, well known to B. Franklin, an Indian trader, knocked some Teeth out of their Jaws," Wright wrote with regard to the two specimens, "& Geo. Croghan has been att the Licking Place near the Ohio where the skelletons of six Monstrous animals was standing as they will inform thee." Collinson was already familiar with the legends that the Shawnee Indians later related to James Wright, for he added a telling detail to his own request: "The Indian Tradition [is] that the Monstrous Buffaloes so called by the Indians was all struck dead with Lightning at this licking place."

During the summer of 1762, when the mysterious bones from the Ohio salt lick were becoming sought-after curiosities in both Philadelphia and London, Collinson himself began to think more systematically about the identity of the American *incognitum*. "By my Beloved Friend Benn Franklin, I wrote a Long letter [to Croghan] relateing to the Skeletons of the Animals who are standing in the Licking place down the Ohio," he reminded Bartram, after receiving his copy of James Wright's account. "I Desired Him to show it Thee for There in, is all I have been able to collect relateing to the Existence of thos Surprising Animals."[22]

No copy of this letter has survived, but it clearly represented the beginning of Collinson's efforts to scrutinize more carefully the new American specimens, using the techniques of comparative anatomy recommended more than thirty years earlier by Sir Hans Sloane. For the first time, Collinson cast doubt on the casual assumption, made by everyone from the French mapmakers to Henry Bouquet, that these fossil remains belonged to elephants, long-dead relatives of the living species. "The Good Colonel thought them Elephants Teeth," Collinson wrote to Bartram, "but they have no relation to them for I saw Elephants' Teeth & they are in the British Museum and [I] can be certain on that point."

Like Sir Hans Sloane, whose immense collection of curiosities formed the nucleus of the British Museum, Collinson saw immediately what was needed to solve the riddle of the American *incognitum's* identity: "What they really are is [impossible] to Determine unless there was the strictest Examination by a Man well Qualified & then its more then [likely] they may be found to be an unknown Creature—unless it may be the Rhinoceras whose teeth I have not Seen." He recommended that Bartram seek out the "drawing Masters" among Colonel Bouquet's staff at Fort Pitt to make exact renderings of the teeth so they could be studied systematically. "The Colo[nel] being a Gentleman of Curiosity & to bring one of the Wonders of the World to Light, may be excited to go & take a Survey of these Amazing Subjects."

In the next few years, Bartram's own opinions about the mysterious bones grew bolder in his letters to Collinson, and he speculated that they may have belonged to an unknown animal rather than an elephant. "I am wholy of ye opinion that ye Ohio bones is ye remains of A creature unknown," he declared, stressing the importance of finding a complete skeleton. "If I should go there & have A proper opertunity to observe them, I believe I should want A[s] many bones to make up an intire skeleton, notwithstanding ye rash superficial reports of those incurious persons that hath been there."[23]

Nearly a year later, when he wrote to Collinson about a "monstrous tooth" from the Allegheny Mountains that he had borrowed from a Philadelphia woman, Bartram came close to embracing an even more controversial idea: extinction. After carefully measuring the specimen's size and weight, which he claimed was "heavy as brass," Bartram suddenly, with an enthusiastic turn of phrase, employed a term whose casual use must have disturbed Collinson: "A monstrous creature must this belong to that is utterly extinct as ye Irish [elk]," he declared, alluding to the bones of another creature whose bones had long puzzled English naturalists.[24] Nearly sixty years earlier, Thomas Molyneux, an Irish physician, had published the first scientific paper on the "Irish elk," which some naturalists believed was extinct because its antlers had no counterparts among living species.

Despite his desire to visit the fabled salt lick, Bartram never returned to Ohio country, choosing instead, with the outbreak of Pontiac's Indian rebellion in the Great Lakes region, to journey south to Florida, where he pursued butterflies and bull frogs in the orange groves instead of digging fossils from the swamps. The person who finally reached the Ohio salt lick and then dazzled London anatomists with the monstrous teeth and tusks of the American *incognitum* was the Indian trader George Croghan. But with the outbreak in 1763 of Indian attacks on traders and settlers, Croghan himself was forced to flee from Fort Pitt. In Philadelphia, where he took refuge, Croghan won the confidence of Samuel Wharton, a wealthy merchant engaged in the fur trade, who was intrigued by the Croghan's dreams of capturing the Indian trade in Illinois country, Britain's newly acquired French territory.

To pursue this grandiose scheme, Croghan traveled to England with letters of introduction to prominent colonial officials at the Board of Trade, the organization responsible for formulating policies for the new western territories. After two frustrating months in England, Croghan wrote to William Johnson, his friend and colleague at Britain's Indian office in the colonies: "I am sick of London & harttily tierd of the pride & pompe of the slaves in power."[25] Rebuffed by the London authorities, Croghan returned empty-handed to Philadelphia in the summer of 1764, where he continued to lobby with local authorities for permission to travel down the Ohio River.

By the end of 1764, the war in the Ohio valley was winding down, but the British military still found themselves stymied by pockets of resistance in Illinois country and the demands of Indian chiefs angry over the terms of peace. A smallpox epidemic had swept through the Indian villages after the British officers at Fort Pitt handed out blankets infested with the disease, wiping out thousands of native peoples while weakening the resolve of those who survived. With the backing of

Philadelphia merchants, Croghan went to New York to gain approval
for an expedition to Illinois country from General Thomas Gage, commander of the British forces in the colonies, who, he hoped, would help
pay for the trade goods supplied by the merchants to pacify the Indians.
Faced with the mounting costs of military operations in the western territories, General Gage and his officers decided that negotiation rather
than armed intervention was the best solution, and as Colonel Bouquet
informed him, "Mr. Croghan is the fittest person in America to trans-
act that business."[26]

Accordingly, several months before a formal peace with France had
been ratified, Croghan set out for Fort Pitt, hiring sixty-five packhorses
along the way to carry the gifts and trade goods for the Indians that
were to be shipped later from Philadelphia. After convening an Indian
congress at Fort Pitt to win the support of more than five hundred Indian chiefs and warriors, mainly Senecas, Delawares, and Shawnees,
Croghan set off down the Ohio River on May 15, 1765, in two large
flatboats laden with merchandise, along with several Shawnee deputies. His party also included boatmen and personal servants, along
with his friend Dr. George C. Anthons and his cousin Thomas Smallwood, a novice Indian trader whom, after he was released from a year
and a half's captivity by the Shawnees, Croghan had helped open a
small store at Fort Pitt.

For the first few days, the flatboats floated down the Ohio through
lush, well-timbered bottomland filled with game. "The country here-
abouts abounds with buffalo, bears, deer, and all sorts of wild game, in
such plenty, that we killed out of our boats as much as we wanted,"
Croghan noted in his journal.[27] Finally, after nearly three weeks on the
water, the little flotilla passed the mouth of the Great Miami River
and, "in the evening arrived at the place where the Elephants' bones
are found."

Early the next morning, Croghan led his party along the well-worn
path about four miles inland to the celebrated salt lick. "In our way we
passed through a fine timbered clear wood," he wrote. "We came into a
large road which the Buffaloes have beaten, spacious enough for two
waggons to go abreast, and leading straight into the Lick."[28] After an
hour's walk, Croghan arrived at the scene of the mystery that anatomists in London and Paris were busy attempting to solve, the disappearance of an entire species whose bones lay strewn across the marshland. "It appears that there are vast quantities of these bones lying five

or six feet under ground, which we discovered in the bank, at the edge of the Lick."

Not being a trained naturalist himself or a religious man to whom the monstrous teeth conjured up images of Noah's Flood, Croghan spent only a few hours at the lick, hastily collecting several tusks and teeth and hauling a six-foot-long tusk and some other unidentified bones back to the flatboats before setting off again downriver later the same day. Unfortunately, Croghan's prized specimens never got out of the Ohio valley. Instead, they were scattered from his flatboats a week later by a hostile band of eighty Kickapoo and Macouten warriors, who attacked the party at daybreak while they were camped at the mouth of the Wabash River, on the edge of Illinois country. In the melee, Croghan himself was wounded and three Shawnee Indians and two of his servants were killed before all the white men were taken prisoner and carried away to the warrior's village north of Fort Vincennes. There Croghan was befriended by sympathetic French traders, who extended enough credit to him to reoutfit his party. Croghan then managed to convince his captors—Illinois Indians fearful of retaliation by the Shawnees—that their best hopes lay with Croghan's own intercession on their behalf.

Within a few months, at a council meeting with deputies from the four Illinois nations and his old acquaintance the aging Wyandot chief Pontiac, who had led the rebellion against the British, Croghan was able to turn disaster into a diplomatic victory for the British. His shrewdness and high standing among the Indians enabled him to persuade all five Wabash tribes to agree to England's occupation of the French forts in Illinois country. In doing so, Croghan rekindled hopes for westward expansion while at the same time presenting new opportunities for collectors of the mysterious bones, which were now associated indelibly with the prospects for land grants and settlement in the Ohio valley.

News of Croghan's exploits spread rapidly throughout the British colonies, making him a celebrity by the time he reached New York in November 1765. In the highly charged political atmosphere, when American colonists were violently protesting Britain's newly enacted Stamp Act, colonial officials welcomed Croghan, hoping his pacification of the Indians in Illinois country would lessen the expense of empire. Returning to Philadelphia, Croghan, whose aim now was to promote his own land speculation in Illinois country, began immediately to lay the foundation for a second trip down the Ohio River.

In this endeavor, he involved Benjamin Franklin and his son, William, who was governor of New Jersey, sending them both private versions of his journal, specially designed to solicit support for the new colony. "The Illinois country far exceeds any other part of America, that I have seen—both as to soil and climate," he wrote to Benjamin Franklin, who quickly became the most ardent American lobbyist in London for an Illinois colony.[29] But Franklin's lobbying proved ineffectual in the face of the British colonial officials' opposition to new settlement beyond the Alleghenies. Nonetheless, with the approval of British military commanders and the financial backing of the Philadelphia firm of Baynton, Wharton and Morgan, Croghan set out again on June 18, 1766, from Fort Pitt, down the Ohio River to Illinois country. This time his expedition contained thirteen flatboats, all laden with gifts for the Indians and provisions for British troops at Fort Chartres.

No journal written by Croghan survives from this second trip, but Captain Harry Gordon, the chief engineer at Fort Pitt, sent by General Thomas Gage to survey the course of the Ohio River, kept a diary that provides glimpses of the journey. His assistant, the young ensign Thomas Hutchins, later became one of the principal American mapmakers of the region, publishing in 1778 the first map to designate the Ohio salt lick as "Big Bone." Among the other members of Croghan's party was George Morgan, the junior partner of the Philadelphia trading company of Bayton, Wharton and Morgan that underwrote the expedition's trade goods.

"The Country is Every where pleasant," wrote Captain Gordon, of the terrain below Fort Pitt; "in the bends of the Rivers course are large level Spots of the richest Land, and on the whole is remarkably healthy, by the Accounts of Traders who have been some time with the Indians hunting in those Parts."[30] Nearly a month after departing, the oarsmen halted at the landing near the renowned salt lick, where Croghan's party spent the night before walking inland the next morning to the site. Captain Gordon described the wide paths made by large game animals through the wilderness to the lick: "The beaten Roads from all quarters to it easily Conducted us, they resemble those to an Inland Village where Cattle go to and fro[m] a large Common. The Pasturage near it seems of the finest kind, mixed with Grass and Herbage, and well watered." The muddy part of the lick covered only about three-quarters of an acre, yet Captain Gordon understood immediately the extent of its popularity among the large quadrupeds of the region: "This Mud being of a Salty Quality is greedily lick'd by Buffaloe, Elk, and Deer, who come from distant parts, in great Numbers for this purpose."

Unlike Croghan's hurried visit to the salt lick the previous year, this time his party lingered for an entire day, collecting hundreds of pounds of bones. Revealing his familiarity with the debate over the specimens, Captain Gordon observed, "We discovered laying about many large bones, some of which [were] the Exact Patterns of Elephants Tusks, and others of different parts of a large Animal." During the day-long visit, Thomas Hutchins sketched the area. By the time they departed the next morning, George Morgan himself had a large box of mud-caked bones, including a massive jawbone with three molars still intact. In addition, he carried away two tibia, two broken scapula, a femur broken into two parts, a jawbone fragment with one tooth, and an assortment of gigantic molars and fragments of teeth.[31]

Illness, not Indian attacks, cut short this expedition, when Croghan came down with malaria on the upper Mississippi at Fort Chartres, after his party had reached its final destination. Along with several crates filled with bones from the salt lick, Croghan went down the Mississippi to New Orleans with Captain Gordon and then traveled by boat to New York, arriving in January 1767. Having achieved a kind of notoriety and fame, Croghan's travels were monitored in the press, and according to his biographer, Nicholas Wainwright, "no name appeared more frequently than his in the scant columns provided for local affairs by Philadelphia's three newspapers."[32] In New York, after conferring with General Thomas Gage, Croghan turned to the task of informing his influential supporters in London of his latest success, always with an eye for furthering his dreams of acquiring land grants in Illinois country.

Less than a week after his arrival in New York, Croghan sent letters about the bones to Benjamin Franklin and Lord Shelburne, the British minister responsible for the American colonies, who, he hoped, would look favorably on the plans for the new colony. For Lord Shelburne, he selected two tusks, several large molars, and a lower jaw with two teeth, along with a letter briefly describing where they had been found. His letter to Shelburne reveals Croghan's penchant for grandiose statements, not to mention his ignorance of the salt lick's history:

There were some extraordinary Bones [at the Lick]. I immediately discovered, They were those of Elephants, and as They were the first ever met with, in any part of North America, and the oldest Indians, have not the least traditional Trace of Them. . . . I shall do myself the Honor, of sending your Lordship, a Box containing some Tusks, Grinders &c.[33]

Croghan saved his best specimens for Franklin, his influential lobbyist, to whom he sent four ivory tusks, one of them six feet long, along with a vertebra and three large molars.

In February, while the uncrated fossils were still in New York, a visitor to the city saw them, perhaps at a public showing that Croghan had organized. As the visitor reported in the *Pennsylvania Chronicle* nine months later, "Several Gentlemen, who had the opportunity of seeing Ivory Tusks in *Africa* and elsewhere, pronounced them, *Elephants' Teeth*."[34] Identifying himself only as "G.W.," the anonymous correspondent invited readers to comment on the fossils, and the ensuing exchange of views demonstrates how news of Croghan's curiosities created a stir among the colonial gentry. One comment extracted from an unidentified journal was reminiscent of Croghan's manner of expression:

At the Distance of about Six Hundred Miles S.W. of *Fort Pitt*, and near the Banks of *Ohio*, is a Salt-Lick, in a clear open Plain, having a Road leading to it beat by Buffaloes, and other wild Game, spacious enough for Three Coaches to go a-breast, here we found the Remains of those huge Animals called *Elephants*, and by holy Job named [the] *Behemoth*, in such Quantities that several Waggons might be soon laden with excellent Ivory.[35]

The allusions to Job's story of the "behemoth" from the Bible and the roadway "Three Coaches" wide were probably Croghan's creation, and his exuberance foreshadowed the arrival of the American monster. In these early stages, the American *incognitum* did not exist yet in the mind of the colonists, for most people accepted the common assumption that the bones belonged to elephants rather than unknown creatures. For them, the great mystery was why these animals had disappeared and how their fossil remains could have found their way into the Ohio valley, far from elephants' usual habitat. "They feed on Grass and

Herbage, and browse on Shrubs, taking the Water, and going in Droves like other wild Beasts," "G.W." surmised.

> But of the Dissolution of such a vast Number of these sagacious Animals, and of their Existence at one Place, and on this Land, where no other Trace or Vestige of them remain, nor has it been known to *Spaniards, French* or *English,* in *South* or *North America,* from their first Investigation thereof to this Time—[this] is the Query?[36]

Many thoughtful observers imagined elaborate scenarios to explain how elephants had come to Ohio country. In this instance, the anonymous author offered a farsighted speculation: "Therefore may not any Gentleman of Capacity, on this side the *Atlantic,* account for the Migration of the Elephants, and Dissolution, at this remarkable Salt-Lick, or Spring, and from reasonable Conjectures, conclude *Asia* to be the Place of their first Existence." Then he added a pragmatic twist to his argument by suggesting that an understanding of how these animals had migrated from Asia to North America might "throw some Light on the Practicableness of finding out a N.W. Passage, by Land, to that Quarter of the Globe, so ardently wished for."[37]

Of course, as Peter Collinson already realized, these animals were not elephants. Within a few years, through Franklin's correspondence with European naturalists, these new relics from the Ohio salt lick aroused controversy from London to Paris, as learned gentlemen and theologians pondered the question of the monster's identity and the reality of extinction.

The first French collection of bones from Ohio country had already reached Paris, where they were being examined by France's leading anatomists. Meanwhile, the American colonists were beginning to dream of their own continental empire, and the bones of the American *incognitum,* like the wilderness landscape itself, were already being assigned symbolic values extending far beyond their scientific significance. Although Croghan himself had little sense of the impact the bones would later have on American national consciousness, his exploits greatly augmented public awareness of the mysterious creature, whose size and girth brought many people their first foreboding image of prehistoric nature.

5

The American *Incognitum* in Paris

This species was certainly the foremost, the largest, the strongest of all the quadrupeds. Since it has disappeared, how many others— smaller, weaker and less noticeable—have also perished without having left us either evidence or information about their past existence?
—Buffon, 1761

DESPITE ENGLAND'S VICTORY over France in the Ohio valley, the French got a head start in the hunt for the bones of the American *incognitum*. Long before George Croghan shipped his fossils from Big Bone to London, an earlier collection of fossils from the same salt lick reached Paris, where they were placed in the cabinet of curiosities belonging to France's King Louis XV. These specimens, including a tusk, a femur, and several molars, were brought back to France by Baron de Longueuil, whose expedition from Canada down the Ohio River in 1739 had led to the discovery of the Big Bone Lick.

The rising interest among Anglo-American naturalists in the bones from the Ohio salt lick was paralleled by the first French theories about the unidentified beast, advanced by the famous French naturalist George Louis Leclerc de Buffon and his anatomist Louis Jean-Marie Daubenton. By the late 1760s, when the mystery of the American *incognitum* began to deepen with realization that the bones did not belong to elephants, Buffon was nearing the peak of his career and had already published the first fifteen volumes of his encyclopedic *Histoire naturelle, générale et particulière*. Based on a comparison of bones from the Ohio salt lick with those of Siberian mammoths and living elephants, these two French academicians put forward the first "scientific" theories about the American *incognitum*, using comparative anatomy to identify its fossil remains.

The bones brought back to Paris by Baron Longueuil were soon examined by Buffon, then a thirty-two-year-old mathematician and natural philosopher who had been recently appointed director of the Jardin du roi, the king's garden and cabinet of curiosities (figure 13). But Buffon and his anatomist Daubenton did not offer any theories about the remains until the early 1760s, a few years before Anglo-American naturalists saw similar specimens from Big Bone. In the meanwhile, Buffon devoted all his time to his *Histoire naturelle*, whose first volumes were published in 1749. Begun as a catalog of the king's cabinet of curiosities, the work eventually became a new history of nature, numbering some forty-four volumes in Buffon's lifetime. The *Histoire naturelle* made Buffon a celebrated literary figure and provoked many controversies among European naturalists and American patriots in the decades before the American Revolution.

The central issue for the founding fathers was Buffon's humiliating theory of American degeneracy, an elaborate environmental explanation for the alleged inferiority of all life-forms in the New World. In Buffon's opinion, the supposed cold and humidity of the New World's climate were responsible for the diminutive size of all creatures there, both animal and human. The notion that animals species degenerated was itself a controversial theory, since it introduced into natural history the new idea of changes within individual species or even the extinction of whole species. Even though Buffon himself did not embrace the idea wholeheartedly, his oblique references to the possible disappearance of the American *incognitum* gave new life to speculation about the previous existence of now extinct species.

The possibility of extinction added another element to Buffon's natural history—his view of the natural world as a violent place, where warring species were present. His descriptions of the terror and violence of wild nature encouraged naturalists later to envision the American *incognitum* as a terrifying monster whose extinction was a blessing for the human race. Buffon's dynamic view of nature and theory of degeneracy thus set the stage for the later transformation of the American *incognitum* into a symbol of national pride for many American patriots. For this reason, Buffon's career constitutes an important phase in the early history of the nation's first prehistoric monster.

In the early 1740s, Buffon already had established his reputation in Paris with his translations of Isaac Newton, and his studies in law, medicine, mathematics, and physics enabled him to enter the Academy of

Naturam amplectitur omnem.

FIGURE 13. Portrait of the French naturalist Buffon, age fifty-four, from the oil painting by F. H. Drouais, 1761. Collection of Paul Farber.

Sciences in 1731, at age twenty-six. Following in the tradition of English natural philosophers like John Locke, Buffon rejected the idealism of Descartes and the abstractness of mathematics, which he felt were divorced from reality. Instead, he based his own scientific methodology on observations of the physical world, approaching nature in an encyclopedic but somewhat old-fashioned manner, inspired by classical scholars of natural history like Aristotle and Pliny. His originality stemmed from the fact that he was neither a scientist nor a theologian but, rather, a literary figure with wide philosophical interests in the history of nature.

In the summer of 1739, while Baron Longueuil was in the Ohio valley, Buffon's rapid rise to prominence among Parisian academics took a surprising new turn. In that year, King Louis XV appointed him to oversee the Jardin du roi, including the king's small cabinet of curiosities, where the bones from the Ohio salt lick were placed the following year. The botanical garden was still small, less than twenty acres, dominated by a seventeenth-century chateau. The acquisition of the fossils from the Ohio was part of Buffon's efforts to expand the king's collection, which in 1740 occupied only two rooms, consisting of a herbarium, a pharmacy, a few minerals, and several anatomical specimens, either fossilized or preserved in jars.[1]

At first, Buffon gave little attention to the bones of the American *incognitum*, perhaps because his new official status enabled him to devote himself to his ambitious project of writing a complete history of the natural world. The first volumes of Buffon's *Histoire naturelle* explained his methodology and presented his views of the earth's history. In 1742, he hired the physician and anatomist Louis-Jean-Marie Daubenton to undertake the formal description of the king's cabinet, and his collaboration became a vital element in the expansion of the catalog into an encyclopedic survey of the natural world. A young physician from Buffon's hometown, Daubenton brought to Buffon's project the sensibility of a comparative anatomist whose clinical descriptions contrasted sharply with Buffon's elegant and episodic history of nature.

When the first three volumes of *Histoire naturelle* appeared in 1749, they created a sensation in the Paris salons, selling out in only six weeks. They made Buffon famous overnight, especially among the French connoisseurs of natural history, many of whom were fashion-conscious aristocrats. With characteristic brashness, he dismissed many of the leading methods for classifying flora and fauna, including the new system of binary classification recently developed by the Swedish botanist Carolus Linnaeus, whose *Systemae Naturae* had first appeared in 1735. With an elegant, corrosive wit that became his trademark, Buffon ridiculed the Linnaean system for grouping the hedgehog, the mole, and the bat under the category of "ferocious beasts" while placing "man, monkeys, sloths, and scaly lizards" under the *Anthropomorpha* order. "One must really be obsessed with classifying to put such different beings together," he pointed out while denouncing all methods of classification as arbitrary systems imposed on nature.

In his *Histoire naturelle*, Buffon challenged Newton's static worldview, the harmonious, perfectly synchronized, mechanical universe that had become the norm for many natural philosophers and theologians in the early eighteenth century. Essential to this view of nature was the concept of the "Great Chain of Being," an imaginary hierarchy in God's creation that ranked everything in the natural world, from the rocks and minerals at the bottom through the plants, insects, shellfish, fish, birds, and quadrupeds to the monkeys and humankind at the top.

Popular among English authors from John Locke to the poet Alexander Pope, the Great Chain of Being was a traditional concept with roots in classical science and medieval Christian doctrine. "Nature," Aristotle stated, "passes from lifeless objects to the highest animals in such unbroken sequence, interposing between them beings which live and yet are not animals, so that scarcely any difference seems to exist between two neighbouring groups owing to their close proximity."[2] For Christians who believed in the perfection of God's creation, the crucial characteristic of this chain was its unbroken character, or the permanence of the species. All created things, from stones to angels, constituted an uninterrupted series passing imperceptibly, without any gaps, from one degree to the next.

In the binary system of nomenclature that Linnaeus proposed, all flora and fauna were products of God's creation, and the purpose of classification was to arrange the animals in a natural system according to their greater or lesser likeness. In the first editions of *Systemae Naturae*, Linnaeus defended the immutability of species from the period of their first creation as described in the Bible, a permanence and perfection that he felt had been summed up by the German natural philosopher Gottfried Wilhelm Leibniz as *natura non facit saltum*, or "nature makes no jumps."[3] The popularity of the Linnaean system among theologians and naturalists stemmed partly from its scientific articulation of the un-changing perfection of God's creation, a hierarchy of nature that the existence of the fossilized creatures without living counterparts seemed to challenge.

The Great Chain of Being found widespread expression among American theologians and natural philosophers during the eighteenth century. In his late work *The Christian Philosopher*, published in 1722, Cotton Mather embraced the idea:

> There is a *Scale of Nature*, wherein we pass regularly and proportion-ably from a *Stone* to a *Man*, the Faculties of the Creatures in their *various Classes* growing still brighter and brighter, and more capacious, till we arrive to those noble ones which are found in the *Soul* of MAN.[4]

The same idea later took a more prosaic form in Benjamin Franklin's parable "An Arabian Tale," in which the principal character, Albu-mazar, is asked to contemplate "the scale of beings, from an elephant down to an oyster."[5] In 1764, in his *Contemplation de la nature*, the Swiss naturalist Charles Bonnet provided a concise diagram of the Great Chain of Being that was widely reproduced. It pictured the intercon-nected character of the natural world as a ladder ascending from the basic elements of air, water, and earth through the various categories of nature (figure 14).

Ironically, even though Buffon attacked the Linnaean system of classification, he still used the Great Chain of Being as a unifying con-cept in the early volumes of his *Histoire naturelle*, maintaining that "one could descend by almost imperceptible degrees from the most perfect creature to the most shapeless matter, from the most organized animal to the crudest mineral."[6] Buffon's primary interest, however, was in the history of nature, both that of individual animal species and of the earth itself. This interest led him away from the static concept of the Chain of Being toward a far more dynamic view of natural history, which eventually influenced the discovery of prehistoric nature and the Darwinian idea of evolution. More important, Buffon's view of natural history underscored the idea that nature was a violent place inhabited by warring species, where the existence of carnivores was nature's way of creating an equilibrium in the natural world.

In the first volumes of his *Histoire naturelle*, Buffon's new emphasis on the dynamic character of natural history took two forms that later

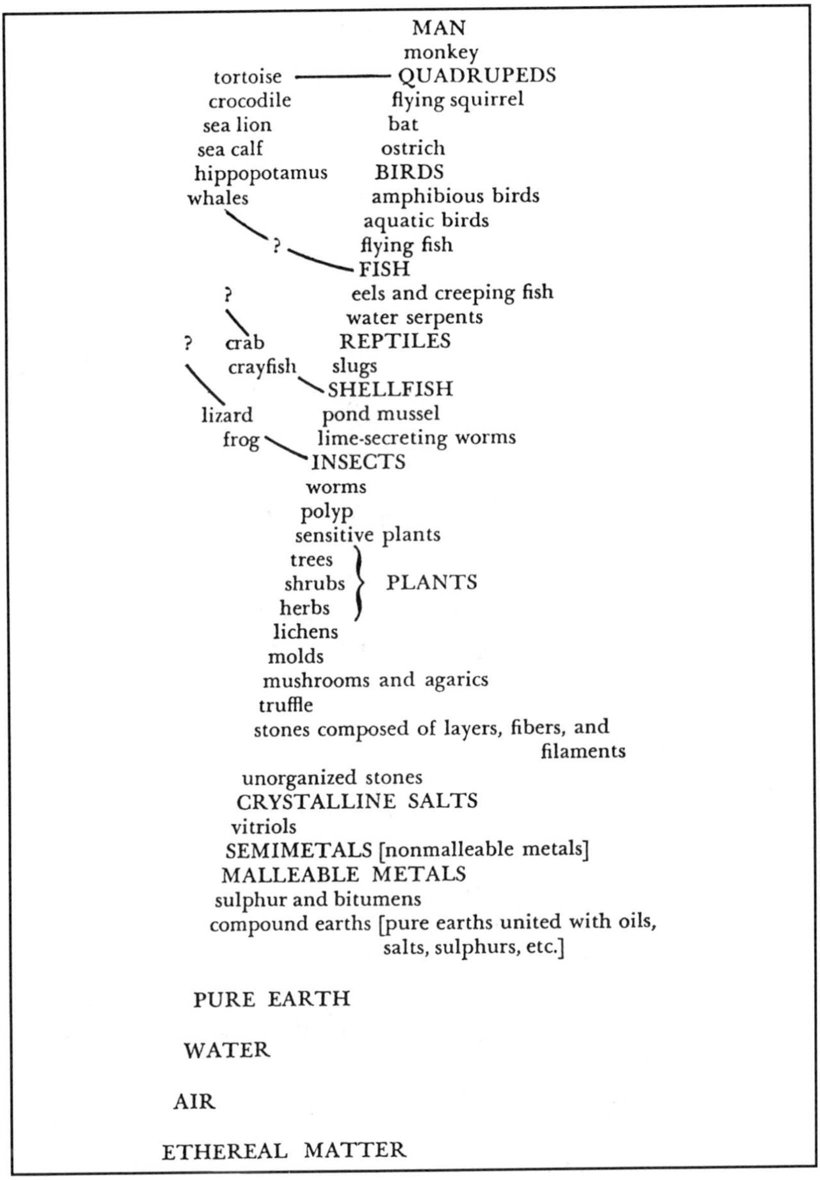

MAN
monkey
tortoise ——————— QUADRUPEDS
crocodile   flying squirrel
sea lion   bat
sea calf   ostrich
hippopotamus   BIRDS
whales   amphibious birds
                              aquatic birds
          ?   flying fish
                           FISH
     ?   eels and creeping fish
                              water serpents
  ?   crab   REPTILES
     crayfish   slugs
                           SHELLFISH
  lizard   pond mussel
     frog   lime-secreting worms
                      INSECTS
          worms
          polyp
     sensitive plants
     trees   ⎫
     shrubs   ⎬   PLANTS
     herbs   ⎭
     lichens
     molds
     mushrooms and agarics
     truffle
     stones composed of layers, fibers, and
                                        filaments
     unorganized stones
     CRYSTALLINE SALTS
     vitriols
     SEMIMETALS [nonmalleable metals]
     MALLEABLE METALS
     sulphur and bitumens
     compound earths [pure earths united with oils,
                           salts, sulphurs, etc.]

PURE EARTH

WATER

AIR

ETHEREAL MATTER

FIGURE 14. The "Great Chain of Being" from Charles Bonnet's *Contemplation de la nature*, 1764. An idea with roots in classical Greek philosophy and medieval theology, the scale of beings was used by Christians during the eighteenth century to defend the fixity of the species and the perfection of God's creation.

helped shape views of the American *incognitum* and the bones from the Ohio salt lick. First, he challenged the prevailing theories embraced by the diluvialists Thomas Burnet, William Whiston, and John Woodward, who had made Noah's Flood the central focus of the earth's history. Instead, Buffon ridiculed the idea that the biblical flood explained the earth's land-forms, although he conceded that the presence of fossil seashells on the highest mountains proved that the continents—though not necessarily the entire earth—had once been submerged under water.

Rejecting catastrophism, Buffon called attention to nature's less dramatic processes—the ocean's currents and surf, the winds and rivers, and other forces of erosion—all agents that he believed had created the earth's topography:

> The causes of rare, violent, and sudden effects must not concern us; they are not found in the ordinary workings of Nature. It is with effects that happen every day—the movements that succeed one another and renew themselves without interruption, the constant and always repeated operations—that we must consider our causes and reasons.[7]

First, Buffon explained the disposition of strata and the presence of fossils as having natural and observable causes rather than being remote accounts of catastrophic events from the Bible. In this manner, without making any heretical statements about the timetable of the earth's history, he subtly implied that the latter had been infinitely longer than the history of humanity: "Human life, stretched as much as it can be, is only one point in the total duration, one single event in the history of God's actions."[8]

The second new approach in Buffon's general methodology was his emphasis on reproduction, or "generation," as he called it, for which he proposed, in a completely novel way, a natural basis for defining animal species. Instead of relying exclusively on the similarity of physical traits as the basis for classification, he defined a species as any group of animals that could reproduce themselves through copulation. This meant that internal forces working in the natural world might cause animal species to change over time as the animals adapted to changing environmental conditions. This idea was at the heart of Buffon's view of the history of nature. His definition of species was fundamental to the emerging controversy over the identity of the American *incognitum* because the discovery and identification of an extinct species hinged on defining the creature's uniqueness with regard to other living animals. In addition, his emphasis on the relationship between the reproduction of species and environmental conditions laid the foundation for the later development of his theory of American degeneracy.

By proposing that a species was defined by its members' ability to reproduce by means of copulation, Buffon's theory gave new prominence to the environmental conditions and internal forces shaping the natural world. In other words, reproduction had a natural and physical origin that did not depend on divine creation. In addition, Buffon introduced into the debate over reproduction the idea of heredity, having deduced from his microscopic study of seminal fluids and the resemblance of children to their parents that both parents contributed to the creation of an offspring in sexual reproduction.

The fossil elephants of Siberia and America were virtually absent from the first volumes of Buffon's *Histoire naturelle*, and the bones of the American *incognitum* brought from the Ohio valley by Baron Longueuil went almost unnoticed among the many specimens described in the king's collection of curiosities. The first person to comment publicly on the bones from the Ohio salt lick was the French mineralogist Jean-Étienne Guettard, a critic of Buffon's unscientific methods who had stunned European naturalists in 1752 with his discovery of extinct volcanoes in eastern France.

In 1756, Guettard published a memoir comparing the geology of Switzerland and North America. His article, which contained the first crude mineralogical map of North America, also provided his readers with the first illustration of the fossil elephant's tooth from the Ohio salt lick, an elegant specimen that paleontologists later identified as the third molar of the American mastodon (figure 15). The detailed drawing, which showed the tooth's long roots and the knobby protrusions on its masticating surface, was accompanied by a smaller figure of a rock from Quebec containing fan-shaped creatures that Guettard identified as fossil moths.

The giant tooth undoubtedly came from Longueuil's collection, for Guettard claimed that the specimen was from the place near the Ohio River designated on French maps of Canada by the words "where the elephant bones were found." The animal's identity was still a great mystery, and its existence raised questions about the

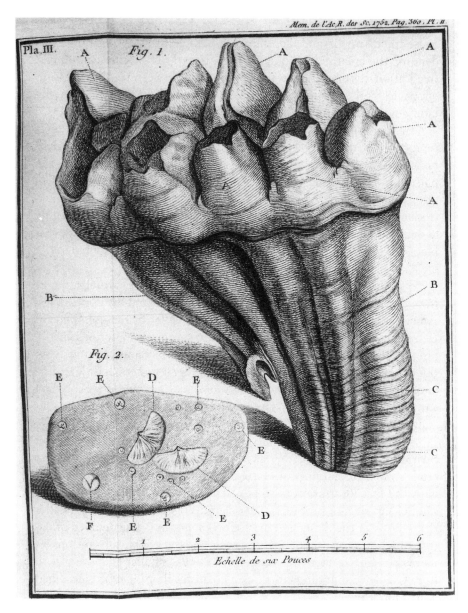

FIGURE 15. Drawing of a giant grinder by the French mineralogist Jean-Étienne Guettard, 1756. Later identified as the third molar of the American mastodon, this was the first figure of a tooth from the Ohio valley salt lick brought back to Paris by Longueuil's expedition. Courtesy of Bibliothèque centrale du Muséum national d'histoire naturelle, Paris.

120

relationship of these bones to other large fossil remains from Europe: "From what animal is this? And does it resemble the fossilized teeth of this size that have been found in different places in Europe?" Guettard asked rhetorically. "These are two points that I have not been able to clarify."[9]

In the 1750s, when war broke out between England and France, cutting nearly everyone off from the Ohio salt lick, Buffon immersed himself in writing his natural history of the quadrupeds, the four-footed beasts that formed the subject of the next twelve volumes of the *Histoire naturelle*. In keeping with his classical training, he began with the domesticated animals most useful to humankind, the horse, the ass, and the bull. Like many storytellers, Buffon anthropomorphized the animal world, giving each creature human characteristics and making them metaphors for human values and behavior.

Domestic animals were the "slaves" of civilized man, the result of his dominion over the natural world, and Buffon celebrated this domination in language blending natural rights doctrine with religious beliefs: "The empire of man over animals is a legitimate empire that no revolution can destroy. It is not only a right of Nature, a power founded on inalterable laws, but it is also a gift of God."[10] In this perspective, natural history itself is a metaphor for dominance, an idea readily accepted by enlightened clergymen and political philosophers in eighteenth-century Europe and America even as they opposed monarchy and absolutism.

While he celebrated man's dominion over nature, Buffon challenged some of the conventional assumptions about the character of wild animals and the savagery of the natural world. For him, terror and wildness were things that man also introduced into nature, not things simply inherent in the natural world. "These animals that we call savages, because they have not submitted to us, do they need anything more to be happy! They still have equality, they make no slaves, nor tyrants among themselves." Portraits of their prey, herbivorous animals like deer and rabbits, provided suitable images of vulnerability and heightened the effect of Buffon's rhetorical device.

In his view, the violence of the natural world was at least partly the result of man's attempt to subjugate creatures who lived in harmony with one another, despite their inevitable fate in the food cycle—that of being eaten by predators. "On the contrary, in countries where men settle, terror seems to live with them. Therefore, it is man who disturbs them, who drives them away, who scatters them, and who makes them a thousand times wilder than they ordinarily be."[11]

With the publication of his volume on the carnivores, the wolf, the fox, and other predators made their appearance. They also served as vehicles for condemning certain human abuses and deepening the metaphorical character of the natural world. "He [man] alone slays, annihilates more living individuals than all carnivorous animals devour. Born destroyers of beings who are below us, we would exhaust Nature if she were not inexhaustible."[12] The theme of man's tyranny over domestic animals is found throughout the *Histoire naturelle*, occasionally serving as an indictment of civilized society, or at least its worst abuses and arrogant assumptions of superiority.[13] However, while Buffon condemned these excesses and abuses, he maintained that nature's cycle of death and destruction, like man's dominion, was ultimately part of the forces of equilibrium in nature and, in the end, made the brutality of predators necessary and natural: "In this manner, violent death is a practice almost as necessary as the law of natural death; these are the means of destruction and renewal which serve to maintain the perpetual youth of Nature."[14]

The overriding effect of Buffon's treatment of the carnivores gave new life to the metaphor of war associated with wild nature and the flesh-eating predators. His introductory essay, "The Carnivorous Animals," begins as follows: "Until now, we have spoken only of the useful animals, [but] the harmful animals are in much greater number."[15] Because they had the same appetite and taste for flesh, the carnivores were rivals of the human species, whose stomachs, according to Buffon, were not designed to be nourished by plants alone. Throughout his description of carnivores, Buffon strengthened the notion that the natural world contained warring species whose voraciousness might even result in the annihilation of weaker animals. "The violent death of animals is a legitimate, innocent happening, since it is based in Nature, and they are only born under that condition," Buffon explained, using the logic of his own earlier statements about the rejuvenating effect of nature's cycle of death and destruction.

Buffon's French critics immediately recognized the subversive character of this essay, since Buffon himself alluded to the possibility that the war among animals might have led to the extinction of weaker species. In 1759, shortly after its publication, the journalist Friedrich Melchior Grimm directly attacked Buffon's view of the carnivores precisely on these grounds, calling the essay "the weakest part of the *Natural History*."[16] Interestingly, Buffon did not apply this idea of a struggle for existence to human society, whose industry and civilized behavior he saw as the antithesis of the violence of the natural world. Instead, he chose to portray the war among the species simply as nature's way of maintaining the equilibrium of the natural world.

In many respects, England was the true home of this metaphor of warfare among the species, as the philosophies of Adam Smith and Charles Darwin later revealed. In fact, Buffon's rationale for the normality of violence in the natural world dramatized ideas already articulated by English clergymen in the early eighteenth century. At that time, the role of predators in nature was a widely discussed moral issue among theologians attempting to explain the existence of bloodshed and suffering in God's creation. In the seventeenth century, during Cromwell's rule after England's civil war, the English political philosopher Thomas Hobbes described the natural condition of humankind as being an animalistic state of conflict and violence, "such a war, as is of every man, against every man."

Since then, Anglican advocates of God's benevolence in the natural world had struggled to counter this harsh Hobbesian view of nature as a chaotic scene of cruelty and conflict. In 1702, William King, the bishop of Derry, published *De Origine Mali*, a Latin treatise on the origins of evil, which sought to reconcile Hobbes's violent view of nature with the idea of divine harmony and the Great Chain of Being. Although King's treatise received favorable reviews on the Continent, the work had little impact in England until a translation appeared in 1731, edited by Edmund Law, bishop of Carlisle. This edition deeply influenced many apologists for God's benevolence in nature, from the Swedish botanist Linnaeus to the English poet Alexander Pope.

Predatory animals were among the problems that these Anglican prelates discussed at length. They claimed that the carnivores' rapaciousness was simply part of God's nature and that their victims' fate was the sacrifice that inferior creatures made to ensure the survival of those above them in nature's hierarchy. "If you insist that a lion might have been made without teeth or claws, a viper without venom, I grant it, as a knife without an edge," Bishop Law observed, "but then they would have been of quite another species and have had neither the nature, nor use, nor genius, which they now enjoy."[17]

In other words, the God of *De Origine Mali* loved the lion and the lamb equally, even though each was destined to fulfill its divine purpose in a different way. However, while these clergymen sought to justify the benevolent design of the God's nature, they also accepted and helped perpetuate the underlying view of violence in the natural world. "Let us not be surprised, then, at the universal war as it were among animals, or that the stronger devour the weaker," Edmund Law remarked, voicing acceptance of the metaphor that Buffon's view of the natural world later helped popularize in England.[18]

The most majestic of the carnivores, the lions and tigers, were the subjects of the ninth volume of Buffon's *Histoire naturelle*, published in 1761, a few years before Croghan's shipment of fossils arrived in London. This volume was also notable because it marked the further development of Buffon's theory of American degeneracy and his first mention of the fossil elephants from Siberia and North America. For Buffon, the lions of Africa and India were the most ferocious of God's creatures, terrifying beasts whose great ferocity he attributed to these regions' excessive heat. His new emphasis on the role of climatic conditions led him for the first time to compare the life-forms of the Old World—Europe, Asia, and Africa—with those in the New World: "In general, all the animals there are smaller than those of the old world, & there is not any animal in America that can be compared to the elephant, the rhinoceros, the hippopotamus, the dromedary, the giraffe, the buffalo, the lion, the tiger, etc."[19]

Even though his remarks were largely descriptive rather than theoretical, Buffon marshaled an array of examples illustrating the inferiority of animal life in the New World. In these passages, Buffon's theory of American degeneracy began to take shape, gathering momentum with each degrading reference to the inferior size of animal life in the New World. Buffon also applied this analogy to the animals brought to America from Europe, like horses, sheep, goats, and hogs. "Even those which, from the kindly influences of another climate, have acquired their complete form and expansion, shrink and diminish under a niggardly sky and an unprolific land, thinly peopled with wandering savages, who, instead of using this territory as a master, had no property or empire."[20]

Predictably, Buffon extended the manifestations of this inferiority of the animal species in America to include the Indians, who became the true guinea pigs for his theory of American degeneracy. Even though the indigenous peoples were about the same height as their counterparts in the Old World, he found other ways to diminish their size: "The Savage has weak and small organs of generation; he has neither hair nor beard and no ardor for his female," he wrote, revealing again the centrality of reproduction in his theory of the earth's history.[21]

Harking back to John Locke's belief that the Indian territories were wilderness wastelands inhabited by hunter-gatherer tribes ignorant of farming, Buffon traced their inferior stature to the fact that they allegedly had not cultivated the earth and domesticated their animals.

> It is thus principally because there were few men in America and because the majority of these men, leading an animal-like existence, left nature in its wild state and neglected the earth, that it has remained cold, incapable of producing active principles, developing the seeds of the great quadrupeds, for whose growth and multiplication there are required all the warmth and activity that the sun can give to the loving earth.[22]

In this wasteland, only the insects, snakes, and frogs were larger than their counterparts in the Old World, whereas the butterflies, spiders, and beetles of Brazil were unsurpassed in their size and beauty.

The physical agents responsible for this degeneration of the animal and human species in America were the humidity, wetness, and cold; the marshy terrain; and the dense foliage whose suffocating effects Buffon described:

> In this state of abandon, everything languishes, decays , [and] stifles. The air and earth, weighed down by the moist and poisonous vapors, cannot purify themselves, nor profit from the influence of the star of life. The sun vainly pours down its liveliest rays on this cold mass, which is incapable of responding to its ardor; it will never produce anything but humid creatures, plants, reptiles, and insects, and will only be able to nourish cold men and feeble animals.[23]

Powerful images of American inferiority emerged from Buffon's robust prose, offering his readers the image of a wild nature, raw and savage. "His main purpose," observed literary historian Gilbert Chinard, "was to illustrate the point that, in its original condition, Nature is not the kind and generous mother of the poets, but that, in order to survive and develop a civilization, man must curb and domesticate the blind forces around him."[24] In Buffon's eyes, the savagery of nature, whether animal or human, became the premise on which all the achievements of European civilization rested, from its industry and commerce to the scientific thought and rationalist doctrines of its Enlightenment philosophers.

In a brief passage toward the end of the ninth volume of the *Histoire naturelle*, on lions and tigers, Buffon alluded to the fossil elephants from Siberia and North America, whose remains, he acknowledged, dwarfed those of even the largest of quadrupeds—the elephant.

> The prodigious *mahmout*, a four-footed animal, whose enormous bones we have viewed with astonishment, which we have judged to be at least six times bigger than the largest elephant, no longer exists anywhere, although its remains have been found in several places, at great distances from each other, like Ireland, Siberia and Louisiana.[25]

The mysterious bones from Ohio country were no more than a footnote to his comparison of animals of the Old World and America, but Buffon seized the opportunity to make a remarkable conjecture about the possible extinction of these unknown animals. "This species was certainly the foremost, the largest, the strongest of all the quadrupeds. Since it has disappeared, how many others, smaller, weaker and less noticeable, have also perished without having left us either evidence or information about their past existence!"[26] For Buffon, the animal's disappearance eliminated the dilemma that the monstrous creature posed for his theory of American degeneracy, a consequence that helps explain why he suddenly made them vanish by embracing boldly and unequivocally, but without any elaboration, the idea of extinction.

Buffon attributed the extinction of this species to climate change, without delving further into the momentous implications of such an event except to reaffirm his view of the earth's history and the natural world: "Nature, I admit, is in a continual movement of flux."[27] This dynamism in Buffon's history of nature was perhaps the most subversive aspect of his encyclopedic survey, although its significance was constantly undermined by the concessions he made to orthodox views of the earth's history.

Nonetheless, the metaphor of warring species reappeared again with his assertion that "the least perfect, most delicate, heaviest, least active, least armed, etc. species have already disappeared or will disappear."[28] When he talked about the hapless sloths, which he felt were unfit for survival, the outlines of a Darwinian struggle for life appear: "Everything reminds us of these monsters by their failure, these imperfect rough drafts, a thousand times tried and executed by Nature, which, having barely the ability to exist, must only have survived for a time, and have since been erased from the list of creatures."[29]

While acknowledging the mystery of the enormous bones from Siberia and the North America, Buffon still hesitated to declare these animals separate species from the elephants, probably because their remains had not yet been subjected to systematic examination by his anatomist Louis-Jean-Marie Daubenton. In 1762, while preparing the eleventh volume of the *Histoire naturelle*, which included Buffon's history of the elephant, Daubenton presented to the Royal Academy of Sciences in Paris the first truly scientific paper on the bones from the Ohio salt lick, more than twenty years after they had been deposited in Louis XV's cabinet of curiosities. Trained as a physician, Daubenton joined Buffon in 1742 to supply anatomical descriptions for each of the animals mentioned in the *Histoire naturelle*, often basing his observations on dissections of cadavers and clinical examinations of the animal's internal organs.

Daubenton tried to bring the clinical exactness of comparative anatomy to bear on the question of the American monster's identity by comparing the femur, or thighbone, from the Ohio salt lick with those of the Siberian mammoth and a living elephant. Following in Sir Hans Sloane's footsteps, he first showed scientifically that the bones were animal, rather than human, arguing that on close inspection all animal bones had characteristic forms that clearly identified them. Illustrating his thesis with an anatomical drawing of the three femurs, including the thighbones of an elephant from the royal menagerie and a Siberian mammoth brought to Paris by a French astronomer, Daubenton concluded that the specimens were essentially similar, despite their slight variations in size and thickness (figure 16).

In his opinion, these bones belonged to animals of the same species, that of the elephants, although the teeth collected from the Ohio salt lick presented a dilemma. The masticating surface of the giant molar from America, with its knobby protrusions and thick enamel, was quite different from the elephant's grinders, resembling instead the teeth of the pig family, at least those of living animal species. Upon careful

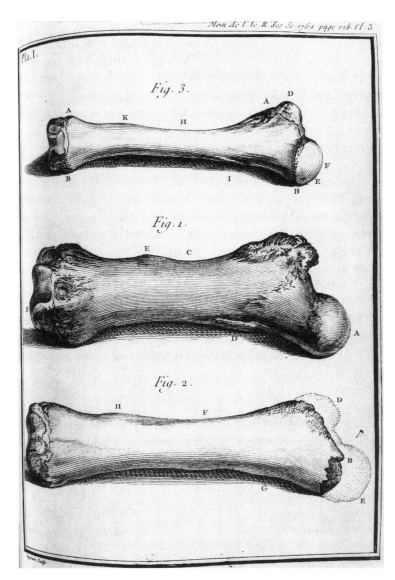

FIGURE 16. Comparison of the thighbones of the American *incognitum* (figure 1), the Siberian mammoth (figure 2), and the elephant (figure 3), from an article by Buffon's anatomist Louis-Jean-Marie Daubenton, published in 1764. The French anatomist claimed the specimens were essentially similar and belonged to the elephant species rather than an unknown, extinct species. Courtesy Bibliothèque centrale du Muséum national d'histoire naturelle, Paris.

study, Daubenton concluded that the molars were those of a large hippopotamus and had somehow become mixed together with the femurs and tusks of the fossil elephants. After all, he pointed out, the bones from the Ohio valley had been collected haphazardly by "savages" unaware of the importance of their disposition at the salt lick.

Although his article launched a new era of clinical exactness in the study of these American specimens, Daubenton refused to consider that the femur, tusk, and tooth from the Ohio valley could be the remains of a separate, extinct species larger than the elephant. In his view, the problem was to find a living animal, or animals, whose bones were like those from the Ohio salt lick. Even to a morphologist accustomed to the methodical dissection of cadavers, these bones excited fanciful images of tropical animals like the hippopotamus roaming the Ohio valley in ancient times. Unlike Buffon, who had already alluded to the great beast's extinction, Daubenton approached the matter more cautiously, unwilling to admit the existence of an extinct species even when confronted with clinical evidence to the contrary.

In the eleventh volume of Buffon's *Histoire naturelle*, published in 1764, the elephant reigned supreme in the kingdom of the quadrupeds, being described from the outset as "the world's most formidable creature," the largest of all terrestrial animals. But Buffon contrasted the animal's great size with its benign character: "In wild nature, the elephant is neither bloodthirsty nor ferocious, he is naturally gentle and never abuses his weapons or his force."[30] As always, he paid special attention to the elephant's sex life, on whose reproductive powers his definition of animal species depended: "Naturalists and travelers agree that the elephant's genital member is hardly longer than that of the horse," he wrote, while applauding the modesty of the females, who never coupled when there was anyone watching.[31]

Toward the end of this essay on the elephant, Buffon again referred briefly to the "prodigious bones" of the "Mammout" and confessed his own doubts about the existence of this enormous creature: "I admit that I myself was uncertain with regard to them. Several times I have examined these enormous bones and I have compared them with the elephant's skeleton which we have in the King's Cabinet, a skeleton I know to be that of an almost adult elephant." In accordance with Daubenton's anatomical study, Buffon expressed skepticism about his earlier belief that the Siberian and American monsters were extinct creatures, larger than the elephant:

Before knowing the history of these animals, I was not persuaded that there could exist elephants six or seven time larger than the one whose skeleton I see. However, since the enormous bones did not have the same proportions as the corresponding bones in the elephant's skeleton, I believed, like the vulgar Naturalists, that these great bones belonged to a much bigger animal, whose species was lost or had been destroyed.[32]

Strangely, Buffon did not refer at all to the teeth and grinders from Siberia or to those from the Ohio salt lick, which Daubenton had claimed two years earlier belonged to the hippopotamus. In his anatomical description of the femur from Siberia, Daubenton now reiterated Buffon's skepticism about the fabled bones of the *mammout*:

The difference in size, which appeared excessive, seemed sufficient to attribute this bone to another animal that ought to be larger than the elephant. But, since no one knew of any larger animal, it was necessary to resort to the fictitious *mammout*: this fabulous animal has been imagined in the northern countries, where there are found very frequently the bones, teeth and tusks of the elephant.[33]

Describing the specimens in the king's cabinet, Daubenton briefly mentioned the thighbone and tooth brought from Canada by Longueuil and provided a sketch of the expedition, only to reaffirm his earlier conclusion that the tooth belonged to the hippopotamus family, whereas the femur resembled those of the living elephants. Evidently, at this juncture, neither Daubenton nor Buffon wished to accept the idea that the bones from Siberia and North America may have belonged to an extinct species, an opinion that would have exposed them to further criticism from the religious authorities.

An extraordinarily complex figure whom Darwin later labeled as the first author in modern times to treat species in a scientific spirit, Buffon was clearly not a revolutionary thinker himself, despite his willingness to provoke controversy. His philosophy of nature evolved episodically, with many twists and turns, fluctuating with each new volume and often articulated in thoughtful, if contradictory, essays sprinkled throughout the individual histories of different animal species. The theory of American degeneracy reflected many of the conflicting ideas in Buffon's philosophy of nature, oscillating over the years between two very different views of its causes, with vastly different implications for views of America and the New World.

In essence, the question Buffon wrestled with was whether the conditions on the American continent were the product of a process of degeneration from an older, ideal form or were due to the immaturity of the New World, where—in the poetic image of the nineteenth-century novelist and poet Victor Hugo—America was "still soft and sodden from the flood."[34] As the Peruvian historian Antonello Gerbi noted, Buffon found it difficult to choose between a world in embryo and a world already rotting, both characterized by the same physical manifestations of stagnant waters, marshlands, and putrescence, swarming with the larvae of inferior life-forms, insects, snakes, and spiders.

In the last volumes of his *Natural History of the Quadrupeds*, published in the 1760s, when the bones of the American *incognitum* had raised the possibility of extinction, Buffon sought to erase any hint of heresy in his view of the natural world. In 1764, the twelfth volume appeared, dealing with the zebra and hippopotamus, among others, and it contained a remarkable essay that put God, the Creator, prominently back into the picture while simultaneously presenting powerful images of the dynamic forces at work in the natural world. Without naming the place America, Buffon described nature in the raw, augmenting with his poetic imagery the dreadful degeneracy existing on the American continent.

> Thus Nature, which everywhere else glistens with youthfulness, here appears decrepit; the earth overburdened by its weight, overwhelmed by the debris of its own produce, offers, instead of a place of flowering greenery, an overcrowded space, crisscrossed by old trees laden with parasitic plants, lichens, [and] fungi, the impure fruits of corruption.[35]

Here he reveals the purpose of his violent view of the natural world—it served as the perfect foil for glorifying the industry and imperial rule of European civilization: "Primitive Nature is hideous and dying, it is I, *I* alone, who can make it pleasant and living: let us dry up these swamps, let us vivify these dead waters by making them run." Images of the conquering spirit and egotism of European civilization tumble out with an unrestrained violence that takes the reader's breath away, even today: "Let us use this active and devouring element that was hidden from us and that we owe only to ourselves; let us set fire to this superfluous waste, these old forests already half dead; let us finish destroying with iron, what the fire was not able to burn."[36] Buffon's affectionate portraits of the quadrupeds, whether wild or domesticated, are really hymns to the grandeur of civilized man, to the domestication of the natural world, which transformed wild nature into a productive Garden of Eden. "How beautiful is this cultivated Nature!" he exclaimed, revealing in a single expression the artificiality of his natural world.

But Buffon's songs of praise are not without words of warning, for his landscape is filled with the ruins of empires destroyed by man's avarice and ambition:

> However, [man] reigns only by right of conquest, he rejoices rather than possesses, he conserves only by ever constant care; if he ceases, everything languishes, everything alters itself and changes, and returns under the hand of Nature. She takes back her rights, erases the works of man, covers with dust and moss his most sumptuous monuments, destroys them with time, and leaves him only with the regret of having lost by his mistakes what his ancestors conquered by their works.[37]

In words reminiscent of Thomas Burnet's apocalyptic landscape, Buffon mingles the imagery of ancient Greece and Rome, the empires of antiquity and the source of European civilization, with the powerful forces of nature, the source of natural rights doctrine, soon to become the banner of American and French revolutionaries.

Buffon's natural history was illustrated with elegant copper engravings of the drawings of Jacques Eustache de Seve which reveal the influence of the Romantic vistas inspired by Thomas Burnet's Gothic landscape. Indeed, the popularity of Buffon's *Natural History of Quad-rupeds* stemmed partly from its sumptuous illustrations, often depicting the four-footed beasts with theatrical effect in cavernous landscapes filled with picturesque ruins, broken statues, pedestals, and columns, the trademarks of the classical revival associated with Romanticism and, more important, republicanism. "Whether the animal depicted is a lion or a pig," noted art historian S. Peter Dance, "it is shown as if in a tableau revealed to our curious gaze by the drawing aside of a curtain."[38] In a Dutch edition of Buffon's *Histoire naturelle*, we see a mongoose crouched over the cornerstone of a col-

FIGURE 17. Engraved illustration of the mongoose from Buffon's *Histoire naturelle*, 1765. Buffon's use of ruins from classical antiquity as settings for his animal specimens helped create an archaeological view of the earth's landscape and natural antiquity.

lapsed temple, unaware of the folly of the comic figure whose broken statue lies at its feet (figure 17). The original edition, illustrated with similar engravings, shows a mongoose with a sphinx and a broken pyramid in the background, images of the Egyptian civilization's mystery and grandeur.

Near the end of Buffon's *Natural History of Quadrupeds*, the bones from the Ohio salt lick seem quite remote from his efforts to sum up his philosophical views of the history of nature. In 1766, while preparing the next-to-last volume, on monkeys, Buffon returned to the problems of classifying the species. His theory of interfertility, which defined species as animals that could reproduce through copulation, now seemed inadequate to explain the changes that had occurred within various species over time. In an essay entitled "On the Degeneration of Animals," he therefore proposed a new natural system of classification that grouped certain species according to their geographic origin, rather than simply their morphological similarities and hereditary traits. Environmental concerns had led Buffon to revise his definition of species in a fashion that added to the dynamism of his own view of the earth's history and prefigured Darwin's theory of natural selection.

For the first time, Buffon envisioned the modification of individual species, a phenomenon that had first puzzled him when he compared the animals of the Old World with those in America. He introduced new terms to distinguish the different varieties that had degenerated from the original species and attempted to create a system of classification by which certain animals could be traced to a common ancestor, a formula that greatly extended the timeline of his history of nature. "It is therefore necessary, to explain the origin of these animals, to go back to the time when the two continents were not yet separated; it is necessary to recall the first changes that happened on the surface of the globe."[39]

Perhaps without realizing at first its implications, speculation about "degeneration" had led Buffon to discern the outlines of an antiquity that extended far beyond the story told by Moses of God's creation:

> Even though the state of Nature back then is not the one that has reached us and that we have represented, even though it is, on the contrary, a much older state, which we can hardly imagine except by means of inductions and relationships, we shall nevertheless try to go back in time using facts and the still-existing vestiges of these first ages of Nature, and to represent only those epochs that seem clearly delineated to us.[40]

From this moment, as John Lyon and Philip R. Sloan have remarked, "Natural history was no longer to be an inquiry dedicated to the collection of facts, but a science concerned broadly with the 'history of nature.'"[41]

The American *incognitum* played a central role in the discovery of this time beyond time that Buffon's theory of degeneracy had conjured up in his imagination. In fact, shortly before the last volume of his *Natural History of Quadrupeds* appeared in 1767, Buffon received a giant grinder from the Ohio valley salt lick, sent to him from London by Peter Collinson, along with a letter describing the excitement created there by the arrival of the bones that George Croghan had gathered at the lick. The giant tooth, as he informed Buffon, "appeared to indicate, even demonstrate, that these bones do not belong to elephants."[42] At age sixty, Buffon was forced to revise his own ambiguous opinions about the great beast whose existence he had virtually ignored in his history of the elephants. With the arrival in London of the new specimens from the Ohio salt lick, the trumpeting of the American *incognitum* could be heard all the way to Paris.

In the next few years, while examining bones from the Ohio salt lick, the London anatomists stole Buffon's thunder in their search for the identity of the American *incognitum*, applying more accurately the principles of comparative anatomy and imagining for the first time that the animal was at once an extinct species and a ferocious carnivore. Buffon's assertions of American degeneracy and the savagery of primitive nature left, however, indelible imprints on the minds of Anglo-American naturalists, especially the founding fathers, who were deeply offended by his naturalistic images of their own inferiority. With the American revolution and the birth of the new nation approaching, the stage was set for the transformation of the American *incognitum* into a prehistoric monster, whose mighty jaws symbolized simultaneously the savagery of prehistoric nature and the American nation's dominion over the natural world.

6

The Anatomy of a Carnivore

Vast chain of being! which from God began,
Nature's ethereal, human, angel, man,
Beast, bird, fish, insect, what no eye can see,
No glass can reach; from infinite to thee,
From thee to nothing. —On superior powers
Were we to press, inferior might on ours;
Or in the full creation leave a void,
Where, one step broken, the great scale's destroy'd:
From Nature's chain whatever link you strike,
Tenth, or ten thousandth, breaks the chain alike.

—Alexander Pope

THE ARRIVAL OF George Croghan's shipments of tusks and teeth in London gave Anglo-American naturalists their first opportunity to examine closely the fossil remains that had led Buffon and Daubenton to offer their theories about the creature's identity. In the summer of 1767, Peter Collinson told Buffon about the excitement that the specimens had generated among London anatomists. In letters to John Bartram and Buffon, Collinson was among the first to declare that the bones did not belong to elephants, though he had little scientific proof for his assertion. The existence of an unknown creature posed an even more troubling question—the anomaly of an extinct species, anathema to those who believed in the perfection of God's creation.

The flurry of excitement in London triggered a furious effort during the next few months by the city's leading naturalists to discover whether the animal in question was actually an unknown species. In November, Collinson presented the first scientific paper on the bones to the Royal Society, stating that the tusks and grinders were from a distinct species, probably herbivorous, that differed from the Asian and African elephants. By the end of the year, after comparing its jawbone and teeth with those of every elephant-like creature in London, William Hunter, the queen's physician, presented the Royal Society with convincing scientific evidence that the specimens from the Ohio salt lick belonged to an unknown, extinct species. In his essay, he labeled this mysterious animal the "American *incognitum*," giving birth formally to the creature whose skeleton the founding fathers pursued until the end of the century. Besides acknowledging the idea of extinction, Dr. Hunter's article also launched a new debate about the great beast's diet by suggesting for the first time that the American *incognitum* was a carnivore.

None of this speculation came easy to London naturalists when they first viewed the magnificent specimens sent from the Ohio salt lick by George Croghan. Benjamin Franklin, the foremost American authority on the bones, had received several choice fossils directly from Croghan, owing largely to his role as a lobbyist for the Indian trader's campaign for a new colony in Illinois country. Disgusted with Pennsylvania politics, Franklin himself had become involved in several ambitious land speculation schemes soon after returning to London in the winter of 1764, toward the end of the French and Indian Wars. In fact, London had become Franklin's preferred place of residence, the cosmopolitan social world in which his wit and influence flourished and where he hoped his fame as a scientist would be followed by a fortune in land speculation.

During the French and Indian Wars, Franklin spent five years in London, enjoying his reputation as a scientific celebrity and his role as a representative of the American colonies. He had arrived there in 1757 already famous for his treatise on electricity, thanks to Buffon who had popularized the essay in Europe by having it translated into French. Franklin carried out his personal lobbying in London on behalf of the Pennsylvania assembly through a steady round of wining and dining with colonial officials while sporting velvet suits and silver shoe buckles. Recognizing the importance of projecting a genteel image to the English aristocracy, Franklin had his portrait painted by Benjamin Wilson, a London artist who was also one of England's leading authorities on electricity (figure 18). Also an enthusiastic supporter of the British monarchy, Franklin had attended the coronation of George III in 1761 before returning the next year to Philadelphia. Two years later, when he returned to London, he was an elegant, if outspoken, American gentle-man, proud of the leisure that his prosperity as a printer had bought him, especially because it gave him time to pursue his scientific studies and to contemplate curiosities like the bones of the fossil elephants.

In early August 1767, Franklin wrote to Croghan thanking him for the box of "elephants' tusks and grinders": "They are extremely curious on many accounts. No living elephants having been seen in any part of America by any of the Europeans settled there, or remembered in any tradition of the Indians."[1] Franklin put his finger on the most puzzling aspect of these specimens, the failure of the fossil molars to conform to those of living elephants:

> The tusks agree with those of the African and Asiatic elephant in being nearly of the same form and texture, and some of them, not withstanding the length of time they must have lain, being still good ivory. But the grinders differ, being full of knobs, like the grinders of a carnivorous animal; when those of the elephant, who eats only veg-etables, are almost smooth.[2]

In the rainy London summer, Franklin's suspicion that the grinders might belong to a carnivore reflected the new currents of thought set in motion by the arrival of the teeth of this unknown creature from Ohio country. The rising levels of excitement and wonder among the Lon-don naturalists were reported by Peter Collinson, whose circle of far-flung correspondents were the first to hear the news: "What fills us with admiration is the wonderful fossil presents of Elephants Teeth &c, sent over to Lord Shelburn & our Fr[ien]d Benj[amin] Franklin by George Croghan," he wrote to John Bartram in September. "Some of these Great Tusks or Teeth were intire near seven foot long and of the thick-ness of common Elephants teeth of that Size & Length."[3] Having al-ready sent a giant grinder to Buffon in Paris, Collinson's enthusiasm stemmed at least partly from his doubts about the animal's identity: "But what Increases the wonder & Surprise, is that with these long Teeth (which are fine Ivory), is found great numbers of Grinding Teeth, but the marvel is they are not the Grinding Teeth of Elephants, as we have recent Elephant grinders to compare them with."

Unwilling to admit the existence of an extinct species, Buffon and Daubenton had maintained that the grinders from the Ohio valley be-

FIGURE 18. Mezzotint portrait of Benjamin Franklin in London by James McArdell from Benjamin Wilson's painting, 1761. Print collection, Miriam and Ira D. Wallach Division of Art, Prints and Photographs, New York Public Library. Astor, Lenox, and Tilden Foundation.

longed to a member of the hippopotamus family. But the open-mindedness of Collinson's Quaker faith and his own comparison of bone specimens led him to conclude that these fossil remains "are some Vast Creatures with the long Teeth or Tusks of Elephants but with Great Grinders belonging to some animal not yet known." Perhaps the real difference lay in the easy access that the London naturalists had to the new specimens, along with the weaker influence of the Anglican Church over their speculations. In Paris, the Ohio monster's bones lay in the king's cabinet of curiosities, available to only a few privileged anatomists, while the numerous London specimens were scattered among a wide variety of collectors, including government ministers, physicians, and members of the Royal Society. "I daresay a Dozen have come Over & Two of them in the Original Jaw which is of Monstrous size," Collinson wrote to Bartram, adding that "this affords room for Endless reflection & Admiration."

The bones that Croghan sent from Ohio country no doubt enlivened Franklin's conversation when he dined in late August with Lord Shelburne, the secretary of state for the American colonies, whose support he sought in swaying British officials toward the creation of an Illinois colony. Shortly before leaving for a trip to Paris, Franklin wrote to his son William, governor of New Jersey, reporting the details of his dinner with Lord Shelburne. "I took the opportunity of urging it as one means of saving expence in supporting the out-posts, that a settlement should be made in the Illinois country," Franklin wrote, addressing the concern of British ministers about the cost of westward expansion.[4] On the same day that Franklin wrote to his son William about his dinner with Lord Shelburne, he set out for Paris with his close friend Sir John Pringle, the queen's physician, whom he had met through his membership in the Royal Society. Indeed, Franklin's election to the Royal Society gave him access to some of the most powerful politicians in the country, since many of the society's fellows were wealthy aristocrats who wielded influence at the English court.

Over the years, Franklin's principal correspondent in France had been Thomas-François Dalibard, the botanist and geologist whom Buffon had asked to translate his treatise on electricity. Surprisingly, Franklin seems to have had little direct correspondence with Buffon himself, although the latter had lavishly praised Franklin's writings about electricity. In 1755, Dalibard had sent Franklin the first four volumes of Buffon's *Histoire naturelle*, along with an account of Buffon's own experiments with lightning rods. Dalibard, however, had given up "Electrical Experiences" after the shocks made his arms shake so convulsively he was barely able to raise a glass to his lips or sign his name.

There is little evidence that Franklin ever met Buffon, perhaps because the French naturalist was at his summer home in Montbard, several days travel south of the French capital. Unfortunately, therefore, they had no opportunity to discuss the controversy over the bones from the Ohio valley. However, in the Parisian salons, among the French aristocracy and his admirers, Franklin made ample use of the gigantic teeth and tusks in his conversation. There, he met Abbé Chappe, a famous French astronomer who had recently traveled to Siberia, where he collected the teeth and bones of a mammoth while observing the transit of Venus at Tobolsk. The tooth of the Ohio monster was so intriguing to Chappe that he asked Franklin to obtain a jawbone of the beast for him when he returned to London.

In early October, Franklin's friend Peter Collinson completed an inventory of the tusks and teeth that Croghan sent to London and was busy comparing their configuration with that of the bones of living elephants in Royal Society's own collection. The next month, he presented the first scientific paper describing the new specimens to the society's monthly meeting. Drawing on details from Croghan's earlier account of the Ohio salt lick, Collinson described the "prodigious number of bones and teeth," repeating Croghan's extravagant claim that the site contained no fewer than thirty skeletons.

With the tusks and teeth laid out before the society, Collinson passed lightly over the tusks, some nearly seven feet long, which he assured everyone definitely belonged to elephants. But he did inform his audience that the identity of the grinders was in doubt:

> It is very remarkable, and worthy [of] observation, [that] none of the molares, or grinding teeth of elephants, are discovered with these tusks. But great numbers of pronged teeth of some vast animals are only found with them, which have no resemblance to the molares, or grinding teeth, of any great animal yet known.[5]

For the first time, Collinson brought to the attention of London's scientific community convincing evidence of an unknown creature whose existence he had only hinted at earlier in his correspondence. Despite the caution with which he advanced this radical idea, his willingness to accept the idea of an unknown creature in God's nature marked a turning point in speculation about the American *incognitum*'s identity.

The paradox of finding elephant tusks and teeth far from their tropical habitat enabled Collinson to cast further doubt on the animal's identity. Because no living elephants had been seen or heard of in

America and there was no probability of their having been brought from Africa or Asia, "it seems incomprehensible how they came there." Knowing his audience was familiar with the tusks of fossil elephants from Siberia, Collinson argued that these fossil remains had very likely been swept by the Great Deluge into the region from nearby Asia: "By the violent action of the wind and waves, at the time of the deluge, these great floating bodies, the carcasses of drowned elephants, were driven to the Northward, and, at the subsiding of the waters, deposited where they are now found." In contrast, the presence of fossil elephants in America, a territory far from Asia and Africa, could not, in his view, be explained so readily by Noah's Flood: "But what system, or hypothesis, can, with any degree of probability, account for these remains of elephants being found in America, where those creatures are not known ever to have existed, is submitted to this learned Society."[6]

Collinson's speculation injected new uncertainty into the debate over the teeth and tusks from the Ohio salt lick. Having posed several disturbing questions about them, he attempted to provide his own answers in a sequel to his first paper, delivered a week later at the Royal Society's next meeting. In all probability, Franklin was in attendance when Collinson pointed to the masticating surface of the teeth, or grinders, as decisive proof the bones belonged to an unknown creature:

> But as the biting or grinding teeth, found with the others, have no affinity with the molares of the elephant, I must conclude, that they, with the long teeth [i.e., tusks], belong to another species of elephant, not yet known, or else that they are the remains of some vast animal, that hath the long teeth, or tusks, of the elephant, with large grinders peculiar to that species, being different in size and shape from any other animal yet known.[7]

His cautiously worded characterization of the unknown creature carefully avoided the issue of extinction that he seemed on the verge of proposing.

Instead, Collinson shifted his argument to the more manageable terrain of the great beast's diet, relying on elephants' eating habits to argue that the Ohio fossils belonged to a herbivorous animal. "The elephant is wholly supported by vegetables; and the animal to which these grinding teeth belong, by their make and form, seemed designed for the biting and breaking off the branches of trees and shrubs for its suste-

nance."[8] Everyone in his audience knew that Collinson was contradicting the opinion of London anatomists and also Franklin that the
knobby protrusions on the teeth, the characteristics that distinguished
them from elephants' teeth, were evidence that the unknown creature
was a carnivore.

Large, unwieldy animals like elephants and rhinoceros were not
carnivorous, Collinson pointed out, because they were "unable, from
want of agility and swiftness, to pursue their prey, so are wholly confined to vegetable food."[9] When his papers were published in the Royal
Society's journal the following year, they were illustrated by two exquisite drawings of an enormous grinder, showing the striking prominences
on the crown of the tooth that had led other English anatomists to conclude the same animal was a carnivore (figure 19).

In the few months since the arrival of George Croghan's specimens,
the climate of opinion among the London naturalists had become quite
unstable with regard to the fossil elephants. The teeth and tusks from
the Ohio salt lick spurred anatomists bent on determining the true
identity of the American *incognitum*. Franklin's own ruminations about
the fossil remains reflected the shifting current of opinion, especially
about the beast's diet. In late January, Franklin sent one of the precious
grinders from Croghan's collection to the French astronomer Abbé
Chappe, with whom he had discussed the fossil elephants during his
visit to Paris. After briefly summarizing the circumstances surrounding
the tooth's discovery, Franklin turned to the issue being debated in
London:

> Some of Our Naturalists here, however, contend, that these are not
> the Grinders of Elephants, but of some carnivorous Animal un-
> known, because such Knobs or Prominences on the Face of the Tooth
> are not to be found on those of Elephants, and only, as they say, on
> those of carnivorous Animals.[10]

Six months earlier, Franklin had favored this notion, but now, after
Peter Collinson's testimony, he was skeptical of this view, which
seemed to defy logic and common sense: "But it appears to me that Animals capable of carrying such large & heavy Tusks, must themselves be
large Creatures, too bulky to have the Activity necessary for pursuing
and taking Prey," he wrote to Chappe. "I am inclin'd to think those
Knobs are only a small Variety, Animals of the same kind and Name

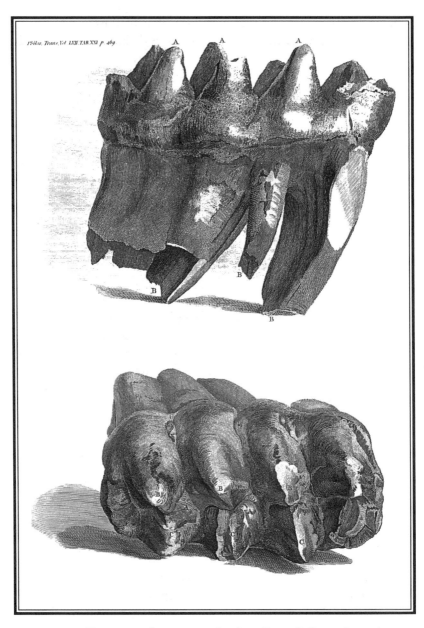

FIGURE 19. Two views of a giant grinder from Peter Collinson's article on the fossil elephants in America. Collinson was among the first to maintain the American *incognitum* was a species distinct from the Siberian mammoth and the African elephant.

often differing more materially, and that those Knobs might be as useful to grind the small branches of Trees, as to chaw Flesh."

Neither Collinson nor Franklin were trained physicians like the London anatomists speculating about the identity of the American *incognitum*. In fact, Collinson's comparison of the giant grinders with those of living elephants provided little clinical evidence to support his assertion that the mysterious creature was a herbivorous animal. But the new controversy over the beast's diet reflected the emergence of an entirely new theory that permanently altered the terms of the debate in both London and the American colonies. No one yet had the courage to suggest publicly, and with scientific authority, that the enormous teeth belonged to a carnivorous animal, much less one that might also be extinct. But Franklin's flirtation with this idea and Collinson's rejection of it were responses to the new opinion being voiced, mostly in private conversations, by London's foremost anatomist, Dr. William Hunter, who had launched his own investigation of the mystery.

In social prestige, professional competence, and perseverance, no one in London could match the Scottish doctor's pursuit of the American *incognitum*'s identity or the authority of his opinions when presented to the Royal Society. Having specialized in the new field of obstetrics, or man-midwifery, as it was derisively called by female midwives, Dr. Hunter was at the pinnacle of his profession, serving as physician-extraordinary to Queen Charlotte, whom he had attended throughout most of her many pregnancies.

The son of a Scottish grain merchant who encouraged his sons to enter the professions to escape the poverty of rural Scotland, Dr. Hunter's rise to prominence at the English court was remarkable given his humble origins. In 1740, at age twenty-two, the young surgeon's apprentice came to London to study obstetrics with Dr. William Smellie, London's best-known man-midwife. As an apprentice, Dr. Hunter early showed an interest in preparing realistic anatomical specimens and learned the latest techniques from Dr. Frank Nichols, the originator of a new method of injecting brightly colored wax into the vascular system to make the veins visible.

In 1746, Dr. Hunter began his own series of anatomical lectures, "The Art of Dissecting," and quickly prospered, enabling him to adopt the lifestyle of an aristocrat. He cultivated friendships with London's leading scholars, authors, and artists, from the novelist Henry Fielding and the Shakespearean actor David Garrick to the caricaturist William Hogarth and the painter Joshua Reynolds, many of whom became his patients.

In 1748, Dr. Hunter brought his younger brother John to London, where he taught him the art of dissection and employed him as an assistant, despite his lack of education and polish. At age twenty, wayward and pugnacious, John had ended his schooling at age thirteen, leaving him barely able to write coherent English and contemptuous of academic life. Nonetheless, under his brother's patient tutoring, he quickly blossomed into an accomplished anatomist, with an astute eye for anatomical detail that soon surpassed his brother's and eventually led to an illustrious career in his own right. The two brothers worked together for twelve years until 1760 when John was drafted into service during the Seven Years War, initiating a period of tension and animosity between them that later complicated their many common endeavors.

Although he had built up a fashionable practice in obstetrics among the English aristocracy, the real source of Dr. Hunter's wealth and renown were his lectures on anatomy, often attended not only by medical students but also by London's most celebrated cultural figures, from Edward Gibbon to Adam Smith. By the time George Croghan visited the Ohio salt lick, William Hunter was clearly the reigning authority in London in the field of comparative anatomy, and after returning from the Seven Years War, his brother John had established himself independently as an anatomist. Dr. Hunter had begun his own inquiry into identity of the American *incognitum* several months *before* George Croghan's shipment of bones arrived in London. In the spring of 1767, learning that a considerable number of elephant's teeth from America had been deposited in the royal family's cabinet in the Tower of London, Hunter asked the curator of the collection there for information about any bones that had been brought from the banks of the Ohio River. These were probably among the same specimens sent to London earlier by the Indian traders and colonial officials that had first created doubts in Peter Collinson's mind.

The curator at the Tower of London sent Dr. Hunter a tusk and a grinder to examine. "The tusk, indeed, seemed so like that of an elephant, that there appeared no room for doubt," Dr. Hunter later explained.[11] However, like Peter Collinson's experience, doubts arose almost immediately about the grinders. Dr. Hunter showed the specimens to his brother John, who agreed that the tusks belonged to an elephant but offered an unexpected verdict on the grinders: "Being particularly conversant with comparative anatomy, at the first sight he told me that the grinder was certainly not an elephant's."[12] By Dr. Hunter's own testimony, his brother seems to have been the first person to make the surprising claim that the grinders belonged to a carnivore: "From the form of the knobs on the body of the grinders, and from the disposition of the enamel, which makes a crust on the outside only of the tooth, as in a human grinder," Dr. Hunter recounted, "he was convinced that the animal was either carnivorous, or of a mixed kind."[13]

His brother's conviction led Dr. Hunter to doubt whether even the tusks belonged to elephants, and to resolve this issue he went to the Tower of London to examine the entire collection of tusks and teeth sent from the Ohio. There he found that all the other specimens were the same as those he had already studied. Dr. Hunter then looked at a wide variety of other specimens in London: two elephants' jaws in his brother's collection, the tusks and grinders of the queen's two elephants, and numerous elephant teeth from Africa at a London warehouse. "From all these observations I was convinced that the grinder tooth, brought from the Ohio, was not that of an elephant, but of some carnivorous animal, larger than an ordinary elephant. And I could not doubt that the tusk belonged to the same animal."[14]

Evidently, Dr. Hunter came to this conclusion before Benjamin Franklin and Lord Shelburne received their shipments of bones from George Croghan. During the summer, shortly after Croghan's shipment arrived, Dr. Hunter visited Franklin with some friends to examine the newly acquired specimens, which he found were exactly the same as those he had previously studied. They only confirmed his belief that the animal was not an elephant.

His political connections at the court and easy access to the English nobility also enabled Dr. Hunter to examine Lord Shelburne's collection, providing him with what appeared to be a decisive confirmation of his new theory. Besides the tusks and grinders, Lord Shelburne possessed a unique specimen, half of the animal's lower jaw with one large grinder still embedded in the jawbone.

> This jawbone was so different from that of an elephant, both in
> form and size, and corresponded so exactly with the other bones,
> and with my supposition, that I was now fully convinced, that the
> supposed American elephant was an animal of another species, a

pseud-elephant, or *animal incognitum*, which anatomists were unacquainted with.[15]

Slowly and methodically, Dr. Hunter was moving toward the truly radical notion of extinction, although this idea does not seem to have been the central focus of the theory that he was discussing privately with London naturalists like Franklin and Collinson. Instead, what created the first ripples of controversy among his fellow naturalists was his assertion that the American *incognitum* was a carnivore. Both Franklin and Collinson were critical of this view before Dr. Hunter formally presented his ideas to the Royal Society in February 1768. Before this date, he seems to have downplayed the idea of extinction by suggesting in private conversations with Lord Shelburne and others that the American *incognitum* was related to the Siberian mammoth. "I imagined farther, that this *animal incognitum* would prove to be the supposed elephant of Siberia, and other parts of Europe," he later explained, "and that the real elephant would be found to have been in all ages a native of Asia and Africa only."[16]

In the fall of 1767 while preparing his formal paper, Dr. Hunter pursued the American *incognitum* with increased vigor, greatly expanding his pool of specimens beyond the tusks and grinders from the Tower of London and the private collections of Lord Shelburne and Franklin. He examined all the fossil teeth in the Royal Society's own museum and those in the British Museum, where Lord Shelburne had deposited his jawbone and grinders. He visited several of London's ivory dealers, examining hundreds of elephants tusks, and consulted with these experts about the texture and substance of the Ohio monster's tusks. Three ivory dealers, who visited Dr. Hunter's home to examine his tusks, concluded that they belonged to African elephants, and ivory carvers who cut through a tusk from Lord Shelburne's collection claimed that its grain and texture were identical to true elephant ivory. Undeterred by their opinions, Dr. Hunter still maintained, however, that true or genuine ivory could be the product of two different animals and not just the elephant.

After surveying the teeth and tusks in London, Dr. Hunter reviewed the scientific literature pertaining to the American *incognitum*. Among the documents he consulted were the writings of the French academicians, namely, Buffon and Daubenton, whose influential theories greatly disappointed him. "Instead of meeting with facts which could disprove my opinion, I found observations which confirm it," he observed of Daubenton's memoir.[17] Daubenton's comparison of the tusks and femurs from the Ohio salt lick with those from Siberia and living elephants had led him to conclude that all three belonged to the elephant species and that the teeth were from members of the hippopotamus family.

Dr. Hunter used the French anatomist's own evidence to refute his theory that the teeth and tusks belonged to two separate animals, the elephant and the hippopotamus. After studying Daubenton's drawing of the three thighbones belonging to a Siberian mammoth, the American *incognitum*, and a living elephant, Dr. Hunter boldly reversed Daubenton's conclusions. In Hunter's opinion, the drawings showed obvious differences in the shape and thickness of these bones, which proved that they belonged to distinct species.

> To my eye, there is nothing more evident, than that the two *femora* differ widely in the shape and proportion of the head, in the length and direction of the neck and in the figure and in the direction of the great trochanter, so that they have many character[istic]s, which prove their belonging to animals of different species.[18]

Except for a few brief citations, Buffon's comments about the American *incognitum's* disappearance made little impression on Dr. Hunter, even though these remarks appeared to support the theory of extinction. In many respects, this idea remained incidental to both men's main arguments. Instead, they seemed primarily concerned with establishing the existence of an unknown creature rather than dwelling on the implications of its possible extinction.

Capping a year of speculation about the bones from the Ohio salt lick, Dr. Hunter delivered his manuscript to the Royal Society shortly before Christmas, barely a month after Peter Collinson had presented his own brief remarks on the teeth and tusks of the American *incognitum*. However, owing to the holiday season and the usual delay in scheduling formal presentations, Hunter's paper was not read before the society for two more months. By then, many members of London's natural history circle were already familiar with his controversial opinions, having discussed the matter with him in private conversations. Hunter's paper, entitled "Observations on the Bones, commonly supposed to be Elephants Bones, which have been found near the River

Ohio in America," reviewed all the details of his year-long research and provided his audience with an authoritative new theory about the fossil remains.

Illustrated by meticulous drawings of the jawbone of the American *incognitum* from Lord Shelburne's collection and those of a full-grown African elephant, showing three different views of each, Dr. Hunter proved conclusively that they belonged to different species (figure 20). In the end, as so many anatomists had suspected, the drawing masters won the day, providing graphic evidence that the American *incognitum* was an unknown species. Finally, after nearly forty years of dispute, Sir Hans Sloane's predictions about the anatomical study of such fossils had been borne out, confirming the validity of his scientific method while disproving his contention that the bones of the Siberian mammoth belonged to the elephant species. Scientifically minded scholars everywhere were now faced with a new dilemma, the existence of an enormous, unknown creature whose teeth and tusks could not be found anywhere among the living beings in God's creation.

Having identified the Ohio creature as an unknown species, Dr. Hunter was still mystified by the true identity of the monster. Eager to prove the American *incognitum* and the Siberian mammoth were related, Dr. Hunter tried to expel from scientific thinking any remnants of myth and folklore surrounding the unknown creatures. "We had information from Muscovy, that the inhabitants of Siberia believed them to be the bones of the mammouth, an animal of which they told and believed strange stories," he told the Royal Society. "But modern philosophers have held the mammouth to be as fabulous as the centaur."[19] Indeed, even while his anatomizing of the monstrous grinders cast out the folktales of the Ostiak tribesmen, Dr. Hunter's own theory created new myths that haunted the scientific imagination for generations to come.

Everyone who contemplated the emerging history of the fossil elephants in Siberia and North America also had to confront the cosmological questions that their existence posed about the earth's history. The presence of seashells on mountaintops and the discovery of enormous bones in northern territories had sparked controversy over the possibility their displacement was caused by catastrophic floods or the Great Deluge. Although Dr. Hunter's own remarks on these matters were brief, they harked back to the speculation of the seventeenth-cen-

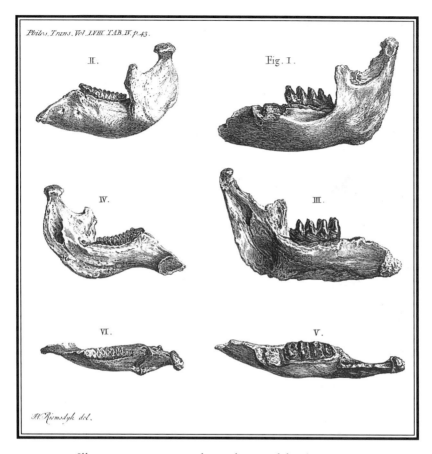

FIGURE 20. Illustration comparing the jawbones of the American *incognitum* and the African elephant from William Hunter's article in 1768 on the "elephant bones" found in the Ohio valley. Dr. Hunter was the first anatomist to give scientific authority to the idea that the unknown creature was an extinct carnivore.

tury English naturalist Robert Hooke, who attempted to explain such anomalies through primitive geological concepts involving volcanic upheavals and climate changes. "From the first time that I learned this part of natural knowledge, it appeared to me to be very curious and interesting," Dr. Hunter declared, "inasmuch as it seemed to concur with many other phaenomena, in proving, that in former times some astonishing change must have happened to this terraqueous globe." Like so many of his contemporaries, from Bartram to Buffon, he was coming to accept, for his own reasons and in his own manner, the notion

> that the highest mountains, in most countries now known, must have lain for many ages in the bottom of the sea, and that this earth must have been so changed with respect to climates, that countries, which are now intensely cold, must have been formerly inhabited by animals which are now confined to the warm climates.[20]

Even though his ideas were leading toward a new geological view of the earth's history, they were not what most readers found most alarming about Dr. Hunter's controversial article. The most memorable and incendiary idea came in the last sentence of his treatise, almost as an afterthought. He joined together for the first time two ideas whose volatility depended partly on their juxtaposition—the twin concepts of the extinct species and the carnivore. "And if this animal was indeed carnivorous, which I believe cannot be doubted," Hunter concluded, "though we may as philosophers regret it, as men we cannot but thank Heaven that its whole generation is probably extinct."[21] It was this last word that provoked the controversy. Unlike Buffon, to whom the disappearance of the fossil elephants had suggested, if only fleetingly, the extinction of multitudes of other animals, this was the only use of the term *extinct* in Dr. Hunter's entire essay. Rather, what made his assertion so influential, especially among the American patriots, was his linking of extinction to the idea that the *incognitum* had been a monstrous carnivore whose disappearance was God's blessing on the human race.

In this way, violence became a part of the earliest perceptions of prehistoric nature, just as predators were the rulers of the natural world. The American *incognitum*'s diet, along with the configuration of its teeth, became a central point of dispute and was discussed by everyone in colonial society from the country parson struggling to fit the fossils into his Sunday sermon to the farmers and frontiersmen who often dug up the bones. With Dr. Hunter's essay, the debate over extinction had become enmeshed in the question of whether the American monster was a carnivore, opening the way to speculation by the founding fathers that the beast was the largest of all terrestrial beings, a "Monarch of the Wilderness" worthy of patriotic admiration.

FIGURE 21. Portrait of Dr. William Hunter lecturing on anatomy at the Royal Academy of Arts, by Johann Zoffany, 1775. The audience included the famous British painter Joshua Reynolds who listens through his ear trumpet. By kind permission of the Royal College of Physicians of London.

Dr. Hunter's theory of extinction in no way tarnished his high standing with the royal family, whose good graces continued to lend an aura of nobility to his endeavors. In 1767, he was elected to the Royal Society—probably as a result of his research on the fossil elephants in America—crowning his rising stature in London society. The following year he was appointed the first professor of anatomy at the newly founded Royal Academy of Arts, created by George III to train the country's classical artists. Dr. Hunter's witty and ascerbic anatomy lectures were immortalized in Johann Zoffany's portrait of him demonstrating the muscles of the human body to his audience, which included the eminent British painter Joshua Reynolds, who is listening intently through his ear trumpet (figure 21).

Dr. Hunter had not intended to cause such a stir. Rather, his new emphasis on extinction and the carnivorous character of the American *incognitum* reflected a larger matrix of ideas then gaining favor in European society during the era of colonization and empire. Just as Buffon had used the cycle of death and destruction in the natural world to justify civilized man's dominance over the "savagery" of wild animals, the extinct carnivore later came to symbolize the superiority of Europeans over the "weaker species" of the human race, whose extinction was viewed as a naturalistic process, analogous to the extermination of inferior life-forms by the dominant species. In words anticipating Charles Darwin's theory of natural selection, Dr. Hunter envisioned this violent process as a means of perfecting God's creation:

> Many animals, from the imperfection of their fabric, are necessarily to perish before the common natural period. Whatever may happen, in a particular instance or with regard to an individual, the most perfect and sound animal upon the whole, will have the best chance of living to procreate others of his kind: in other words, the best breed will prevail.[22]

The American *incognitum* and the Siberian mammoth were not the only mysterious animals whose fossil remains forced English naturalists to consider the existence of extinct species. Ever since Sir Thomas Molyneux had published the first scientific account of the "Irish elk" in 1697, naturalists had been trying to find a living specimen in America to prove that the fossil antlers found in Ireland belonged to the American moose. But as Peter Collinson explained to John Bartram, the recent arrival in England of some American moose antlers seemed to prove just the opposite, spurring instead further speculation about existence of extinct species:

> As to the Fossil Horns Dig'd up in Ireland, that Long contested Point, is now setled—for Last year my Friend the Duke of Richmond had a Large Pair of Your Country Moose Deer Horns sent Him from Quebec. At the first Sight they have not any Affinity with the Irish Fossil Horns but come very near to the European Elk.[23]

The physical evidence now suggested that the Irish elk was extinct, although many people still held out hopes that the living creature would be found in the uncharted regions of northern Canada. "Whether they Exist, God Almighty knows," Collinson declared in exasperation, reluctant to accept the animal's apparent disappearance, since as he reminded Bartram, "it is contrary to the common Course of Providence to suffer any of his Creatures to be Annihilated."

While the London naturalists were busy pursuing the American *incognitum*, the duke of Richmond obtained a young American moose, the first such living specimen to enter Britain. After publishing his article about the Ohio bones, the dispute over the Irish elk captured Dr. Hunter's interest, and he began his own investigation into the elk's possible extinction. In 1770, he commissioned George Stubbs, England's foremost painter of horses, to paint the young bull moose that the duke had brought to Britain.

Stubbs's idealized but anatomically detailed paintings of horses were based on his own dissection of the animals. Intent on giving his patrons anatomically accurate images, he devised a mechanical apparatus for hoisting the corpses of horses into a standing position, where, in the process of dissecting them, he could meticulously peel off the layers of tissue. Like Dr. Hunter and his brother, Stubbs used the latest techniques of dissection, including the new method of injecting liquid wax into the veins. The publication of his book *The Anatomy of the Horse* in 1766 established Stubbs's reputation not only as a painter but an accomplished anatomist as well.[24]

Stubbs's portrait of the American bull moose reflected Dr. Hunter's uncertainty concerning the animal's true identity and its possible extinction. Hunter had been critical of illustrations published by French academicians, especially those of Buffon in 1764, and he considered Stubbs's picture to be the first accurate portrayal of the American moose. In the foreground of the painting are the pair of adult moose antlers that had convinced Peter Collinson that the American moose and the Irish elk were not the same animal. "Whoever will take the trouble to compare the horns upon the ground of the picture with the figure of the Irish horns which Dr. Molyneux has published will see that the two animals must have been of different species," Dr. Hunter wrote in his own manuscript. However, he added to the controversy by stating that "the Irish Deer then was a noble animal of an unknown species, which like the American elephant or *incognitum* is still now probably extinct."[25] But Dr. Hunter never published this paper, perhaps because he could not be certain that the Irish "elk" was not living somewhere in the North American wilderness.

In the decade before the American Revolution, these ideas were still in their infancy. Even at this early stage of scientific debate, when extinct species only loomed on the horizon, the Great Deluge remained a powerful cultural medium through which early geological conscious- ness was filtered. The many popularizers of Buffon's natural history who brought the first images of the fossil elephants to wider audiences in England and the colonies were themselves defenders of traditional Christian views of the antediluvian world.

Paradoxically, Buffon's ideas about the violence of primitive nature were first promoted among English readers by apologists for God's benevolence, theologians who opposed the absolute monarchy that Thomas Hobbes had felt man's natural selfishness and greed made nec- essary. In 1768, John Bruckner, a Lutheran minister who had emigrated to England from Belgium, published his book *A Philosophical Survey of the Animal Creation*, one of the early compendiums modeled on Buf- fon's natural history. Rev. Bruckner described his own work as "An Essay wherein the general devastation and carnage that reign among the different classes of animals are considered in a new point of view, and the vast increase of life and enjoyment derived to the whole from this necessity is clearly demonstrated."

Bruckner's view of the natural world as an animated mass of vital- ity clearly echoed Buffon's own language and outlook, especially the latter's view of the cycle of death and destruction in nature: "One part of life is perpetually at war with the other; one half of this living sub- stance feeds upon another." Like Buffon, Bruckner pictured this car- nage not as an evil to be deplored but, rather, as an integral part of the self-propagating dynamism of the natural world, or "the wonderful economy of nature," as he called it, which "after it is extinguished in one class of animals, immediately rekindles itself in another, and burns with fresh lustre and strength."[26]

The Lutheran minister stopped short of imagining the permanent disappearance of any creatures from the earth's history, invoking in- stead the principle of plenitude to defend the inviolability of God's cre- ation : "It is, I say, five thousand years at least that one part of the liv- ing substance has waged war with the other, yet we do not find that this Law of Nature has to this day occasioned the extinction of any one species." Then, paraphrasing Buffon's image of nature's eternal youthfulness, he offered this consolation: "Nay, we may add, it is this which has preserved them in that State of perpetual youth and vigor in which we behold them."[27] In the end, the carnivores served as symbols of the rejuvenating power of God's nature and, at the same time, man's divinely ordained dominion over the natural world.

In 1771, the popular English author Thomas Pennant published his *Synopsis of Quadrupeds*, which also borrowed heavily from Buffon. He was already the most prolific of the many popularizers of Buffon's natural history in England, having published the first volumes of his influential *British Zoology* in 1766, illustrated with handsome engravings. The year before its publication he had visited Buffon, where he received his encouragement. Pennant was a successful literary figure, not a trained scientist, although he had studied mineralogy and fossils during his dabblings in natural history. His real talents lay in transforming the dry language of scientific treatises into easily digestible and entertaining prose, often through derivative works like *Synopsis of Quadrupeds*.

In Pennant's *Synopsis*, the specter of the American *incognitum*, Dr. Hunter's carnivore, entered the literary world, creating further controversy over its diet while spreading the news of its arrival on the scene. Pennant rejected the idea that the *incognitum* was an extinct creature, naming the unknown species instead the "American Elephant" in an effort to protect the inviolability of God's nature. Nonetheless, its fossil teeth were displayed prominently in his description of the animal, where he briefly reviewed the history of their discovery and revealed that he himself had collected them: "The teeth of this animal [are] often found in a fossil state; some years ago two great grinding teeth, and part of the tusk of an elephant, were given to me by some miners, who discovered them at the depth of 42 yards in a lead-mine in Flintshire."[28]

Even though the curvature of this animal's tusks and the configuration of the fossil grinders differed from those of living elephants, Pennant still insisted that the "American Elephant" belonged to the elephant species. He discussed the issue of the animal's diet in terms that were clearly shaped by Dr. Hunter's article, offering his readers a vivid description of the controversial grinders:

> The great and specific difference consists in the shape of the *molares* or grinders, which are made like those of a carnivorous animal, not flat and ribbed transversely on their surface like those of the

recent elephant, but furnished with a double row of high and conic processes, as if intended to masticate, not to grind their food.[29]

Calling attention to other distinguishing features, like the shape and thickness of the thighbones, Pennant opposed the idea that they belonged to an extinct species. "As yet the living animal has evaded our search. It is more than possible that it yet exists in some of those remote parts of the vast new continent, unpenetrated yet by Europeans."[30] He did not accept the disappearance of any of God's creatures, largely because so much of the earth's terrain remained unexplored, but he did express doubt about extinction in poetic images drawn from the Bible: "Providence maintains and continues every created species, and we have as much assurance, that no race of animals will any more cease while the Earth remaineth, than seed time and harvest, cold and heat, summer and winter, day and night."[31]

Pennant's eloquent plea for the perfection of God's creation was typical of the resistance that the idea of extinction encountered in England and the colonies following Dr. Hunter's article on the American *incognitum*. Few popularizers of natural history were willing to embrace this radical notion because it undermined the rationale for the Great Chain of Being, or *scala naturae*, the overarching metaphysical concept used by many naturalists to give the natural world a harmonious and hierarchical structure. In his poems, a generation earlier, Alexander Pope celebrated this concept in rhyming couplets, warning his readers of the destructive effect that extinction would have on the natural order: "From Nature's chain whatever link you strike, Tenth or ten thousandth, breaks the chain alike."

The most spirited defense of the Great Chain of Being came from Oliver Goldsmith, the English novelist and poet whose *History of the Earth and Animated Nature* appeared in 1774 on the eve of the American Revolution, based on Buffon's *Histoire naturelle*. In 1763, only two years after Buffon's initial suggestion that the fossil elephants from the Ohio valley were an extinct species, Goldsmith had been among the first to alert English readers to this unsettling news. Hired by a book publisher to write an introduction to an inexpensive six-volume natural history, he summarized Buffon's comments:

Those monstrous bones of the Mahmout, as the *Siberians* call an animal, which must have been at least four times as big as the elephant, which are dug up in that country, and which by no means belong to the Whale, as has been falsely imagined, may serve to convince us, that there were once animals existing, which have been totally extirpated.[32]

Indeed, the seeds of Dr. Hunter's conclusion can be found in Goldsmith's early remarks about the large quadrupeds:

> The wisdom of providence in making formidable animals unprolific is obvious; had the Elephant, the Rhinoceros, and the Lion, the same degree of fecundity with the Rabbet, or the Rat, all the arts of man would soon be unequal to the contest, and we should soon perceive them become the tyrants of those who affect to call themselves the masters of the creation.[33]

In England's literary world, extinction emerged hand in hand with the struggle for existence, where domination and violence were naturalistic truths like Buffon's cycles of death and destruction.

Even before Dr. Hunter's article had appeared, all eyes were focused on the carnivores' teeth: "The teeth of carnivorous animals differ in every respect from those which feed upon vegetables," Goldsmith wrote. "In the one the teeth serve as grindstones, in the other, as weapons of offence."[34] The carnivores gave his natural world its violent character, creating the fundamental premise for the dichotomy between civilization and savagery, an idea that influenced the thinking of England's natural philosophers for many generations. "The rapacious animal is in every respect formed for war; yet the various kinds make their incursions in very different ways," Goldsmith explained, and "the beasts of the forest . . . are formed for a life of hostility, and, as we see, possest of various methods to seize, conquer and destroy."[35]

Aware that Buffon's dynamic view of animal species threatened Christian doctrine and the stability of the natural world, Goldsmith defended in his *Animated Nature* the integrity of the Great Chain of Being. He used this concept as the organizing principle of his own history of nature but discarded Buffon's idea that the natural world could be divided into separate species, whose character might change over time or, in some cases, disappear altogether.[36] To provide an aesthetically pleasing and simpler system of classification for his popular audience, Goldsmith created a "literal chain" rather than a metaphysical one, in which the natural world was arranged in a steadily descending scale from man at the top to the zoophyte at the bottom.

Both Buffon and Goldsmith assumed that diminishing size reflected inferiority, with smaller creatures being more numerous because that ensured their survival. The one exception to this system of imperceptible gradations was the human species, since man did not, in Goldsmith's view, "shade" imperceptibly into other classes of species. Like Buffon, Goldsmith followed the Christian tradition, making man the apex of God's creation, separated from all other creatures by his rationality and anatomical perfection. "Every creature becomes more important in the history of Nature in proportion as it is connected with man," he explained, ranking all animals according to their usefulness to humans, from the domestic to the savage.[37]

Goldsmith's colorful history of the elephants, drawn mainly from Buffon's portrait of them, devoted a few paragraphs to the new discoveries of fossil teeth and tusks in Siberia and North America that had created so much controversy among London's natural history circles. Relying heavily on Thomas Pennant's earlier assessment, Goldsmith reviewed the now familiar details, highlighting the two creatures' distinctive features, the spiral curvature of their tusks and the disproportionate thickness of their thighbones. His final commentary on the fossil elephants, however, revealed his reluctance to accept the idea that they belonged to an extinct species. "It is the opinion of Doctor Hunter that they [the bones] must have belonged to a larger animal than the elephant, and differing from it, in being carnivorous. But as yet this formidable creature has evaded our search."[38]

Goldsmith's closing remarks demonstrate how useful and appealing the other half of Dr. Hunter's equation was to English naturalists faced with the dilemma of an unknown species, not to mention the anathema of extinction: "And if, indeed, such an animal exists, it is happy for man that it keeps at a distance, since what ravage might not be expected from a creature [endowed] with more than the strength of the elephant, and all the rapacity of the tiger."[39] In America, this imaginary creature was welcomed with open arms as a dramatic refutation of Buffon's humiliating theory of American degeneracy. When Dr. Hunter's article appeared in the Royal Society's journal, England's monarchy was entering the early stages of the colonial crisis that led to the outbreak of the American Revolution seven years later. Although neither William Hunter nor his brother John sympathized with the American colonists, the ferocious carnivore they invented soon became an emblem of the rebellion even while the Revolutionary War was in progress.

7

The "Monstrous Grinders" in the American Revolution

> To whatever animal we ascribe these remains, it is certain such a
> one has existed in America, and that it has been the largest of ter-
> restrial beings.
>
> —Thomas Jefferson, 1785

SPECULATION ABOUT THE identity of the American *incognitum* in Europe and America intensified with the rebellion against British authority in the American colonies. The end of the English monarch's rule coincided with an increased interest on the part of the patriots in the mysterious animal, whose great size and ferocity were gradually coming to symbolize the new nation's own spirit of conquest.

During the Revolutionary War, the search for the animal's identity shifted from Big Bone Lick to the Hudson River valley, where the first giant tooth had been found nearly seventy-five years earlier. The discovery there of new fossil remains near the battlefields of the American Revolution was witnessed by General George Washington, the commander and chief of the Continental Army, who took time off from his wartime duties to view some "monstrous grinders" unearthed on a farm near his headquarters north of West Point. By then, Washington himself had a grinder from Big Bone Lick, acquired on one of his many trips to Ohio country before the war for independence.

Land speculation and settlement by the colonists beyond the Allegheny Mountains, along with the Indian attacks they provoked, led to the collapse of British authority in the western territories shortly before the outbreak of hostilities. In April 1775, when the first shots of the Revolution were fired at Lexington and Concord, the Ohio River was filled with the canoes and flatboats of squatters and surveyors searching for choice bottomlands in Kentucky. The following year, the tusks and teeth of the American *incognitum* were topics of conversation among the members of the Continental Congress who met in Philadelphia to draft the Declaration of Independence.

Awareness of the debate in London and Paris over the great beast's identity was heightened by the arrival of bones from the Ohio valley and the stories of surveyors and scouts who had visited Big Bone Lick on behalf of land speculators like Benjamin Franklin and George Washington. In Philadelphia, during the Congress's deliberations, Dr. William Hunter's theories about the American *incognitum* were amusing small talk, as were the wax models of anatomical parts fashioned by his American students, who were now successful surgeons in the city. Many delegates to the Congress were familiar with Buffon's theory of American degeneracy, which gained currency among European critics of the New World during the Revolutionary War.

Upon his return from the Ohio valley nearly a decade earlier, George Morgan, the junior partner in the firm of Baynton, Wharton, and Morgan, brought to Philadelphia a box of bones from Big Bone Lick. These bones, collected on the expedition led by George Croghan, arrived in Philadelphia about the same time as Croghan's own specimens reached London. Not being an enthusiastic naturalist himself, Morgan gave his collection of bones to his brother Dr. John Morgan, a young Philadelphia physician who had recently been appointed a professor of physic at the newly established medical school in Philadelphia.

In 1760, John Morgan sailed for Europe to obtain a medical degree at the University of Edinburgh, carrying letters of introduction to several prominent Pennsylvanians in London, including Benjamin Franklin. With Franklin's assistance, he was introduced to Dr. John Fothergill, a key figure in Peter Collinson's natural history circle. Before going to Edinburgh for his medical studies, Morgan spent the winter studying anatomy with Dr. William Hunter and became quite skilled in making the anatomical wax models displayed in Hunter's teaching museum. In 1763, after completing his degree, Morgan departed for his grand tour of the Continent, a rite of passage for members of the polite society to which he aspired. During his travels, he continued to collect curiosities, returning home to Philadelphia with a small cabinet of curios he found in France and Italy. After his brother returned from Ohio country with the fossil remains, Dr. Morgan added them to his collection of coins and medals from ancient Rome and bits of lava from Mount Vesuvius.

Dr. Morgan was only mildly intrigued, however, by the jawbone, tusk, and teeth from Big Bone Lick, so they remained unwashed in their box, serving mainly as oddities brought out occasionally to entertain dinner guests. Even though he was familiar with the controversy surrounding the American *incognitum*, Dr. Morgan never examined the bones closely nor offered any theories about their identity. His lack of interest very likely stemmed from his weak national consciousness and limited sympathy for the patriot cause. "He respected English law and liked English ways and had no wish to overturn or shake the political or social order in which he was prosperous and secure," observed his biographer Whitfield J. Bell Jr.[1]

In the years before the outbreak of hostilities, as British authority began to crumble in the western territories, many American colonists looked enviously on the Indian lands beyond the Allegheny Mountains. News of the gigantic bones from the Ohio salt lick filtered back to the coastal towns with the flood of surveyors and squatters who crossed the Alleghenies seeking land in defiance of the British prohibition against settling in Ohio country. In 1770, George Washington made another trip down the Ohio River, traveling by canoe from Pittsburgh to the mouth of the Great Kanawha, where he surveyed lands on behalf of his Virginia regiment, the soldiers who had been promised 200,000 acres there as compensation for their services in the French and Indian Wars (figure 22). In Pittsburgh, before his departure down the Ohio, Washington dined with George Croghan, who had set up his own private land office and was busy selling titles in a huge tract of land he had acquired directly from the Indians, without authorization from either the Crown or a colony.

Traveling down the Ohio in two large canoes, Washington's small party took eleven days to reach the mouth of the Kanawha, where he marked off a tract of choice bottomland on both sides of the river to meet the claims of the Virginia regiment. Among Washington's companions on this trip was his childhood friend and land agent William Crawford, a Virginia surveyor who lived on the upper Ohio River. In 1771, Crawford selected and surveyed for Washington some ten thousand acres running seventeen miles along the south bank of the Kanawha, which the two probably had spotted during their trip together the previous year. Unfortunately, Washington's party stopped

FIGURE 22. Portrait of George Washington in the uniform of a British colonel, by Charles Willson Peale, 1772. Shortly before this portrait was painted,
Washington traveled to the Ohio valley to survey land for the Virginia regiment. Washington-Custis-Lee Collection, Washington and Lee University,
Lexington, Virginia.

several hundred miles upriver from Big Bone Lick, and as result, there
is no mention of the American *incognitum* in the diary of his journey
to Ohio country. There can be little doubt, however, that the elephant bones from this celebrated landmark in the Ohio valley figured
in Washington's conversations with the traders and travelers that he

encountered along the way. In addition, the trip gave Washington yet another opportunity to acquire the giant grinder from the Ohio salt lick that was in his possession by the time of the Revolutionary War.

The collapse of English authority in Ohio country, together with the unwillingness of British ministers to authorize settlement west of the Alleghenies, created a vacuum in the Ohio valley, opening the way for a flood of squatters and surveyors into the region. Rival groups from Pennsylvania and Virginia moved farther down the Ohio River, vying for claims to huge tracts of land in Shawnee country near the mouth of the Scioto River. During his trip down the Ohio, Washington had been alarmed at the number of surveyors and squatters from Pennsylvania in the region. Upon his return, therefore, he warned John Murray, the earl of Dunmore and the new governor of Virginia, of the inroads being made into Ohio country. In the summer of 1772, the governor defied royal authority by sending Washington's friend William Crawford to survey lands on the upper Ohio on behalf of Virginia's military claimants. In Virginia, members of the Ohio Company decided to focus on land in Kentucky, south of the Ohio River, after the Privy Council in London, fearful of westward expansion by the colonists, sought to curb all groups seeking large imperial land grants in Ohio country.

In the summer of 1773, Lord Dunmore, who was personally in- volved in land speculation, sent Thomas Bullitt, a Virginia surveyor with connections to the Ohio Company, to survey lands farther down the Ohio River, opposite the mouth of the Scioto River and near the center of the Shawnees' settlement. When he made these earliest offi- cial surveys of Kentucky, Captain Bullitt was accompanied by Hancock Taylor, a deputy surveyor of Fincastle County, Virginia, and three brothers, James, George, and Robert McAfee, who lived with their fam- ilies in the frontier settlements in western Virginia. Several years ear- lier, Taylor had gone with a party of explorers to the falls of the Ohio, and so he was able to guide Bullitt's party when they turned south from the Scioto to Big Bone Lick in early July 1773.

By then, numerous other parties of surveyors and squatters had vis- ited the famous salt lick, though without leaving any record of their impressions. This time, however, Robert McAfee kept a journal briefly describing the party's encounter with the American *incognitum*:

> On the 5th [of July] we went to see the Big Bone, which is a wonder to see the large bones that lie there, which have been of several large

big creatures. The lick is about 200 yards long and as wide, and the waters and mud are of a sulphur smell.[2]

These men had little scientific interest in the bones, for they used the fossil elephants' gigantic ribs and vertebrae to make seats and tent poles, although they undoubtedly carted away a few specimens as souvenirs.

Soon a steady stream of squatters and surveyors moved downriver from Pittsburgh to settle along the Ohio, creating an unstable and violent social world in which the constant removal of families farther west was often an attempt to escape the chaotic conditions created by the land rush. In early 1774, the rivalry between Virginia and Pennsylvania erupted into open warfare when Dr. John Connolly, Lord Dunmore's agent at Fort Pitt, suddenly asserted Virginia's claims to Ohio country by seizing the fort and declaring all the lands west to Kentucky to be part of Virginia. Almost simultaneously, Virginia hunters and squatters launched several brutal attacks on Indian parties in Ohio country, including the massacre of the family of a Mingo chief named Logan, whose eloquence Thomas Jefferson later celebrated in his *Notes on the State of Virginia*. These raids quickly escalated into full-scale war when Lord Dunmore came to Fort Pitt himself in September to lead a military campaign against the Shawnee territories to the south.

In the spring of 1774, several months before the outbreak of Dunmore's war, the Virginia governor had authorized new surveys of the lands claimed by Washington's Virginia regiment in the Ohio valley. Having become friends with Washington, the governor agreed to permit a party led by John Floyd, a young schoolteacher and surveyor from Fincastle County, and James Douglas, a Virginia surveyor, to journey to Ohio country to locate the lands Washington had claimed for his soldiers and officers during his trip down the Ohio four years earlier. Among the other members of the surveying party was Thomas Hanson, who kept a private journal documenting their visit to Big Bone Lick.

After encountering some twenty-six squatters and surveyors already poaching on Washington's lands in the Kanawha, the party pushed farther downriver, surveying bottomlands along the Ohio, until they reached Big Bone Lick several weeks later. "The Land is not so good as the other Bottoms, likewise a little broken," Hanson remarked about the landmark site. "There is a number of large Teeth [i.e., tusks] to [be] seen about this Lick, which the People imagined to be Elephants."[3] During their visit, John Floyd and his assistant James Douglas made the first survey of Big Bone Lick, claiming one thousand acres at the site for Colonel William Christian, a Virginia Indian fighter and militia officer, who represented Fincastle County in the Virginia assembly. The original plat of John Floyd's survey of the tract includes a crude sketch of the site and clearly identifies "the large Buffalo Lick and Salt Spring known by the name of Big Bone Lick being about four miles from the Ohio River."[4]

Amid all the turmoil surrounding the rebellion in the colonies when the outbreak of the Revolutionary War was only months away, Nicholas Cresswell, a twenty-four-year-old English traveler, decided to go to Ohio country, where he hoped to stake his own claims to a large landed estate. He arrived in Alexandria, Virginia, in October 1774, when the townspeople were busy preparing for hostilities against England. "Independent Companies are raising in every County on the Continent, appoint[ing] Adjutants and train[ing] their Men as they were on the Eve of a War," he wrote in his diary.[5]

Forced to conceal his own Tory sentiments, Cresswell spent the winter ingratiating himself with the local gentry while making arrangements for his trip to Ohio country. Finally, having formed a partnership with two Virginians, who offered him a five-thousand-acre parcel in exchange for going to view the land at his own expense, he obtained a surveyor's warrant and purchased his provisions—some blankets, gunpowder, lead, flints, a camp kettle, frying pan, and tomahawk, along with silver trinkets to trade with the Indians. Fearful of being arrested as a spy by the "liberty-mad" patriots, he hurriedly set out for Fort Pitt on April 3, 1775.

Within a few weeks, after a cordial reception from Major John Connolly at Fort Pitt, Cresswell's party was drifting down the Ohio River in two thirty-foot, heavily loaded canoes made from hollowed-out walnut trees. Not far downriver he was joined by a young Virginia militia captain and surveyor named George Rogers Clark, who was heading toward Kentucky with a surveying party. The tall red-headed frontiersman had first come to Ohio country three years earlier at age nineteen and was already a veteran surveyor and military figure, having served as a guide with several surveying expeditions and as a militia captain under the Virginia forces during Dunmore's war. In 1775, when Cresswell met him, he was working as an assistant to Hancock Lee, who was surveying land for the Ohio Company under the supervision of Washington's land agent William Crawford.

Despite being tormented by ticks, torrential rains, and fears of Indian attacks, Cresswell's party eventually made its way down the Ohio to the mouth of the Kentucky River, missing Big Bone Lick in the night. Ascending the Kentucky River to the newly founded settlement of Harrodsburg, they came upon a frontier "town" of thirty rough-hewn log cabins established the previous year by James Harrod, a Pennsylvania-born pioneer. News of Indian attacks nearby created panic among his nervous companions, and their quarreling and timidity led the exasperated Cresswell to join forces with a group of Virginia militiamen and surveyors who offered to accompany him back upriver to Fort Pitt. After only a few days on the Ohio, they arrived at the landing near Big Bone Lick. Fortunately, the hardships and disappointments Cresswell had endured had not dulled his powers of observation, for he left a vivid description of the fabled salt lick in the journal that he had continued to keep.

Setting out the next morning for the salt lick, Cresswell's party lost its way in the hilly woodlands, walking for several hours before reaching the muddy pond, a little more than knee-deep, where to his delight a profusion of bones still lay.

> Found several bones of a Prodigious size, I take them to be Elephants, for we found a part of a tusk, about two feet long, Ivory to all appearance, but by length of time had grown yellow and soft. All of us stripped and went into the pond to grabble for teeth and found several.[6]

Admiring an eighteen-inch-long fragment of an ivory tusk and a jaw tooth weighing some ten pounds, Cresswell viewed his specimens with an educated eye, carefully noting the dimensions of the ribs and thighbones scattered nearby. His commentary, however, reveals a somewhat muddled understanding of Indian traditions, for his opinion about them seems to reflect that of the backwoodsmen around the campfire: "What sort of animals these were is not clearly known. All the traditionary accounts by the Indians is that they were White Buffaloes that killed themselves by drinking salt water." Though familiar with the controversy over the beast's diet and identity, he took a commonsense approach, contradicting the London anatomist Dr. William

Hunter. "It appears to me from the shape of their teeth that they were Grass-eaters."[7]

Like many educated English gentlemen contemplating these specimens, Cresswell was puzzled by the discovery of ivory tusks similar to those of African elephants so far from their usual tropical habitat. "There neither is or ever were any Elephants in North or South America, that I can learn, or any quadruped one tenth the part as large as these was." Returning to the Ohio River during a thunderstorm, he arrived wet and tired only to discover that one of his tusks had been damaged in transit. "A D[amn]d Irish rascal has broken a piece of my Elephant tooth, put me in a violent passion, can write no more," he fumed.[8]

Two weeks later, when the party approached the mouth of the Kanawha River, where thousands of acres of Washington's land lay, several settlers informed them that "the New Englanders have had a battle with the English troops at Boston and killed seven thousand."[9] That is, three months after the first shots were fired at Lexington and Concord, Cresswell had heard a garbled account of the beginning of the American Revolution.

For many Virginians, assertion of their land claims in Ohio country had become part of the larger struggle against Britain's colonial rule. In December 1773, the Boston Tea Party had ended the prospect of large imperial land grants sought by the Ohio Company of Virginia and lobbyists in London like Benjamin Franklin. When Lord Dunmore launched his campaign against the Shawnees in the fall of 1774, George Washington was in Philadelphia attending the first Continental Congress, where resentment against British aggressiveness on the frontier was intensified by Washington's fear that Dunmore's actions now threatened his own land claims in the region. Increasingly, the delegates were coming to see the issue of independence in terms of continental expansion, as Thomas Paine's pamphlet *Common Sense* made evident two years later.

In Philadelphia, during the meetings of the first Continental Congress, news from the frontier about the American *incognitum* reached the delegates caught up in debate over the land rush in the Ohio valley. Based on natural rights doctrine and evangelical beliefs, the rhetoric of republicanism was filled with prophecies of an empire in the West, ordained by both God's will and the natural progress of societies from savagery to civilization. "It requires but a small portion of the gift of discernment for anyone to foresee, that providence will erect a mighty empire in America, and our posterity will have it recorded in history," Sam Adams, a Boston patriot, wrote to a friend.[10] In 1771, two graduating seniors at the College of New Jersey, Hugh Brackenridge and Philip Freneau, delivered a poetic commencement address celebrating the westward movement of empire from Athens to Rome to England and, finally, America. "We too shall boast / Our Alexanders, Pompeys, heroes, kings," they declared while claiming that America's cultural supremacy would last exactly a thousand years.[11]

The motives for the founding fathers' preoccupation with America's cultural ascendancy lay partly in their awareness of the barrenness of their own past. For many classically educated patriots, the absence of ruined temples and monuments to mark the grandeur of antiquity was a sign of the New World's cultural inferiority. Revolutionary republicanism meant turning their backs on Europe's decadence, and their beliefs in their own racial superiority and the westward course of civilization and empire led them to reject the antiquity of Indian America as a savage state of social development. In the decades before the American Revolution, European critics of the New World, like the French philosopher Abbé Raynal, used Buffon's theory of American degeneracy to further humiliate the founding fathers: "Through the whole extent of America," Raynal claimed in 1770, "there had never appeared a philosopher, an artist, a man of learning, whose name had found a place in the history of science or whose talents have been of any use to others."[12] And as historian Joseph J. Ellis noted, Abbé de Pauw, the author of the entry for America in the *Encyclopédie*, "argued that the inhabitants of the New World were permanently condemned to live as diseased semisavages incapable of refinement."[13]

In the fall of 1774, with the colonies in political crisis, delegates from the thirteen colonies convened in Philadelphia. Benjamin Franklin and John Bartram had made this city a symbol of American ingenuity and industry, especially among connoisseurs of American curiosities. Philadelphia-based merchants and Indian traders had played key roles in the transfer of the tusks and teeth from Big Bone Lick to the scientific community in England and Europe. Upon their arrival in the city, many delegates to the Continental Congress were welcomed by local physicians, who were among the strongest proponents of natural history studies in the colonies.

The bones of the American *incognitum* lay unwashed in Dr. Morgan's collection, still caked with mud from Big Bone Lick. His own lack of interest in the new scientific theories about the unknown creature contrasted sharply with the founding fathers' growing fascination with the bones. During the meetings of the first Continental Congress in the fall of 1774, John Adams, a Harvard-educated Boston lawyer, dined with Dr. Morgan, who, many Philadelphia patriots suspected, was a Tory at heart. In his diary, Adams labeled Dr. Morgan, "an ingenious physician" and noted that after dinner he had showed his guests "some curious paintings upon silk which he brought from Italy, which are singular in this country, and some bones of an animal of enormous size found upon the banks of the river Ohio."[14] In New England, the bones from the Kentucky salt lick were less well known than similar specimens from the Hudson River valley, which continued to fascinate scholars like Ezra Stiles, even though few new tusks or teeth had been found in the region since the discovery of the Claverack monster.

The bones gathering dust in Dr. Morgan's cabinet were part of the wider interest in curiosities being cultivated by the American gentry who saw their knowledge of natural history as a stepping-stone to social status in colonial society. The breadth of this interest was demonstrated by the other diversions that John Adams found in Philadelphia during the deliberations of the Continental Congress. He visited the display of Dr. Abraham Chovet's wax models in his anatomical museum on the same day before he dined with Dr. Morgan. An eccentric, London-trained barber-surgeon who had recently fled Jamaica after a checkered career, Dr. Chovet quickly established himself in Philadelphia as a showman, with witty lectures and elegant anatomical models, including a pair of male and female figures with removable parts. "Went in the morning to see Dr. Chovet and his skeletons and waxworks," Adams noted in his diary, "most admirable, exquisite representations of the whole animal economy. Four complete skeletons; a leg with all the nerves, veins and arteries injected with wax; two complete bodies in wax, full grown; waxen representations of all the muscles, tendons, etc. of the head, brain, heart, lungs, liver, stomach, etc."[15]

In the private cabinets of curiosities, the founding fathers encountered the artifacts of a new museum culture in the making, collections of natural history specimens that were not only evidence of scientific endeavors but also symbols of the new nation's natural antiquity. Known as the "Paris of the New World," Philadelphia was the center of

America's natural history culture, offering to the delegates more cabinets of curiosities than any other colonial city. Among the several different private collections, there was one with which the founding fathers were especially familiar, since its owner had recently begun documenting the history of the Revolution itself. This was the private museum of Pierre Eugène Du Simitière, a Swiss-born émigré who had come to the colonies a decade earlier with the express purpose of creating a comprehensive collection of American curiosities.

Born in Geneva of French Protestant parents, Du Simitière was the son of a wealthy merchant in the Dutch East Indies, where the young naturalist first developed his artistic talents and taste for curiosities. Before settling in Philadelphia in 1774, Du Simitière traveled for some ten years throughout the American colonies, collecting natural history specimens and occasionally painting portraits to earn his living. In 1768, while still a peripatetic artist and collector, he had been elected to the American Society for Promotion of Useful Knowledge, an early scientific group nurtured by Benjamin Franklin. Returning to Philadelphia in September 1774, when the Continental Congress was about to begin its deliberations, Du Simitière quickly realized the gravity of the revolutionary events and began to collect pamphlets and broadsides, clippings, and many other forms of ephemeral literature associated with the American Revolution. Du Simitière's extensive private collection of curiosities had been open since 1775 and was already perceived by Philadelphia's genteel classes as a "museum." The Continental Congress had paid Du Simitière to translate some documents into French, and the young Swiss curator was already courting delegates whose financial support he sought in hopes of becoming official historiographer of the American Revolution.

While John Adams was in Philadelphia the following year to draft the Declaration of Independence, he visited Du Simitière's collection and wrote to his wife Abigail afterward about it: "This M. Du Simitière is a very curious man. He has begun a collection of materials for a history of this revolution."[16] In fact, Du Simitière had begun to collect materials related to the rebellion a decade earlier with the first news about the riots against the Stamp Act and the attacks on tea ships in Boston harbor. By the time Adams visited his museum, he already envisioned making them a permanent historical collection.

In 1777, shortly before the British occupied Philadelphia, Du Simitière was drafted into the Pennsylvania militia, but he earned the scorn of many patriots by shunning military service on the grounds that he was a foreigner. Despite his ambiguous citizenship, he submitted a formal proposal to the Continental Congress two years later asking for a subsidy to write a natural and civil history of the American Revolution. His request was ultimately denied by the full Congress, although the congressional committee considering his proposal had recommended that he be appointed "historiographer of the U.S. Congress," with an annual stipend of $2,000 in continental bills. Faced with financial difficulties, Du Simitière sought to defray his expenses by painting portraits of the founding fathers. He drew a series of thirteen profile portraits of Revolutionary leaders, including George Washington, who sat for Du Simitière on February 1, 1779, while visiting Philadelphia for consultations with the Congress.

Before the Revolution, Du Simitière had also begun collecting published articles about the American *incognitum*, making manuscript copies of William Hunter's article on the enormous bones from Ohio country and extracts from Buffon's commentaries on the fossil elephants. In October 1774, Benjamin Rush, a young Philadelphia physician and revolutionary patriot, gave Du Simitière a copy of John Woodward's scheme for classifying fossils. Troubled by Buffon's theory of American degeneracy, Du Simitière began to compile the first recorded statistics on longevity in America. In a letter to a French philosopher, he lamented the lack of interest in natural curiosities by many settlers on the frontier, who he felt were motivated largely by the lucrative Indian trade and fertile land: "Self interest is the only motive that Spurs the white people to penetrate the boundless American forests. If perchance we meet in the Journals . . . some short account of natural or artificial curiosity, it is all nay more than we could reasonably expect from them, everything considered."[17] No doubt Du Simitière had in mind the short descriptions of Big Bone Lick in Christopher Gist's *Journal* that he had copied from Thomas Pownall's edition of Evans's famous "Map of the Middle British Colonies," published in 1776.

Du Simitière's pessimistic view was contradicted by evidence that the enormous bones from the Kentucky salt licks were still valuable curiosities to New England clergymen during the Revolutionary War. In the late summer of 1777, Ezra Stiles, the grandson of Edward Taylor, examined a monstrous grinder from Big Bone Lick, which had reached New Haven despite the turbulence of the Revolution: "I weighed a large Tooth which Rev. Mr. Macclure bro't from the Ohio & found it *fifty Ounces*."[18] Even though Stiles was closely following the scholarly debate about the discovery of these bones, he still shared his grandfather's opinion that such remains might be those of human giants: "It is the Grinder Tooth of some great Animal, but whether an Elephant or Gyant, is a Question."[19]

In September 1780, when the outcome of the Revolutionary War was still in doubt, several workmen hired by Rev. Robert Annan to drain a shallow swamp on his farm dug up several "monstrous grinders" which they tossed aside carelessly from the ditch they were digging.[20] Rev. Annan's farm was located near the village of New Windsor in the Hudson River valley, about seventy miles north of New York just above the Continental Army's fortifications at West Point and only a few days' travel downriver from Claverack, where the first tooth of the American *incognitum* had been found seventy-five years earlier.

When the Reverend found the huge molars near the drainage ditch, he was well aware of the controversy then swirling around the bones in Europe and America. After washing the pearly white teeth, Annan showed them to a neighbor native to the New Windsor area, who returned with him to the marl beds to dig up more bones. News of these curiosities spread quickly throughout the New Windsor neighborhood, especially among the local physicians, lawyers, and clergymen. With the help of his neighbors, Rev. Annan dug up some twenty fragments of bones and teeth, many of which simply crumbled away into dust when removed from the marl.

In late September, General Washington traveled to Hartford, Connecticut, to meet with Count de Rochambeau, the commander of a large French expeditionary force that had landed at Newport, Rhode Island, during the summer. In the tense months before France's intervention turned the Revolutionary War against the British, Washington's principal concern was with the British stronghold in New York City, which he contemplated attacking with forces from the American fortress at West Point. Less than a week after his meeting with Rochambeau, while inspecting West Point, he learned of the betrayal of Benedict Arnold, whose plot to surrender this strategic Hudson River fortress to the British was foiled by the capture of an enemy spy by American militiamen. During the ensuing months, General Washington established the winter quarters of the Continental Army near West

Point, setting up his own headquarters in the farmhouse of Thomas El-
lison at New Windsor, overlooking the Hudson River about ten miles
from Rev. Annan's farm (figure 23).

In all likelihood, Washington first heard reports about the fossil remains unearthed at Annan's farm from the local gentry with whom he
fraternized at New Windsor. Or his curiosity about the bones may have
been piqued by the visit shortly before Christmas of the marquis de
Chastellux, a French officer involved in negotiating France's intervention in the war. The marquis was a personal friend of the French naturalist Buffon, whose peculiar theory of American degeneracy had made
the bones of the American *incognitum* an emblem of national honor in
the eyes of the founding fathers. Washington himself welcomed the diversion that Chastellux offered: "I am in very confined Quarters; little
better than those of Valley Forge," he had written to General Lafayette
a week before the marquis arrived, "but such as they are I shall welcome
into them your friends on their return from Rhode Island."[21]

Traveling overland by carriage from Philadelphia through the backcountry to New Windsor, Chastellux imagined that he saw a monstrous
creature in the wilderness as he neared Washington's headquarters:

> I was now in the wildest and most deserted country I had yet passed
> through; my imagination was already enjoying this solitude and my
> eyes were searching through the woods for some extraordinary ani-
> mals, such as elk or caribou, when I perceived in a clearing a
> quadruped which seemed to me very large. I started with joy and cau-
> tiously approached, but on closer observation of this monster of the
> wilderness, I discovered to my great disappointment that it was only
> a forlorn horse peaceably grazing there; and the clearing was nothing
> less than a field belonging to a new settlement.[22]

Intent on visiting Saratoga, the site of British General John Bur-
goyne's defeat, Chastellux later crossed the Hudson River in General
Washington's barge and then traveled north along a route that took
him through the village of Claverack, fearful that his trip would be fore-
stalled by the snow that had begun to fall. Three days before Christmas,
barely twenty-four hours after he left Washington's camp, he awoke to
find "the ground entirely covered with snow, which continued to fall in
abundance, mixed with ice and sleet."[23] Despite the inclement weather,
he traveled north on horseback through Livingston manor and de-

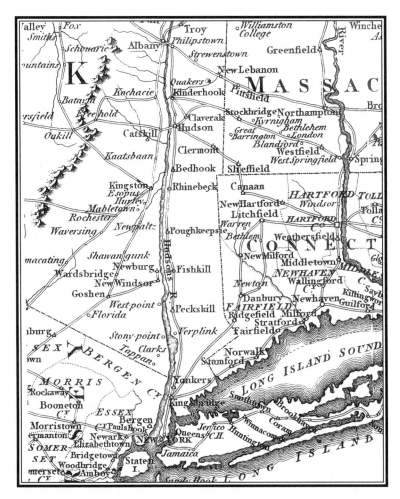

FIGURE 23. Detail from a map of the Hudson River valley from a
reprint of William Strickland's *Journal of a Tour in the United States,
1794–1795*, published by the New York Historical Society.

scended from the hills to the Hudson River, passing the Claverack
meetinghouse, near the site where the first tooth of the American *incognitum* had been discovered.

The snowfall that the marquis observed may well have occasioned
a holiday outing by General Washington, who evidently traveled to
Rev. Annan's farm in late December to see the giant bones dug up there

a few months earlier. From the small frame house overlooking the Hudson River that served as his headquarters, Washington rode to the site across the snow-covered countryside in two sleighs, accompanied by several of his officers, including his aide-de-camp Colonel David Humphreys. Although Washington himself left no record of the visit, Rev. Annan's account, published several years later, offers evidence of the general's own fascination with the American *incognitum*: "His Excellency, General Washington, came to my house to see these relicts. He told me, he had in his house a grinder which was found on the Ohio, much resembling these."[24] At the site, Colonel Humphreys examined a tooth weighing about two pounds and some bone fragments measuring nearly a foot in diameter.

News of Washington's viewing of the bones quickly reached other parts of New England, thanks to the travels of his aide-de-camp. In February 1781, only a few months later, Colonel Humphreys went to New Haven to visit Ezra Stiles, president of Yale University and gave him a firsthand account of the general's encounter with the fossil elephants. He confirmed that Washington had mentioned having some of the Ohio teeth at his estate in Virginia that resembled the specimens discovered at Annan's farm. At Annan's farm, Washington had apparently recounted a story that he had heard about the Ohio valley site: "[A]Gentleman informed him who saw the Ohio Bones on the spot, when they raised up the Head out of which they took the Teeth, & found it to be nearly of [a] Man's Height, or a man stand[in]g by it, it reached up to the middle of his Face."[25] The anecdote elicited a private comment by Stiles in his diary revealing that the New England scholar still believed the fossil remains belonged to human giants: "They all take these Bones to belong to Quadrupeds. I suppose them to be human—like the Bones & Teeth at Claverack."[26]

About the same time that George Washington visited Rev. Annan's farm, Thomas Jefferson began writing his *Notes on the State of Virginia*, which contained a long section on the fossil elephants in America. When it was published five years later, Jefferson's *Notes* helped make the American *incognitum* a symbol of national identity for the citizens of the new republic. The significance of this literary work seems all the more remarkable given the turmoil surrounding its conception, when, during the darkest moments of the American Revolution, Jefferson could hardly have been certain of the war's outcome.

In the fall of 1780, while governor of Virginia, Jefferson received a questionnaire circulated among members of the Continental Congress by the secretary of the French legation in Philadelphia seeking information about the rebellious states that France was supporting. The capital of Virginia had recently been moved from Williamsburg to Richmond, a picturesque town of eighteen hundred people, which Jefferson felt would be more accessible to western farmers and thus would weaken the power of Virginia's Tidewater aristocracy. In December, while a large British expeditionary force under the turncoat Benedict Arnold approached the Chesapeake, Jefferson began answering the twenty-three questions posed by the French consul while confiding to his friends his desire to resign his office to devote himself to his scientific studies.

Jefferson was driven out of Richmond by Arnold's forces shortly after the new year, and in June 1781, he retired as governor, humiliated by accusations that he had fled in a cowardly manner from his home at Monticello as the enemy troops approached. Embittered by Virginia politics and physically debilitated by a broken wrist suffered as a result of a fall from a horse, Jefferson sought refuge at "Poplar Forest," his summer retreat in the Blue Ridge Mountains, where he resumed working on his manuscript.

As a young lawyer who had been born and raised in the foothills of these mountains, Jefferson built his law practice on processing land patents in the frontier territories where the settlers frequently fought over titles to Indian lands. A classically educated planter himself, Jefferson owned some five thousand acres in western Virginia near his home at Monticello. Elected to the Virginia House of Burgess in 1769, at the age of twenty-seven, he had gained political stature in the colony as an opponent of the wealthy planters of the Tidewater region, who were less concerned than the western farmers about the British prohibition of settlement beyond the Appalachian Mountains. In 1774, his pamphlet summarizing the political rights of the Virginia colonists condemned, among other things, British restrictions on westward expansion. Its eloquence greatly enhanced his reputation as a spokesman at the Continental Congress for frontier democracy.

Jefferson's role in drafting the Declaration of Independence added to his reputation as a writer capable of articulating the new nation's dreams of continental expansion, which were then focused on the Ohio valley, where the bones of the American *incognitum* had been found. In 1778, during the Revolutionary War, Jefferson was involved in secret efforts by Virginia to support George Rogers Clark's campaign against British forts in the northwest. In the eyes of Virginians, the goal of Clark's maneuvers was to secure their own state's claims to territories in the Ohio valley. In 1779, while governor of Virginia, Jefferson offered to Colonel William Christian a military grant to Big Bone Lick and its environs, a tract of one thousand acres based on the earlier survey by John Floyd. The value of this property became evident the following year when Colonel Christian sold it for 1,350 pounds, its value based on its widely known salt springs.[27]

Most of the first draft of Jefferson's *Notes* had been written in 1781, during the decisive months of the American Revolution, when French intervention enabled General Washington's Continental Army to defeat Lord Charles Cornwallis at Yorktown. Jefferson's desire to remain in seclusion with his literary pursuits was so powerful that he refused the Continental Congress's request to go to Europe with John Adams and John Jay as ministers plenipotentiary to negotiate a peace. In December, when he went to Richmond to defend himself against charges of malfeasance by the Virginia assembly, Jefferson took with him his completed manuscript, which he delivered to the French consul.

In his utilitarian survey of Virginia's resources, Jefferson addressed some of the issues raised by Buffon, whose theory of American degeneracy had offended his sensibility, especially since he was an ardent admirer of Buffon's natural history. In a section entitled "Productions Mineral, Vegetable and Animal," Jefferson eloquently rebutted Buffon's theory, using clever innuendos about the illogic of his argument and incontrovertible physical evidence to challenge his central thesis that life-forms in America were inferior in size to those of the Old World.

The American *incognitum* played a central role in Jefferson's rebuttal. "It is remarkable that the tusks and skeletons have been ascribed by the naturalists of Europe to the elephant, while the grinders have been given to the hippopotamus, or riverhorse," he observed, referring to the argument by Buffon and his chief anatomist Daubenton.[28] Jefferson then demonstrated how the bones' immense size, as Buffon documented in his own treatise, belied his claim that the *incognitum* was an elephant or a hippopotamus.

The skeleton of the mammoth (for so the *incognitum* has been called) bespeaks an animal of six times the cubic volume of the elephant. The grinders are five times as large, are square, and the grinding surface studded with four or five rows of blunt points: whereas those of the elephant are broad and thin, and their grinding surface flat.[29]

Clearly, Jefferson had benefited from William Hunter's clinical study, and he chose carefully the terrain on which he engaged his French adversary. The question of size was critical to his essay because, despite the many uncertainties with regard to the beast's actual identity, its enormous bones offered irrefutable evidence that American animals were not necessarily smaller than those of Europe. "But to whatever animal we ascribe these remains, it is certain such a one has existed in America, and that it has been the largest of all terrestrial beings," Jefferson declared, knowing the consequences these bones had for Buffon's overarching theory of American degeneracy.[30]

Aware of the many contradictions in Buffon's sprawling *Histoire naturelle*, Jefferson chose not to challenge the French naturalist's controversial opinions about the American climate. In his own view, there had not been enough meteorological observations to disprove Buffon's contentions about the deleterious effects of the alleged moisture and cold in the New World. Instead, he questioned whether there was any valid evidence that dampness and cold actually inhibited an animal's growth. After all, as Jefferson pointed out, Buffon himself had shown that the oxen of Denmark, Ukraine, and Siberia, which certainly had cold and damp climates, were the largest of their species. "The truth is, that a Pigmy and a Patagonian, a Mouse and a Mammoth, derive their dimensions from the same nutritive juices," Jefferson insisted. "The difference of increment depends on circumstances unsearchable to beings with our capacities."[31] In this passage, Jefferson used the traditional notion of the Great Chain of Being to ridicule Buffon's environmental argument, revealing in the process his own conservatism with regard to hierarchy of God's creation. "What intermediate station they take may depend on soil, on climate, on food, on a careful choice of breeders. But all the manna of heaven would never raise the Mouse to the bulk of the Mammoth."

The centerpiece of Jefferson's rebuttal consisted of statistical tables comparing the weights of American animals with those of their counterparts in Europe. Ultimately, in true Lockean fashion, he relied on the greater bulk of American quadrupeds to disprove Buffon's theory rather than on any arcane arguments about the effects of the New World's climate. Using the physical measurements collected by his correspondents and reports from naturalists like Mark Catesby, Peter Kalm, and John Bartram, Jefferson's list of quadrupeds extends from the largest to the smallest, from the buffalo, moose, and elk down to water rat, weasel, and shrew mouse. In this systematic manner, he offered concrete evidence that among the many animals common to both continents, there was no pattern of inferiority with regard to the size of New World creatures. On the contrary, as his table shows, the American bear was twice as heavy as its European counterpart, and the Old World had nothing comparable to the buffalo, which weighed some eighteen hundred pounds.

Predictably, the "mammoth" is at the top of Jefferson's list of quadrupeds, and its presence among the living creatures reveals an anomaly in Jefferson's own view of the American *incognitum*. Even though he followed the English anatomists in their assertion that the animal was definitely a separate, unknown species, he rejected the idea of its extinction. "It may be asked, why I insert the Mammoth, as if it still existed? I ask in return, why I should omit it, as if it did not exist?"[32] Like many other Americans who believed in the inviolability of God's nature, he still clung to the belief that this animal might be found wandering somewhere in the unexplored wilderness. "Such is the economy of nature, that no instance can be produced of her having permitted any one race of her animals to become extinct; of her having formed any link in her great work so weak as to be broken."[33]

Just as Edward Taylor used Indian folktales to confirm the bones belonged to human giants, Jefferson used these traditions to strengthen his idea that the "mammoths" were living creatures. He was skeptical about the reliability of Indian testimony but did not dismiss their legends about the beast, choosing instead to use them to spur exploration of the uncharted wilderness where he believed the *incognitum* might still be lurking in the forests. In fact, at the outset of his discussion of the mammoth, he featured an Indian legend about the Ohio salt lick that he himself had heard from a delegation of Delaware chiefs during the Revolutionary War. "Their tradition is, that he was carnivorous, and still exists in the northern parts of America," Jefferson observed, giving credence to Dr. Hunter's controversial claim that the American *incognitum* was a carnivore.

When asked what they knew about the bones found at the salt lick on the Ohio, the Delaware chiefs had told him a legend handed down by their ancestors. It explained how the "Great Man above," enraged by the great beast's destruction of the bear, deer, elks, and buffaloes at the salt lick, had killed off all the gigantic creatures with lightning bolts, except for a wounded bull that had "bounded over the Ohio, over the Wabash, the Illinois, and finally over the great lakes, where he is living at this day."[34] Jefferson's version of the story gave public literary expression to an Indian folktale that had appeared earlier in only a highly fragmented form in the private correspondence and reports of Indian traders to naturalists like John Bartram and Peter Collinson. It was one of the mostly widely reproduced passages from his *Notes* and was instrumental after the war in creating the symbolic meaning of the *incognitum*.

For American patriots searching for symbols of their own superiority, the most significant aspect of Jefferson's use of the Indian myth was the way it strengthened the belief that the *incognitum* was a carnivore. However, his acceptance of the Indian traditions regarding this controversial issue presented him with the practical problem of explaining the animal's disappearance and led him to scramble fact with folklore in his speculations about the causes of the creature's disappearance:

> If he be a carnivorous animal, as some Anatomists have conjectured, and the Indians affirm, his early retirement may be accounted for from the general destruction of the wild game by the Indians, which commences in the first instant of their connection with us, for the purpose of purchasing matchcoats, hatchets, and fire locks, with their skins.[35]

In this way, Jefferson blended the scientific opinion of the London anatomist William Hunter, who imagined the beast was a carnivore, with Indian legends to produce a compelling new image of the American *incognitum*'s awesome stature.

To substantiate the Indian legends about the living mammoth, Jefferson himself recounted the testimony of a settler captured by the Indians near the Tennessee River, who had heard similar stories from his captors after being carried over the mountains west of the Missouri River. The settler claimed to have seen many bones while a prisoner of tribes in the western territories where "the natives described to him the animal to which they belonged as still existing in the northern parts of their country."[36] According to Jefferson, similar bones had recently been found on the banks of the North Holston River, a branch of the Tennessee: "From the accounts published in Europe, I suppose it to be decided, that these are of the same kind with those found in Siberia."[37]

Like so many naturalists who contemplated the mystery of the fossil elephants in America, Jefferson was especially perplexed by the alleged existence of tropical animals in cold northern climates. In fact, this was one of the arguments he used to undermine the claims that the American *incognitum* was an elephant: "I have never heard an instance, and suppose there has been none, of the grinder of an elephant being found in America. From the known temperature and constitution of the elephant he could never have existed in those regions where the remains of the mammoth have been found." Rather than accepting the conventional notion of climate change as an explanation for this anomaly, Jefferson was inclined to believe the *incognitum* was an entirely different species, perhaps one capable of living in the cold Northwest: "For my own part, I find it easier to believe that an animal may have existed, resembling the elephant in his tusks, and general anatomy, while his nature was in other respects extremely different."[38]

For Jefferson, who was unaware of the new discovery on Rev. Annan's farm, the answers to many of these questions lay in obtaining more specimens from the famous Kentucky salt lick. On December 19, 1781, the day before he sent his completed manuscript to the French consul in Philadelphia, Jefferson wrote to his friend George Rogers Clark in the Ohio valley requesting some specimens from Big Bone Lick. By then, Clark, a native of Jefferson's Albemarle County in Virginia, was the commanding officer of the Army of the West, famous for his capture of Fort Vincennes from the British three years earlier in a daring winter campaign, secretly supported by the Virginia patriots. Remarkably, Jefferson's letter to General Clark was conveyed to him by another hero of the Kentucky frontier, Daniel Boone, who had served as a militia captain during the war fighting Indians loyal to the British.

> Having an opportunity by Col. Boon I take the liberty of calling to your mind your kindness in undertaking to procure for me some teeth of the great animal whose remains are found on the Ohio. Were it possible to get a tooth of each kind, that is to say a foretooth, grinder, &c, it would particularly oblige me.[39]

Unfortunately, the threat of Indian attacks made travel to the salt lick too dangerous, even for an experienced soldier, and in February 1782, General Clark wrote to Jefferson, explaining why he had not been able to fulfill his request. In the interim, though, he had managed to collect a thighbone, jaw bone, grinder, and tusk from travelers on the frontier, but he would not be able to collect more specimens until the spring. His reply indicated his own willingness to challenge Jefferson's views of the American *incognitum*: "The animal has no foreteeth that I could ever discover and [was] by no means Carnivorous as many suppose."[40]

Clark had a wide knowledge of the curiosities found on the Kentucky frontier, including the ruins of Indian mounds that he associated with the fossils: "You scarcely ride a day through many part[s] of the Western Cuntry but you meet with some Curios work of Antiquity," he wrote to Jefferson. In his opinion, the Indian mounds were remnants of powerful nations that had inhabited the region at the same time as the mysterious beasts whose bones Jefferson so eagerly sought.

Owing to disruptions by the war, Jefferson did not receive General Clark's reply until August 1782, nearly six months later when peace negotiations with the British were entering their final phases. With the independence of the new American nation assured, the bones of the American *incognitum* had become even more highly prized. Writing to Clark in November, Jefferson spared no means in his pursuit of the bones: "A specimen of each of the several species of bones now to be found is to be the most desirable object in Natural History, and there is no expence of package or of safe transportation which I will not gladly reimburse to procure them safely."[41] Even though General Clark had doubts about the existence of a carnivore at the Kentucky salt lick, his opinions about the region's natural history had won Jefferson's respect: "Any observations of your own on the subject of the big bones or their history, or on any thing else in the Western country, will come acceptably to me, because I know you see the works of nature in the great, and not merely in detail."

While the manuscript of Jefferson's *Notes* circulated initially among a small circle of friends, his correspondence demonstrates how knowledge of these bones spread during the Revolutionary War. The ideas outlined in his report to the French consul at Philadelphia did not become public until after the war, but by then many other citizens had become involved in the search for the American *incognitum*.

8

The Doctrine of Monsters Reborn

How formidable an enemy to the human species, an animal as large
as an elephant, the tyrant of the forests, perhaps the devourer of man!

—John Filson

DURING THE WAR for Independence, patriotism and prehistoric nature became intertwined as the American *incognitum* acquired new
symbolic meaning in the national consciousness of the emerging republic. In the waning years of the war, the monstrous bones began to
take their place in the nation's public culture, moving beyond the status of private curiosities and scientific specimens to become objects celebrated in American literature and displayed in the nation's first natural history museums. The surrender of Lord Cornwallis at Yorktown in
October 1781 enabled Thomas Jefferson the following winter to revise
the unpublished manuscript of his *Notes on the State of Virginia*. While
he continued to solicit specimens from Big Bone Lick, a young Pennsylvania schoolteacher named John Filson came to the Ohio valley and
made the famous salt lick a landmark in his own book about the Kentucky frontier and its pioneer hero Daniel Boone. The new nation's first
best-seller, Filson's romantic treatment of Kentucky's natural history
mingled Thomas Burnet's view of the landscape as a Gothic ruin with
allusions to William Hunter's image of the American *incognitum* as a ferocious carnivore.

Before the hostilities had formally ended, the etiquette of war allowed General George Washington to help an enemy officer, Dr. Christian Friedrich Michaelis, excavate bones at Rev. Annan's farm while
negotiations of the peace treaty took place in Paris. Frustrated in his efforts at this site, Dr. Michaelis, physician-general to the Hessian mer-

cenaries employed by the British, then hired Charles Willson Peale, Philadelphia's foremost portrait painter and patriotic artist, to make drawings of the bones from the Ohio valley. Late in his illustrious life, Peale attributed the founding of his own natural history museum in Philadelphia to the public interest sparked by the presence of these bones in his studio.

Finally, as the search for the bones became a national quest after the war's end, Jefferson, the new American ambassador in Paris, began a correspondence about the American *incognitum* with Ezra Stiles, the president of Yale College. Jefferson convinced Stiles that the bones did not belong to human giants, and in a few years, the carnivore envisioned by Dr. William Hunter truly began to resemble a prehistoric monster as the "Doctrine of Monsters" was reborn in a new form in the eyes of the founding fathers and the citizens of the new republic.

The American *incognitum* entered the museum world before the war ended, when Pierre Eugène Du Simitière, the Swiss collector of curiosities living in Philadelphia, began to solicit information about the new discoveries at Rev. Annan's farm. Denied official status as historiographer of the American Revolution by the Continental Congress, Du Simitière continued to collect natural history specimens throughout the conflict, receiving gifts from both leading revolutionary figures and enemy officers. The rapid growth of his collection was spurred by the publicity surrounding his petition for funding from the Continental Congress which occasioned visits by delegates to view his private collections.

The Congress's rejection of his petition in the summer of 1780 dealt a devastating blow to Du Simitière's hopes for official patronage, and in the wake of this setback, he catered increasingly to visiting foreign dignitaries, many of them European aristocrats serving with the military on both sides of the conflict. In early December, shortly before he visited General Washington at New Windsor, the marquis de Chastellux, a French officer and friend of Buffon, visited Du Simitière, noting in his journal that his cabinet of curiosities "was rather small and rather paltry [but] very renowned in America because it has no rival there."[1]

The walls of Du Simitière's painting rooms were decorated with frames of butterflies and shelves full of glass jars containing snakes and other creatures preserved in spirits. His collections of coins and medals were displayed in cabinets amid the Native American headdresses, arms, and artifacts. Compared with the lavish cabinets of European roy-alty and the French aristocracy, Du Simitière's collection of curiosities appeared meager, but to many citizens of the new republic, the cabinet was a great achievement. In 1781, the College of New Jersey [now Princeton] awarded Du Simitière an honorary degree of master of arts, which deeply touched the Swiss émigré, who had no formal university education. Burdened by mounting debts, this formal recognition of his achievements encouraged him to open his collections to the public. The surrender of Lord Cornwallis at Yorktown in the early fall of 1781 made this decision logical, since the outcome of the war then was no longer in doubt. Six months later, Du Simitière announced the open-ing of his "American Museum," located in his house on Arch Street. "For the first time in American history," notes historian Joel J. Orosz, "a private cabinet had been transformed into a public museum."[2]

In June 1782, while formal peace negotiations were still in progress at Paris, Du Simitière boldly advertised his "American Mu-seum" in a series of small notices in newspapers. His announcement was addressed to "Gentlemen and Ladies" and "Strangers in this City," and his restricted hours of admittance and admission fee of "Half A Dollar" limited his audience largely to the educated gentry rather than Philadelphia's numerous artisan classes. He further re-stricted tours of the museum, open only four days a week, to small groups of eight persons, who were shepherded through the collec-tions in about one hour. Du Simitière's fossil collection was com-posed mainly of the ores of various metals; unusual mineral sub-stances like onyx, crystal, quartz, and rare figured stones; petrifac-tions including shells, sea eggs, sea worms, and shark's teeth; and an assortment of reptiles, insects, and petrified plant life.

Through his extensive network of contributors, Du Simitière learned of the discovery of the enormous bones at Rev. Annan's farm during the war, and his efforts to acquire them began nearly six months before his museum was opened to the public. In October 1781, while the siege of Yorktown was still under way in the Chesapeake region south of Philadelphia, Du Simitière wrote to William Deming, who lived near New Windsor where the fossil remains had been found:

> As you are well acquainted with the nature of my pursuits in what re-lates to the history of North America and have Seen my collections of natural and artificial curiosities, I hope and flatter myself that you

will oblige me in procuring the answers from some intelligent observer to the inclosed Queries.[3]

Du Simitière wanted a detailed account of the discovery of the bones, such as how they were discovered and the disposition of the bones at the site, as well as information about "what sort of animal are they supposed to have once belonged."

Although his personal fortunes continued to decline after the opening of his American Museum, Du Simitière continued to pursue the American *incognitum*, writing to another correspondent in New York the following summer asking for help in acquiring information about the bones. After further correspondence with acquaintances around New Windsor, he finally received a shipment of bones from Rev. Annan in the spring of 1783. His reply to Rev. Annan was delayed, however, by the amputation of the first joint of one of his fingers, which caused him extreme physical pain and added to his financial troubles. But on May 28, 1783, he wrote to Annan thanking him for a grinder, a kneecap, and a fragment of ironstone with impressions of bivalve shells.

In January 1783, Britain, France, and Spain signed the preliminary peace treaty agreed to by the British and American peace commissioners in Paris. General Washington set April 19, 1783, the anniversary of the battles of Lexington and Concord, as the official date for the end of hostilities, although his triumphant entry into New York did not take place until November 25, after the British evacuation of the city. Between these events, Du Simitière struggled to keep his museum afloat, moving to a larger house on Arch Street to accommodate his expanding collection. His continued reliance on foreign visitors, especially aristocratic military figures, was evident in his extravagant description of Philadelphia at the war's end as "the Paris and Hague of America, where the brilliancy of our *beau monde* and the sumptuosity and elegancy of their entertainments rivals those of the old world."[4]

In late July, a German physician named Johann David Schoepf arrived at Du Simitière's doorstep with high praise for his small collection, which he claimed contained "a not inconsiderable number of well-executed drawings of American birds, plants and insects." A surgeon who had served with the allied troops from Anspach, Schoepf was typical of the well-educated, scientifically minded "Strangers" on whom the Swiss collector depended for his livelihood. By then, Du Simitière was already complaining about the insufficient ticket sales that were compounding his financial difficulties. "It is to be regretted that his activities, and his enthusiasm for collecting, should be embarrassed by domestic circumstances, and that he should fail of positive encouragement from the American publick," Schoepf observed.[5] In fact, the lagging attendance at Du Simitière's American Museum was due largely to the self-imposed exclusiveness of his clientele, dictated by his own preference for polite society and dependence on cosmopolitan European visitors.

In Pittsburgh during his travels, Schoepf had seen a thighbone, a tusk, and a molar that an American artillery officer had brought from the Ohio salt lick. "The molar-tooth, which I received as a gift, weighed six full pounds, and its crown was armed with three high, wedge-shaped apophyses," Schoepf later wrote.[6] Having seen similar specimens elsewhere in his travels, including those from Rev. Annan's farm on display at Du Simitière's museum, Schoepf noted in his journal the many new discovery sites, from the Tar River in North Carolina to the marshlands of Hudson River valley: "It has only recently become known that these places on the Ohio are not the only ones in North America where remains of this sort are to be found."[7] Previously, the bones had been hard to obtain, owing to the remoteness of the Ohio valley salt licks, "but Kentucky now becoming more settled, there are better hopes of soon securing an exact knowledge of these remarkable accumulations of bones."[8] For the time being, the greatest store of these fossils from Ohio, as Schoepf pointed out, was the collection owned by Dr. John Morgan in Philadelphia.

Du Simitière himself continued to pursue the unknown creature whose bones were gaining stature among connoisseurs of curiosities in Philadelphia with the new discoveries at Rev. Annan's farm and elsewhere. In August, Du Simitière wrote to Captain Stephen Adye of the Royal British Artillery, an old friend from the days of Philadelphia's occupation who was now stationed in New York. His letter was undoubtedly occasioned by his continuing quest for further information about the discovery of large animal bones in North America:

> [I have] for Several years past collected every information that I could procure respecting that uncommon natural production and have transcribed out of every author what they have wrote in professo or accidentally on that Subject, from the time of the first discovery of these skeletons by the baron de Longeuil to the present day. I have

also by me the drawings I have made of some of the most interesting pieces of them but whether I shall ever be able to publish my memoirs on that other Subject from my present Situation is very doubtful and uncertain.[9]

Du Simitière's acquisition of the bones from Rev. Annan's farm coincided with the arrival in Philadelphia of Dr. Christian Friedrich Michaelis, fresh from his own attempts to excavate bones at Rev. Annan's farm. Stationed in New York during the hostilities, the doctor had become acquainted with several local physicians from whom he very likely heard early reports about the bones discovered in the Hudson River valley. Through his American friends, Dr. Michaelis traveled up the Hudson River to General Washington's headquarters at Newburgh, where he sought the general's assistance in excavating bones from Annan's marl pits.

With the American victory in the Revolutionary War, Washington had moved his headquarters in 1782 to the Hasbrouck House, on a bluff overlooking the Hudson River at Newburgh, about fifteen miles east of Rev. Annan's farm. Dr. Michaelis was received with due courtesy by General Washington, who provided a dozen men with tools and wagons to help dig for the bones. Unfortunately, Dr. Michaelis's efforts were frustrated by heavy rains that flooded the excavation, forcing him to return to New York empty-handed, except for a few previously excavated specimens donated by Rev. Annan.

Undeterred by his misfortunes, Dr. Michaelis traveled to Philadelphia intent on going to Ohio country to obtain bones of the American *incognitum*. During his stay in New York, he had sent reports of his own medical experiments to a scientific journal at Göttingen, where his father, Johann David Michaelis, was a famous Orientalist. The elder Michaelis, who had met Benjamin Franklin on his tour of the Continent in 1767, was among a group of European scholars deeply interested in the fossil elephants in America, and he had urged his son to bring back some bones from the Ohio valley. In Philadelphia, Dr. Michaelis met George Morgan and Thomas Hutchins, two veterans of George Croghan's trip to Ohio country in 1766, who gave him detailed instructions for finding the bones there, including a map of Big Bone Lick drawn by Hutchins himself.

When reports of Indian attacks curtailed his travel plans, Dr. Michaelis decided to examine Dr. John Morgan's collection of bones from the renowned Kentucky salt lick. To his dismay, he found the precious bones lying in a box still caked with mud, more than seventeen years after their discovery. Although he was unable to buy Morgan's impressive collection, he did have the bones cleaned and obtained permission from their owner to have anatomical drawings made of them. For this purpose, he hired Charles Willson Peale, Philadelphia's leading portrait painter, who made between thirty and forty full-scale renderings of the specimens, each from several different views (figure 24). Du Simitière's friend Johann David Schoepf mentioned having seen Peale's specimens in the painter's studio: "I saw a collection of great bones brought from the Ohio, which Mr. Peale was just then painting, natural size, for Counsellor Michaelis."[10]

Among the other "Large Fossil Bones" listed in Du Simitière's *Memoranda Book* were several fossils found near Yorktown, Pennsylvania, and his copy of a letter to Thomas Jefferson describing some large bones found the previous year in "North Holstein" in western Virginia. Near the war's end, Jefferson received a large jaw tooth of an unknown animal sent by Arthur Campbell, whose father had been among the earliest Scotch-Irish settlers on the North Holston River. The bone had been found by workmen digging trenches to reach salt veins or springs in a dried-up marshland near the river. "In sinking one of these Pits, several feet under the surface was found Bones of an uncommon size, of which the Jaw Tooth now offered you is one," Major Campbell wrote to Jefferson.[11]

Traveling to Richmond with his gift for Jefferson, Major Campbell showed the giant tooth to Colonel William Preston, a veteran Virginia surveyor and militia officer who had settled at Draper's Meadows shortly before the Revolutionary War, after a long career in land speculation on the frontier. Thirty years earlier he had obtained a similar tooth from the Ohio salt lick which had been sent to the Royal Society in England. Evidently the Virginians were familiar with the opinions of London anatomists, for according to a subsequent letter from Campbell, Dr. Arthur Lee, a Virginian who had studied medicine at Edinburgh and settled in London, was present at the meeting of the Royal Society when Dr. William Hunter presented his famous paper on the Ohio bones, demonstrating "that the species was of the carnivorous kind."[12]

These remarkable letters to Jefferson concerning the jaw tooth from North Holston show the wide range of discussion being generated

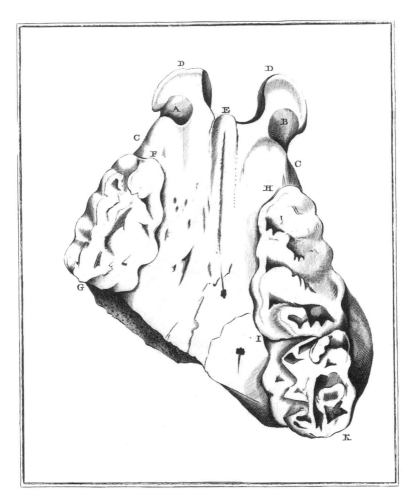

FIGURE 24. Charles Willson Peale's drawing of a jawbone from the Ohio valley salt lick in the collection of Dr. John Morgan, 1783. This drawing was later reproduced by the Dutch anatomist Petrus Camper in an article maintaining that the American *incognitum* had neither tusks nor trunk. Courtesy of Bancroft Library, University of California at Berkeley.

by the bones during the last years of the Revolutionary War. Even the opinions of African slaves on the specimens were reported by Major Campbell: "Several sensible Africans have seen the tooth, particularly a fellow at your neighbour Colo[nel] Lewises, all of whom pronounced it an Elephants."[13] Fifty years earlier, the English naturalist Mark

Catesby had reported similar opinions among African slaves in South Carolina concerning such fossils.

Major Campbell's letter also provided the factual basis for one of the most important passages in Jefferson's *Notes*, the account of a settler captured in this region who was transported west of the Missouri River, where he heard stories from the Indians about living "Elephants" in the West:

> A certain Mr. Stanley was captivated by the Indians, some years ago, near the mouth of the Cherokee River on his way to the Mississippi. I have been told by different persons that since his return, he relates, that after being transferred from one Tribe to another, he was at length carried over Mountains west of the Missouri, to a River that runs Westwardly; that the natives told him there were animals in the Country which from the description he judges to be Elephants.

In his *Notes*, Jefferson used this anecdote to corroborate his own belief that the American *incognitum* might still be found roaming the unexplored northwest territories.

Du Simitière's copy of the letter to Jefferson was very likely the source of the Swiss collector's own dreams of traveling west of the Mississippi to the Missouri in search of the American *incognitum*. In December 1783, he had taken Jefferson's eleven-year-old daughter Martha as a drawing pupil while Jefferson was serving as a delegate to the Continental Congress. These contacts with Jefferson may have given Du Simitière an opportunity to obtain a copy of the letter about the large fossils recently discovered in the western territories.

In January 1784, Du Simitière wrote to Isaac Melcher thanking him for the gift of six empty bottles and remarked about his anticipated trip to the West: "Whether you sent [them] for my intended Journey to the West of the Mississippi, up the Missouri to view the enormous quadrupeds who are said to be still existing there I can no[t] say."[14] Unfortunately, illness and poverty cut short his ambitious plans. Nine months later, his health ruined by adversity, Du Simitière died in Philadelphia at age forty-seven, and the following spring the contents of his collection were auctioned off to the highest bidders.

Jefferson was polishing the manuscript of his *Notes* and had recently submitted copies of his rebuttal to Buffon to his friend Thomas Walker, one of the first Virginians to explore Kentucky: "That part particularly which relates to the positions of Monsr. de Buffon, I would wish to have very correct in matters of fact."[15] Some of the columns in Jefferson's table comparing the American quadrupeds with those of Europe were still blank, so he asked Walker to give him "the heaviest weights of our animals . . . from the mouse to the mammoth as far as you have known them actually weighed." In October, he received a long letter from his friend Colonel Archibald Cary, a prominent Virginia legislator, enumerating the weights of many animals, including a bear weighing 410 pounds.[16] Jefferson's presence among the delegates to the Continental Congress, with the completed manuscript of his *Notes* and the recently acquired jaw tooth of the great beast, contributed to the greater awareness of the mysterious bones at the war's end.

In the summer of 1783, Charles Willson Peale had begun drawing the enormous bones at Dr. John Morgan's house, but he later moved the specimens to his painting studio where they remained after Dr. Michaelis departed in the late summer with the completed drawings. The level of excitement generated by the bones of the *incognitum* was made manifest the following summer by Peale's brother-in-law Colonel Nathaniel Ramsay, who saw the specimens still lying in the corner of the painter's studio: "[I] would have gone 20 miles to behold such a collection. Doubtless, there are many men like myself who would prefer seeing such articles of curiosity than any paintings whatever," Peale recalled him exclaiming.[17] Peale later attributed the impetus for the foundation of his own "American museum" to this remark by his brother-in-law in the early summer of 1784, although his museum did not open for two more years, after Du Simitière's death and the public auction of his collection of curiosities.

In early 1783, Thomas Jefferson wrote once again to George Rogers Clark in Kentucky, reminding him to send bones from the Ohio salt lick east. Governor Benjamin Harrison of Virginia had sent Colonel William Fleming to the Ohio valley to check into Clark's expenditures for the western military campaigns and to report on his personal conduct. Not surprisingly, the governor's emissary ended up gathering fossils with Clark despite the severe winter weather: "Set out in the morning dry cloudy, cold, snowing and Threatening a Storm, crossed the Salt River and Chaplains Fork, came on Simpsons run where at a spring branch, Genl. Clark collected some petrified Cockles," the colonel later wrote in his journal. "Those I got were the sea cockle, some wholy petrified, others half petrified."[18] His comments reveal how widely knowledge of these curiosities had spread among both the educated gentry and the frontier soldiers: "They seemed either to be real Antediluvians, or to have lain there since that part of this country was possessed by the sea, as these were real marine shells."

Several days later, Clark and Fleming rode down to the lower end of the falls of the Ohio River, where they collected "Buffalo dung turned to perfect stone [and] goose dung turn'd to Stone," along with the petrified roots of trees and a Buffalo horn. In his journal, Colonel Fleming described the rock formations at the falls, noting the striations in the flat rocks covering the river bottom where the petrifications had been found. The dim outlines of prehistoric nature and geological consciousness were thus beginning to emerge from these rocks and fossils, even on the Kentucky frontier. Several months later, General Clark sent several of the petrified cockleshells to Jefferson, with apologies for not having been able to reach Big Bone Lick, owing to the presence of hostile Indians. By then, the salt lick had been picked clean of bones. General Clark had visited the site the previous fall with a hunting party without being able to dig up any new specimens from the frozen ground. "The mud and banks [that] those bones lay in was so frozen that it was impossible they could get them[,] having nothing to dig with but their small Tomahawks[,] all those lying on the surface being formerly carried off," he wrote to Jefferson.[19]

Before the final peace treaty was signed, the land rush to Kentucky resumed as settlers from Pennsylvania and Virginia crossed the Alleghenies searching for choice bottomland in the Ohio valley. After the surrender of Cornwallis at Yorktown, General Clark launched a military campaign against the Shawnee settlements north of Big Bone Lick, opening the way for acquisition of the Northwest Territory by the United States in the treaty concluded in Paris. Daniel Boone's adventures on the Kentucky frontier took place during the Revolutionary War when he was a militia captain fighting Indians allied with the British. Born into a Quaker family in Pennsylvania, Boone's father was a farmer and blacksmith who had migrated to North Carolina in 1750, when his son Daniel was twelve years old. In 1755, at age seventeen, as a teamster and blacksmith, the young Boone accompanied General Braddock's ill-fated campaign during the French and Indian Wars, narrowly escaping on one of his horses from the disastrous defeat near Fort Duquesne.

In this campaign, Boone met John Finley, a Virginia hunter who piqued his interest in Kentucky with stories of his own exploits there before the war. In 1767, after marrying, Boone set out for the Kentucky wilderness, where he again encountered Finley, now an itinerant Indian trader wandering the territory with his wares. Two years later, as agents of the Transylvania Company, the two men led a party through the Cumberland Gap into Kentucky to locate sites for a permanent settlement, which they finally established at Boonesborough in 1775, on the eve of the Revolutionary War. Throughout the war, while engaged in surveying and Indian fighting, Boone continued his efforts to acquire land titles in Kentucky, making several trips to Virginia to purchase land warrants for himself and the settlers at Boonesborough. In December 1781, when returning from one of his trips to Virginia, he carried a letter from Thomas Jefferson to George Rogers Clark requesting bones from the Ohio salt lick, located north of the town of Lexington, the principal settlement of Fayette County.

Toward the end of the war, a young Pennsylvania schoolteacher named John Filson, who later became Boone's first and most famous chronicler, suddenly left his classroom for Kentucky to seek his own fortunes on the frontier. Filson's biographer John Walton characterized him as a melancholic figure, a self-conscious poseur filled with "necrophilic Gothicism" from reading *Admonitions from the Dead in Epistles to the Living,* a collection of letters from the grave "steeped in the romantic spirit of the last eighteenth century."[20] From a family of Scotch-Irish settlers who had come to Pennsylvania in the early eighteenth century, Filson's melancholy outlook stemmed at least partly from his childhood. As a young boy he learned a little Latin, Greek, and French and read widely in Romantic literature while growing up in southeast Pennsylvania, where his father had inherited a two-hundred-acre farm and accumulated a respectable estate before the outbreak of the Revolutionary War. The Scotch-Irish immigrants in the Brandywine Valley in Chester County were New-Side Presbyterians, supporters of revivalism and resentful not only of British colonial policy in America but of Ireland as well.

As a child, Filson attended school in Maryland at the West Nottingham Academy, founded by Rev. Samuel Finley, later president of the College of New Jersey, the seat of Presbyterian liberalism in America. Filson's Gothic literary taste probably made him seem quite learned, if not foreign, to the farm boys around Chester, who may have been his first students. Before departing for Kentucky, he taught school

briefly in nearby Wilmington, where he probably acquired a thin ve-
neer of refinement that added to his naïve romanticism. In the course
of his own studies, he also acquired a rudimentary knowledge of surveying, which was often taught as part of natural philosophy, as it involved geometry and mathematics.

By late 1783, thanks to General Clark's brutal campaigns against
the Shawnees, the Indian Wars had subsided, and the formal end to
hostilities with the British in September unleashed a new wave of migration to Kentucky. No record of military service has been found for
Filson, but according to his biographers, his coming to Kentucky may
have been to take up land on certain Virginia military warrants that
had come into his possession. After surveying on the Ohio River from
Pittsburgh to the falls, Filson formally filed in December 1783 claims for
several large parcels of land, including five thousand acres about ten
miles east of Big Bone Lick.

In the next months while preparing a book promoting land sales
and settlement on the Kentucky frontier, Filson traveled around the
area gathering information from prominent pioneer settlers, including
Daniel Boone, Levi Todd, and John Harrod. For his book, he drew the
first detailed map of Kentucky, with Lexington at its center, which
clearly designated the Ohio salt lick to the north as "Large Bones are
found here" (figure 25). In the spring of 1784, Filson succeeded in getting Boone, Todd, and Harrod to endorse his completed manuscript. In
the early summer, he returned to Wilmington where his book, *The Discovery, Settlement and present State of Kentucke,"* a thin volume of only
118 pages, was published in an edition of fifteen hundred copies.

The publication of Filson's book marked a milestone in the developing mythology of the American *incognitum* since the Ohio salt lick
was featured among the region's landmarks. In addition to an essay on
the area's geography and resources, the book contains an account of the
Indians, a table of distances, and, most notably, the first biography of
Daniel Boone. In Filson's florid prose, Boone emerges as the prototype
for later stories of American frontier heroes, from James Fenimore
Cooper's *Leatherstocking Tales* to Davey Crockett.

The book's structure bears a striking resemblance to Jefferson's
Notes, with which Filson was apparently familiar, even though Jefferson's work was still only a manuscript being circulated among his close
friends. However, Filson's pedantic and melodramatic prose contrast
sharply with Jefferson's erudition and polished style. His naïveté lends

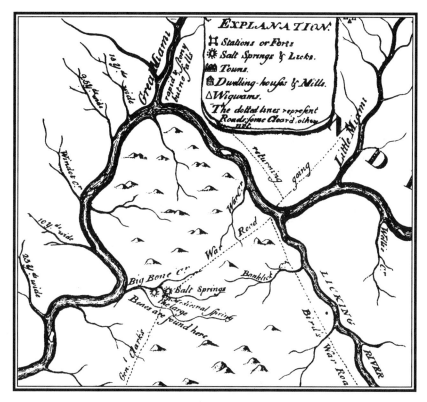

FIGURE 25. Detail from John Filson's map of Kentucky, 1784. The famous Ohio valley salt lick is identified by the words "the large Bones are found here," an echo of the term first used by the French geographer Bellin a generation earlier.

a folkloric aspect to the imagistic prose and the drama of his story, which overshadow his stilted allusions to scholarly speculations about the American *incognitum*, from Dr. William Hunter's theory of extinction to Thomas Burnet's Gothic view of the landscape.

Styled as a "Compleat Guide" for travelers to Kentucky, Filson's description of the region's natural history includes a lengthy section on "Curiosities," ranging from the area's impressive limestone precipices and subterranean lakes to the Indian burial grounds near Lexington full of human skeletons. From the Indian graves he turned to Big Bone Lick, the burial site of the American *incognitum*: "The amazing herds of Buffalos which resort thither, by their size and number, fill the traveler with amazement and terror, especially when he beholds the prodigious roads they have made from all quarters, as if leading to some populous city."[21] In a rather melodramatic manner, Filson summarizes the main ideas being debated by the European naturalists, highlighting the unknown creature's status as a nondescript animal: "What animal this is, and by what means its ruins are found in regions so widely different, is a question of more difficult decision." With a sense of awe, he conveyed to his readers fragments of the scholarly debate on the "Elephants" in America: "These bones have equally excited the amazement of the ignorant, and attracted the attention of the philosopher."[22]

According to Filson, the learned London anatomists had rejected the fabulous tales of Siberian tribesmen while puzzling over the resemblance of the tusks to those of living elephants, but the disappearance of the species raised unsettling questions about the animal's identity. Filson repeats the opinions of Dr. William Hunter regarding the diet of American monster:

> He observed from the form of the teeth, that they must have belonged to a carnivorous animal; whereas the habits of the elephant are foreign to such sustenance, and his jaws totally unprovided with the teeth necessary for its use. And from the whole he concluded to the satisfaction of naturalists, that these bones belonged to a quadruped now unknown, and whose race is probably extinct, unless it may be found in the extensive continent of New Holland, whose recesses have not yet been pervaded by the curiosity or avidity of civilized man.[23]

Filson's Romantic treatment of the American *incognitum* set the tone for its depiction decades later as a ferocious beast, for he was one of the first American authors to amplify Hunter's celebration of the animal's extinction as a triumph over savage nature: "Can so great a link have perished from the chain of nature? Happy we that it has. How formidable an enemy to the human species, an animal as large as the elephant, the tyrant of the forests, perhaps the devourer of man!"[24] In keeping with Indian legends about the beast, Filson imagined its extermination to have been the work of tribes united against its threat to their existence. "To such circumstance we are probably indebted for a fact, which is perhaps singular in its kind, the extinction of a whole race of animals from the system of nature."[25]

The lasting significance of Filson's book was the influence of his tale of Daniel Boone's adventures on the creation of the prototypical hero of the American frontier. His Boone narrative, which occupies more than a quarter of the text, is supposedly the words of the Kentucky pioneer himself, although Filson attributes to him classical allusions clearly drawn from his own fragmentary knowledge of scholarly articles and Romantic literature: "We had passed through a great forest, on which stood myriads of trees, some gay with blossoms, others rich with fruits. Nature was here a series of wonders and a fund of delight."[26]

The strength of Filson's writing lies in its imagistic prose and dramatic action, not in its intellectual pretense. His story combines key elements of the Puritan literary tradition, from the personal testimonial to the captivity narrative, creating a new mythical hero of the American wilderness whose character is fashioned out of natural history, religious doctrine, Indian legends, and the rhetoric of Romanticism. "Filson revolutionizes the Puritan forms by substituting nature or the wilderness for Jehovah as his symbol of deity," historian Richard Slotkin observes in his study of the mythology of the American frontier, *Regeneration through Violence*.[27]

This substitution of natural history for the new nation's antiquity was achieved through a fusion of the evangelical tradition, which saw the conquest of nature as ordained by God, with the Enlightenment belief in the progress of nations from savagery to civilization—that is to industry, commerce, and Christianity. "In the eyes of Filson's Boone," Slotkin points out, "the beauty of wild nature lies in the extent to which it imitates cultivated nature and implies that civilization is itself the crown of natural evolution."[28] In Filson's complex symbolism, his frontier hero introduces new images of the wilderness and the Indians as sources of American identity while celebrating at the same time the inevitability of their violent conquest. In many respects, this new mythology of the frontier enshrined the violence and savagery of wild nature as basic realities of American cultural life, something that helped the citizens of the new nation define the meaning of the American *incognitum* in the coming decades.

Literary historians like Richard Slotkin have emphasized the sympathy for Indian life that Filson's Boone story introduced into the captivity narrative and American consciousness. The ambiguities of Boone's love of the wilderness, however, were revealed by the American poet William Carlos Williams, whose essay on the frontier hero in his anthology *In the American Grain* inspired the title of Slotkin's book, *Regeneration through Violence*. According to Williams,

> With the sense of an Indian, Boone felt the wild beasts about him as a natural offering. Like a savage he knew for such as he their destined lives were intended. As an Indian to the wild, without stint or tremor, he offered himself with a great appetite, taking the lives of the beasts into his quiet murderous hands as they or their masters, the savages, might take his own, if they were able, without kindling his resentment.[29]

The basic premise in the Boone myth is the wildness of the natural world, including the Indians, who come to symbolize in the frontier hero's eyes his own individuality and the authentic cultural values of the conquerors of the New World.

For Filson's Boone, Kentucky was still a "howling wilderness" inhabited by "savages" that only lately had become the site of civilized settlement. The howling wolves that haunted Buffon's wild nature were never out of earshot, nor were the Indians' horrible war cries. In the end, no matter how noble the savage, this implacable belief in the violence of wild nature was the common ground of American culture, shaping both the view of the wilderness and prehistoric nature.

The immense popularity of Filson's Daniel Boone narrative stemmed largely from the way he romanticized the wilderness hero, but the setting for his adventures includes many elements of the Gothic landscape that had become so much a part of the natural history genre since the days of Thomas Burnet's sacred theory. The Boone narrative itself contains a few artistic conventions clearly indicating that the author's literary style was influenced by the emerging Romantic sensibility inspired by Burnet's view of the landscape as a ruin itself. Entering Cumberland Gap with his band of settlers, Filson's Boone evokes an exotic metaphor drawn from the author's own reverence for the classical ruins of antiquity:

> The aspect of these cliffs is so wild and horrid, that it is impossible to behold them without terror. The spectator is apt to imagine that nature had formerly suffered some violent convulsion; and that these are the dismembered remains of the dreadful shock; the ruins, not of Persepolis or Palmyra, but of the world![30] (figure 26)

FIGURE 26. Nineteenth-century engraving of the Cumberland Gap showing the rocky prominences described by John Filson as a Gothic landscape in romantic language reminiscent of Thomas Burnet's view of the earth as a natural ruins. Cumberland Gap print by D. Appleton & Co., New York, 1872, Filson Club Historical Society, Louisville, Kentucky.

The echo of Burnet's ruined landscape in Kentucky might seem an artless literary convention in Filson's hands, but a similar view of the American landscape appeared almost simultaneously in the polished prose of Jefferson's *Notes*. Viewing the Potomac River water gap in the Blue Ridge Mountains, Jefferson refers to the same terror and awe:

> The first glance of this scene hurries our senses into the opinion, that this earth has been created in time, that the mountains were formed first, that the rivers began to flow afterwards, that in this place particularly they have been dammed up by the Blue ridge of mountains, and have formed an ocean which filled the whole valley; that continuing to rise they have at length broken over at this spot, and have torn the mountain down from its summit to its base.[31]

In this lyrical view of the landscape, Jefferson's geological consciousness gives rise to an aesthetic feeling normally associated with Romanticism:

> For the mountain being cloven asunder, she presents to your eye, through the cleft, a small patch of smooth blue horizon, at an infinite distance in the plain country, inviting you, as it were, from the riot and tumult roaring around, to pass through the breach and participate in the calm below.[32]

Indeed, the apocalyptic spirit of Burnet's natural history of the earth is the source of such Romantic images of the American landscape. In John Filson's *Kentucke*, a landscape full of fossils and Indian bones, the unacceptable ancient history of the New World's original inhabitants is replaced by the ruins of nature's antiquity.

Shortly before Filson's *Kentucke* was published in Philadelphia, Thomas Jefferson was appointed by the Continental Congress as minister plenipotentiary to France, where he was to join Benjamin Franklin and John Adams in negotiating commercial treaties with European nations. The prospect of traveling to Paris pleased Jefferson, especially since it would give him an opportunity to meet the French naturalist Buffon, for whom he had prepared a sophisticated rebuttal in his unpublished *Notes*.

While a delegate to the Congress, Jefferson had looked into having his manuscript published in Philadelphia, but the costs were prohibitive, so he decided instead to have it published in Paris. Throughout the winter, he continued to revise the manuscript, soliciting information from correspondents about American quadrupeds in order to strengthen the facts in his refutation of Buffon's theory of American degeneracy. In June 1784, when Jefferson set out by stagecoach from Philadelphia to Boston with his young daughter and servant to meet the ship for France, he carried with him the revised manuscript, which had already tripled in size in the last three years.

En route from Virginia to Boston where he sailed for Paris, Jefferson stopped briefly in New Haven to visit with Ezra Stiles, the president of Yale College, with a letter of introduction from Roger Sherman, the Connecticut delegate to the Continental Congress. An ardent antiquarian with a strong taste for scientific inquiry, the Congregational minister at Yale had established a reputation for being the most learned

PRESIDENT STILES Ætat.59. 1786.

FIGURE 27. Pencil sketch of Ezra Stiles, age fifty-nine, by St. John Honeywood, 1786. In this year, after correspondence with Thomas Jefferson, Stiles abandoned his belief that the bones from Claverack belonged to human giants. Courtesy of Beineke Library, Yale University.

man in New England (figure 27). He was a classical and biblical scholar who gave speeches in Latin and studied Hebrew and Arabic, but whose pursuit of scientific knowledge included raising silkworms, experimenting with electricity, and corresponding with Benjamin Franklin.

In a display of admiration that revealed the shared sensibility of the

Calvinist and the Deist, Stiles wrote in his diary that Jefferson was "a truly scientific and learned Man." After visiting the college library to see the electrical apparatus donated by Benjamin Franklin in 1749, Jefferson described the simple new electrical machine left by a British officer in Philadelphia.[33] During the visit the conversation apparently turned briefly to their mutual interest in the bones of the American *incognitum:* "Gov. Jefferson has seen many of the great Bones dug up on the Ohio," Stiles noted in his diary. "He has a thigh-bone *Three Feet long*—& a Tooth weighing *sixteen Pounds*."[34]

Stories of the Hudson River bones were legendary in this old New England family, for Stiles's mother had been Edward Taylor's daughter, and her brother Eldad had heard tales about the giant of Claverack when he was a young boy: "Uncle Eldad adds about the Giant," Stiles wrote in 1760, "that he remembers hearing his Father [Edward Taylor] conversing about it with the Dutchmen, and that the Tradition among the Indians was that the Giant 'was peaceable and would not hurt the little Indians.'"[35] In June 1750, at age twenty-three while working as a tutor at Yale, Stiles himself had examined a giant tooth weighing four pounds brought to New Haven by a gentleman delivering the specimen to England. His interest aroused by the huge tooth, he subsequently discovered Edward Taylor's unfinished "Epic Poem" on the monster of Claverack among the four hundred pages of his grandfather's unpublished manuscripts. In 1760, he extracted from his grandfather's diary Taylor's account of the first article from the *Boston News-Letter* and the visit of a Dutchman named Koon in 1706.[36]

Even though Stiles had faithfully followed the scholarly debate about the discovery of mysterious bones, including reports about fossil remains found in a cave in Austria and tusks from Siberia and Sumatra, he still agreed with his grandfather that the remains from Claverack were those of human giants. When Colonel David Humphreys came to visit several years later, with his firsthand account of General Washington's sleigh ride to Annan's farm, Stiles had been far more insistent that the bones belonged to human giants: "They all take these Bones to belong to Quadrupeds. I suppose them to be human—like the Bones & Teeth at Clavarack."[37]

During his visit to Yale College, Jefferson was apparently unaware of his host's extensive knowledge of the American *incognitum.* But two days later, after being informed of Stiles's expertise, Jefferson wrote to him from Hartford requesting "whatever facts you may have become acquainted with as to this animal."[38] Since Jefferson was still revising the manuscript for his *Notes*, he referred to his efforts to fortify his own rebuttal to Buffon's theory which was, as he informed Stiles, so degrading to America. "Having therefore on a particular occasion drawn his opinion into question I am still anxious of getting every additional information on the subject which may serve either to confirm or to correct the conclusion that I had formed." Jefferson offered Stiles a few details about the recent discovery of fossil remains in the "Salines of North Holston," near the Tennessee River, the southernmost site yet reported. "I understand from different quarters that the Indians beleive [*sic*] this animal still existing in the North and North West tho' none of them pretend ever to have seen one," he added, revealing again his own reliance on Indian testimony to confirm his belief the animal was not extinct.

Three days after receiving Jefferson's letter, Stiles answered with a remarkably detailed letter giving Jefferson a history of his own investigation. Then he stated in no uncertain terms his belief that the bones were those of human giants:

> I will hazard my Reputation with you, Sir, and give it as my opinion that the huge fossil Bones, Teeth and parts of Skeletons dug up in Siberia, in Germany, France and other parts of Europe, and finally those on the Ohio and elsewhere in America, appertain, *not to Quadrupeds, not to Sea-Animals, but to Bipeds* of huge and immense Stature.[39]

For Jefferson's benefit, Stiles reviewed the reasoning and evidence that had led him to embrace what he called the "Doctrine of Monsters." He began with a summary of his grandfather Edward Taylor's testimony, whom he described affectionately as "a physician, and very Learned in Chemistry and Natural History, and of vast reading, of nice and curious Observation, tho' very much a Recluse from the World." Having read Taylor's verses about the giant of Claverack to his friends, Stiles was well aware they contained "such wonderful Facts and Speculations as would seem to indicate credulity and Imagination." "Yet this was not his Reputation, which was that he was a grave, solid, judicious learned old man."

Like his grandfather before him, Stiles attempted to use scientific evidence to confirm the existence of giants mentioned in various

historical accounts, from the anomalies of nature reported in the Scriptures and by the Roman author Ovid to the stories of the medieval giants slain by Scandinavian heroes in Norwegian chronicles. "What
struck me first, was an instant Conviction about 24 years ago, that there
was in these ages *no Animal on Earth or in the Ocean* of the Magnitude
adequate to these Bones and Teeth." Stiles also was familiar with the
numerous scholarly articles on the matter published by the Royal Society, including Francis Nevile's account of the bones and teeth dug up in
Ireland and Thomas Molyneux's analysis of them. Curiously, he did not
refer to Dr. William Hunter's article, which established that the American *incognitum* was not an elephant but, rather, an unknown creature,
probably extinct.

Throughout his letter, the measurement of the bones was the bal-
last that kept Stiles's argument from capsizing in a sea of speculation. It
added weight to an argument influenced by classical chronicles and
Protestant beliefs, doctrines that reflected the durability of Noah's Ark
and the Flood as vehicles for scientific ideas: "The Flood might bring
Elephants, or the Monoceros, to Ireland, Saxony, the Ohio, or Siberia,
as well as carry inland Shells and other Marine fossils dug in the Appalachian Mountains and other parts of Continents," Stiles wrote in
language reminiscent of John Woodward's *Natural History of the Earth*.
"But the Question is whether any animal of the terraqueous Globe now
exists with Teeth and Bones of these Magnitudes: If not we must go into
the Doctrines of gigantic forms whether of Quadrupeds of men."

In contrast to both Edward Taylor and Jefferson's sympathetic use
of Indian traditions, Stiles dismissed them outright and embraced
rather impulsively the far more radical idea of extinction: "I give no
Credit to the Indian Fable that this great Animal now exists in the
N.W. Parts of America. I believe the Race extinct: and I am surprized
that any should exist so late as 240 Winters before 1705." Acknowledging Jefferson's own extensive inquiries, he briefly alluded to the
giant grinder owned by General Washington and provided a few details
of the general's visit to Annan's farm, which he had heard from Colonel
Humphreys.

The friendly first meeting between the Calvinist Stiles and the
Deist Jefferson had thus developed into an enthusiastic correspondence
reflecting the widening awareness of the American *incognitum*. Shortly
after Jefferson sailed for France, Pelatiah Webster of Philadelphia vis-

ited Stiles with news of a tooth and thighbone found at the salt licks in Kentucky, which Stiles noted in his diary: "A sensible Gent[leman] lately there assured him he found in the Salt Licks a Tooth weigh[ing] Eight Pounds, and a Bone supposed a Part of Thigh Bone 3 or 4 feet long broken off, whose *knob* at the end where it entered the socket was as big Diam[eter] as his *Hat Crown*."[40] The appearance of John Filson's promotional tract later that same year, with its dramatic description of Big Bone Lick, made the bones of the *incognitum*, not to mention those of the herds of buffalo, deer, and elk gathered at the licks, a lure for prospective settlers.

Without supplying many details of the event, Stiles's letter to the departing Jefferson mentioned the discovery several years earlier of similar bones near General Washington's encampment on the Hudson River. He referred Jefferson directly to the "Revd. Mr. Anan of Boston" for a description of the specimens, which Stiles claimed had been promised to him but that he had not yet received. In the fall of 1785, nearly a year later, Rev. Annan, who had become minister of a Presbyterian church in Boston after leaving New Windsor in 1783, visited New Haven. He finally gave Stiles a more detailed account of the bones discovered on his farm, including his encounter with "a large Quantity of Matter which had the appearance of fresh Dung as in the Paunch of an animal," which Stiles also noted in his diary.[41]

About this time, Rev. Annan had drafted his own memoir about the skeletal remains found on his property, which soon rivaled those of the fossil elephants from Kentucky. His remarks, although not published for eight more years, provide glimpses of these New England ministers' speculations: "What could this animal be? Certainly not a marine monster, for it lay above a hundred miles from the sea; unless we can suppose, that not many centuries ago, that part of the country was covered by the sea."[42] Evidently, he was inclined to doubt the theory that the creatures were extinct, although he admitted having discussed this matter with several persons who accepted the idea: "Some gentlemen, with whom I have conversed, have supposed that their extinction . . . is owing to some amazing convulsion, concussion, or catastrophe, endured by the globe. But I know of none that could produce such an effect, except the flood."

Annan's wavering opinions reflected an undercurrent of doubt creeping into the biblical explanations for such anomalies, doubt that probably also disturbed Ezra Stiles. "Shall we, sir, suppose the species to be extinct over the face of the globe? If so, what could be the cause?" Annan mused in his memoir, contemplating the collapse of the Great Chain of Being. Not surprisingly, to avoid this catastrophe, he fell back on the same idea that still kept alive Jefferson's hopes of finding the unknown creature somewhere in the unexplored American wilderness. "It is next to incredible, that the remains of this animal could have lain there since the flood. May there not be some of the kind yet surviving in some interiour part of the Continent?"[43]

Not long after Annan's visit, Stiles received Jefferson's long-awaited reply, written on July 17, 1785, but delayed for more than a year by his preoccupations in Paris: "I thank you for your information as to the great bones on the Hudson's river," Jefferson wrote, before offering with disarming cordiality his contrary opinion of the identity of the creature to which they belonged: "I suspect that these must have been of the same animal with those found on the Ohio: and if so, they could not have belonged to any human figure, because they are accompanied with tusks of the size, form and substance of those of the elephant."[44] Jefferson then turned quickly to other topics, but his dismissal of the "Doctrine of Monsters" began Stiles's reevaluation of his own views of the monster's identity, which soon led him to a realization of his error and a reversal of his opinion.

Earlier the same year, a well-known French printer in Paris had agreed to publish Jefferson's *Notes on the State of Virginia* for one-quarter the cost asked by American printers, and an edition of two hundred copies appeared in May, intended solely for private distribution by the author. An American edition of *Notes* was not published until 1788, and in the interim the literary work shaping many people's views of the American *incognitum* was John Filson's *Kentucke*, which was already circulating among literary salons in Paris when Jefferson arrived. The popularity of Filson's *Kentucke* in both Europe and America turned all eyes toward the Ohio valley as reports of new discoveries at the salt licks there reached Philadelphia in the wake of the land rush to Kentucky. Filson himself had remained in Philadelphia after the publication of his book, attempting unsuccessfully to obtain an endorsement from George Washington. In the spring of 1785, he traveled to Pittsburgh and down the Ohio River to explore lands along the Wabash River in Illinois country, where he narrowly escaped an Indian attack the following year.

Among the land speculators then flocking to the Ohio valley was the Revolutionary War veteran General Samuel H. Parsons, a Harvard-educated lawyer from an old Connecticut family, who had been appointed by Congress as a commissioner to terminate Indian claims to the territory northwest of the Ohio. His eagerness to profit from land speculation stemmed from his own loss of a sizable investment in government securities during the war. When the new Ohio Company was formed to secure lands for Revolutionary War soldiers, he became one of its promoters, launching a new career at the age of fifty-one.

In November 1785, Parsons's own expedition down the Ohio River stopped at Big Bone Lick to search for bones. He spent half a day with his servants digging up some four hundred pounds of bones, including several large teeth that he donated to museums at Yale and Harvard the following year upon his return.[45] "We found the place to be a flatt [sic] of about 20 acres inclosed with rising lands on all Sides, through which is running a stream of water; the soil is a yellow, soft Clay, the Bones are found in and near this stream under the Earth at different depths."[46]

Returning to New England the following spring, General Parsons brought his "curiosities" to New Haven to show his friend Ezra Stiles at Yale College. There the two traded theories about the strange bones. "What species of animal this was I am unable to conjecture, and being wholly Unknown to the Natives we are not aided by tradition," Parsons wrote in his own memoir, drafted the day after he visited New Haven.[47] Stiles was already beginning to abandon his belief in human giants, for his diary entry describing the visit refers to "two Elephants Teeth" that his guest brought with him: "They were Grinder Teeth with I think six protuberances atop each. The Fangs or Roots much broken off, yet the Tooth was above six Inches high. I saw them weighed; and afterwds sent them to an Apothecary's shop to be weighed."[48]

As always, Stiles recorded the exact measurements of the specimens, together with the dimensions of a thighbone six inches in diameter and the fragment of a tusk "longer than a long Pipe I was then smoking." While he seemed ready to accept Dr. William Hunter's theory of extinction, he made no direct mention of the London anatomist: "They were the Teeth of a carnivorous Animal: The Lacunae & Protuberances on the Summit of the Teeth were such as I think could not be suited for eating Grass."[49] With regard to the identity of the creature, he noted that General Parsons deferred judgment to the "literati," although from the general's own memoir, it is evident that he himself assumed that the animal in question was extinct: "Of what species they were, by what means, and at what time they became extinct, I leave to the enquiry of Others."[50]

Barely a week after General Parsons brought these bones to New Haven and only three days after Stiles received his memoir about the discoveries in Ohio country, the Calvinist wrote a letter to Jefferson in Paris that marked a momentous shift in his own views of the American *incognitum*: "I was mistaken in thinking the Ohio Teeth and Bones did not belong to the Elephant. Your learned Letter led me to re-examine the Skeleton of the Elephant. But what is most decisive with me is the *Tusks* found at the Ohio, which are indubitably Elephants."[51] As testimony to the empirical evidence, Stiles enclosed copies of General Parsons's letter describing his adventures in the Ohio valley, along with his drawing of some ancient ruins he encountered at the mouth of the Muskingum River.

Having changed his opinion about the bones of the American *incognitum*, Stiles then journeyed to the Hudson River valley several months later in the autumn of 1786, to the site of the original discovery that had inspired his grandfather's lyrical verses about the giant of Claverack. En route, he visited the eighty-year-old patriarch Robert Livingston at Livingston manor, near the riverbank where the fossil remains of the *incognitum* were first found in 1705. "He told me of the Great Bones dug up at Clavarack," Stiles noted in his diary, "that his Father sent a Tooth weigh[in]g 3 or four pounds & a Thigh Bone three feet long to the Royal Society, when he was a young man."[52]

The correspondence between Ezra Stiles and Thomas Jefferson brought together the two main currents of thought about the American *incognitum* as well as the two principal sources of its fossil remains—the Big Bone Lick on the Kentucky frontier and the marshlands of the Hudson River valley, which were soon to yield the first complete skeleton of the unidentified animal. The publication of Jefferson's *Notes* and John Filson's *Kentucke* heralded the rebirth of the American monster, not as the human giant celebrated by Cotton Mather and Edward Taylor, but as the "tyrant of the forests," a ferocious carnivore whose existence and extinction were welcomed by many citizens of the new republic. Still, the mystery of the creature's identity remained unsolved, although nearly everyone now agreed with Jefferson's assertion that it was the largest of terrestrial beings to have ever walked the earth. Its enormous size made the animal an even more inviting prey for nature lovers on both sides of the Atlantic, especially the founding fathers who saw the great beast as a symbol of the New World's superiority and a repudiation of Buffon's theory of American degeneracy.

9

American Degeneracy and
White Supremacy

White, then, appears to be the primitive color of Nature, which
may be varied by climate, by food, and by manners to yellow, brown
and black.

—Buffon

IN THE SUMMER of 1784, Thomas Jefferson sailed for Paris with his
young daughter Patsy and his slave James Hemings. The voyage took
only nineteen days in the new merchant ship *Ceres*, making its first trip
across the Atlantic. The party landed first on the coast of England and
then crossed the channel to the French port of La Havre where they
spent three days before departing for Paris in Jefferson's black phaeton
carriage. In his luggage, Jefferson carried the manuscript of his *Notes on
the State of Virginia* and a large panther skin from America with which
he intended to do battle with Buffon. Indeed, during the five years Jefferson spent in Paris, the American *incognitum* was overshadowed by
the stuffed carcasses of living quadrupeds that Jefferson used to combat
Buffon's theory of American degeneracy.

For the American ambassador, Buffon proved to be an elusive prey.
In his latest masterpiece, *Époques de la nature*, a recapitulation and re-
vision of his ideas about the earth's history published in 1778, Buffon
abandoned many elements of his theory of American degeneracy. Publication of his *Époques* was a seminal event in the discovery of prehistoric nature because it revealed the dark, unexplored geological time
where many lost species like the American *incognitum* were hidden
from view. For the first time, naturalists in Europe and America began
to perceive dimly the possibility of a prehuman past. In addition, the

FIGURE 28. Portrait of Benjamin Franklin in London by John
Trumbull, 1778. Franklin wore his fur cap as an emblem of
American national identity and to alleviate irritation of his
scalp from wearing powdered wigs. Yale University Art Gallery, John Hill Morgan, B.A. 1893, Fund.

racial overtones of the debate over American degeneracy erupted into
a full-blown controversy with the publication of Jefferson's *Notes*,
which combined a defense of life-forms in America with an assertion of
the natural inferiority of its Negro population.

Four days after his arrival, Jefferson rode out to Passy on the out-
skirts of Paris to meet with Benjamin Franklin, who was serving as
head of the American delegation in France. He was now seventy-
nine years old, his face tired and drawn, and his body nearly immobi-
lized by a gout-stricken foot and a large kidney stone (figure 28).

With Franklin's help, however, Jefferson found a printer who agreed to publish a private edition of his *Notes on the State of Virginia* at a quarter the cost quoted to him by American printers in Philadelphia. In the spring of 1785, therefore, he had two hundred copies of his book printed anonymously, largely for distribution among a small circle of friends and acquaintances.

This extremely small, private printing reflected Jefferson's apprehension about how his criticism of the institution of slavery would be received in America, especially among politicians in the slave-holding states. In his *Notes*, under "Manners," Jefferson made an unusually bold statement about the detrimental effects of slave holding on American society: "The whole commerce between master and slave is a perpetual exercise of the most boisterous passions, the most unremitting despotism on the one part, and degrading submissions on the other." He used a child's view of this degradation to stress the corrupting influence of slavery on the slaveholders themselves in addition to the suffering of the slaves. "The man must be a prodigy who can retain his manners and morals undepraved by such circumstances."[1] Such circumstances conjured up a specter of social upheaval should justice prevail: "Indeed I tremble for my country when I reflect that God is just: that his justice cannot sleep for ever: that considering the numbers, nature and natural means only, a revolution of the wheel of fortune, an exchange of situation, is among possible events: that it may become probable by supernatural interference!"[2]

The first copies of his *Notes* had only begun to circulate when Jefferson wrote to his friend James Madison in Virginia asking his advice about *limiting* its distribution: "I beg you to peruse it carefully because I ask your advice on it and nobody's else. I wish to put it into the hands of the young men at the college, as well on account of the political as physical parts."[3] Fearful that his condemnation of slavery would elicit censure by the Virginia assembly, Jefferson expressed the same concerns a month later to his protégé, the young Virginia lawyer James Monroe: "I fear the terms in which I speak of slavery and of our constitution may produce an irritation which will revolt the minds of our countrymen against reformation of these two articles and thus do more harm than good."[4] Writing to his Parisian friend the marquis de Chastellux in early June, Jefferson explained why he wished to send copies to students at the College of William and Mary: "It is to them I look, to the rising generation, and not to the one now in power for these great reformations."[5]

The publication of his *Notes* made Jefferson a literary celebrity among the French aristocracy, whose salons he began to frequent after being introduced to their hostesses by Benjamin Franklin. In May 1785, only a week after his *Notes* was printed, with Franklin's retirement imminent, Jefferson was ushered into the king's bedchamber at Versailles to present his papers as the sole American ambassador to the French sovereign, Louis XVI. Nonetheless, despite his rising social status, an invitation from Buffon, the principal target of his criticism, eluded Jefferson's grasp.

As soon as his *Notes* was printed, Jefferson sent a copy to the marquis de Chastellux, a French nobleman and a member of the academy whom he had entertained at Monticello. Knowing that the marquis was a personal friend of Buffon's, Jefferson enclosed a second copy of his book which he asked Chastellux to pass onto him. In early June, the marquis enthusiastically praised Jefferson's book and informed him that he had forwarded the volume to Buffon's anatomist Daubenton, since Buffon had already left Paris to spend the summer at his country estate.

The issue uppermost in Jefferson's mind at this time was not the pursuit of the American *incognitum* but the alleged inferiority of the inhabitants of the New World, whether of European descent or Native Americans. In his *Notes*, he acknowledged that Buffon had not extended his theory of degeneracy to Europeans in the New World, although he had come close to doing so. For this reason, Jefferson's rebuttal focused on the supposed inferiority of the American Indians, whom he defended as being equal to Europeans at a similar stage of development. "Before we condemn the Indians of this continent as wanting genius, we must consider that letters have not yet been introduced among them," he wrote, comparing them with the northern Europeans when the Romans first invaded. "How many good poets, how many able mathematicians, how many great inventors in arts or sciences, had Europe North of the Alps then produced?"[6] Nonetheless, Jefferson's testimony contained the seeds of a more pernicious racial doctrine that became evident only when he discussed the condition of the people of African descent in America. "I do not mean to deny, that there are varieties in the race of man, distinguished by their powers of both body and mind. I believe there are, as I see to be the case in the races of other animals."[7]

In contrast to his defense of the American Indian's innate abilities, Jefferson used his sophisticated powers of reasoning to maintain the natural inferiority of the Negroes in America. Perhaps to compensate for his condemnation of slavery, Jefferson erected an elaborate new edifice of natural inferiority to justify the expulsion of the African slaves after their emancipation. His discussion of Virginia's laws and the administration of justice led him to put forward strong arguments opposing the integration of freed slaves into American society. "Deep rooted prejudices entertained by the whites; ten thousand recollections, by the blacks, of the injuries they have sustained; new provocations; the real distinctions which nature has made; and many other circumstances, will divide us into parties, and produce convulsions which will probably never end but in the extermination of the one or the other race."[8]

Besides the prospect of this immense social upheaval, the logic of his argument pivoted on a deeper, almost "scientific" conclusion based on what he viewed as Negroes' "natural" deficiencies: "The opinion, that they are inferior in the faculties of reason and imagination, must be hazarded with great diffidence," he cautiously asserted, calling for further scientific study to confirm his hypothesis. "To justify a general conclusion, requires many observations, even where the subject may be submitted to the Anatomical knife, to Optical glasses, to analysis by fire, or by solvents."[9]

But no matter how guarded his commentary or how deep his anxiety, he drew the following conclusions about natural inferiority: "I advance it therefore as a suspicion only, that the blacks, whether originally a distinct race, or made distinct by time and circumstances, are inferior to the whites in the endowments both of body and mind."[10] Then applying to the human races the same scientific principles used by European and American naturalists to categorize varieties within animal species, he called on natural history to confirm his argument:

> It is not against experience to suppose, that different species of the same genus, or varieties of the same species, may possess different qualifications. Will not a lover of natural history then, one who views the gradations in all the races of animals with the eye of philosophy, excuse an effort to keep those in the department of man as distinct as nature has formed them?[11]

Skin color ranked high among the physical characteristics under-pinning his argument that the differences between the races were fixed in nature rather than simply the product of environmental conditions and social circumstance. Despite his own reservations about embracing this biological premise, Jefferson's *Notes* contained an unambiguous statement of his belief in the natural inferiority of the Negroes, all the more authoritative due to its aura of scientific fact. In the end, the bluntness of his argument against the incorporation of the Negroes into American society after emancipation rested on his fear of miscegenation: "When freed, he is to be removed beyond the reach of mixture."[12] Elsewhere, Jefferson's choice of words made it clear that these judgments also reflected the breeder's eye for fine livestock as well as a certain aesthetic sense: "The circumstance of superior beauty is thought worthy [of] attention in the propagation of our horses, dogs, and other domestic animals; why not in that of man?"[13] In fact, he employed aesthetic criteria as if they were scientific facts in his discussion of skin color and the physical differences between the races. "Are not the fine mixtures of red and white, the expressions of every passion by greater or less suffusions of colour in the one, preferable to that eternal monotony, which reigns in the countenances, that immoveable veil of black which covers all the emotions of the other race?"[14]

Jefferson even invoked apocryphal reports of sexual relations between apes and humans to demonstrate the superiority of white skin: "Add to these, flowing hair, a more elegant symmetry of form, [and] their own judgment in favour of whites, declared by their preference of them, as uniformly as is the preference of the Oran-ootan for the black women over those of his own species."[15] In this analogy, Jefferson equated the alleged ardor of black males for white women with aberrant sexual behavior in the animal world, in which interbreeding supposedly marked the boundary between species. Ironically, his familiarity with the assumed sexual preferences of the orangutan came straight from Buffon's own writings, which described these animals as "equally ardent for women as for its own females" and cited instances of African women who reportedly had intercourse with apes.[16]

Following the publication of his *Notes*, Jefferson was preoccupied with diplomatic affairs, especially after the departure of Benjamin Franklin, when the responsibility for representing the United States' interests in France rested solely on his shoulders. Having sent off copies of his *Notes* to his closest friends in America, he waited anxiously for news of its reception at home. In September, a young Dutch nobleman, Count Gijsbert Karel van Hogendorp, to whom he had sent his *Notes*, responded with warm praise for his refutation of Abbé Raynal and Cornelieus De Pauw, two of Buffon's disciples who were the most outspoken exponents of American degeneracy. Van Hogendorp had come to America near the end of the Revolutionary War with letters of introduction from an American military clothier in the Netherlands. Impressed with his knowledge and manners, Jefferson recommended him highly to George Washington as "the best informed man of his age I have ever met."[17]

But van Hogendorp's inquiry about Jefferson's contacts with Buffon made Jefferson uneasy at the absence of any reply from the French naturalist. "I have never yet seen Monsr. de Buffon," the exasperated Jefferson replied several weeks later. "He has been in the country all the summer." Evidently, Jefferson had heard secondhand reports of Buffon's reaction to his arguments, but they revealed only how out of touch he was with Buffon's latest thinking on the subject. "I sent him a copy of the book and I have only heard his sentiments on one particular of it, that of the identity of the Mammoth and Elephant," Jefferson wrote to van Hogendorp. "As to this he retains his opinion that they are the same."[18]

Meeting his Parisian adversary was an event for which Jefferson had carefully prepared before his departure for France more than a year earlier. In his view, Buffon had mistakenly identified the American panther as a cougar in his *Histoire naturelle*, and shortly before leaving for France Jefferson had acquired what he felt was convincing evidence of Buffon's error:

> Being about to embark from Philadelphia for France, I observed an uncommonly large panther skin at the door of a hatter's shop. I bought it for half a Jo [$16] on the spot, determining to carry it to France to convince Monsieur Buffon of his mistake in relation to this animal.[19]

At some point after the publication of his *Notes*, Jefferson sent the panther skin to Buffon through the good offices of Chastellux, hopeful that the gift would provoke a response. The strategy seems to have had its desired effect, for at the year's end he received a terse note from Buffon thanking him for the animal skin, though he still insisted that it belonged to a "cougar" rather than a panther. No doubt Jefferson found it easy to forgive the aging Buffon's stubbornness, since his letter also contained a much coveted invitation to dine with him, along with the marquis de Chastellux.

Jefferson's recollections of his first encounter with Buffon provide a vivid picture of the deference he showed to his adversary. It was Buffon's practice to remain in his study until dinnertime without greeting his guests, but his house and grounds were open and a servant showed them to the visitors. Even though they encountered Buffon in the garden, Jefferson and the marquis carefully avoided conversing with him until he appeared for dinner. Jefferson clearly was apprehensive about the reception he would receive, as he had dared to challenge Europe's leading authority on natural history.

Surprisingly, Buffon proved to be an affable host, engaging his visitors in a gracious, if condescending, manner, typical of the patronizing politeness of the French aristocracy: "He proved himself, as he always did, a man of extraordinary powers in conversation," Jefferson later recalled. "Instead of entering into an argument, he took down his last work, presented it to me, and said 'When Mr. Jefferson shall have read this, he will be perfectly satisfied that I am right.'"[20] Very likely, Buffon's gift to Jefferson was his *Époques de la nature*, summarizing his new theory of the earth's history, which had been published in 1778.

By the time Jefferson met Buffon, he had probably heard from Franklin an anecdote about Franklin's ingenious rebuke of Abbé Raynal, who had become the most outspoken proponent of the New World's inferiority. At a dinner party hosted by Franklin, when Raynal began his usual fulminations about the degeneracy of life-forms in America, Franklin observed that the American and European guests seated on opposite sides of the table were of strikingly different sizes. "Come, M. l'Abbé, let us try this question by the fact before us," he proposed. "Let both parties rise, and we will see on which side nature has degenerated." In Jefferson's recollection of the anecdote years later, the tall Americans dwarfed their European counterparts, and "the Abbé himself particularly, was a mere shrimp."[21] Franklin's intervention was unusual, since before going to Paris, he had shown little concern for the scorn heaped on America's inhabitants during the Revolution.

Evidently, the panther skin convinced Buffon of his error with regard to this animal, since he promised Jefferson that he would correct his mistake in future editions of his *Histoire naturelle*. Seizing the initiative, Jefferson promptly took issue with other aspects of Buffon's theory of American degeneracy, boasting that the American deer had much larger horns than Buffon suspected and claiming the European reindeer could walk under the belly of the American moose. "He replied with warmth," Jefferson remembered, "that if I could produce a single specimen with horns one foot long, he would give up the question."[22]

Buffon's cavalier attitude spurred Jefferson to acquire from his own correspondents in America more physical evidence of the Frenchman's errors. Shortly after his dinner with Buffon, Jefferson wrote to his Virginia friend Archibald Cary, who had supplied information for his *Notes*, asking him to find a large pair of buck's horns to prove the American animal's superior size.

> In my conversations with the Count de Buffon on the subjects of Natural History, I find him absolutely unacquainted with our Elk and our deer. He has hitherto beleived [sic] that our deer never had horns more than a foot-long. Will you take the trouble to procure for me the largest pair of bucks horns you can, and a large skin of each colour, that is to say a red and a blue?[23]

Jefferson's first encounter with Buffon thus triggered a flurry of activity, including a letter to Governor John Sullivan of New Hampshire reiterating his desire to obtain the skin, skeleton, and horns of a moose, caribou, and elk. Before leaving for France, Jefferson had traveled to New Hampshire to acquire information about these animals from the governor, who had then asked for detailed reports from several New England hunters.

> The readiness with which you undertook to endeavor to get for me the skin, the skeleton, and the horns of the moose, the caribou, and the original or elk, emboldens me to renew my application to you for those objects which would be an acquisition here, more precious than you can imagine. Whatever expence you incur in procuring or sending these things, I will immediately repay.[24]

The urgency of his request for an elk arose directly from his conversations with Buffon, as revealed several weeks later in yet another of Jefferson's letters to Virginia: "I have made a particular acquaintance here with Monsieur de Buffon, and have a great desire to give him the best idea I can of our elk," he wrote to Archibald Stuart, who had also provided considerable information on American animals for Jefferson's *Notes*. "Were it possible, you could not oblige me more than by sending me the horns, skeleton, and skin of an elk." As always, Jefferson supplied explicit instructions for gutting the animal and packing the carcass, to best preserve the skin for stuffing in Paris.

In the coming months while Jefferson awaited replies from his American correspondents, he began to receive the first commentaries from home on the privately published edition of his *Notes*. Only a few weeks after dining with Buffon, he received a letter from his friend James Madison cautioning him about the planned distribution of the book among students at the College of William and Mary. Owing to the controversy surrounding Jefferson's condemnation of the institution of slavery, certain words in Madison's commentary on this subject were written in a cipher used by Jefferson for sensitive communications. "We are all sensible that the *freedom* of *your strictures* on some *particular measures* and *opinions* will displease *their respective abettors*," Madison wrote, using the code for the italicized words. "But we equally concur in thinking that this consideration ought not to be weighed against the *utility of your plan*."[25] In Madison's opinion, an *"indiscriminate gift"* of his *Notes* directly to the students might offend *"some narrow minded parents,"* whereas donating the book to the college's library would allow professors discretion in making it available to their students.

Events in the publishing world were fast overtaking such efforts to limit the distribution of Jefferson's *Notes*. Even though Jefferson had written, in every copy he gave out, a restraint against its publication, a Paris bookseller was about to bring out an unauthorized French translation that Jefferson felt was unworthy. To prevent the pirating of his work, he reluctantly made arrangements with a French clergyman, Abbé Morellet, a member of the Academy, to translate the book instead, with strict provisions for his own review of the galleys.[26] In August, Madison added to Jefferson's anxiety by recommending that he have an authorized English edition published, since the risk of a pirated version's appearing at home was increasing.

News of the enthusiastic response to his *Notes* at home soon allayed Jefferson's fears that the book would result in his censure. In August 1786, he received encouragement from Rev. James Madison, the president of the College of William and Mary, who welcomed the opportunity to offer his students the book: "Such a work should not be kept private. Let it have the broad light of an American sun."[27]

Two months earlier, Dr. David Ramsay, a Pennsylvania-born physician and naturalist living in South Carolina, had sharply criticized Jefferson's views of the Negroes. In his opinion, their lowly condition was a product of their degradation in society, not simply the result of nature: "I admire your generous indignation at slavery; but I think you have depressed the negroes too low. I flatter myself that in a few centuries the negroes will lose their black color. I think they are less black in Jersey than Carolina, their [lips] less thick, their noses less flat."[28] But in his praise of Jefferson's refutation of Buffon, Ramsay revealed how sensitive educated Americans were to charges of their own inferiority made by Buffon's disciples in Europe: "Europeans affect to under value Americans. I acknowledge an inferiority but this is chargeable on the state of society. Less industry, less perseverance and less knowledge will answer the purposes of our country than in old established countries, but human nature is certainly radically the same in both."[29]

The proposed French translation of the *Notes* was delayed for nearly a year by the production of a new map and Jefferson's dissatisfaction with his translator's rendition of the text. In fact, the problems with the translations convinced Jefferson of the necessity of publishing an authoritative English edition of the book to prevent further adulteration of his ideas. In February 1787, he sent the corrected manuscript to John Stockdale, a London bookseller who agreed to publish an edition of four hundred copies, which finally came out during the following summer. Any doubts about the wisdom of making his *Notes* public were eased by Rev. James Madison's letter in February further praising the eagerly awaited English edition: "Your Book is read here, by every one who can get a View of it, with the greatest Avidity."[30] By the summer, when Stockdale's English edition came off the press, Jefferson's friend Francis Hopkinson had already published excerpts in his journal the *Columbian Magazine*, especially those sections refuting Buffon's theory of degeneracy.

In Jefferson's own mind, true vindication could only come through physical evidence of the superior size of American animals, namely, the stuffed skin and bones of his country's largest quadrupeds. In September, with both editions of his *Notes* available to the public, he finally received from John Sullivan, the governor of New Hampshire, the long-awaited skin, horns, and skeleton of an American moose, along with the antlers of the caribou, elk, deer, and a spike-horned buck. Even though the moose stood some seven feet tall, the animal's skin had lost much of its hair during the voyage to Europe, and the antlers of the other animals were unusually small. But despite their disappointing appearance, Jefferson wasted no time in sending them to Buffon with a lengthy letter apologizing for their poor condition and uncharacteristically small size. "The skin of the Moose was drest with the hair on, but a great deal of it has come off, and the rest is ready to drop off," he wrote in early October. "The horns of the elk are remarkably small. I have certainly seen of them which would have weighed five or six times as much."[31]

Unfortunately, Buffon's failing health denied Jefferson the satisfaction of an unequivocal retraction of his doctrine of American degeneracy. Even though he could not personally respond to Jefferson's latest attempt to disprove his theory of degeneracy, several weeks later, Buffon's assistant, the comte de Lapécède, politely thanked Jefferson for the *"beau present,"* complimenting him on his artful uniting of "the knowledge of the naturalist with the science of the statesman."[32] Buffon died six months later in April 1788, ending Jefferson's hopes of a public vindication from his adversary, and his recollections of Buffon's death attest to his disappointment: "He promised in his next volume to set these things right also, but he died directly afterward."[33]

Surprisingly, the American *incognitum* was not part of Jefferson's discussions with Buffon, which focused mainly on comparisons of the living animal species of Europe and America. Thus the monstrous grinders from the Ohio salt lick were not brought up to contradict his theory of the natural inferiority of the American species. This omission represents a curious lapse on Jefferson's part, since the great beast's identity was still a mystery and its fossil remains played such a prominent role in his *Notes on the State of Virginia*. Even while American journals were reprinting excerpts from *Notes* extolling the unsurpassable size of the fossil elephants in America, Jefferson was forced to rely on his hairless moose as evidence of his country's equal stature.

Moreover, Jefferson had not read Buffon's latest works with sufficient attention, for they outlined a surprising new role for the American *incognitum* in the earth's history. The dawning awareness of extinction provided an impetus to discovering the prehuman era of the earth's history, but it was not until Buffon alluded to the lost species that the earth's true timeline really began to emerge. As historian

Martin Rudwick observed in his study of the early perceptions of geological time, a deep prehuman time became conceivable for the first
time in Buffon's *Époques*. Jefferson's own lack of interest in this subject may have derived from his rejection of the idea of extinction and
his expectation that the American *incognitum* would be found in the
unexplored American wilderness.

Publication of Buffon's *Époques de la nature* in 1778 represented the
culmination of his career as a natural philosopher, the final summation
and revision of his ideas about the history of nature on earth. In deference to the prevailing religious doctrine, Buffon's overview of the
earth's antiquity took the conventional form of seven epochs obviously
inspired by the creation narrative of Christianity found in Genesis.
This device enabled Buffon to lengthen the timeline of the earth's history while outwardly conforming to the biblical story of God's creation.
Each day of God's creation became an epoch in Buffon's scenario,
which was conceived in geological terms beginning with the formation
of the planets, including the earth, during the first epoch and ending
with the appearance of humankind in the seventh and final epoch.

For the first time, the geological dimensions of the earth's history
were framed in a systematic theory based on natural science not overtly
incompatible with religious doctrine. Elements of the Mosaic story like
Noah's Flood were absorbed into a larger panorama of naturalistic
events, in which individual phases of the earth's creation, from the formation of the continents to the volcanic upheavals which gave birth to
the mountains, took thousands of years instead of a single day.

The naturalistic principle governing Buffon's vision of the earth's
history was the cooling of the planet after the cataclysm of the earth's
creation when a meteor plunged into the sun, throwing off molten fragments that became the planets of the newly created solar system. The
earth's natural history then became an irrevocable process of slow cooling until the globe eventually became habitable by humans. Buffon's
timeline for the earth's prehuman history was based on his own experiments with the cooling of molten metals, which gave him his estimates
of the duration of the various epochs. Unfortunately, the inevitable end
of Buffon's naturalistic process was the final extinguishing of the earth's
climate, along with all its life-forms, at some undetermined time far in
the future.

Buffon's notebooks on the manuscript reveal that he privately
imagined the overall process to have required hundreds of thousands, if

not millions, of years. But when his published work appeared, he estimated the age of the earth to be only 75,000 years, though still quite long, even heretical, compared with the biblical standard of six thousand years. By his calculations, 25,000 years passed before the earth cooled sufficiently to allow bodies of water to form on the planet.[34] In this time, the earth remained a luminous, molten body whose incandescence lasted another 2,936 years before being consolidated all the way to its center. "For thirty-five thousand years our globe has only been a mass of heat and fire which no sensible being could get close. Then, for fifteen thousand or twenty thousand years, its surface was only a universal sea."[35] Eventually, after 36,000 years, the continents had been covered with water for some twenty thousand years, with only the highest peaks exposed above a warm "universal sea" containing the earth's first primitive forms of marine life.

The presence of seashells on the highest mountain peaks from the Andes to the Alps was testimony to the extent of this flooding of the earth before the receding waters left these fossil remains far from any existing oceans. "Consequently, it has been shown through attentive observation of these authentic monuments of nature, like the shells in marbles, the fish in slates and plants in coal mines, that all these organized beings have existed long before animals on earth," Buffon announced, anchoring his sweeping new timeline in the fossil evidence observed by naturalists since antiquity.[36]

Echoing the archaeological metaphor of Robert Hooke, Buffon's *Époques* begins with the commonplace analogy between the ruins of ancient empires and the fossils or "monuments" of the earth's natural antiquity:

> In civil History, just as we consult the titles, research the coins, and decipher the ancient inscriptions, to determine the course of human revolutions and to record the dates of moral events, it is the same in Natural History. It is necessary to mine the archives of the world, to pull old monuments from the entrails of the earth, to collect their ruins, and put together in one body of evidence all the signs of the physical changes that can let us go back to the different ages of Nature.[37]

Buffon's natural history helped popularize the idea that fossils, petrifactions, and rock formations could be viewed as monuments of the earth's antiquity, opening the way for the fusion of natural history and nationalism in the minds of the founding fathers, who saw them as ingredients in the natural antiquity of the new American nation.

In Buffon's theory, the receding waters of the "universal sea" gave way to an era of volcanic activity that saw the raising up of the landmasses by subterranean electrical storms, spewing molten rocks on the ravaged landscape. God had spared humans from witnessing this violent upheaval and devastation, since living organisms did not appear on the land until the volcanic eruptions had subsided, about fifteen thousand years ago. Because the earth's rotation caused the planet to cool from the poles toward the equator, the first terrestrial animals inhabited the polar regions where the landmasses, though still quite hot, had cooled sufficiently to support living organisms.

Being a firm believer in the degeneration of species, Buffon claimed that the first life-forms on earth were not simple organisms but giant creatures—huge ammonites in the seas, elephants and hippopotamuses on land—all of which were much larger than their contemporary counterparts. In this fashion, Buffon was able to explain the existence of the fossil elephants found in Siberia and the Ohio valley, whose monstrous grinders he now introduced as evidence supporting his theory that the earth was once in a liquid state and had cooled gradually from the poles toward the equator.

In many ways, Buffon's new theory of the earth's history helped resolve the dilemma posed by the remains of the fossil elephants found in northern climates far from their normal habitat in the tropics. Previously, he had linked the size of these large quadrupeds to the higher temperatures in the tropics. With his new scheme of cooling from the poles, he could explain the existence of the lost species, including the Siberian mammoth and the American *incognitum*, which he himself had claimed were six times the size of a living elephant. For Buffon, these giant fossil remains now proved that in antiquity, the northern regions had been a torrid zone, although he left unresolved the question of the animals' extinction except for his assertion that they had migrated south as the earth cooled.

Buffon's acknowledgment that the fossil remains in Siberia and North America belonged to an extinct species marked a further revision of his earlier claim, inspired by Daubenton's clinical study, that the tusks from the Ohio valley were elephants and the grinders came from

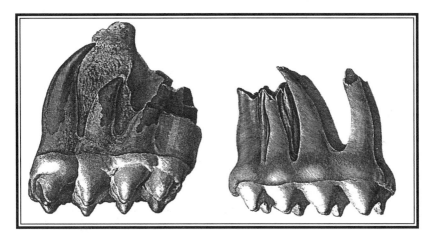

FIGURE 29. The grinder of the American *incognitum* (left) sent to Buffon by Peter Collinson and a tooth from Siberia (right) pictured in Buffon's *Époques de la nature*, 1778. In this volume, Buffon accepted the idea that the bones of these creatures belonged to separate species that were extinct.

hippopotamuses. To prove his new point, Buffon published several elegant engravings of the molars in question—enabling his readers to compare for themselves the grinders of the Siberian mammoth and the specimen from the Ohio salt lick sent to Paris by Peter Collinson, whose letter Buffon published along with the illustrations (figure 29). "It seems certain that these big teeth have never belonged to the elephant or the hippopotamus. Therefore, I am able to declare with supportive arguments that this great animal species is lost."[38]

Jefferson chose not to acknowledge this shift in Buffon's thinking with regard to the American *incognitum*, probably because Buffon's disciples continued to promote the notion of American degeneracy. In addition, geology was not Jefferson's strong suit in regard to natural history, and he later claimed it mattered little to him whether the earth was six hundred or six thousand years old.[39] However, before going to France, he already was familiar with Buffon's theory of the earth's cooling, since he discussed the idea with his friend James Madison. Taking issue with Buffon's assertion that the planet would cool unevenly from the poles toward the equator, Jefferson maintained that the cooling would occur equally from the extremities to the center, affected only by

the unequal distance of the mountains and valleys from the earth's center: "If my idea of the process of cooling be right, his is wrong and his
whole theory in the *Epochs of Nature* is overset."[40]

Many passages in his *Notes* testify to the influence of the emerging
geological consciousness on Jefferson's view of the American landscape. His description of the Potomac River water gap was couched in
terms hinting of a cataclysmic event, the violent breaching of the
mountain range by the river's pent-up waters. Discussing the existence
of seashells on the mountaintops in Virginia, Jefferson evaluated the
two leading scientific explanations for the origin and formation of the
earth's surface—the theory of a universal deluge and the opposing view
emphasizing the role of convulsions or cataclysms. Based on his own
scientific calculations of the volume of water available for the Great
Deluge, he rejected this geological event as an explanation for the
anomaly while at the same time casting doubt on the claims of the "vul-
canists" that violent upheavals of the earth's crust had displaced the
seashells.

Jefferson's belief in the economy of nature and his rejection of the
idea of extinction led him to embrace temporarily the anachronistic
notion that such formations may not have been the fossil remains of
living organisms at all but, rather, replicas of them formed in the soil by
a strange mineral process by which likenesses of shells grew in stone. "It
might be asked, whether it is more difficult for nature to shoot the calcareous juice into the form of a shell, than other juices into the forms
of chrystals, plants, animals? Have not Naturalists already brought
themselves to believe much stranger things?[41] These passages aroused
so much controversy when they appeared in the original Paris edition
of his *Notes* that Jefferson revised his comments in the English edition.
In the final analysis, even though he was clearly influenced by early geological views of the landscape, Jefferson withheld judgment on these
matters, preferring instead to focus on the pragmatic search for the
bones of the American *incognitum*.

Contrary to his earlier views, Buffon went to great lengths in his
new scenario to downplay the degeneration of either human or animal
species. Instead, he maintained that while the size of certain species
had changed, the form remained the same. Even though he repeatedly
alluded to the disappearance of various animals, Buffon defended the
essential fixity of the species with renewed vigor, abandoning his earlier
ideas about the transformation of animal life. In this respect, his revi-

sion of the earth's history moved away from the notion of a struggle for existence that his earlier writings on degeneration had implied with their emphasis on the relationship of climate to the survival of certain life-forms.

The most striking manifestation of this shift in Buffon's thinking was the modification of his theory of American degeneracy in *Époques*: "Nature, far from being degenerate through old age there, is on the contrary recently born and has never existed there with the same force, the same power as in the northern countries."[42] Perhaps Jefferson overlooked this modest revision of his theory because Buffon's explicit repudiation of the notion appeared in a less well known volume dealing with the natural history of man, published the year before his *Époques*. Dissatisfied with Cornelius de Pauw and Abbé Raynal, who had extended his original argument to include people of European descent in America, Buffon publicly repudiated the doctrine in 1777 while discussing revisions of his views. In a special section, "The Americans," he rejected unequivocally the notion that the inhabitants of North America were inferior beings: "In a country where Europeans multiply themselves so promptly, where the view of the natives of the country is broader than elsewhere, it is hardly possible that men degenerate."[43]

The document that had altered Buffon's thinking on this matter was Benjamin Franklin's essay on population growth in the British colonies, *Observations concerning the Increase of Mankind*, published in 1755. Written in an effort to convince Britain's colonial authorities that the American colonies were important to their empire, this essay showed that the American population had doubled in a single generation. According to Franklin, this rapid population growth was due to not merely the favorable climate but also the superior subsistence provided by the industrious Americans, which enabled them to marry and create families with greater frequency: "What an accession of power to the British empire by sea as well as land!"[44] Besides their impact on Buffon's theory of degeneracy, Franklin's ideas helped shape early views of prehistoric nature because they influenced the English economists Adam Smith and Thomas Malthus, whose writings on the relationship between population growth and competition for natural resources were the seedbed for Darwin's theory of natural selection and the struggle for existence.

At the conclusion of his essay, Franklin placed population growth squarely within the framework of the nascent theories of scientific racialism still in their infancy. He pointed out "that the number of purely white People in the World is proportionably very small" and that the Saxons and the English constituted the "principal Body of White People on the Face of the Earth." Under those circumstances, he cautioned his countrymen against the deleterious effects of the continued importation of African slaves into the British colonies:

> And while we are, as I may call it, *Scouring* our Planet, by clearing America of Woods, and so making this Side of our Globe reflect a brighter Light to the Eyes of Inhabitants in Mars or Venus, why should we in the Sight of Superior Beings, darken its People? why increase the Sons of Africa, by Planting them in America, where we have so fair an Opportunity, by excluding all Blacks and Tawneys, of increasing the lovely White and Red?[45]

This controversial passage, which was expunged from later editions of his pamphlet, was a harbinger of things to come, since scientific racialism soon took root in discussions about the origins of humankind accompanying early speculation about the geological history of the earth.

As naturalists in Europe and America pondered the origins of humankind and the emerging reality of a prehuman past, Buffon's theory of the degeneration and disappearance of various animal species heightened awareness of racial differences among the human species. Despite his repudiation of American inferiority, Buffon's earlier ideas about the degeneration of animal species deeply influenced a new generation of European anatomists who sought to define scientifically the hierarchy of the human races. In this endeavor, they drew on Buffon's own articulation of the racial differences within the human species that had appeared in the earliest volumes of his *Histoire naturelle*.

In the last chapter of his *Natural History of Man*, published in 1749, entitled "Variations in the Human Species," Buffon outlined his early views of the different ethnic groups, what many European natural philosophers were coming to view as the separate races of humanity. His ethnographic tour of the world, based largely on travel literature, used certain physical characteristics—like skin color, hair type, and facial features—to differentiate the various human types. Unlike Voltaire and other Enlightenment philosophers, Buffon rejected the concept of polygenesis, the idea that the various races existed before Adam and

Eve and were the result of a separate and unequal creation, an assertion frequently used to declare them irredeemably inferior.

Even though Buffon defended the unity of the human species and used racial terminology sparingly, his description of the human races incorporated into the scientific study of the origins of man certain aesthetic criteria reflecting the common assumptions Europeans made about their own superiority, not only in mental capacity, but also in physical beauty. "White, then appears to be the primitive color of Nature, which may be varied by climate, by food, and by manners, to yellow, brown and black."[46] In his opinion, the temperate climate extending through Europe from Georgia and Circassia to northern Spain had produced the world's most beautiful people, with the ideal human living in the vicinity of the Caspian Sea: "It is from this climate that the ideas of the genuine color of mankind, and of the various degrees of *beauty* ought to be derived."[47]

These assertions at the outset of Buffon's *Histoire naturelle* constituted important preconditions for his theory of American degeneracy that later became so offensive to the founding fathers. Non-European races were identified as degenerate forms of humanity, whose inferiority, or "ugliness," was produced by the influence of climate, together with their customs and cultural life. His emphasis on environmental conditions was combined with aesthetic judgments about the beauty of various races, for civilization itself was an important factor in the development of racial types: "Coarse, unwholesome and ill prepared food, makes the human species degenerate. All those people who live miserably, are ugly and ill made," he declared in his essay on variations in the human species.[48]

Predictably, Buffon described the black, tawny, yellowish, brown, and so-called degenerate white peoples as being superstitious, stupid, effeminate, indolent, and parasitic—terms that had become commonplace among both European travelers and Enlightenment intellectuals. Degeneracy theory, especially with regard to America, could be traced back to the writings of John Locke, who viewed the inferiority of Native Americans as a product of their personal failings and customs, particularly their alleged unwillingness to cultivate the earth and to create private property. The same ideas were embedded in the Swedish naturalist Linnaeus's system of classification, in which Europeans were described as being gentle, acute, and inventive, and Africans, Asians, and American Indians were obstinate, covetous, crafty, and lazy.

Buffon's theories of degeneracy provided a new model for the ideas of scientific racialism being formulated by anatomists in northern Europe, especially those associated with the new school of *Naturphilosophie* in the German city of Göttingen. In the 1770s, the Prussian philosopher Immanuel Kant fostered the critical perspective among Buffon's disciples there by urging them to adopt more rigorous scientific criteria to define the races based on Buffon's theory of degeneration. "The only work in which the history of nature is properly handled is Buffon's *Époques de la nature*. However, Buffon gave free rein to his imagination and therefore has written more of a romance of nature than a true history of nature," observed Kant.[49] Under Kant's prodding, the anatomists at Göttingen applied Buffon's principles of degeneration to the human species while seeking to understand the origins of man and the racial history of humanity.

In European scientific circles, Jefferson and Buffon were being eclipsed by Dutch and German anatomists who saw the comparative anatomical study of bones as a means to establish a hierarchy of the human races as well as to identify the American *incognitum*. Toward these ends, they became avid collectors of both the fossil remains of the *incognitum* and human skulls from the different races. The latter were used to bolster the theories of white supremacy in the new field of craniology, the scientific study of the size and configuration of human crania. In this fashion, they linked the debate over the fossil elephants in America to the problem of ranking the various races within the human species, which Buffon had said was largely determined by the effects of climate and mode of living over long periods of time.

The speculation in Jefferson's *Notes* about the natural inferiority of the Negroes and the gigantic stature of the American *incognitum* had already fused these two issues in the American imagination when European anatomists began to develop their own scientific explanations for the racial superiority of the white race. With the lengthening of the earth's history in Buffon's *Époques*, the questions of extinction and geological time forced new consideration of the origins of man, an endeavor paralleling the search for the American *incognitum's* identity and the creation of the nation's first prehistoric monster.

10

The Savagery of Prehistoric Nature

Does not the natural gradation of animals, from one to another, lead
to the original species? And does not that mode of investigation gradually lead to the knowledge of that species? Are we not led on to the
wolf by the gradual affinity of the different varieties in the dog?

—John Hunter

BUFFON'S *ÉPOQUES DE LA NATURE* opened the way to the discovery of prehistoric nature and geological time, but the American *incognitum* still remained an unknown creature. The Parisian naturalist
called attention to the great beast's existence and its extinction without resolving the question of its identity. Every aspect of Buffon's
sweeping theory provoked controversy among those still reluctant to
abandon the perfection of God's creation and the fixity of the species,
not to mention the Bible's timetable for the earth's history. For most
Americans, Noah's Flood continued to be the predominant explanation for the anomalies in the earth's history, from the so-called lost
species to the seashells and marine fossils found on mountaintops in the
Alleghenies. For a few naturalists, the fossil remains were incontrovertible evidence of the earth's undiscovered antiquity, the millions of
millennia beginning to haunt the imagination of theologians and natural philosophers in Europe and America.

In an age of uncertainty and revolutionary violence, when fossil
elephants threatened to undermine the authority of the Scriptures, scientific racialism offered a new paradigm of dominance for European
and American civilization. Contemplation of the existence of extinct
species and the reality of a prehuman past led many European anatomists to develop an entirely new field of comparative anatomy—

craniology, or the study of human skulls. These natural philosophers believed that the configuration of human crania provided clues not only to the origins of man but also to the formation of a hierarchy of races within the human species. The search for the American *incognitum* was linked to the development of these ideas of racial superiority because its existence dramatized the reality of extinction, an event that in the eyes of many anatomists confirmed the degeneration and disappearance of various species.

With the advent of the idea of extinction, the benevolence of God's creation and its "natural" hierarchy were challenged by images of powerful predators and warring species, both animal and human. Images of animal terror and violence appeared in the static harmony of the Great Chain of Being, a concept already weakened by the discovery of lost species like the American *incognitum*. In effect, the savagery of prehistoric nature emerged simultaneously with the first scientific theories suggesting the biological inferiority of the so-called savage races. Thus the search for the bones of the American *incognitum* coincided with the development of a new symbol of white supremacy in Europe and America—the size and shape of human crania.

The most avid European collectors of grinders and tusks now were a group of Dutch and German anatomists who took the lead among naturalists searching for the American *incognitum*'s identity. In early 1787, Jefferson's diplomatic duties at Paris included sending a certificate of membership in the American Philosophical Society to Dr. Christian Friederich Michaelis, a German physician who had taken an interest in the *incognitum* while serving with British troops during the Revolutionary War. Dr. Michaelis had returned from America to the German university town of Göttingen with a set of drawings of the bones from the Ohio salt lick made by the Philadelphia artist Charles Willson Peale.[1]

After a careful study of Peale's drawings and further correspondence with European anatomists, Dr. Michaelis published a comprehensive article on the American *incognitum* two years later. Like Peter Collinson, he ridiculed Daubenton's thesis that the bones from the Ohio valley were those of elephants and hippopotamuses mixed together. While he accepted Dr. William Hunter's hypothesis that the American *incognitum* was an extinct species, he rejected the idea that the giant grinders belonged to a carnivore. Because the animal resembled the Siberian mammoth, he named the unknown creature *mam-*

mout giganteus, but his own physical description of the animal introduced some strange new elements.

In Dr. Michaelis's opinion, the creature had neither tusks nor trunk, an assertion that seemed more illogical and farfetched than Daubenton's own theories, given the abundant fossil evidence to the contrary. The most impressive specimen in Dr. John Morgan's collection was the massive upper jawbone with three molars still intact, which Peale's drawing depicted accurately. Unfortunately, while studying this drawing, Dr. Michaelis looked at the jawbone backward, mistaking the front for the back, an error that led him to conclude that there was no place for tusks.

This aberrant image of the American *incognitum* gained credibility owing to its confirmation by another of Europe's leading comparative anatomists, Petrus Camper, a Dutch physician and authority on the fossil elephants. A personal friend of Dr. Michaelis's father, Johann David Michaelis, a famous Orientalist at Göttingen, Camper received a bone specimen and copies of the Peale's drawing from the doctor upon his return from America. A professor of anatomy at Groningen University in Holland, Camper was actively involved in the debate over the identity of the American *incognitum*, having published an article in 1775 summarizing the scholarly opinions about the mysterious beast. His fossil collection included at least one tusk sent to him from London by William Hunter, with whom he corresponded. In this early article, Camper claimed that the unknown creature had a trunk and giant grinders similar to those of an elephant rather than a hippopotamus, as Buffon and Daubenton had proposed.

In 1784, after receiving copies of Peale's drawing of the jawbone, along with Dr. Michaelis's comments, Camper reversed himself, agreeing with his colleague that the animal had no tusks: "It is evident in this maxilla superior, there was no room for any exerted teeth, nor has this creature ever had any."[2] The following year he visited England, where he examined and sketched "very many beautiful specimens of the *incognitum*," including an upper jawbone in the British Museum, the specimen sent to Lord Shelburne by George Croghan nearly twenty years earlier.

Despite his extensive examination of numerous specimens, Camper's investigation produced a scholarly paper shaped largely by the ill-conceived theories of his friend Dr. Michaelis. Camper now claimed Peale's drawing of the jawbone proved that "the animal never had tusks, and that the tusks found intermixed with the bones of the *incognitum* belonged most certainly to Elephants."[3] His confusion over the beast's appearance was evident when his article was published in St. Petersburg in 1788, for he stated that he did not know what to make of an animal that apparently had a pointed snout and no tusks and did not resemble an elephant.

In 1784, after learning from Dr. Michaelis about Dr. John Morgan's box of old bones, Camper asked Dr. Michaelis, who was still in America, to offer the Philadelphia physician one hundred guineas for the collection. Unsure of Camper's ability to pay this amount, Dr. Morgan turned him down, stating that "it would be a pity to remove [these] rare and surprizing Curiosities of Nature" from the country where they were found. But Dr. Morgan reconsidered after Camper renewed his offer during the summer of 1787, because he was worried that his own failing health would prevent him from undertaking any studies of the bones himself. In addition, the specimens were no longer the unique curiosities they had been twenty years earlier, since numerous other bones from the Ohio salt lick were now making their way to Philadelphia. In the summer or early fall of 1788, Dr. Morgan had the bones crated and shipped to Holland, where they arrived shortly before Camper's death the following year, at age sixty-seven. Among the items listed in the inventory was the massive upper jawbone that had led Dr. Michaelis to conclude that the animal had no tusks or trunk, a specimen now in the paleontology collection of the University of Groningen.

The accelerating demand in Europe for bones of the American *incognitum* from the Ohio valley brought American citizens into closer contact with the European anatomists who were heirs to Buffon's theory of degeneracy. Instead of applying his theory to Americans, his disciples were using the field of comparative anatomy to create new theories of scientific racialism based on the study of human skulls. Craniology was central to this new field of study, which first became known to English and American naturalists during the last phases of the search for the American *incognitum's* identity. Through comparative anatomical study of human skulls, these anatomists sought to establish scientific criteria for a hierarchy of the human races and the superiority of the Caucasian race.

At the time he purchased Dr. Morgan's collection of bones, Petrus Camper was one of the leading architects of the new field of

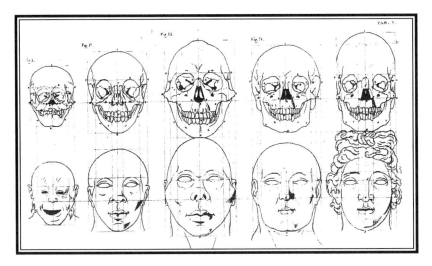

FIGURE 30. Progression of skulls from the monkey through the African to the European and the Greek ideal type in Camper's "Dissertation," 1791. European and American anatomists used such aesthetic concepts in their scientific theories to create a hierarchy of the races.

craniology, and his ideas concerning the configuration of human skulls had established the model for the early theories of scientific racialism. Besides being a skilled anatomist, Camper had been trained as a painter and had won the Gold Medal of the Amsterdam School of Art in 1770. His interest in craniology originally grew out of his belief that Dutch masters like Rubens had misrepresented the shape of the African skull in their paintings of the Eastern Magi. To correct this distortion, Camper developed a technique for measuring the facial angle of human skulls, a plane extending from the lip to the forehead, which varied from the nearly vertical angle of classical Greek statuary and the ideal European skull to the deeply slanted angle of the Africans which Camper felt was closer to the lines of apes and dogs than to men. Two illustrations of this progression appeared in his *Dissertation sur les variétés naturelles*, published in 1791, two years after his death. Camper incorporated into this scientific measurement of the human skull an image of the Apollo Belvedere, the classical Greek ideal of beauty, creating in the process a physical standard for European racial superiority that influenced the field of craniology for many generations (figures 30 and 31).

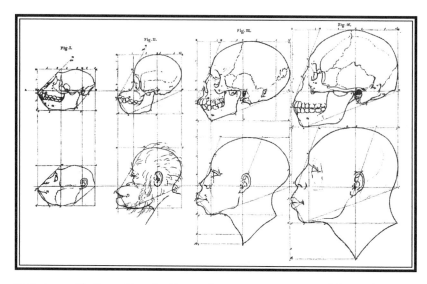

FIGURE 31. Skulls and heads of a monkey, an orangutan, an African American, and a Kalmuck from Petrus Camper's "Dissertation sur les variétés naturelles," 1791. Camper used these diagrams to illustrate his theory of the facial angle, which related innate intelligence to the cranial capacity of the different human races.

Camper's treatise contained ideas about the physical characteristics of the human races that had been developing for several decades. He had completed the first draft in 1768 when the earliest notions of scientific racialism were in their infancy, although theories of the superiority of European civilization were already commonplace. Perhaps the first true scientific theory of race was proposed by the Prussian philosopher Immanuel Kant in his essay "On the Distinctiveness of the Races in General," published in 1775. Scarcely five feet tall, with a deformed chest, he taught mathematics at Königsberg University in East Prussia before being appointed in 1770 to the chair of metaphysics and logic.

Influenced by Isaac Newton's philosophy, Kant's first major work was the *Universal Natural History and Theory of the Heavens,* a general theory of cosmic evolution published in 1755, which startled the academic world by proposing the existence of an infinite universe composed of innumerable star systems beyond the Milky Way. Even though he was a devout believer in the divine contrivance of this vast natural system, Kant hinted at an equally infinite time dimension necessary for its existence: "Millions and whole myriads of millions of centuries will flow on, during which always new worlds and systems of worlds will be formed. It needs nothing less than an eternity to animate the whole boundless range of the infinite extension of space with worlds, without number and without end."[4] At first, Kant's early natural history of the universe attracted little attention, owing to his publisher's bankruptcy, but his nebular hypothesis later helped extend the horizons of geological time among naturalists concerned with the origins of the solar system and the earth's history.

In his essay on the human races, Kant offered a more rigorous scientific interpretation of Buffon's theory of degeneracy, which proposed interbreeding as the principal criterion for identifying a species.[5] Like Buffon, Kant defended the unity of the human species, although he placed more emphasis on the biological factors differentiating the "varieties," or races, within the human species. For Kant, racial classification had to be based on the hereditary traits passed from each generation to the next. Skin color was the only physiological trait that seemed to be transmitted in this manner, and using it, he identified four basic races from which all other were derived by crossing or hybridity: White or European, Copper-red or American Indian, Black or African, and Olive-Yellow of the Asiatic or Oriental Indian.

An important aspect of his theory was the new scientific authority it gave to Buffon's notion of the white race as the original *Stamm*, or stem type, from which all the other races had descended, or "degenerated," to use the French naturalist's term. In defending the unity of human species, Kant introduced biological criteria essential to scientific racialism, although he himself approached the subject in clinical terms, without open advocacy of European superiority. By emphasizing the role of hereditary factors rather than climate and mode of life, biology became one of the primary factors in deviations from the white norm. More important, the formation of the human races was considered analogous to the process of degeneration associated with similar alterations in the animal kingdom, in which differentiation among species, like the American *incognitum* and living elephants, had become the basis for declaring the unknown creature an extinct animal. The larger question of the age of the earth was essential to all speculation about the origins of man, since the deviations described by Kant occurred over long stretches of as yet unimagined time.

Through the auspices of Dr. Christian Friedrich Michaelis, the search for the identity of the American *incognitum* in the United States was linked directly to the University of Göttingen, the new center of comparative anatomy in Europe. While Dr. Michaelis was pursuing the American *incognitum* in New York and Philadelphia after the Revolutionary War, local physicians gave him the skulls of several African Americans and a Native American. Eventually, he brought them back to Göttingen where he gave them to Dr. Johann Friedrich Blumenbach, the university's renowned anatomist, whose growing collection of anatomical specimens included both human skulls and the bones of the American *incognitum*. Blumenbach's large skull collection was well known, and he used it to arrive at a more precise scientific classification of the various races within the human species.

In his doctoral thesis, "De generis varietate humani nativa" (On the natural variety of mankind), presented a decade earlier in 1775, Blumenbach defended the unity of the human species. This notion was then under attack by the advocates of polygenesis, who maintained that the various human races other than the European were actually separate, naturally inferior species, created so from the beginning of time. Polygenesis originally grew out of criticism of biblical texts by the French heretic Isaac La Peyrère, whose book *Preadamitae*, published in 1655, claimed that Adam was the ancestor only of the Jews, whereas other ancient peoples—like the Chaldeans, Egyptians, Chinese, and Mexicans—had descended from other pre-Adamite ancestors. Defenders of polygenesis like the French philosopher Voltaire later cast doubts on the authenticity of the Mosaic history by denying that all humanity had descended from Adam and Eve and attributing racial differences instead to separate acts of creation. "The idea of the plurality of human species has found particular favor with those who made it their business to throw doubt on the accuracy of Scriptures," Blumenbach observed, acknowledging the religious doctrines inherent in his own belief in the unity of the human species.[6]

Twenty years later, after examining the teeth of the fossil elephants, Blumenbach rejected Buffon's definition of species based on the ability of animals to interbreed, because he felt that this factor alone was inadequate to determine whether certain similar animals distant from one another, like the Indian and African elephants, were separate species or only varieties of the same species. "I see, for example, that the molar teeth of the African elephant differ most wonderfully in their conformation from those of the Asiatic. I do not know whether these elephants, which come from such different parts of the world, have ever copulated together."[7]

Blumenbach preferred to rely on dissection and a close scrutiny of the bones to answer the species question.

> But since, so far in all the specimens which I have seen, I have observed the same difference; and since I have never known any example of molar teeth so changed by mere *degeneration*, I conjecture from analogy that those elephants are not to be considered as mere varieties, but must be held to be different species.[8]

To resolve the matter of degeneration within the human species, he applied the same methodology that was used to differentiate varieties, or "races," in the animal kingdom: "We must therefore assign the same causes for the bodily diversity of the races of mankind to which we assign a similar diversity of body in the other *domestic* animals which are widely scattered over the world."[9] Buffon's theory of degeneration, which now extended far beyond his original insult to the Americas, proved to be a broad tool of analysis applied not only to the definition of extinct animal species but also to the development of races within the human species. In 1775, when Kant pleaded for a more precise scientific differentiation of the human races, Blumenbach was already proposing to make craniology the means for attaining this goal and proving scientifically that all men of every race were of the same species, instead of separate species.

Following Buffon, Blumenbach based his own theory of degeneration and racial identity on a combination of environmental factors, including climate, food, and mode of life, whose effects he felt produced physiological changes in the human body over long periods of time. Influenced by Kant, Blumenbach assigned new importance to heredity and genetic patterns, which could be studied objectively by means of comparative anatomy, especially the comparison of human skulls from the various races. In his view, the configuration of the skulls, among other physiological traits, revealed the processes of interaction with the environmental conditions responsible for creating the varieties of races within the human species.

The basic hypothesis underlying Blumenbach's classification of the human races was the assumption, made originally by Buffon, that white was the original skin color of humanity from which all other racial types had degenerated through a complex process of interbreeding and inter-action with the environment. Blumenbach divided humankind into five varieties or races—Caucasian, Mongolian, Ethiopian, American, and Malay, each with its own predominant skin color of white, yellow, black, copper, and tawny. Along with other physiological traits like hair, facial features, and skull configuration, these characteristics formed the basis for the five major categories. However, his scientific theory contained aesthetic criteria similar to those shaping the racial views of his friend Petrus Camper, whose influence Blumenbach read-ily acknowledged in subsequent editions of his dissertation.

Like Buffon, who identified the archetypal white skin color with people living near the Caspian Sea, Blumenbach located the original home of the ideal human skull on the southern slopes of Mount Cau-casus in nearby Georgia. As a result, he coined the term "Caucasian" to describe the archetypal European cranium, "the most beautiful form of the skull, from which, as from a mean and primeval type, the others diverge by most easy gradations on both sides to the two ulti-mate extremes, that is on the one side the Mongolian, on the other the Ethiopian."[10] The third edition of Blumenbach's dissertation, published in 1795, was illustrated with five skulls from his collection, then numbering eighty-two. In 1790, his *Decades cranorium* was pub-lished, a handsomely illustrated volume with accurate engravings and an account of how each skull came into his possession. Among his specimens were the skulls of a Negro and an American Indian sent from America by Dr. Michaelis, along with news about the American *incognitum*.

Blumenbach was a critic of those who held that Africans—or any other racial group—were innately inferior, arguing instead that their inferiority was a result of their mode of life and lack of education. He dismissed the popular notion that the Ethiopian race was a degenerate form of the ape or a hybrid mix of monkey and Homo sapiens, an idea favored by certain Enlightenment philosophers. Nonetheless, as histo-rian George Mosse points out, Blumenbach's scientific writings associ-ated the perfect European skull with the classical Greek ideal.[11] Despite Blumenbach's defense of the unity of humankind, the aesthetic judg-ments implicit in his own theories contained the seeds of a form of sci-entific racialism that took root in European and American culture dur-ing the early nineteenth century. In fact, the same patterns of thought were already present in American national consciousness, as Thomas Jefferson's views of the Negro in America demonstrate.

In February 1787, shortly before the first excerpts from Jefferson's *Notes* appeared in American magazines, a Presbyterian clergyman in Pennsylvania traveled to Philadelphia to deliver to the American Philosophical Society a scholarly paper on the unity of the human species, articulating many of the same ideas defended by Blumenbach. Samuel Stanhope Smith, who taught moral philosophy at the College of New Jersey in Princeton, was unaware then of Blumenbach's treatise, although he clearly was familiar with Buffon's theories about the effects of climatic conditions and the state of society on the formation of racial types. Smith was already a controversial figure at the institution known to be the seat of liberal Presbyterianism, of which he became president eight years later.

Smith's defense of the unity of the human species was written in response to the treatise *Sketches of the Natural History of Man* by Lord Kames, an Edinburgh jurist and literary critic who was a leading advocate of polygenesis among the Scottish Enlightenment authors. Published in 1774 on the eve of the American Revolution, this influential book broke with Christian tradition by assuming the human races were separate species and that human history was characterized by the progress of societies from savagery to civilization. Lord Kames strongly defended the hierarchical arrangement of the natural world and the fixity of the species, or what had come to be known during the eighteenth century as the Great Chain of Being. Even though he tried to reconcile his theory with Christian doctrine by dating the creation of the separate races from the events surrounding the Tower of Babel, his unorthodox interpretation of biblical texts brought criticism by Protestant theologians and natural philosophers in Europe and America.

Published in 1787, Smith's *Essay on the Causes of the Variety of Complexion and Figure in the Human Species* relied heavily on Buffon's theory of climatic conditions in the formation of races within the human species. "The minutest causes, acting constantly, and long continued, will necessarily create great and conspicuous differences in mankind," he noted, rejecting, as Buffon had done, catastrophism in favor of the imperceptible modification of human constitution by heat and cold and the transmission of new traits by means of heredity. "The complexion in any climate will be changed toward black, in proportion to the decree of heat in the atmosphere, and to the quantity of bile in the skin."

He was convinced that the Negro's pigmentation was the result of an oversupply of bile stimulated by the "putrid exhalations" of tropical climates.[12]

Smith was greatly influenced by Buffon's view that white was the original skin color of humankind and that this ideal form of pigmentation was the product of temperate climates. In this respect, his treatise contained the same aesthetic criteria and standards of beauty employed by Buffon and his European disciples. Without engaging in any polemic, Smith tried to counter the theory of American degeneracy by claiming that the temperate zone of North America would eventually reproduce the primordial and perfect skin color of Adam and Eve, even among people of color: "When time shall have accommodated the constitution of its new state, and cultivation shall have meliorated the climate, the beauties of Greece and Circassia may be renewed in America," he asserted, alluding to the regions of Europe where Buffon himself had located the ideal human racial types.[13]

Smith's faith in the eventual amelioration of the Negro's alleged inferiority contrasted with Jefferson's claim that these deficiencies were permanently fixed by nature, irredeemable by any degree of education and improvement. Instead, Buffon's emphasis on the beneficial effects of civilization in transforming the savagery of the natural world into cultivated nature was clearly the source of Smith's own assertion that the state of society was a causal factor in the perfectibility of the human races. Historian John C. Greene elucidates Smith's logic: "The human form could not retain or achieve its original perfection apart from civilization. Savages living exposed to the influence of raw nature and habituated to uncleanliness, neglect, and the practice of painting and anointing their bodies could never be fair in complexion."[14] Within the cultural framework of any civilization, the standard of beauty in a society played an important role in perfecting the human form. Like Jefferson, Smith invoked the breeding of thoroughbred horses to illustrate his point: "We continually see the effect of this principle on the inferior animals. The figure, the colour and the properties of the horse are easily changed according to the reigning taste."[15]

Preoccupation with human origins and scientific racialism reflected the desire for timeless truths in an era of skepticism and impermanence, when the discovery of prehistoric nature threatened to undermine the stability of God's creation, particularly in the new American nation

where the founding fathers' insecurity led them to look for their symbols of antiquity in the earth's natural history. Their revival of the classical ideals drew on centuries-old stereotypes found in England's medieval romances, in which the physiognomy of Greek sculpture and
"skin of dazzling whiteness" were symbols of personal beauty.[16] The immutability and permanence of scientific racialism appealed especially
to Enlightenment thinkers for whom the classical Greek ideal of beauty
was based on the laws of nature, the new symbol of universal authority
in an age of nationalism and revolutionary violence.

The ideas of European anatomists like Blumenbach reached influential naturalists in the new United States in a variety of ways, often
through the continuing influence of British scientific culture there after
the Revolution. In 1793, Blumenbach's *Introduction to Physiology* was
published in Philadelphia shortly after he visited England, where he
had direct contact with American expatriates. Blumenbach traveled
very little, but in early 1792 he went to London where he spent several
weeks talking with the country's leading artists and anatomists, an
event that brought his renown to the attention of Americans unfamil-
iar with his pioneering work in craniology at Göttingen. While there,
Blumenbach also discussed the physiognomy of the Jewish face with the
foremost American painter of the era:

> The great artist Benj[amin] West, President of the Royal Academy of
> Arts, with whom I conversed about the racial face of Jews, thought
> that it above all others had something particularly goat-like about it,
> which he was of opinion lay not so much in the hooked nose as in the
> transit and conflux of the septum which separates the nostrils from
> the middle of the upper lip.[17]

In England, Blumenbach was entertained by the country's leading naturalists, including Sir Joseph Banks, president of the Royal
Society, the English naturalist who had accompanied Captain James
Cook on his first voyage to the South Pacific. With the death of Sir
Hans Sloane, Banks had emerged as England's preeminent collector
of natural history specimens, particularly those related to the anthropology of humankind, the booty brought back from the voyages
of exploration accompanying England's imperial expansion. Among
the trophies he passed on to Blumenbach were the skull of a Carib

chief from the island of St. Vincent in the Caribbean and the skull of a Tahitian, the only example of the Malay race in Blumenbach's collection. These two specimens were especially prized by his German colleague because they were good examples of the American and Malayan races, and Blumenbach used them to illustrate these races in the 1795 edition of his dissertation.[18]

Blumenbach was a critic of the Great Chain of Being, the system of classification still used by many theologians and naturalists who believed in an uninterrupted gradation in the natural world from the lowest forms of matter through the plant and animal kingdoms to the epitome of God's creation—humankind. Debate over the existence of extinct species, like the American *incognitum*, had intensified some anatomists' efforts to defend the Great Chain as proof of the inalterable perfection of God's creation. Being a strong believer in the divinity of nature and the dominance of man, Blumenbach drew a firm line between the animal species and humans and dismissed the Great Chain on the grounds that there were large gaps in the natural world where the animal kingdoms were plainly separated from one another. Nonetheless, while he was in London, he visited the anatomical museum of John Hunter, the English anatomist whose brother William had coined the phrase "American *incognitum*" and first imagined that it was an extinct carnivore. By then, John Hunter's own theory of gradation in the animal kingdom was transforming the Great Chain of Being into an instrument of analysis to demonstrate through physiological traits the existence of a hierarchy of internal organs, animal and human.

John Hunter had become London's foremost surgeon anatomist following the death in 1783 of his older brother William, and he had become the more accomplished anatomist over the years despite his relative lack of formal training. Even though John had been the first person to suggest that the American monster was a carnivore, he had not ventured further in his speculation about the mysterious animal's identity. Near the end of his career when Blumenbach visited his museum, Hunter was already a legendary figure in the European anatomical world, famous not only for his unparalleled private museum of natural history specimens but also for his surgical feats and knowledge of medical pathology.

Hunter's collection of scientific specimens, which included some three thousand stuffed, dried, or skeletonized animals, were exhibited on the upper floor of long galleried hall where visitors encountered several whale skeletons suspended by wires from the ceiling. The walls were lined with five thousand flint-glass jars filled with specimens preserved in spirits—from the embryos and eggs of silkworms and crocodiles to the larvae of mollusks, bees, and fish—displayed alongside the tatooed arms of South Sea islanders. The anatomist's prize was the skeleton of Charles O'Byrne, the "Irish giant," an eight-foot-tall human curiosity who had been exhibited in London.

For European and American anatomists, the enduring influence of John Hunter's museum lay in the methodology he used to arrange his anatomical specimens. Instead of the conventional Linnaean classification of plant and animal species based on external characteristics, he arranged his specimens according to the similarity of their internal organs. "My design, gentlemen, in the formation of this museum was to display throughout the chain of organized beings the various structures in which the functions of life are carried on," he explained, invoking in a novel way the traditional metaphor of the Great Chain of Being.[19] Each set of organs was arranged in a series from the simplest to the most complex, an arrangement that often brought together an odd assortment of creatures whose internal organs were morphologically similar.

Hunter himself had little interest in scientific racialism, but his arrangement of skulls reflected some of the same assumptions that colored the views of craniologists like Petrus Camper and Blumenbach. Visitors to the museum encountered his skull series carefully set out on a table, beginning with the human varieties—the European, Asiatic, American Indian, and African—and then proceeding from the Australian aborigine through the chimpanzee and macaque monkey to the dog and crocodile. Hunter's own commentary contained few aesthetic judgments about the beauty of the European skull, but his arrangement of the specimens illustrated his latent assumptions about the superiority of the European race implicit in his theory about the gradation of particular organs in the animal kingdom. "The declension of animals from the Human to the brute, or more distant brute, is faster in the head," he observed, with regard to the skulls. Furthermore, when reversed, the pattern of gradation reflected a progression from the imperfect to the perfect: "The declension of animals from the most perfect to the most imperfect is in regular order or progression."[20]

Hunter's display of skulls resembled the profiles of Petrus Camper's theory of the facial angle, minus the classical Greek head that he used to show the ideal form of the European skull. In 1785, the same year that Camper himself visited Hunter's museum, the English anatomist had his portrait painted by Sir Joshua Reynolds, England's foremost artist (figure 32). His painting shows Hunter seated beside his writing table, where several carefully chosen accessories are displayed. In the center stands an open volume with drawings of a graded series of fore-limbs and skulls like those exhibited in his museum. Neither Hunter nor Blumenbach were overt advocates of white supremacy, at least not in the biological sense argued by their adversaries the polygenesists. But other European natural philosophers and anatomists used Hunter's skull series to bolster their claims that non-European races were actually separate species, naturally inferior from the beginning of time. Prodded by the fossil evidence for extinct species and the specter of a vast prehuman past, defenders of the innate inequality of the human races saw in Hunter's schematic gradation of skulls scientific evidence of the superiority of the European race, based on biology rather than simply cultural dominance.

Among the British physicians who visited the John Hunter's anatomical museum was Charles White, an eminent surgeon from Manchester who had been Hunter's fellow student during their early medical training. Like William Hunter, White devoted his career to man-midwifery and surgery, serving as physician at the Manchester Infirmary before founding the Manchester Lying-in Hospital for pregnant women in 1790, where he was employed as a consulting surgeon. Just when Camper's influential dissertation was published (posthumously) and the third edition of Blumenbach's treatise *The Natural Varieties of Man* appeared, White presented his own defense of the Great Chain of Being which showed the influence of all three of Europe's leading comparative anatomists.

Elected to the Royal Society in 1762 at age thirty-four, White was well known for his innovative methods in obstetrics, as well as his active participation in the city's cultural life, being the author of numerous articles and the owner himself of a museum of three hundred anatomical preparations. In 1795, responding to advocates of the unity of mankind, he defended both the Great Chain of Being and the doctrines of polygenesis in a paper delivered to the Manchester Literary and Philosophical Society. Four years later at age seventy-one, he

FIGURE 32. Detail from William Sharp's engraving of a portrait of John
Hunter by Sir Joshua Reynolds, 1788. On the table is an open book illustrating Hunter's theory of the gradation of forelimbs and skulls, which progressed
from the crocodile and dog through the chimpanzee and monkey to the Australian aborigine and European. Courtesy of the Hunterian Art Gallery, University of Glasgow.

published the complete results of his investigation into nature's hierarchy in four volumes under the cumbersome title *An Account of the Regular Gradation in Man and in different animals and Vegetables, and from the former to the latter.* Observing Hunter's cabinet of skulls and his physiological exhibits had led White to apply the anatomist's theory of gradation as a general principle governing the animal and plant kingdoms and the hierarchy of the human races as well, which he insisted were actually separate species.

The man-midwife from Manchester combined Petrus Camper's theories of cranial beauty with Hunter's charting of physiological functions to produce an influential new version of the Great Chain of Being that looks today like a demonstration of Darwin's theory of evolution. Pictured in profiles reminiscent of Camper's facial angle, White's skull series begins with the pointed beak of the snipe and continues in Hunter's familiar sequence from the crocodile through several breeds of dogs to the snub-nosed monkey and orangutan before moving on to the human races, which were arranged in ascending order from the Negro to the Europeans (figure 33). In a tribute to the aesthetic standards of Camper's facial angle, the sequence ended with profiles of Roman and Greek heads, inspired by statuary from classical antiquity: "Ascending the line of gradation, we come at last to the white Europeans; who being most removed from the brute creation, may, on that account, be considered as the most beautiful of the human race."[21]

Hybridity and apocryphal stories of sexual intercourse between apes and humans conjured up fears in the minds of polygenesists that the unity of the human species would elevate monkeys and chimpanzees to the rank of humans while degrading humanity to the level of animals. In White's opinion, the Negro was an intermediate species between the white man and the ape, whose natural inferiority could not be altered by any amount of interbreeding or the effects of environment and mode of life. By defining the human races as different species, he sought to protect the privileged position of the European race, which seemed to be threatened by the dangerous dynamism of interbreeding, the criterion used for defining the unity of the human species by everyone from Buffon to Blumenbach. Behind all these theories lay an even more explosive issue, the eons of geological time necessary for the modification of species, whether animal or human.

John Hunter's scant writings about fossils reveal the existence of a substratum of Anglo-American thought that privately contradicted the

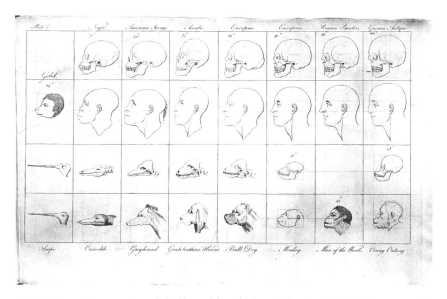

FIGURE 33. Progression of skulls and heads from Charles White's *Account of the Regular Gradation in Man,* 1799. White used Camper's craniological theories and John Hunter's graded skull series to support his theory of polygenesis—the idea that non-European races were separate, naturally inferior species. Courtesy Department of Library Services, American Museum of Natural History.

platitudes and dogma of public culture concerning the age of the earth. Before he died suddenly of a heart attack in 1793, Hunter submitted to the Royal Society a manuscript summarizing his observations of some fossils encrusted with "crystallized earth" that had been sent to England by a Prussian aristocrat in Anspach. Hunter mentioned briefly the fossil remains of elephants found in England, Siberia, and other areas, but the main focus of his remarks was the chemical process of fossilization itself and the long time that it must have taken for the bones to become encrusted with calcareous matter.

> The difference in the state of the bones shows that there was probably a succession of them for a vast series of years. If we calculate how long these must still remain to be as far decayed as some others are, it will require many thousand years, a sufficient time for a vast accumulation.[22]

Recognizing water as the chief agent producing these changes, he proposed rather casually a timeline that far exceeded the accepted biblical standard of six thousand years.

Initially, the editors of the Royal Society's journal rejected Hunter's article because his statement that fossil decay required "many thousand years" contradicted the accepted biblical chronology. But after his death the following year, Hunter's remarks were deemed sufficiently innocuous to allow their publication, possibly as homage to the recently deceased author. During his lifetime, the London anatomist seemed willing, like many of his contemporaries, to accept such restraints on his speculations about the age of the earth, though he clearly held opinions that were at odds with the accepted biblical timeline.

Shortly before his death, Hunter also prepared a second controversial manuscript for the Royal Society entitled "Observations and Reflections on Geology." In this essay, he directly challenged the idea of the Great Deluge, again using the extended time required for the fossilization to cast doubt on its ability to explain the layers of fossil strata in the earth's landmass. "Forty days' water overflowing the dry land could not have brought such quantities of sea-productions on its surface, nor can we suppose thence, taking all possible circumstances into consideration, that it remained long on the whole surface of the earth; therefore there was no time for their being fossilized."[23] Without embracing any elaborate theory of the earth's age, he employed the term "many thousand centuries" to describe the time it took to lay down the complex fossil strata found underground.

The Royal Society's response to Hunter's manuscript this time reveals the private acceptance of an extended timeline among learned Englishmen even while it could not be endorsed publicly. Major James Rennell, a geographer and member of the society, was asked by his colleagues to persuade Hunter to alter his statements in order to placate public opinion:

> Now, although I have no quarrel with any opinions relating to the antiquity of the globe, yet there are a description of persons very numerous and very respectable in every point but their pardonable superstitions, who will dislike any mention of a specific period that ascends beyond 6000 years. I would, therefore, with submission, qualify the expression by many *years,* instead of *centuries.*[24]

Unwilling to change his text or to challenge publicly the orthodox views of the earth's age, Hunter decided instead to withdraw the paper for publication, preferring the silence of his dissecting rooms to the noise of public controversy.

While fossil evidence provoked thought about the origins of man and prehistoric life on earth, the acceptance of extinction and geological time as physical truths remained marginal themes in Anglo-American consciousness. Even the boldest intimations of the earth's antiquity had little impact on speculation about the American *incognitum's* identity during the last decades of the eighteenth century. In 1785, England's first true geological treatise was presented to the Royal Society of Edinburgh by James Hutton, a leading member of the city's famous Oyster Club, whose members included the political economist Adam Smith. Trained as a physician at the Universities of Edinburgh and Leyden, Hutton had stopped practicing medicine in order to settle on his father's farm to study agriculture. During these studies, he became interested in mineralogy and geology, which led him to resettle in Edinburgh where he continued his chemical experiments in the company of other members of the Scottish Enlightenment.

The first sketch of Hutton's *Theory of the Earth,* presented to the Royal Society of Edinburgh in 1785, outlined a complex system of uplift and erosion operating on the earth's crust to produce an almost endless succession of geological epochs, whose character was essentially cyclical rather than historical, in keeping with the chronology of Christianity.[25] For Hutton, granite was an intrusive, igneous rock, not a sediment, and its irregular, vertical beds had been eroded and covered over by horizontal layers of sedimentary rocks to create the striking "unconformities" visible in exposed rock faces. In 1788, when the final version of Hutton's theory was published, this controversial hypothesis was illustrated by an engraving showing the turbulent geological forces lying beneath the English countryside, unbeknownst to the horses and carriages passing overhead (figure 34).

For Hutton, these unconformities represented the restorative principle in the earth's geological system, providing evidence of nature's mechanism for renewal during a succession of geological epochs. "Time, which measures every thing in our idea, is to nature endless and as nothing."[26] But his new concept served mainly to prove the existence of a geological system in nature, not to discredit the biblical timeline.

FIGURE 34. John Clerk of Eldin's engraving of James Hutton's unconformity from the 1788 edition of Hutton's *Theory of the Earth*. In Hutton's geological system, irregular beds of igneous rocks overlain by sedimentary layers reflected the earth's cyclical process of renewal.

> For having, in the natural history of this earth, seen a succession of worlds, we may from this conclude that there is a system in nature; in like manner, as from seeing revolutions of the planets, it is concluded, that there is a system by which they are intended to continue those revolutions,

he announced, invoking the metaphor of Newton's celestial system. In memorable but often misinterpreted words, Hutton actually discouraged speculation about God's creation of the heavens and the earth: "But if the succession of worlds is established in the system of nature, it is in vain to look for any thing higher in the origin of the earth. The result, therefore, of our present enquiry is, that we find no vestige of a beginning, no prospect of an end."[27]

Even though he had an extensive collection of fossils, Hutton made little use of this type of evidence in his treatise on the geological processes at work in the earth's crust. The existence of fossil beds served mainly to explain the disposition of sediments rather than to mark historical epochs in the earth's history. The issue of extinction and the identity of many unknown fossil creatures remained unresolved during his lifetime, and his few comments on the subject suggest that he still believed that many of these creatures were living animals as yet undiscovered in the earth's unexplored territories.

Nonetheless, Hutton did introduce an important new distinction between human history and the prehuman past of prehistoric animals and geological time. In his opinion, natural history provided little evidence that the antiquity of man extended further back in time than Mosaic history:

> But this is not the case with regard to the inferior species of animals, particularly those which inhabit the ocean and its shores. We find in natural history monuments which prove that those animals had long existed; and we thus procure a measure for the computation of a period of time extremely remote, though far from being precisely ascertained.[28]

Despite the implications of this declaration for the history of nature, Hutton refused to speculate on the origins of any species, human or animal, choosing instead to focus on the timeless cyclical processes of the earth's natural history.

Hutton's *Theory* drew immediate criticism from several learned naturalists in London, who accused him of subverting the Scriptures. But the overall impact of his geological treatise was muted by the ponderous detail of his writing, which became even more cumbersome in the two-volume edition of his work published in 1795, two years before his own death. Not until his good friend John Playfair, a professor of mathematics at the University of Edinburgh, published a shorter volume in 1802 explaining the theory more clearly and concisely did Hutton's ideas have wider impact. Even then, the uniformitarian principles of his theory did not become part of the geological canon for thirty more years, when they were affirmed by Charles Lyell's *Principles of Geology*.

The relative obscurity of Hutton's theory of the earth's history illustrates the extent to which the discovery of prehistoric nature still lay buried beneath overlying layers of scientific thought and religious doctrine during the last decades of the eighteenth century. When the founding fathers were pursuing the American *incognitum*, their hunt for the bones took place largely in a national culture shaped by evangelical assumptions and Enlightenment doctrines far removed from Hutton's unconformity, the intrusive, igneous rocks of a revolution in geological thought that eventually led to the upheaval of Darwin's *Origin of Species*. In many respects, Buffon's theory of degeneration had a more far-reaching effect on American national consciousness than did Hutton's scientific principles and the awareness of geological time.

Perhaps the first primitive elaboration of an evolutionary idea appeared about this time in the eccentric literary works of the London physician and poet Erasmus Darwin, grandfather of the celebrated author of *Origin of Species*. His *Zoonomia: or the Laws of Organic Life*, published in 1794, extended Buffon's theory of generation to include the evolution of organisms through a biological process analogous to the transformation of life-forms from microscopic organisms in the seminal fluids to adulthood.

> By considering in how minute a proportion of time many of the changes of animals described have been produced, would it be too bold to imagine, that in the great length of time, since the earth began to exist, perhaps millions of ages before the commencement of the history of mankind, would it be too bold to imagine that all warm-blooded animals have arisen from one living filament?[29]

The extinction of animal species and the fossil record were evidence of "this gradual production of the species and genera," which he envisioned as a progression from lower forms of life to more perfect beings. Erasmus Darwin thus reversed Buffon's theory of the degeneration of species, introducing an optimistic scenario of gradual perfectibility, although the struggle for survival played little role in his view of the evolutionary process.

None of Europe's leading anatomists could be considered true iconoclasts with regard to the existence of geological time and the earth's prehuman past. Efforts to introduce scientific evidence for a longer timeline were often inhibited by religious authorities as well as the cautiousness of anatomists unwilling to bring down on themselves the opprobrium of the scientific establishment. Like John Hunter, many chose to pursue their empirical studies without drawing controversial conclusions, at least not publicly through publications. "As Moses derives his authority from powers we cannot admit to natural causes and effects," Hunter pointed out, "we must leave the first formation of things, and take them as formed."[30]

Evidently, Hunter viewed the antediluvian world with the same clinical detachment with which he dissected cadavers, preferring not to engage in philosophical questions about the origin of man and the earth's antiquity. His collection of fossils was extensive, but unlike his brother William, he seldom speculated about the extinction of species or the identity of the American *incognitum*. Nevertheless, transcripts of his own notes, published posthumously, contain a section, "On the origin of species," that does link his theory of gradation to the degeneration of species from a primeval archetype:

> Does not the natural gradation of animals, from one to another, lead to the original species? And does not that mode of investigation gradually lead to the knowledge of that species? Are we not led on to the wolf by the gradual affinity of the different varieties in the dog?[31]

At his rural estate, where ostriches roamed the lawn and the roar of lions and tigers chained in subterranean dens could be heard, Hunter kept several wolves, jackals, and dogs penned up together to see what kind of hybrid creatures they might produce. This experiment augured the approach of the Darwinian era when the concept of a violent struggle for survival and the bared fangs of carnivores replaced the static harmony of the Great Chain of Being that naturalists from Buffon to Charles White had defended.

In fact, an unsettling image of this carnivorous nature had already appeared in English painting, heralding the arrival of Darwin's warring species. Beginning in the 1760s, George Stubbs, England's most famous painter of horses, produced a series of paintings depicting a magnificent thoroughbred stallion being attacked by a lion (figure 35). In many of these paintings, the lion has sunk its teeth and claws into the flanks of one of England's finest equestrian specimens. For decades, the self-taught Stubbs had made his living painting portraits of thoroughbred horses belonging to English aristocrats, always picturing them in harmony with the serene English countryside. His elegant paintings were visions of the cultivated nature celebrated by Buffon, in which the horse was the noblest of the domestic animals, a symbol of the dominance of European civilization over the natural world.

FIGURE 35. George Stubbs's painting *Horse attacked by a Lion*, ca. 1762. One of a series of paintings on this theme, these works foreshadowed the later arrival of warring species and the struggle for existence in the era of Darwin and the dinosaurs. Courtesy Yale Center for British Art, Paul Mellon Collection.

In 1770, William Hunter commissioned Stubbs to paint the first American "moose" brought to England as part of his investigation into its possible extinction. Hunter's younger brother John, whose patronage was especially strong in the last decade of Stubbs's life, owned two different versions of his lion paintings, *A Horse frightened by a Lion* and *Lion devouring a Stag*. According to Judy Egerton, a curator at the Tate Gallery in London, the opening of John Hunter's museum was probably the chief reason that Stubbs resumed his own anatomical work.[32] Exotic wild animals were becoming more fashionable than bucolic scenes filled with domesticated animals and prize-winning racehorses.

As Stubbs's biographer Basil Taylor points out, these "Lion and Horse" paintings are images of animal violence and terror without precedent in English art and contrast sharply with the spirit of his earlier horse paintings. Rather than viewing them as proto-Romantic works foreshadowing the style of Gericault and Delacroix, Taylor traces their inspiration to a classical Roman sculpture of a lion attacking a horse that Stubbs may have seen in 1754 during a visit to Rome. Even Buffon, who romanticized the animal kingdom and celebrated the ferocity of the carnivores in his *Histoire naturelle*, offered no images to match the violence and terror of Stubbs's *Horse attacked by a Lion*. To explain the appearance of this alarming image in Stubbs's repertoire, we must probe deeper into the cultural psyche of late-eighteenth-century England and the changes wrought by industrialism and commercial life.

Indeed, as art critic Peter Fuller noted, the harsh ethos of industrialism and urban commercial life—with its celebration of competition in the marketplace and Adam Smith's impersonal law of supply and demand—was eroding the old aristocratic order based on noble birth and military prowess. In many ways, the vision of a static, unchanging hierarchical order in nature associated with the Great Chain of Being, which was idealized in Stubbs's earlier horse paintings, reflected the values of a bygone era. The divinely ordained natural order was being replaced by the new ethics of *caveat emptor*, the dog-eat-dog world of industrialism and commerce, in which the wealth of nations was generated by industry and self-interest.

The true source of Stubbs's obsession with the "Lion and Horse" paintings, as Fuller explained, lay in the problems that predatory animals posed to his anachronistic vision of a harmonious and hierarchical natural world ruled by divine will and aristocratic good taste: "It is as if, in this theme, Stubbs dimly glimpsed the idea of the struggle for life and the survival of the fittest—evolutionary ideas which were to dominate the following century."[33] In his opinion, the scenes of animal violence have an "unnatural, dream-like quality." Harking back to William King's *De origine mali*, the theologian's justification for the war between the species, Fuller emphasizes the pathos of Stubbs's predicament, viewing his paintings as a lament for the advent of the carnivores, the onset of a natural world ruled by competition and conflict instead of domesticity and deference.

Conflict in nature, symbolized by the extinction of species, was no longer evidence of a divinely ordained natural event but the harbinger of a struggle for survival whose viciousness mirrored the harsh realities of industrial society and the marketplace. Later in life, Stubbs traded the patronage of dukes and duchesses, with their desire for idyllic scenes of "Mares and Foals" and thoroughbred racehorses, for the naturalism of anatomical studies, in which beauty was determined by the scientific accuracy of his lines. Like many of his contemporaries, Stubbs did not really want to dwell on the horror of the lion's jaws or the horse's fate, preferring instead the certainty of scientific truth to class war and the conflict between the species.

For all its powerful premonitions of things to come, Stubbs's paintings remained an anomaly in the Anglo-American cultural world, since the war among species was still a marginal theme in the emerging awareness of prehistoric nature. In the new American republic, where the *incognitum* was already an icon of national identity, people looked upon its monstrous grinders with a mixture of envy and awe, enjoying the sense of superiority the massive jaws gave them. As the quest for a complete skeleton of the unknown creature gained momentum, they seemed to take a certain pride in the fact that the mysterious beast was reputed to be a ferocious carnivore, the largest of all terrestrial beings. In their eagerness to embrace the extinct species as an emblem of nationhood, many Americans transformed the *incognitum* into an elephant with claws, a voracious predator that leaped on deer and elk with the ferocity of Stubbs's lion attacking the horse, savagely crushing the flesh and bones of these large animals between their monstrous grinders.

11

"Monarch of the Wilderness"

The Pines crashed beneath their feet; and the Lake shrunk when they slaked their thirst; the forceful Javelin in vain was hurled, and the barbed arrow fell harmless from their side. Forests were laid waste at a meal, the groans of expiring Animals were everywhere heard; and whole Villages, inhabited by men, were destroyed in a moment.

—*The American Museum*, 1790

THE RISING INTEREST in American antiquity—whether the ancient ruins of Indian mounds, the fossil remains of the "mammoth," or the natural wonders of the wilderness landscape—found an ideal synthesis in the overlapping themes of natural history and nationalism in the new republic. Publication of Jefferson's *Notes* led many Americans to imbue the missing creature's bones with a political purpose. Excerpts from Jefferson's eloquent rebuttal of Buffon were soon published in the *Columbian Magazine*, a Philadelphia journal devoted to the creation of a national culture. The young nationalists who contributed to it were already ridiculing the theory of American degeneracy in their poems and essays. In 1787, during the Constitutional Convention at Philadelphia, sarcastic rebukes of Buffon's theory even found their way into the *Federalist Papers*, the compendium of political writings advocating adoption of the new constitution.

In many respects, Buffon's influence on American national consciousness was positive. He gave new recognition to the powerful internal forces operating in the natural world by making nature itself a historical reality rather than a static, idealized entity. From the geological epochs to the dynamism of degeneration, Buffon's romance of nature unleashed a new sense of the potent symbolism of the laws of nature and nature's God. Without the grandeur of Buffon's spectacle, the American *incognitum* could not have become an icon of national identity, nor would natural history have emerged so boldly as an ideology of conquest. Even as Americans railed against European arrogance, they eagerly embraced naturalism as either evidence of God's glory or the rationale for the empire they sought to create. In American eyes, the unsettled western territories, like the *incognitum's* habitat, were a savage wilderness destined to be conquered by piety and progress.

Despite the European anatomists' convincing case for extinction, many Americans still believed in a divinely established natural order. In fact, the idea of extinction was applied almost immediately to the Indians, whose own disappearance, like that of the American *incognitum*, was viewed as a natural event that had God's blessing. For citizens of the new republic, extinction came to have a moral purpose, opening the way for their own triumph over the savagery of the natural world. Drawing on the romanticized treatment of an Indian legend that was first popularized in Jefferson's *Notes*, an anonymous author in Mathew Carey's monthly magazine *American Museum* depicted the legendary animal as a beast of prey that had once threatened man's existence. The monster's long period of gestation was about to end as its immense skeletal form began to take shape in the imagination of American patriots.

Several weeks before Washington's inauguration in 1789, Rev. Dr. Nicholas Collin, rector of the Swedish Churches in Pennsylvania, gave a speech to the American Philosophical Society mixing nationalistic rhetoric with natural history and calling on his countrymen to find the unknown animal's complete skeleton. Enlightened clergymen and their congregations drew a moral lesson from the disappearance of the "mammoth" that was instrumental in its transformation into a monstrous carnivore in the eyes of many American citizens. They viewed the extinction of the nation's first prehistoric monster as a parable of God's benevolence and the American nation's own mastery of the natural world, including its subjugation of the nations and races they considered "savages."

Even before the delegates to the Constitutional Convention gathered in Philadelphia to strengthen the federal government's powers, Jefferson's *Notes* began to affect the nation's public culture. Emboldened by the success of the American Revolution, the young American poets Joel Barlow and Philip Freneau published political satire mocking

European exponents of American degeneracy. They depicted Cornelius de Pauw, Buffon's Dutch disciple, announcing the invention of a miraculous new telescope that made things look smaller the farther away they were, including all the creatures in America, which appeared infinitely smaller than those in Europe.[1]

Educated Americans were sensitive to the insinuations of American inferiority largely because they were unsure of their own national identity. They still measured their own achievements against European standards and the classical literature of Greece and Rome, envisioning themselves as the heirs to a civilization and empire that had traveled westward from its origins in Mediterranean antiquity. In 1779, David Ramsay, a Pennsylvania-born physician living in South Carolina, eloquently expressed these sentiments, joining in a single phrase his countrymen's evangelical beliefs and dreams of empire: "Ever since the flood, true religion, literature, arts, empire, and riches, have taken a slow and gradual course from east to west, and are now about fixing their long and favourite abode in this new western world."[2]

In the eyes of the founding fathers, the creation of a new society entailed a separation from the past—a rejection of Europe's decadence and despotism—but they viewed this act of rebellion as a rebirth of the grandeur of Christian civilization shorn of the corrupting influence of the Catholic Church and monarchical rule. The rhetoric of republicanism was a complex mosaic of religious beliefs and political philosophy linked by the common assumption of the nation's messianic purpose, jointly conceived in terms of a redeemer nation favored by God and the Enlightenment idea of the progress of societies from savagery to civilization.

Natural history, whether God's nature or natural law, served to legitimate the nation's expansion, providing citizens at the same time with a vision of their own antiquity, one rooted in the universal history of nature itself. "America as a political concept came into being as antihistory, as the power of nature—in spite of all the European [abuse]—reaching out toward the future and already proud of its titanic primitivism," according to historian Antonello Gerbi.[3] In this perspective, the bones of the American *incognitum* were emblems of empire, symbolizing the extinguishing of the savagery of nature by the civilizing forces of Christianity and commerce.

The principal vehicles for this cultural nationalism in American intellectual life after the Revolution were the magazines created by the educated classes who were self-consciously aware of the lack of a national culture. Among the twenty new journals, the most important was the *Columbian Magazine,* a monthly founded in Philadelphia during the summer of 1786 by five journalists and printers, including Mathew Carey, an Irish émigré who had come to America just after the Revolution. Modeled on the popular British monthly the *Gentleman's Magazine,* the journal quickly achieved a circulation of some twelve hundred subscribers, mainly lawyers, physicians, clergymen, merchants, and politicians. The forty-eight- page format, "elegantly printed on a very neat paper, of American manufacture," contained copperplate engravings of picturesque American scenes, including views of natural wonders in the landscape.

Striving to promote a distinctively national literature, the magazine's editors mixed biographies of famous American patriots with descriptions of the country's landscape. The second issue set the tone in October 1786 by juxtaposing a biography of the Revolutionary War hero Nathaniel Greene and an article about the structure of the earth in Pennsylvania by David Rittenhouse, a Philadelphia mathematician and astronomer who had been celebrated as one of America's geniuses in Jefferson's *Notes.* The first page faced an engraving of the great seal of the new republic, and its opening lines demonstrated the way the American Revolution could be incorporated into the cycles of the earth's history: "There is nothing, perhaps, which would gratify the curiosity of man in a higher degree, than the history, if it could be obtained, of the globe we inhabit—its formation and the various revolutions it has undergone."[4]

The revolutions to which Rittenhouse referred were the geological epochs that were coming to be perceived as violent upheavals in the formation of the earth's crust, like those that Jefferson described in his view of the Potomac River water gap. In language reminiscent of Thomas Burnet's *Sacred Theory of the Earth,* Rittenhouse pointed to the nearly vertical limestone beds in the Allegheny Mountains as evidence of such an upheaval: "In short, the whole face of the country seems strongly to confirm a supposition, that the former shell, or outward crust of the earth, has been broken to pieces, and its fragments thrown confusedly in every direction."[5]

Without trying to present a general theory of the earth's formation, Rittenhouse's geological view of the landscape mixed the gradual process of erosion and sedimentation with catastrophism, although he stopped short of rejecting the Great Deluge. In fact, among the catastrophic natural processes he envisioned shaping the landscape was an immense flood: "I have, indeed, no conception of any cause which could leave the face of the country in the conditions we now find it, but the most prodigious rains, and these, too, falling perhaps before vegetation had covered the face of the earth."[6] Like Buffon, Rittenhouse saw the flood occurring *before* the creation of mankind. However, his own scientific views still contained elements of the biblical narrative, thereby facilitating the identification of the new nation's antiquity with the revolutions in God's nature.

Rittenhouse contrasted the turbulence of the upended beds forming the Allegheny Mountains with the vast, extended plain to the west, where the layers of stone, sand, coal, and clay seemed to lie undisturbed, perfectly horizontal, in unbroken beds. The flat beds of coal were once a vegetable substance as the imprint of common tree leaves, "pressed together, like cakes of saffron," clearly indicated to him. Struggling to explain how beds of sand and clay formed into masses of solid stone, he encountered the anomaly that had stimulated so much geological thought over the years—the presence of seashells fossilized in stone. "Some very ingenious philosophical gentlemen, are of the opinion, that these apparent remains of shells were never real shells, but original productions of nature, in stone, in imitation of animal shells."[7]

This was the same explanation that Thomas Jefferson briefly used in the first private edition of his *Notes on the State of Virginia*. Having received an early copy of this edition, Rittenhouse had been among the first to challenge his friend's anachronistic views: "Nothing has hitherto occurred to me in it contrary to my own Philosophical notions," he wrote to Jefferson in September 1785, "except that of Stones growing in imitation of Shells without real animal Shells to give them that form."[8] In the *Columbian*, Rittenhouse felt confident enough of his beliefs to contradict Jefferson: "Besides the arguments against this hypothesis, which will occur to every one who examines such petrifactions, there is one which to me appears perfectly conclusive. Pieces of these petrified shells, lightly calcined, have precisely the same taste with fresh shells heated."[9] Interestingly enough, he applied the same empirical test to animal bones found embedded in stone: "And, pieces of bone and horn, lodged in stone, and so completely petrified as to strike fire plentifully with steel, will nevertheless, if moistened and rubbed together, emit the same strong smell as the raspings of fresh horn and bone."[10]

In the summer of 1786, Rittenhouse accompanied Andrew Ellicott, a Philadelphia surveyor commissioned by Congress to determine the northern border of Pennsylvania, on an expedition up the Susquehanna River. At Tioga, on the banks of the Susquehanna, they found a giant tooth, which Rittenhouse brought back to Philadelphia and had Charles Willson Peale draw. Published in the *Columbian*, the engraving of Peale's sketch showed, as the artist himself noted, the tooth's grinding surface which was quite different from the molars brought from the Ohio salt lick: "The others had several conical nobs of about one inch and an inch and an half prominency, but in this we find some waiving, but little elevated ridges, which part, as well as the nobs of the other teeth, are hard enamel."[11] In December 1786, Rittenhouse read a short paper at the American Philosophical Society on the curiosity but offered little speculation about the identity of the creature to which it belonged.[12]

Even before excerpts from Jefferson's *Notes* were published in the *Columbian Magazine*, descriptions of the gigantic bones from the Ohio salt licks appeared in its pages. In November 1786, the journal featured an anonymous article entitled "Description of Bones, &c found near the River Ohio," describing a tusk, thighbone, and grinder brought to Philadelphia several years earlier by Major Isaac Craig, an American officer serving on the Ohio frontier during the Revolutionary War.[13] These specimens had already been the subject of a paper delivered to the American Philosophical Society on March 5, 1784, by General Lewis Nicola, an ambitious military figure active in the society's affairs.[14]

The article in the *Columbian Magazine* had a strongly religious tone in keeping with the close association of these curiosities with evangelical thought in the American national consciousness. Echoing the defenders of the Great Chain of Being, the anonymous author identified these natural wonders as evidence of the Creator's inestimable powers. For him, natural history was tangible proof of the existence of God's power: "Abstracted from the doctrine of revelation, which is as yet but partially believed by the world, the book of nature is the only record from which the existence, power, &c. of the great former and governor of the universe can be deduced."[15]

Not surprisingly, the author dismissed the idea that the American *incognitum* was an extinct creature, although he quoted directly Dr. William Hunter's famous assertion to this effect, which he felt clearly impugned God's benevolence: "This sentence, I apprehend, conveys an idea injurious to the Deity; who, at the creation, wanted neither foresight to discover how detrimental so powerful an enemy to the human, as well as animal race, or benevolence to prevent the evil, without requiring or depending on experience."[16] But the underlying problem was that extinction implied an imperfection in God's creation: "I believe our globe, and every part thereof, came out of the hand of its creator as perfect as he intended it should be, and will continue in exactly the same states, as to its inhabitants at least, till its final dissolution." The forcefulness of this rebuttal reveals how formidable a topic Dr. Hunter's idea of extinction had become among America's educated classes.

The jawbone with grinders, a femur, and part of a tusk had been displayed at the city's library for several months, giving Philadelphians the opportunity to examine the specimens firsthand. Disappointed that no qualified person had offered to analyze the bones, the anonymous author provided a detailed description himself, including exact measurements of each specimen, along with illustrations drawn to scale. Puzzled by the tusk's texture, which seemed different from an elephant's, he had taken several pieces to a local ivory turner, who examined the specimen under a magnifying glass but could not determine its identity. "Major Craig, the gentleman who brought these fossils from the Ohio, says there were others, of the same kind, much larger," the author declared, still unsure that the encrustation on the tooth's roots was petrified ivory as the major claimed.

What gave this article in the *Columbian Magazine* its real impact was not the author's defense of God's creation but the engraving that the editors chose to illustrate his text. Readers were greeted with a large, two-page foldout depicting the tusk, thighbone, and tooth of the American *incognitum* alongside two other widely discussed American curiosities, a paddlefish and the rattle of a rattlesnake (figure 36). Through a curious distortion of scale, the rattlesnake's rattle appeared to be the same length as the enormous thighbone and tusk, giving an ominous presence to this delicate anatomical organ often associated with America in the eyes of European naturalists. The large scale of these specimens, all unique to the American continent, reflected the editor's desire to rebut any insinuations of smallness and inferiority in the new nation's creatures.

The enormous size of the *incognitum's* bones presented a dilemma— how to explain the disappearance of so large an animal from the American continent. Not wishing to dwell on this, the author attributed its demise to an alteration in the climate and shortage of food, since, as he concluded, humans seemed to have played no role in their disappearance. How to account for the concentration of bones at Big Bone Lick posed another question that he attempted to answer by citing the example of the herds of deer, buffalo, and wild cattle flocking to the site to lick the salt: "These [deposits] are often found in marshy ground, in which many beasts are at certain seasons swamped, and several unable to extricate themselves. And, in a succession of years, or possibly ages, so many of the animals, which produced the bones now found petrified, may have perished in this manner."[17]

The author's cautious, commonsense hypothesis was equally circumspect in its modest appraisal of the amount of time during which the bones were accumulated. He did not emphasize the presence of a ferocious carnivore in America's antiquity, nor was there any indication the author had strong nationalistic sentiments. Compared with Jefferson's *Notes*, his remarks were almost devoid of polemic, since they made no reference to Buffon's theory of degeneracy. However, the size of the illustrations, together with the journal's subsequent articles, suggests that the magazine's editors did have such matters on their minds.

In April 1787, when delegates from twelve of the independent states were gathering in Philadelphia for the historic Constitutional Convention, the first excerpts from Jefferson's *Notes* appeared in the *Columbian Magazine*. By then, his friend Francis Hopkinson, a well-known author of satires and a signer of the Declaration of Independence, had become editor of the journal, although his tenure was short, since he himself became a delegate to the convention. Hopkinson's close friendship with Jefferson no doubt encouraged him to publish excerpts from *Notes* despite Jefferson's explicit instructions not to make his views public. "In the Magazine of this Month, I shall take the Liberty of giving an Extract from your valuable Notes on Virginia, respecting the Comparative Size of European and American Animals,"

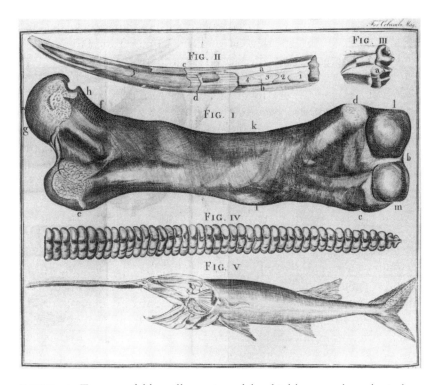

FIGURE 36. Two-page foldout illustration of the thighbone, tusk, and grinder of the American *incognitum* from the *Columbian Magazine*, 1786. Such images helped make the bones of the unidentified American monster a symbol of national identity in the new republic. Courtesy American Antiquarian Society.

Hopkinson wrote to Jefferson in April 1787 while begging forgiveness for doing so.[18] In an article entitled "Thoughts on American Genius," published in the previous issue of the *Columbian*, Hopkinson had already called his readers' attention to the importance of Jefferson's refutation of Buffon's theory of American degeneracy: "The learned Jefferson, in his excellent 'notes on Virginia,' has refuted this thesis, with the urbanity of a gentleman, and the accuracy of a scholar, supported by the sound reasoning of a philosopher."[19]

By the time Jefferson received news of the intended publication of his *Notes*, plans were already well under way to publish an English edition in London. In August, rumors of the imminent appearance of an

American edition alarmed his London publisher John Stockdale: "Just as I was going to ship 400 of your work to Richmond and Philadelphia, I had the disagreeable intelligence to learn that your book was already printed in Philadelphia."[20] Several months earlier, the Connecticut poet Joel Barlow had sent Jefferson a copy of his own book *The Vision of Columbus*, informing him that excerpts from his *Notes* were appearing at home: "Your Notes on Virginia are getting into the Gazettes in different States, notwithstanding your request that they should not be published here."[21] Clearly, many young American nationalists were delighted with the literary elegance of Jefferson's rebuttal of Buffon. "We are flattered with the idea of seeing ourselves vindicated from those despicable aspersions which have long been thrown upon us and echoed from one ignorant Scribbler to another in all the languages of Europe," Barlow told him.

Jefferson's rebuttal of Buffon appeared in the April and May issues of the *Columbian*, complete with his tables comparing the quadrupeds of Europe and America. Along with his extensive comments on the "mammoth," they focused everyone's attention on the American *incognitum*. A few months later, the journal offered the delegates to the Constitutional Convention Jefferson's views of the American landscape. In August, while a committee was finishing the newly drafted constitution, Jefferson's description of the Potomac River water gap provided a diversion for them. He lamented the undiscovered character of such natural wonders which were only beginning to become fixtures in national rhetoric. "Yet, here, as in the neighborhood of the natural bridge, are people who have passed their lives within half a dozen miles, and have never been to survey these monuments of a war between the rivers and mountains, which must have shaken the earth itself to its center."[22]

The invigorating effect of such statements on American national consciousness was revealed by Jefferson's friend Charles Thomson, secretary of the Continental Congress, whose remarks about this passage were published by the journal in the same issue: "The reflections I was led into on viewing this passage of the Patowmac through the Blue ridge were, that this country must have suffered some violent convulsion, and that the face of it must have been changed from what it probably was some centuries ago."[23] Brought to America from Ireland when he was ten years old, Thomson had become a prosperous Philadelphia merchant, active in Pennsylvania politics as a leader of the Sons of Liberty.

Like many of his fellow countrymen, Thomson's response to Jefferson's *Notes* was to speculate about the geological epochs buried in the American landscape:

> I am informed that at Yorktown in Virginia, in the bank of the York river, there are different strata of shells and earth, one above another, which seem to point out that the country there has undergone several changes; that the sea has, for a succession of ages, occupied the place where dry land now appears; and that the ground has been suddenly raised at various periods.[24]

Delegates to the Constitutional Convention were witnessing simultaneously the birth of a new nation and the discovery of prehistoric nature, although their speculation about the latter was still in its primitive stages, being what Thomson himself called "visions of fancy" rather than readily discernible natural laws.

This new geological view of the landscape was closely connected to the incipient Romanticism that eventually helped make the American *incognitum* the terror of the antediluvian world in the eyes of many patriots. In Jefferson's *Notes*, the most lyrical expression of these sentiments came in his description of the Natural Bridge, which he described as "the most sublime of Nature's works." Located on property owned by Jefferson in western Virginia, the rocky arch, through which a small stream passed, prompted a rare display of emotion from the taciturn author: "It is impossible for the emotions, arising from the sublime, to be felt beyond what they are here: so beautiful an arch, so elevated, so light, and springing, as it were, up to heaven, the rapture of the Spectator is really indescribable."[25]

Ever since Thomas Burnet's view of the Alps as the turbulent ruins of God's creation, such rocky prominences had become part of the Romantic sensibility. As defined by novelists and poets, the experience itself of seeing the mountains involved an element of terror rooted in Thomas Burnet's view of the powers of upheaval responsible for the earth's landforms. These sentiments were especially significant for the editors of the *Columbian*, who were trying to create a national culture out of the landscape, using elements of the Romantic literary style becoming fashionable among English poets and painters. In September, inspired by Jefferson's *Notes*, the *Columbian* published its own description of the Natural Bridge, illustrated by a large, foldout engraving of the arch: "If we consider this bridge simply as a picturesque object, we are struck with the majesty with which it towers in the valley" was how the anonymous author described Virginia's natural wonder[26] (figure 37).

The influence of Jefferson's *Notes* could even be found in the national debate about ratifying the new constitution after the Constitutional Convention. The polemic with Buffon and his disciples found its way into the *Federalist Papers*, a series of essays written by James Madison, Alexander Hamilton, and John Jay to promote its ratification in New York. To justify the creation of a powerful new federal government, these authors used sophisticated constitutional arguments favoring the expansion of the nation into the western territories. By enlarging the electorate, James Madison contended, westward expansion would neutralize the power of any factions that might attempt to gain control of the government. Published first in New York newspapers, these essays revealed how the founding fathers translated opposition to the theory of American degeneracy into nationalist rhetoric.

In November, Alexander Hamilton's essay on the commercial benefits of a strong federal government mocked the charges of American degeneracy while advocating funding a federal navy to counter Britain's dominance over Africa, Asia, and America. "The superiority she has long maintained has tempted her to plume herself as the Mistress of the World, and to consider the rest of mankind as created for her benefit." Then, with obvious reference to Buffon's theory of degeneracy, he referred sarcastically to the rationale behind Europe's arrogance. "Men admired as profound philosophers have, in direct terms, attributed to her inhabitants a physical superiority and have gravely asserted that all animals, and with them the human species, degenerate in America, that even the dogs cease to bark after having breathed awhile in our atmosphere."[27] To make sure his readers understood his allusion to the voiceless dogs, Hamilton added a footnote referring to the infamous work by Buffon's Dutch disciple Cornelius de Pauw, *Recherches philosophiques sur les Américains,* which claimed that in America, dogs lost their bark, the meat of oxen became tough, and the genitals of camels ceased to function.[28]

To counter such insults, the *Columbian Magazine* published excerpts from Charles Thomson's remarks about Buffon's theory of degeneracy. Jefferson had sought Thomson's opinion on the manuscript of his *Notes* when he had first submitted it to the French consul in

FIGURE 37. View of the Natural Bridge in Virginia as pictured in the *Columbian Magazine*, 1787. Thomas Jefferson's vivid description of this rocky arch helped transform the American landscape into the new nation's natural antiquity. Courtesy American Antiquarian Society.

Philadelphia, and he so valued the resulting commentaries that he published selections from them as an appendix to both the privately printed first edition of his *Notes* and the public London edition. By the spring of 1788, when his own commentaries on Buffon's theory of degeneracy appeared in the *Columbian Magazine*, Thomson was thus already a familiar figure in its pages.

Thomson's comments about Buffon portrayed Native Americans as noble savages and an honorable national symbol. Indeed, Thomson's reputation for fairness and integrity in Indian affairs had led to his adoption into the Delaware tribe during the French and Indian Wars after he had served as their secretary at treaty proceedings. His remarks directly addressed each of the aspersions Buffon had cast on the native peoples, from the alleged smallness of their organs of generation and their lack of ardor for their females to their hairless bodies and cowardly behavior in battle. "Mons[ieur] Buffon has indeed given an afflicting picture of human nature in his description of the man of America. But sure I am there never was a picture more unlike the original."[29] The Indians had no beards, he explained, because they plucked out their hair by the roots using tweezers fashioned from brass wire. And rather than being cowardly, they "braved death, like the old Romans in the time of the Gauls." Whatever defects they may have had were the result of cultural differences rather than any natural inferiority. "The seeming frigidity of the men, therefore, is the effect of manners, and not a defect of nature."[30]

In repudiating Buffon's theory of degeneracy, Thomson and Jefferson were not rejecting the inferiority of Indians, only denying that it had a natural cause. Such ambivalent attitudes enabled the *Columbian Magazine* to admire the Indians as Roman warriors, while at the same time publishing accounts of their savage attacks on white settlers, filled with the details of torture and murder. "The Indian appears in the *Columbian* simultaneously as a sadistic savage and as the romantic and naturally virtuous legendary inhabitant of the New Eden," states William J. Free in his study of the journal's role in promulgating American literary nationalism.[31]

Jefferson's *Notes* put the American *incognitum* on the map of American national consciousness, but his defense of the New World species also led to the substitution of the nation's natural antiquity for the monuments of Greece and Rome. For this reason, the common use of the term *monuments* to describe the fossil remains of the mysterious creature was significant, since metaphorically speaking, such language transformed the bones into remnants of a glorious past, all the more powerful for the universality associated with the earth's natural history. To American patriots, who saw themselves as heirs to the greatness of classical antiquity, the bones truly represented an ancient nature whose natural laws had justified the founding of their new society. In their eyes, the noble savage was an uncivilized primitive who had no noble past or any ancient ruins that were acceptable substitutes for the antiquity of Greece and Rome.

For the founding fathers, the only signs of "civilization" among the native peoples in North America were the mysterious mounds they discovered in the Ohio and Mississippi valleys, which were often ignored, if not destroyed, by early settlers looking for farmland. Frontier travelers often looked disparagingly on these curious earthworks, doubting they could have been constructed by the ancestors of the present-day Indians, whom they considered savages. But as the nation began to improvise its own antiquity out of the monuments of nature, these mounds began to attract the attention of travelers to the western territories.

While Jefferson was in Paris, Ezra Stiles had sent him a short memoir by General Samuel Parsons concerning the large earthworks he had seen at the mouth of the Muskingum River in Ohio country in 1785.

> The numerous mounds of Earth erected in conical form, to the height of 70 or 80 F., containing the bones of the Dead, are proofs of this Country's having been peopled heretofore by those who had some knowledge of the Arts. The present Inhabitants having no knowledge of the Arts or tradition respecting the fortifications leaves a doubt whether the present are the Immediate descendants of the former Inhabitants.[32]

The Indian mounds posed a serious problem for Americans constructing the new nation's natural antiquity out of the wilderness landscape, for they suggested that the Indians' ancestors may not have been hunter-gatherers but, rather, agricultural peoples whose "monuments" contradicted the Protestant stereotype of nomadic societies without any legitimate claim to the western lands. In 1788, the Columbian Magazine published another excerpt from Jefferson's Notes describing his experience excavating one of these Indian mounds near his property in Virginia. Despite his sympathetic treatment of living Indians, his remarks reveal the typical bias against evidence of any links with an ancient Indian civilization:

> I know of no such thing existing as an Indian monument: for I would not honour with that name arrow points, stone hatchets, stone pipes, and half-shapen images. Of labor on the large scale, I think there is no remain as respectable as would be a common ditch for the draining of lands: unless indeed it be the Barrows, of which many are to be found all over this country.[33]

To determine whether these "barrows," or mounds, were burial grounds for towns, in which the dead were buried standing, or simply mass graves of those fallen in battle, Jefferson systematically excavated the site. Using techniques later developed by professional archaeologists, he cut across the mound a trench wide enough for a man to walk through, to reveal its various strata. Examining the exposed walls, he found many layers of bones, often jumbled together, covered at irregular intervals with large stones and strata of earth. By his own estimate, there were about a thousand skeletons in the mound. "The bones of which the greatest numbers remained, were sculls, jaw-bones, teeth, the bones of the arms, thighs, legs, feet, and hands. The sculls were so tender, that they generally fell to pieces on being touched."[34]

Jefferson withheld any judgment about the mound's purpose, except to say that from the disposition of the bones, they did not seem to be a common burial ground for a town or the remains of persons fallen in battle. "But on whatever occasion they may have been made, they are of considerable notoriety among the Indians," he added, acknowledging the living Indians' reverence for the site.

> For a party passing, about thirty years ago, through the part of the country where this barrow is, went through the woods directly to it, without any instructions or enquiry, and having staid about it some time, with expressions of what were construed to be those of sorrow, they returned to the high road, which they had left about a half dozen miles to pay this visit, and pursued their journey.[35]

Like most of the founding fathers, Jefferson was reluctant to attribute any monumental antiquity to the living Indians, whom he viewed as noble savages doomed to extinction by the progress of society from barbarism to civilization. To appreciate the bones' symbolic associations, we need to imagine ourselves standing beside Jefferson in the trench with the skeletons of Indian ancestors spilling out at his feet as he methodically examined their earthen tomb. Just as the proponents of the noble savage transformed Indian braves into Roman warriors, Jefferson's thoughts upon seeing these skeletons in the earth were of the burial customs of Greek and Roman soldiers in classical antiquity.

In the margin of his personal copy of *Notes*, alongside his account of the excavation of the Indian barrow, he later inscribed a passage from Homer's *Odyssey*, written in his own hand in Greek, describing a similar burial mound erected over their comrades fallen in battle: "And over them we heaped up a great and goodly tomb, we the mighty host of Argive spearmen, on a projecting headland by the broad Hellespont, that it might be seen from far over the sea both by men that now are and that shall be born hereafter."[36] Through such metaphorical views of America's antiquities, the landscape itself, along with the monuments dug out of it, became a symbol of the nation's natural antiquity, worthy of a race destined to create its own empire in the New World.

This evidence of an Indian antiquity intrigued many of the founding fathers searching for the identity of the American *incognitum*. New England scholars were among the most vociferous opponents of the idea that the mounds were constructed by the ancestors of living Indians. Shortly before Jefferson's description of his excavation appeared in the *Columbian*, Noah Webster wrote several letters to Ezra Stiles at Yale claiming that the mounds and fortifications in the Ohio and Mississippi valleys had been built by the Spanish explorer Hernando de Soto's soldiers in the sixteenth century. Webster's hypothesis was based on an account of de Soto's expedition by the English historian William Roberts, but Benjamin Franklin had already suggested the same idea to Stiles several years earlier.

The controversy erupted into public debate when Webster's letters to Stiles were published in 1789 by the *American Museum*, a new journal edited by the exiled Irish journalist Mathew Carey. The son of prosperous Dublin baker, Carey came to Philadelphia in 1784 at age twenty-four after his career as a journalist was cut short by his political activities and accusations of libel in Ireland. With the help of Benjamin Franklin, whom he had met in Paris during the American Revolution, and a loan from the marquis de Lafayette, he launched the *Pennsylvania Herald* and was one of the founding editors of the *Columbian Magazine*. Less than a year later, he withdrew to form his own monthly journal, the *American Museum*, which quickly became popular among educated Americans.

Noah Webster's letters concerning the mounds invited criticism from one of Carey's most avid readers, George Rogers Clark, the Kentucky militia man who had supplied Jefferson with specimens from Big Bone Lick. From the Kentucky frontier, Clark drafted a long letter to the *American Museum* ridiculing Webster's claims: "So great a stranger to the western Cuntrey as Mr. Webster appears to be, ought to have informed himself better before he ventured to have pa[l]med his conjectures on the World."[37] Even if there had been paved roads connecting all the sites, de Soto's soldiers could not have even visited all the mounds in four years, much less have constructed them.

Clark, who had visited hundreds of these sites himself, provided detailed descriptions of some of the most impressive, including the huge elevated town at Kohokia, on the Mississippi River near the mouth of the Ohio. "Nature never formed a more beautiful [view] than this, several leagues in length and about four Miles in breadth, from the River to the High land."

During the American Revolution, the Kaskaskia Indian chief Jean-Baptiste Ducoyne, who had fought against the British under Clark in the Illinois campaign, had provided Clark with a history of his people. Based on such firsthand accounts and his own examination of numerous sites, Clark strongly supported their claims that the mounds were built by the ancestors of living Indians. "This is their Tradition and I see no reason why it should not be received as good History, at least as good as [a] great part of ours." Clark's common sense and his respect for Indian testimony contrasted with the illogical arguments of New England scholars unwilling to accept the reality of an Indian antiquity. Unfortunately, his opinions on the subject never appeared in the *American Museum*, probably because they further embarrassed Webster, who confessed in a letter of retraction published by Carey in June 1790 that his theory was no longer valid.

Armed with the powerful logic of Jefferson's *Notes*, Buffon's theories no longer stood in the way of the American patriots eager to establish their own noble traditions in the natural world. On the contrary, his theory of degeneracy spurred American nationalists to put natural history to work on their own behalf, enabling them to appropriate the universality of the earth's history to serve as the legitimating force of a nation born without a past. Natural history thus became part of the new nation's mythology, whether it took the form of evangelical beliefs in the country's millenarian destiny or the scientific truths and technology driving continental expansion and the progress of society from savagery to civilization. For this reason, natural history museums came to have a special significance, since they housed the sacred symbols of the nation's conquering spirit, from the Indian headdresses and war clubs to the bones of the American *incognitum*.

During the Constitutional Convention, James Madison was one of the many delegates who visited the newly founded American Museum of Charles Willson Peale, the Philadelphia painter who had made numerous drawings of the bones belonging to the American *incognitum*. Three years earlier, the monstrous bones in Peale's studio had attracted

FIGURE 38. Portrait of Thomas Jefferson by Charles
Willson Peale, 1791. This image was typical of the
portraits of revolutionary war heroes in Peale's museum that joined natural history and nationalism in
the early American consciousness. Courtesy Independence National Historical Park.

so much attention that he began to think of creating his own museum
to serve as a showplace of the nation's natural history. Peale was not a
collector of curiosities himself but instead was an accomplished painter
whose gallery was filled with portraits of American patriots.

Born and raised on the Eastern Shore of Maryland, Peale worked as
a saddler for several years in Annapolis before being sent to London by
a group of wealthy gentlemen to study painting with Benjamin West.
Upon his return two years later, he enjoyed a prosperous patronage as
an itinerant artist, traveling throughout Maryland and Virginia to paint
portraits of the local gentry (figure 38). In 1776, he moved his family to

Philadelphia, where he was elected a lieutenant in the city militia and served with the American patriots against the British at Princeton. During the winter of 1777, while in camp with General Washington's troops at Valley Forge, he painted some forty miniatures of officers to send home, as well as a full-length portrait of the general.

Not being a trained naturalist or a collector of curiosities, Peale had begun to collect natural history specimens as a result of the enthusiasm of his brother-in-law Nathaniel Ramsay, who first saw the bones of the American *incognitum* in his studio during a visit to the portrait gallery. Peale's idea for opening a natural history museum slowly germinated as he began to accumulate specimens, including a large paddlefish donated by his friend Dr. Robert Patterson, a professor of mathematics at the University of Pennsylvania. The cigar-shaped fish, dried and preserved, was among the first stuffed animals acquired by Peale, who taught himself the art of taxidermy in order to mount his collection of American animals.

Peale did not begin to collect natural history specimens seriously, however, until the summer of 1786 when he published an advertisement publicly announcing his intent to make part of his house a "Repository for Natural Curiosities." Thereafter, he received a steady stream of exotic artifacts and animal carcasses from sympathetic supporters, including George Washington, who sent several Chinese golden pheasants, a gift of General Lafayette from the king of France, which had died at his Mount Vernon estate. Having mounted nearly all the ducks from nearby waterways, Peale arranged them in natural settings, on artificial ponds, perched in trees, and suspended in flight. Capitalizing on his artistic skills, Peale pioneered the display of animals in habitat groups, introducing for the first time painted backdrops and naturalistic settings for his lifelike mountings.

Peale's patriotism bordered on religious enthusiasm, and the arrangement of his specimens was designed to display the virtue of republican ideals by demonstrating the order, harmony, beauty, and benevolence of God's creation. Only his fear of organized religion kept him from calling his museum "a temple of wisdom," although he contemplated such a name before settling later on the more nationalistic "American Museum." For many Americans steeped in biblical lore, the array of stuffed animals called to mind the Garden of Eden and Noah's Ark, which had given Christianity its first images of the natural world. When James Madison visited his museum in the summer of 1787, he recommended Buffon's writings to the fledgling curator. The following year, after reading Linnaeus, Peale began to arrange his stuffed animals according to his classifications, a tribute in their own right to the Great Chain of Being and the benevolence of God's creation. There was no hint yet of violence in Peale's arrangement, although the giant tooth found by Rittenhouse at Tioga, which Peale had drawn for the *Columbian Magazine*, was among the curiosities on display.

Ratification of the new Constitution and the inauguration of George Washington as the nation's first president unleashed a new wave of patriotic fervor which intensified the efforts to identify the American *incognitum*. Several weeks before Washington's inauguration in New York on April 30, 1789, Rev. Nicholas Collin, rector of the Swedish Churches in Pennsylvania, called on members of the American Philosophical Society in Philadelphia to join in the search for a complete skeleton. Sent by the king of Sweden to America in 1770 to minister to his fellow countrymen, Collin had only recently been elected to membership in the society, but his paper combined nationalism and natural history in a uniquely American fashion: "Natural history, like a faithful guide, leads us through the mysterious mazes of nature, and opens to our enraptured eye her sublime and beautiful wonders."[38] As his rhetoric readily acknowledged, natural history was a sacred science that lent itself to nationalistic purposes: "Patriotic affections are in this, as in other instances, conducive to the general happiness of mankind, because we have the best means of investigating those objects, which are most interesting to us."[39]

Enlightenment in America entailed the refinement of public manners and the rise of scientific educators, and Collin emphasized the crucial role of museums in the exhibition of natural history specimens: "That of Mr. Peale in Philadelphia, commenced a few years ago, is by his laudable care coming into reputation both at home and abroad, and merits public patronage."[40] Collin's essay ranged over several areas that he felt were important to American natural history, from collecting and cataloging native medicinal plants to preventing the destruction of forests by farmers. In his survey, he called attention to the mystery of the American *incognitum's* identity and the task of finding a complete skeleton: "The vast Mahmot, is perhaps yet stalking through the western wilderness; but if he is no more, let us carefully gather his remains, and even try to find a whole skeleton of this giant, to whom the elephant was but a calf."[41]

The search for the bones of the American *incognitum* thus became a national quest, drawing naturalists together in the creation of an icon whose monstrous grinders were becoming simultaneously the symbols of the savagery of the natural world and the nation's conquering spirit. What captured their fancy now was the existence of a ferocious carnivore in the nation's natural antiquity. It was no longer simply the enormous size of the animal that they celebrated but its ferocity and its terrifying power, bringing to life in their mind's eye the creature John Filson called the "tyrant of the forests, perhaps the devourer of man."

Filson himself had returned to the Kentucky frontier to found a "seminary" in Lexington, after having spent several years promoting his book. But the pedantic public announcement for his new academy was ridiculed by an anonymous author whose letter to the *Kentucky Gazette* made fun of Filson's pretensions to refinement. "In my neighborhood all are illiterate, and unaccustomed to high, flowery language or abstruse reasoning."[42] His academy discredited by the local gentry's resentment, Filson threw his energies into an ill-fated project for a new settlement in Ohio country on the Great Miami River, not far from Big Bone Lick. In October 1788, while traveling up the Little Miami River with a surveying party organized by Judge John Cleves Symmes of New Jersey, Filson disappeared during an Indian attack, his body never found.

Filson's literary view of the Kentucky frontier lived on in his book about Daniel Boone's exploits, whose numerous editions continued for many generations to romanticize views of Big Bone Lick and the American *incognitum*. The interest in this legend and the fossil elephants on the Kentucky frontier grew the following year when new details concerning the monster appeared in the local newspaper. Probably as a result of Filson's influence, the *Kentucky Gazette* published the entire text of Dr. William Hunter's famous article describing the extinct carnivore that had once roamed the Ohio frontier.[43]

No sooner had Rev. Collin issued his call to find a complete skeleton of the American *incognitum* than a new image of the ferious beast appeared in the nation's public culture. In December 1790, the *American Museum*, a monthly magazine founded three years earlier by Mathew Carey, published an article entitled "Of the enormous bones found in America," which contained a remarkable new version of Jefferson's Indian tale. Evidently, Carey's extensive contacts in New England enabled him to find a contributor there whose knowledge of the American *incognitum* led him to submit the short article on the Ohio bones containing a poetic rendering of Jefferson's Indian tale. "There is now in the museum at Yale college, teeth of a monstrous magnitude, sent thither from Muskingum by the late general Parsons," the anonymous author wrote. "The one which the writer of this account saw, was upwards of 15 inches in circumference, and, including its fangs, 12 or 13 inches in length."[44]

Whoever submitted this article also had a detailed knowledge of the bones taken from Rev. Annan's farm seven year's earlier by Dr. Michaelis, with General Washington's assistance:

> In the year 1783, as a labourer was ditching a bog-meadow belonging to a clergyman at Little Britain in Ulster County, he found a mass of bones, not two feet beneath the surface of the ground, of the same kind probably with those observed at the Ohio. A German physician, then with the British army at New-York, just before its departure, procured and took them all to Europe.

According to this account, the thighbone alone measured thirty-five inches in circumference: "Gentlemen of the first character in this country, saw them, and declare that they were astonishingly large."

Various New England clergymen subscribed to the *American Museum*, including Ezra Stiles, several of whose letters appeared in the journal. That fact plus the author's familiarity with the specimens at Yale and the excavation at Rev. Annan's farm suggest that Carey himself may have visited Stiles in New Haven while promoting his magazine in New England. Despite its brevity, the article offered a comprehensive comparison of the bones from Ohio with those from the Hudson River valley. In addition, the author stressed the importance of finding a complete skeleton in order to identify the creature, although there could be little doubt about its immense size: "It is impossible to arrive to the knowledge of the magnitude of an animal from an imperfect skeleton; but no one can hesitate supposing, that the most gigantic quadrupeds at present known, are mere pigmies compared to some of the former tenants of the western world."

In the *American Museum*, the Shawnee legend from Jefferson's *Notes* was recast in a poetic style to give dramatic new stature to the

American *incognitum*. In words reminiscent of John Filson's Romantic imagery, the monster suddenly emerged with a new force and ferocity, its lyrical fury also calling to mind Edward Taylor's use of Indian myth in his poem about the giant of Claverack:

> Ten thousand moons ago, when nought but gloomy forests covered this land of the sleeping Sun, long before the pale men, with thunder and fire at their command, rushed on the wings of wind to ruin this garden of nature—when nought but the untamed wanderers of the woods, and men as unrestrained as they, were the lords of the soil, a race of animals were in being, huge as the frowning Precipice, cruel as the bloody Panther, swift as the descending Eagle, and terrible as the Angel of Night.

Readers of Carey's *American Museum*, like the *incognitum* itself, were now entering the Gothic landscape of English Romanticism, with a violent storm swirling around them while lightning bolts and thunder crashed overhead.

> The Pines crashed beneath their feet; and the Lake shrunk when they slaked their thirst; the forceful Javelin in vain was hurled, and the barbed arrow fell harmless from their side. Forests were laid waste at a meal, the groans of expiring Animals were everywhere heard; and whole Villages, inhabited by men, were destroyed in a moment.

This rewriting of Jefferson's Indian legend has all the earmarks of an American tall tale and is reminiscent of that of England's Romantic novels, which were just beginning to become popular among American readers. More important, the *American Museum*'s tale conjured up an image of animal terror similar to George Stubbs's lion attacking a horse, which hinted at the outbreak of a Darwinian war among the species.

The new imagery of this Indian legend went far beyond the naturalistic wording of Jefferson's own version of the tale. In this romanticized treatment, the first truly violent images of prehistoric nature began to appear in American literature.

> The universal distress extended even to the region of peace in the west, and the good spirit interposed to save the unhappy. The forked lightning gleamed all around, and loudest thunder rocked the globe.

The bolts of heaven were hurled upon the cruel destroyers alone, and the mountains echoed with the bellowings of death.

True to the Shawnee story, there was only one survivor, the wounded bull that escaped across America's wilderness landscape by leaping over rivers and mountains.

The red lightning scorched the lofty firs, and rived the knotty oaks, but only glanced upon the enraged monster. At length, maddened with fury, he leaped over the waves of the west at a bound, and this moment reigns the uncontrouled monarch of the wilderness in despite of Omnipotence itself.

These last words hint that the wounded beast, the American monster, had defied even God's power to become "the uncontrouled monarch of the wilderness" in the western territories. The transformation of the American *incognitum* into a beast of prey whose extinction was a blessing to new nation emerged even more forcefully in this rewriting of Jefferson's Shawnee legend.

Scientific myth joined Indian legend as the monster's image took root in American national consciousness in the first decade of independence. Even though a complete skeleton still eluded the bone hunters, the mythical beast was already appearing in the mind's eye of naturalists, who soon imagined the *incognitum* pouncing on its prey with all the fury of a sabertooth tiger.

12

The Elephant with Claws

With the agility and ferocity of the tiger; with a body of unequaled magnitude and strength, it is possible the Mammoth may have been at once the terror of the forest and of man!

—George Turner, 1797

IN THE 1790s, the image of the American *incognitum* grew even more ferocious in American eyes, augmenting the fearsome creature already depicted in Indian legend and romantic literature. Toward the end of the decade, the discovery of the giant claws of another unknown animal in a Virginia cave added an ominous new dimension to speculation about the fossil elephants. Naming the new beast the "Great Claw or Megalonyx," Thomas Jefferson concluded that its bones belonged to a lionlike animal whose roar had terrorized early settlers in western Virginia. In the heated debate over extinct species, some naturalists now imagined the American *incognitum* to have been an elephant with claws. This argument was first proposed in the summer of 1797 when George Turner, a Philadelphia judge, delivered an influential scientific paper to the American Philosophical Society. He systematically compared the masticating surfaces of grinders from Siberia and North America to prove that the American *incognitum* was an extinct carnivore that had crushed deer and elk in its jaws. Emboldened by such speculation and new discoveries of mammoth bones in the Hudson River valley, American naturalists hastened their search for a complete skeleton of the monster.

In February 1792, at Yale College, Ezra Stiles welcomed a visit to New Haven by his friend Mr. Rensselaer from Claverack, where the first tooth of the monster had been found nearly a century earlier.

The elderly Rensselaer told Stiles about two large bones recently dug up by Joseph Barber near Poughkeepsie, about forty miles south of Albany.[1] Eight months later, owing to his own interest in the American monster, the sixty-five-year-old Stiles journeyed once again to the Hudson River valley to see for himself the newly discovered bones. He traveled up the valley on horseback, passing through Newburgh, near the farm where General Washington had viewed some gigantic bones during the Revolutionary War. At Barber's residence, Stiles saw "a Rib Bone dug up on his Farm at Wallkill," which he measured at four feet and six inches.[2] He left the next day for Albany but returned a week later to visit the site near Claverack where the giant tooth had been found that inspired his grandfather Edward Taylor's remarkable poem. At an inlet named Prawen's Hook, along the banks of the Hudson River, he "inspected & examined the Place of the enormous Bones & Teeth dug up there A.D. 1705."[3]

Near the high bluffs made of soft clay, Stiles met another elderly local resident, the ninety-year-old Francis Hardick, who recounted his boyhood memories of bones: "Saw and conversed with aged Mr. Hardick, who told me that when about [age] 16, he assisted his Father in digging up a Bone, stand[in]g Vertical or erect, which he saw his Father measure *Twelve feet in length,*" Stiles wrote in his diary.[4] The old man, using a metaphor that had become part of the monster's lore in the Hudson River valley, described how "he put his Fist into the Hollow of it & turned round his Fist in it freely—he judged its Diam[eter] bigger than a Hat Crown." His recollection of several teeth found in the vicinity was equally graphic: "His father told him that they had taken two Teeth upon the shore, about 10 or 12 R[o]ds off, one of w[hich] weighed six pounds, the other five pounds & one Ounce; but these he did not see."[5]

New discoveries elsewhere intensified the search for bones of the American *incognitum* as naturalists searched for a complete skeleton. In 1791, Timothy Matlack, a Revolutionary War veteran from Philadelphia who had served as an assistant to Charles Thomson, published a short account in the *Proceedings of the American Philosophical Society* about "a large tusk found in the back country."[6] Four years earlier, Matlack had presented a paper jointly with Caspar Wistar describing "a large thigh bone found near Woodbury Creek in Gloucester County, N.J."[7]

Caspar Wistar was a twenty-six-year-old physician who had returned the same year from a tour of the Continent after completing his medical degree at the University of Edinburgh. Already held in high esteem by his contemporaries, Wistar was immediately elected to the American Philosophical Society, which became the focus in the next decades for his anatomical studies. In the 1790s, he became the society's best-informed authority on fossil bones and was closely associated with Thomas Jefferson's search for the American *incognitum's* identity. The collaboration of Matlack and Wistar illustrates how the torch of natural history was being passed from the founding fathers to a new generation of anatomists who began the formal study of prehistoric animals in the United States.

Every major American city now seemed intent on consolidating its cultural institutions through the formation of new universities and scholarly organizations modeled after the American Philosophical Society. During the Revolutionary War, the Massachusetts legislature had passed an act creating the American Academy of Arts and Sciences, an institution promoting "useful knowledge" in the best Franklinesque tradition. Spearheaded by John Adams, the Boston-based institution's most urgent project after the Revolution was the publication of its scholarly journal *Memoirs*, whose aim was both to publish basic science and to disseminate it to a wider audience.

Like its Philadelphia counterpart, the academy sought to put American science on the map among the world's learned societies by developing a scientific culture. Articles from *Memoirs* were often excerpted by American magazines, especially the *Columbian Magazine* and the *American Museum*, in an effort to bring national attention to scientific ideas. "The language of nature is not written in Hebrew or Greek," Francis Hopkinson told professors at the University of Pennsylvania, who complained of the practice. "The great book of nature is open to all—all may read therein."[8]

In 1793, the academy helped expand public knowledge of the American *incognitum* by publishing two personal accounts of encounters with the fossil elephants that were already well known in New England's academic circles. The more important article was Rev. Robert Annan's "Account of a Skeleton of a Large Animal found near Hudson's River," briefly chronicling the discovery of the bones on his farm during the Revolutionary War. By this time, Annan had moved to Boston where he was pastor at the Presbyterian church. His paper seems to have been drafted in December 1785, shortly after his visit with Ezra Stiles in New Haven. In addition to details of the actual excavation,

Annan's testimonial included his anecdote about George Washington's visit during the Revolutionary War to see the monster's bones.

Written with a clergyman's sense of awe, Rev. Annan's straightforward prose revealed the crosscurrents of speculation among New England's educated classes about the mysterious creature. "What could this animal be? Certainly not a marine monster, for it lay above a hundred miles from the sea: unless we can suppose, that not many centuries ago, that part of the country was covered by the sea."[9] His remarks thus addressed the question of extinction, revealing how this concept was beginning to resonate among American clergymen: "Shall we, sir, suppose the species to be extinct over the face of the globe? If so, what could be the cause?" he asked rhetorically before seeking refuge in the thought the living creature still existed elsewhere. "It is next to incredible, that the remains of this animal could have lain there since the flood. May there not be some of the kind yet surviving in some interiour part of the Continent?"[10]

Genesis and geology came together uneasily in Annan's mind as he attempted to digest the new theories of the earth's history being discussed by New England scholars in connection with such fossil remains. "Some gentlemen, with whom I have conversed, have supposed that their extinction, as it is probable they are extinct, is owing to some amazing convulsion, concussion, or catastrophe, endured by the globe. But I know of none that could produce such an effect, except the flood."[11] As was the case for many American clergymen, Noah's Flood was still the principal reference point in his geological consciousness.

In addition to Annan's article, the academy's *Memoirs* published an important testimonial concerning the Ohio salt licks that had also circulated privately among the New England gentry. In the spring of 1786, Samuel Parsons, a Revolutionary War general from Connecticut, visited New Haven, where he regaled the president of Yale College with a lively account of his travels to the Ohio valley the preceding year. Sent by Congress as a commissioner to extinguish Indian claims to the territory north of the Ohio River, Parsons sought to redeem his own claims to land in the Northwest Territory. In October 1786, after his visit with Stiles, he drafted a short memoir describing in more detail his excursion to the site of an ancient fortress at the mouth of the Muskingum River and the fabled site at Big Bone Lick. "This place is a resort of all species of beasts in that country. A stream of brackish water runs through the land, which is soft clay."[12]

Parsons's prize acquisitions were a thighbone, several jawbones with teeth, a tusk, and two molars, one of which he donated to the Yale College collection. Despite his good fortune, General Parsons was disappointed in the inadequacy of his haul: "An entire skeleton we did not find, but of different parts we brought off about four hundred pounds."[13] Like Stiles, he put little stock in the Indian legends about the American *incognitum*, except for one appealing detail—the beast's appetite for meat: "Of this animal the natives have no tradition, but that which is so fabulous that no conjecture can be aided by it; unless it be, that the animal was a carnivorous one."[14] Learned New Englanders were still inclined to think in these terms and to imagine the unknown creature was carnivorous. Clearly, the bones of the American *incognitum* were becoming a common topic of conversation among those seeking to discover the beast's identity.

Physicians in New York City were among the first to hear about the new bones unearthed in Orange County, since Dr. James Graham had sent several of these specimens to his friend Dr. Richard Bayley, a professor of anatomy at Columbia College. Ever since Dr. Michaelis's exploration of Rev. Annan's marl pits during the Revolutionary War, local doctors had been kept apprised of the diggings there. In 1793, when the academy's *Memoir* appeared, the New York gentry had no comparable learned society, but they could see the "Tooth of the American non-descript animal" at the city's newly opened American Museum. The museum had been founded two years earlier by the Tammany Society, a fraternal organization revived by a group of Federalists, mostly merchants, lawyers, doctors, and master craftsmen caught up in the patriotic fervor after Washington's inauguration as president in New York. Led by John Pintard, a wealthy young New York merchant, the society's museum was dedicated to "collecting and preserving everything relating to the history of America, likewise, every American production of nature or art."[15] Housed initially in the attic of the newly refurbished Federal Hall, above the rooms where the United States Congress first met, the museum's collection brought together natural history and nationalism in a way typical of the early development of the nation's museum culture.

In Pintard's eyes, the museum's purpose was more historical than scientific, mirroring the patriotic sentiments expressed by Charles Willson Peale, whose Philadelphia Museum embodied similar principles. At that time, there was far less distinction made between the world of science and those of religion, political philosophy, and economic thought, since scientific-minded persons shared the same nationalistic outlook with clergymen, politicians, and merchants. For them, American relics and historical artifacts were an integral part of the new republic's own natural history—in the largest sense of the word—since the broad spectrum of natural history culture included everything from religious truths and natural law to the useful arts and scientific investigation. In this perspective, scientific ideas themselves became tools of nationalistic thought, serving in the larger matrix of American national culture to propagate the central belief in the superiority of people of European descent.

By the summer of 1793, the Tammany Society's American Museum had moved into spacious new quarters in the Exchange Building, where the collection flourished under the management of Gardiner Baker, a shoemaker who had become "keeper of the museum" under John Pintard's tutelage. Baker's broadside announcing the museum's new location provided the first detailed listing of the contents of its collection, which included, among other things, a stuffed orangutan, or "Wild Woman of the Woods," an American buffalo, and a South American vulture. Among the other exhibits advertised was the tooth of the American *incognitum*, complete with allusions to Buffon's description of the enormous creature:

> A Tooth of the American non-described animal, called the Mammoth, supposed to be four or five times as large as the modern Elephant. This tooth is upwards of seven inches through, and four thick, and weighs upwards of four pounds [and] was found in April, 1792, at the great Salt Licks, near the River Ohio, in Kentucky.[16]

Self-conscious about his own lack of scientific training, Baker enrolled as an occasional student at Columbia College, where he attended lectures in natural history by Dr. Samuel Latham Mitchill, the most influential of a new generation of New York physicians. Recently appointed to the chair of natural history, chemistry, and agriculture, Dr. Mitchill's lectures provided a direct link to the early European theories of the earth's history that had shaped American views of the fossil elephants. As Baker's friend and classmate Alexander Anderson noted in his diary, the subject of these lectures was "the theories of Burnet, Woodward, Whiston, and Buffon on the Formation of the Earth."[17]

Born of Quaker parents on Long Island, Dr. Mitchill had established himself as the city's leading scientific personality, setting up his
medical practice in 1786 after graduating from the University of Edinburgh. Elected to the state assembly in 1791, he had been among the
earliest contributors to the American Museum and was actively involved in the Tammany Society's promotion of nationalistic sentiments. In the coming decades, Dr. Mitchill emerged as one of the leading authorities on early American geology, publishing in 1797 the first
mineralogical history of New York.

Each spring the Tammany Society celebrated its anniversary with a
ceremony honoring its namesake, the Delaware Indian chief Tammany,
who had become a popular symbol of American nationalism after the
Revolution, especially among master craftsmen and merchants aspiring
to political influence and social status in New York's mercantile society.
At these annual events, members of the society often paraded through
the streets wearing Indian headdresses and warpaint, emblems of the
democratic sentiments embraced by New Yorkers sympathetic to
Thomas Jefferson's new political party.

The popularity of the Tammany cult stemmed at least partly from
the enthusiasm of young nationalists seeking to create an American antiquity out of the new nation's natural history. In the spring of 1795, Dr.
Samuel Latham Mitchill delivered the society's annual anniversary oration, "The Life, Precepts, and Exploits of Tammany; the Famous Indian
Chief." Native American legends about the American *incognitum*
proved to be a useful device in his talk for magnifying Tammany's legendary powers. Published as a pamphlet the same year, Mitchill's anniversary oration transformed Tammany into a Promethean figure at
war with an "evil spirit" who subjected him to many trials, including a
nest of rattlesnakes that the mythical hero easily subdued. Tammany's
exploits were linked to familiar landmarks in the American landscape,
from the salt licks in Kentucky to Niagara Falls, but the most remarkable aspect of the fable was the appearance of the American *incognitum*
as the Indian hero's adversary. "Frustrated in this scheme, [the evil
spirit] brought from the other side of Lake Superior, alarming droves of
Mammoths, carnivorous animals, and especially loving to feed upon
human flesh," Dr. Mitchill wrote, incorporating elements of Jefferson's
tale in his account of Tammany's adventure.[18]

His audience at the Presbyterian church, which included the wives
and children of the society's members, was awed by the ferocity of the

beasts as well as by Tammany's ingenuity in luring these creatures into traps where they were impaled on the sharpened points of trees. "Thus the country was cleared of these monsters, whose bones, discovered to this day at the Licks, confirms the reality of the story,"[19] Dr. Mitchill re-counted, alluding to the fossil remains of the American *incognitum*. An exercise in political mythology, his lengthy speech added new elements to the Shawnee legend first popularized by Jefferson's *Notes,* creating in the process an entirely new fable about the American *incognitum*.

Dr. Mitchill's Quaker upbringing probably contributed to his sym-pathetic treatment of the American Indians, but this exercise in myth-making grew mainly out of the nationalistic sentiments associated with natural history culture during the early days of the republic. Buffon's theory of American degeneracy led many patriots to employ images of the noble savage as emblems of nationhood. "The eastern world has long boasted of the superiority of its people, and the inhabitants of western climes have been spoken of as a feeble or degenerate race of men," Mitchill observed with reference to Buffon's humiliating con-cept.[20] Years later, when his own fable became something of an embar-rassment to him, Dr. Mitchill dismissed the exercise as a youthful in-discretion. Nonetheless, at the time of its conception, his anniversary oration was an important milestone in the American *incognitum's* emer-gence as an icon of national identity.

By then, the bones of the American monster had become a valu-able commodity, largely as a result of the growing realization that only a complete skeleton would answer the riddle of the beast's true identity. In 1795, the same year that Dr. Mitchill's wrote his fable, General William Henry Harrison, governor of the Northwest Territory, visited Big Bone Lick, where he filled thirteen large wooden casks with fossil remains which were shipped up the Ohio River on a flatboat. Unfortu-nately, this valuable cargo, probably the largest single collection to date from the salt lick, was lost when the boat capsized below Pittsburgh.[21]

Perhaps the best indicator of this rising interest in the American *incognitum* comes from Alexander Anderson, a young New York med-ical student and engraver who was in the audience at the Presbyterian church when Dr. Mitchill delivered his anniversary oration.[22] Despite his impatience with Dr. Mitchill's "Indian mythology," Anderson was already an ardent reader of Romantic novels and a frequent visitor to Gardiner Baker's American Museum, where he was developing a taste for curiosities.

The son of a successful Scottish-born printer and auctioneer, Anderson entered Columbia College in 1791 at age seventeen, after his father had discouraged him from taking up a career in engraving. As a young boy, the classically educated master craftsman's son had become skilled in the art of woodcutting and etching on copper plates, two popular new media for illustrating natural history books. Among Anderson's early engravings was a woodcut of an orangutan, a porcupine, and the king of vultures that that his friend Gardiner Baker used as an illustration for the first broadside advertising his American Museum.

The arrival of the first elephant in America in New York in April 1796 created quite a stir among the city's natural history enthusiasts. Only a week after the animal was unloaded from the ship, Anderson went to see the creature brought from India. "She is but 2 years old, but about the size of a bullock and very plump," he noted in his diary. "The sagacity of the animal was astonishing, and its trunk a great curiosity, with this she examined us carefully and search'd our pockets for something eatable."[23] The elephant traveled for several years throughout the country and appeared on stage at the New Theatre in Philadelphis in 1797. Later that same year, the exotic animal was exhibited in New England where a broadside called her "the greatest natural curiosity ever presented to the curious" (figure 39).

Illustrated with a handsome woodcut, the broadside illustrates how news of Jefferson's dispute with Buffon may have spread to a wider audience than the subscribers to the *Columbian Magazine*. The advertisement skillfully used both the elephant and Buffon's opinions to attract patrons: "The Elephant, according to the account of the celebrated BUFFON, is the most respectable Animal in the world. In size he surpasses all other terrestrial creatures; and by his intelligence, makes as near an approach to man, as matter can approach spirit."[24] Exhibited from sunrise to sundown every day of the week, the elephant show undoubtedly stimulated further speculation about the *incognitum*, especially among those citizens who may not have read the scholarly articles and romanticized Indian myths in the literary journals.

Memories of Jefferson's polemic with Buffon were now tempered by the sympathy of many American citizens for the revolutionary movement in France that had overthrown the monarchy and established a republican government shortly after Buffon's death. The beheading of the French king Louis XVI and his wife Marie Antoinette during the

THE
ELEPHANT,

ACCORDING to the account of the celebrated BUFFON, is the moſt reſpeſtable Animal in the world. In ſize he ſurpaſſes all other terreſtrial creatures; and by his intelligence, makes as near an approach to man, as matter can approach ſpirit. A ſufficient proof that there is not too much ſaid of the knowledge of this animal is, that the Proprietor having been abſent for ten weeks, the moment he arrived at the door of his apartment, and ſpoke to the keeper, the animal's knowledge was beyond any doubt confirmed by the cries he uttered forth, till his Friend came within reach of his trunk, with which he careſſed him, to the aſtoniſhment of all thoſe who ſaw him. This moſt curious and ſurpriſing animal is juſt arrived in this town, from Philadelphia, where he will ſtay but a few days.———He is only four years old, and weighs about 3000 weight, but will not have come to his full growth till he ſhall be between 30 and 40 years old. He meaſures from the end of his trunk to the tip of his tail 15 feet 8 inches, round the body 10 feet 6 inches, round his head 7 feet 2 inches, round his leg above the knee 3 feet 3 inches, round his ankle 2 feet 2 inches. He eats 130 weight a day, and drinks all kinds of ſpirituous liquors; ſome days he has drank 30 bottles of porter, drawing the corks with his trunk. He is ſo tame that he travels looſe, and has never attempted to hurt any one. He appeared on the ſtage, at the New Theatre in Philadelphia, to the great ſatisfaſtion of a reſpeſtable audience.

A reſpeſtable and convenient place is fitted up adjoining the Store of Mr. Bartlet, Market-Street, for the reception of thoſe ladies and gentlemen who may be pleaſed to view the greateſt natural curioſity ever preſented to the curious, which is to be ſeen from ſunriſe till ſundown, every day in the week.

☞ The Elephant having deſtroyed many papers of conſequence, it is recommended to viſitors not to come near him with ſuch papers.

Admittance ONE QUARTER OF A DOLLAR———Children ONE EIGHTH OF A DOL-LAR.

NEWBURYPORT, Sept. 19, 1797.

FIGURE 39. Broadside advertising an exhibition at Newburyport, Massachu-setts, of the first elephant brought to the United States, 1797. Touted by its proprietors as the largest of terrestrial creatures, this elephant had appeared the previous year on stage at the New Theatre in Philadelphia. Courtesy New York Historical Society.

Reign of Terror polarized New York politics, pitting pro-British Federalists, who abhorred the violence, against the Francophile "true Republicans" led by supporters of Thomas Jefferson.

The violence of the French Revolution gave new impetus to the
burgeoning Romanticism among English poets and novelists, producing a new generation of Gothic novels whose morbid settings were reminiscent of the landscape of fear associated with the American monster
in Mathew Carey's *American Museum*. Even before France's "Reign of
Terror," Edmund Burke, an eminent British lawyer and political
philosopher, sounded an ominous note in his *Reflections on the Revolution in France*. Published in 1790, the same year the *American Museum's*
refurbished Indian myth appeared, Burke's literary classic described the
new revolutionary regime as a Gothic monstrosity, "a species of political monster which has always ended by devouring those who have produced it."[25] Five years later, in Dr. Mitchill's version of the American
tale, the Gothic monster was slain by a mythical Indian hero who had
become a symbol of American nationalism.

In 1796, when the Asian elephant reached America, the political
situation in France had become more stable with the installation of a
moderate revolutionary faction in Paris called the Directory which
sought to restore France's reputation for scientific studies in Europe.
During the Reign of Terror, many of the old scientific institutions had
been abolished or disrupted, since they had functioned largely under
the patronage of the French aristocracy and the monarchy. However,
the Jardin du roi and the Royal Museum, formerly Buffon's sphere of influence, had managed to survive by becoming the *Muséum national
d'histoire naturelle*, a national museum now devoted to restoring the
prestige of French science after the Revolution. Led by a new generation of scholars and anatomists, the institution quickly focused on
problems relating to the earth's history and the controversy over the
fossil elephants, which many French anatomists felt was the key to un-
raveling the mystery of the prehuman past.

Their renewed interest in this subject was stimulated by Charles
Willson Peale's efforts to begin a correspondence with the leading European naturalists. Nearly a decade after founding his museum, Peale
had mastered the art of taxidermy, and his collection of stuffed animals
was now quite impressive. Visitors to his museum were greeted by a
number of large American quadrupeds mounted in lifelike postures, all
grinning with their teeth bared to show these features of their anatomy

so crucial to their identification. "In any part of this room, a vast variety of monsters of the earth and man, and fowls of the aire are seen, in perfect preservation," an anonymous visitor to the museum wrote. "At the further extremity of this room are to be seen a great collection of bones, jaws, grinders of the incognitum, or non descript animals, royal tyger, sharks, and many other land and marine animals, hostile to the human race."[26]

Peale's patriotism and his success with taxidermy led him to contemplate even the preservation and display of human cadavers in his museum, especially those of the heroes of the American Revolution whose portraits adorned his walls. In fact, in 1792, when he attempted to create a board of directors for the museum, he suggested such an experiment in a broadside outlining the museum's purpose and design. "Sorry I am, that I did not propose the means of such preservation to that distinguished patriot and worthy philosopher, Doctor Franklin, whose liberality of soul was such, that it is not improbable that by the interest which I might have made with his friends, he could have been prevailed on, to suffer the remains of his body to be now in our view."[27]

Although this endeavor remained an unfulfilled dream for the Philadelphia curator, Peale's broadside proposed another equally challenging project that eventually became the crowning achievement of his scientific career. Nearly a decade before his excavation of its bones, the skeleton of the elusive *incognitum* was already a top priority among the quadrupeds that Peale wanted to display in his museum. As he noted, however, this was a daunting enterprise given the fact the animal's identity was still unknown. "But if such a number of those bones were collected together, and made into a complete skeleton, it would lead to an illustration of the animal by analogy." With a word of warning to his patrons, he acknowledged the potential dangers of the increased demand for such specimens. "A work that I believe may yet be executed—but if not undertaken soon, the remaining bones will be so scattered over the whole globe, as to render it scarcely possible to get them together again."[28]

By this time, Peale hoped to make his institution into a "national museum," and he had solicited public patronage, rather unsuccessfully, in order to place the collection on firmer institutional footing. In many respects, the model for his enterprise was the newly founded Muséum national d'histoire naturelle in Paris, which he had contacted about the possibility of exchanging natural history specimens. Events in France had conspired again to make the bones of the American *incognitum* the most sought-after fossils by those French anatomists concerned not only with the question of extinction but also the new notion of evolving species being advanced for the first time by the Parisian zoologist Jean-Baptiste Lamarck. In the late spring of 1797, while the Asian elephant was still traveling around the United States, Peale received an enthusiastic reply to his earlier queries from Lamarck and his young assistant Geoffroy St. Hilaire, two key figures in zoological studies at the new Paris museum.

Lamarck and St. Hilaire welcomed Peale's proposal to exchange specimens and left little doubt about which ones had the highest priority for them. "Those enormous bones which are found in great quantity on the borders of the Ohio. The exact knowledge of those objects is more important towards the theory of the earth, than is generally thought of," they explained, calling attention to pivotal role of the fossil elephants in the debate over the earth's history.[29] Evidently, the upheaval wrought by the French Revolution had not dampened the interest of anatomists in the American *incognitum*, even though by then Buffon's theory of American degeneracy had been thoroughly discredited. For Lamarck, who had worked with Buffon, degeneration no longer included American inferiority or necessarily the devolution of life-forms there. Instead, the term simply signified the mutability of species, which, as a forerunner to Darwin, Lamarck was coming to view as a progression over long periods of time from simple to increasingly complex organisms in response to changing environmental conditions.

In June 1796, when he wrote to Peale, Lamarck had not yet made public his radical theory of evolution, but these ideas were already circulating among his colleagues at the Paris museum and had generated opposition from a young anatomist who later played an instrumental role in the discovery of the American *incognitum's* identity. At this time, Lamarck's colleague Geoffroy St. Hilaire was working closely with Georges Cuvier, an acting professor of anatomy at the museum who was just beginning his illustrious career as a comparative anatomist. Born in a French-speaking Protestant region belonging to the German duchy of Württemberg, Cuvier had come to Paris the preceding year at the age of twenty-six, after several years of fieldwork in mineralogy under the patronage of a French nobleman with estates in Normandy. In Paris, he obtained a minor position at the newly founded museum as an understudy to the institution's elderly professor of animal anatomy.[30]

Cuvier rapidly rose to prominence at the museum, and he quickly exhibited the exacting scientific methodology that became the trademark of his long career in comparative anatomy. Only a week after a brilliant inaugural lecture explaining his conception of organisms as functionally integrated "animal machines," Cuvier was elected to the prestigious National Institute of Arts and Sciences, the successor to the old Royal Academy of Sciences. In April 1796, with characteristic boldness, he chose to deliver his first scholarly paper at the institute on the problem of the fossil elephants, whose unidentified bones were at the center of the debate among European anatomists over the earth's history and the existence of extinct species.

Cuvier's choice of this topic was partly the result of the museum's acquisition of a new collection of bones brought to Paris from the Netherlands as trophies of war by the French army led by the rising young military genius Napoleon. The army's looting of the Netherlands included the Dutch ruler's natural history collection, containing, among many other treasures, two enormous elephant skulls, one from Ceylon and the other from the Cape of Good Hope. These new skulls, with many teeth still intact, enabled Cuvier to prove conclusively that the Asian and African elephants were distinct species and to investigate further the identity and disappearance of the fossil elephants from Siberia and North America.

During his investigation, Cuvier came across the excellent drawing of the Siberian mammoth's skull by Daniel Messerschmidt which had been published in the Royal Society's journal nearly sixty years earlier. This drawing, as Cuvier later noted, was invaluable in helping him determine that the Siberian mammoth was a distinct species, different from living elephants. His examination of the American *incognitum*'s bones, though limited to those specimens collected by Buffon, confirmed the same opinion with regard to the "Ohio animal," as Cuvier called the unknown creature. "These animals thus differ from the elephant as much as, or more than, the dog from the jackal and the hyena," he confidently informed his colleagues in Paris.[31]

Even though Cuvier's examination of the bones was far more careful than that of his European colleagues, what made his analysis convincing was the manner in which he linked this conclusion to the larger issue of the earth's history and the existence of a prehuman past. Judiciously choosing his words, he emphasized the connection between anatomical study of the fossil elephants and the new field of "geology," a term that was just beginning to enter the scientific vocabulary. "In a word, it is only with the help of anatomy that geology can establish in a sure manner several of the facts that serve as its foundations."[32] Thus, the urgency with which Lamarck and Geoffroy St. Hilaire requested bones of the American *incognitum* from Charles Willson Peale a few months later stemmed directly from Cuvier's analysis of this controversy and his conclusion that the fossil elephants from Siberia and North America were extinct species.

For Cuvier, this discovery called into question all existing explanations of how their bones came to be found in such inhospitable regions. Buffon's theory that they were the remains of elephants and hippopotamuses that had migrated as the earth cooled from the North Pole southward was no longer tenable. But rather than offering any grand theory of the earth's history or extinction himself, Cuvier was content to confine himself to the issues at stake in the controversy: "What has become of these two enormous animals of which one no longer finds any [living] traces, and so many other of which the remains are found everywhere on earth and of which perhaps none still exist?" he asked his readers.[33]

In Cuvier's view, the list of missing creatures now included numerous other animals, from the fossil bears of Anspach, whose bones had provoked John Hunter's ruminations on the many thousands of years required for the process of fossilization, to an enormous clawed creature from "Paraguay" recently assembled at the Royal Museum in Madrid. "All these facts, consistent among themselves, and not opposed by any report, seem to me to prove the existence of a world previous to ours, destroyed by some kind of catastrophe." With his parting words, he revealed the deeper dilemma created by the existence of extinct species and the prehuman past: "But what was this primitive earth? What was this nature that was not subject to man's dominion?"[34]

Indeed, as Cuvier's question reveals, the real problem underlying the discovery of prehistoric nature was the existence of a vast realm of natural history not under man's dominion or delineated by God's nature. Neither Buffon nor the Bible could extricate European civilization from this disturbing dilemma should the hypothesis of a prehuman past prove correct. Metaphorically speaking, Christian civilization, the empire of reason and revelation, whether conceived in religious or secular terms, was faced with a weakening of its rationale for dominance, an event whose consequences went far beyond the contradiction of

Mosaic history and the biblical timeline. In many respects, prehistoric nature was a "new found land" that would have to be subjugated like any other newly discovered territory, although the absence of the human species presented an awkward predicament for its would-be conquerors. As a result, monstrous predators later emerged as the surrogate rulers of prehistoric nature, preserving for Christian civilization the paradigm of dominance in the prehuman past.

Ever cautious about the "vast field of conjectures" that his questions opened up, Cuvier himself backed away from further speculation about the consequences of this discovery. In any case, his paper had little immediate impact on American views of the *incognitum* except to intensify the search for bone specimens for shipment to Europe. The full version of his controversial paper was not published for three more years, when many citizens of the new republic were already convinced their monstrous prey was now an elephant with claws. More important, Cuvier's discussion of the fossil elephants represented the beginning of a long period of research on fossils by him which eventually became the benchmark for many American naturalists searching for the identity of the American monster.

During the summer of 1796 while Parisian naturalists were urgently soliciting bones from Peale's Museum, Thomas Jefferson learned of the discovery of the fossil remains of a new monster in a Virginia cave that had a more immediate influence on American views of the *incognitum*. Jefferson, who had withdrawn to his home at Monticello after serving as secretary of state during Washington's presidency, was now the leader of a new political party—the Democratic Republicans—which opposed many of the Federalists' policies and had nominated him as its candidate in the upcoming presidential elections.

Jefferson's friend Colonel John Stuart, who lived in western Virginia, had informed him that workmen digging for saltpeter in the floor of a cave in Greenbriar County had unearthed the bones of a gigantic clawed creature. News of the discovery caused considerable excitement in the neighborhood of the cave, and many of the bones had already been carried away by curiosity seekers. Believing that they may have been bones of the *incognitum,* Colonel Stuart salvaged several specimens and sent them to Jefferson at Monticello. Evidently, Jefferson was able to obtain a few more bones from a "Mr. Hopkins of New York," who had visited the cave upon hearing of the discovery. The meager collection that Jefferson assembled consisted of a small fragment of the femur or thighbone, a radius and an ulna, three enormous claws, and half a dozen other bones from the creature's foot.

Shortly after news of the discovery reached Monticello, Jefferson wrote to the president of the American Philosophical Society, advising him of the new monster's existence and promising a more detailed commentary on the bones. During the fall while studying the specimens, Jefferson was elected vice president of the United States after narrowly losing the presidential race to his New England adversary John Adams, who successfully defended the Federalist Party against the Democratic Republicans. In March 1797, when Jefferson went to Philadelphia for the inauguration, he carried with him a box containing the bones of the unknown creature, along with the manuscript of his commentary on the specimens. His memoir was formally read at the American Philosophical Society on March 10, 1797, shortly before the inauguration ceremony ended his brief respite from public office.

Fascinated by the length of the beast's claw, which was more than seven inches long, Jefferson claimed that the unknown animal was a large lionlike creature and named the new species the "Great-Claw or Megalonyx." Relying on anatomical descriptions in Buffon's *Histoire naturelle*, he constructed an elaborate statistical table showing that the newly discovered American creature's bones were much larger than those of the African lion. "Let us only say then, what we may safely say, that he was *more* than three times as large as the lion," Jefferson concluded. This conservative estimate was more than sufficient to support his more controversial claim that the Megalonyx "stood as pre-eminently at the head of the clawed animals as the mammoth stood at that of the elephant, rhinoceros, and hippopotamus; and that he may have been as formidable an antagonist to the mammoth as the lion to the elephant."[35] Clearly, Buffon's theory of American degeneracy still bothered Jefferson, who relished this new opportunity to repudiate the doctrine.

Despite the mounting scientific evidence for extinction, Jefferson, along with many Americans, refused to accept the idea and still held out hope that such unknown creatures would eventually be found living in the unexplored wilderness. "In the present interior of our continent there is surely space and range enough for elephants and lions, if in that climate they could subsist, and for mammoths and megalonyxes who may subsist there," he informed members of the Philosophical Society. "Our entire ignorance of the immense country to the West and

North-West, and of its contents, does not authorise us to say what it does not contain."[36]

To reinforce his conclusion that the animal was lionlike, Jefferson marshaled an array of circumstantial evidence, from the apocryphal reports of earlier explorers, who claimed lions could be found in American forests, to the rock carvings of "a perfect figure of a lion" near the mouth of the Kanhawa River. Inhabitants of Greenbriar County told a story about the first explorers to this region who were alarmed at their camp on the first night of their arrival "by the terrible roarings of some animal unknown to them" that circled their camp, its eyes glowing in the darkness like two balls of fire. "Their horses so agonised with fear," Jefferson recounted, "that they crouched down on the earth, and their dogs crept in among them, not daring to bark."[37] In 1770, an experienced backwoodsman in Ohio country had fled in terror upon finding his horse half eaten by an enormous catlike animal whose shadowy form he glimpsed darting into the forest.

Reminiscent of Stubbs's lion attacking a horse, these images of animal terror bolstered Jefferson's underlying belief in the plenitude of God's nature, the traditional Christian view of the "Great Chain of Being" that still held sway in the mind of the Enlightenment scholar. "The movements of nature are in a never-ending circle. The animal species which has once been put into a train of motion, is still probably moving in that train," he asserted, recalling the poet Alexander Pope's famous dictum. "For if one link in nature's chain might be lost, another and another might be lost, till this whole system of things should vanish piecemeal."[38]

As Jefferson pointed out, however, terrifying carnivores like "Great-Claw" were little-known, rare animals whose local disappearance did not constitute sufficient evidence for the extinction of an entire species. Even now, long after Buffon's theory of American degeneracy had been discredited, he felt compelled to remind his audience that the "Great-Claw," like the elk's skin and the mammoth's bones, was further evidence of Buffon's errors.

Even though Jefferson's paper was not published for two more years, this new monster had an immediate impact on the way that Philadelphia naturalists viewed the American *incognitum*. In late April, only a few weeks after Jefferson's presentation, Charles Willson Peale wrote to Geoffroy St. Hilaire at the Paris museum telling him about it: "Mr. Jefferson lately presented to the American Philosophical Society a small number of bones found in Virginia which appear to belong to the Cat kind, but of a size vastly larger than any Lion yet discovered."[39] Peale took pride in announcing the future publication of Jefferson's memoir along with drawings of the bones, and he graciously offered to send plaster casts of them to St. Hilaire.

Peale's letter was a formal reply to Lamarck and St. Hilaire's earlier correspondence soliciting American specimens, which had taken more than a year to reach Peale. Their urgent request for bones from the Ohio salt lick evidently led Peale to contemplate sending his son to obtain them. "I am taking the necessary steps to aid my Son in an excursion into the western parts of this Government to collect what number he can of those large bones, and in proportion to his success I shall be able to comply with your request."[40] None of Peale's sons traveled to Ohio country, but this correspondence with the Paris museum brought American naturalists into closer contact with the French anatomists who were to be instrumental in solving the mystery of the *incognitum's* identity.

In the summer of 1799, Jefferson's description of the "Great-Claw or Megalonyx" stirred new speculation among Philadelphia naturalists about the appetite and extinction of the American *incognitum*. The halls of the American Philosophical Society adjacent to Peale's museum were buzzing with talk about the existence of a second unknown animal whose claws were now on display along with the fossil elephant's monstrous grinders. Only a few months after the "Great Claw" appeared on the scene, the American *incognitum* itself acquired a new ferocity inspired at least partly by Jefferson's commentary on the lion-like creature's bones.

In early July, Judge George Turner, who had visited Big Bone Lick himself, presented his own contentious but well-documented paper to the American Philosophical Society on the gigantic bones he had examined there. Elected to the society in 1790 while serving as a federal judge in Ohio country, he had moved to Philadelphia two years later and become active in the society's affairs. Very likely he was in attendance when Jefferson's own paper on the "Great Claw, or Megalonyx" was read to members several months earlier. Turner's eyewitness account of the disposition of the bones at the Ohio salt lick figured prominently in his own memoir which challenged Jefferson's opinions concerning the fossil elephants. In addition, his first-hand experience with the bones was bolstered by a broad survey of scholarly opinion and a careful comparison of both the Siberian and North American tusks and teeth.

Members of the society must have felt a certain uneasiness as Judge Turner spelled out his deferential but sharply critical argument, since Jefferson was now serving as president of the American Philosophical Society. Demonstrating his own familiarity with the scholarly literature, Turner immediately put the controversy into historical perspective by briefly reviewing the opinions of numerous eminent naturalists who had offered conflicting theories over the years about the identity of the American *incognitum*. From Sir Hans Sloane, Daubenton, and Buffon's claims that the bones belonged to elephants or hippopotamuses to Dr. William Hunter's inference that the American *incognitum* was an extinct carnivore, the whole familiar cast of characters was there. Turner even used the learned opinions of the Swedish officers and Dutch diplomats in the service of the Russian czar, which had helped shape early views of the Siberian mammoth.

From the outset, Turner directly criticized Jefferson's *Notes on the State of Virginia*, politely pointing out that the recent discovery of bones during the cutting of the Santee and Cowper River canal in South Carolina had disproved Jefferson's opinion that such specimens found in the South were likely carried there as curiosities rather than being indigenous to the area. Expressing reluctance to contradict so able a writer, Turner attacked Jefferson's inference that the Siberian mammoth and the American *incognitum* may well have been the same animal. Invoking his own scientific evidence, Turner claimed that careful examination of their tusks and grinders revealed that they were clearly distinct species: "The masticating surface of the Mammoth tooth is set with four or five high double-coned processes, strongly coated with enamel, whereas that of the other *incognitum* is flat, nearly smooth, and ribbed traversely, somewhat like the elephant's grinder, but less prominently marked."[41] Independently of Cuvier, who had arrived at a similar conclusion in Paris the previous year, Turner proved unequivocally that the Siberian and North American animals themselves were separate species.

Turner culled a convincing image of the enormous girth of these unknown creatures from the early-eighteenth-century account of the Siberian mammoth by Philipp Johann Tabbert von Strahlenberg, a Swedish officer employed by Czar Peter the Great. In contrast to the dry, anatomical comparison of the grinders, Strahlenberg's description of a carcass discovered in Siberia gave Turner's audience a vivid picture of a whole skeleton, whose rib cage was so large that "a man standing upright on the concavity of a rib, as the skeleton rested on its side, could not quite reach the opposite one, though with the aid of a pretty long battle axe which he held in his hand."[42]

Relying heavily on such writers, Turner used these dramatic tales to challenge his learned colleagues at the Philosophical Society to find a complete skeleton of the American *incognitum*.

> It is to be regretted, that the world has not yet been favored with a particular and scientific description of the whole skeleton of an *incognitum* so interesting as the Mammoth. The person who shall first procure the complete skeleton of this *incognitum*, will render, not to his country alone, but to the world, a most invaluable present.[43]

The very size of these animals, along with the discovery of the fossil remains of other large unknown creatures in Germany, South America, and Virginia, led Turner to question another central tenet of Jefferson's *Notes*, the idea that the American *incognitum* would be found to be living in the remote, unexplored areas of the North American continent. In Turner's opinion, both the Siberian mammoth and the *incognitum* were extinct. By his count, there were now five such animals whose bones were unknown, including the mysterious clawed creature recently discovered in a Virginia cave. "Can we believe, then, that so many and such stupendous creatures could exist for centuries and be concealed from the prying eye of inquisitive man?" Then, with a pointed reference to Jefferson's opinion, he hinted at the misconceptions fostered by his belief in the perfection of God's nature. "The benevolent persuasion, that no link in the chain of creation will ever be suffered to perish, has induced certain authors of distinguished merit, to provide a residence for our Mammoth in the remote regions of the north."[44]

The skepticism about extinction in Jefferson's *Notes* derived at least partly from the Indian legends, particularly the Shawnee tale of the great beast's escape to the northern territories by leaping over the Ohio River and the Great Lakes. "But their belief rests on mere tradition," Turner claimed, disputing another of Jefferson's arguments. "For none of them will venture to declare they have seen the animal themselves, or that their information concerning him, is drawn from any person who had."[45] Even though he summarized the legend once again for the society's members, Turner cast doubts on the reliability of such evidence: "There is little or no dependence to be placed on Indian traditions. They are so clouded with fable, as to obscure any truths they may contain."

Turner's personal acquaintance with Big Bone Lick enabled him to detect one aspect of the Indian traditions that he felt did contain an element of truth. His scrupulous comparison of the tusks and grinders there had led him to conclude that the Siberian mammoth was a herbivorous animal, whereas the American *incognitum* was definitely a carnivore, as Dr. Hunter had first claimed more than thirty years earlier. In the soft clay on either side of the stream flowing from Big Bone to the Ohio River, Turner had found a stratum composed entirely of the bones of buffaloes and other smaller animals mentioned in the Indian legends as having been the monster's victims.

> But, judge my surprize, when attentively examining them, I discovered, that almost every bone of any length had received a fracture, occasioned, most likely, by the teeth of the Mammoth, while in the act of feeding on his prey. Now, may we not from these facts infer, that Nature had allotted to the Mammoth the beasts of the forest for his food?[46]

The swiftness and size of these smaller animals presented an elusive prey for the elephant-like American monster that these specimens conjured up in Turner's mind. From the bones of fleet-footed deer, elk, and buffalo, he concluded that the *incognitum* itself must have had great strength and agility, an improbable trait given the animal's great girth and ponderous size, but a puzzle that he resolved with unusual audacity using the Indian legend.

> May it not be inferred, too, that as the largest and swiftest quadrupeds were appointed for his food, he necessarily was endowed with great strength and activity? That, as the immense volume of the creature would unfit him for coursing after his prey through thickets and woods, Nature had furnished him with the power of taking it by a mighty leap?—That this power of springing a great distance was requisite to the more effectual concealment of his bulky volume while lying in wait for his prey?[47]

The Indian legend was correct, Turner argued, in attributing great leaping powers to the extinct monster. With a single bound of his own fertile imagination, he greatly enhanced the ferocity of the American monster, adding additional drama to the violent imagery of the Romanticized version of Jefferson's Indian myth that had appeared in the *American Museum* nearly a decade earlier. "The Author of existence is wise and just in all his works. He never confers an appetite without the power to gratify it."[48]

In Turner's impressionistic view of extinction, the American monster had been killed off by humans in self-defense—a theme first introduced obliquely by the English anatomist William Hunter thirty years earlier when he suggested the *incognitum* was an extinct species whose disappearance was God's blessing on the human species. The beast's increased ferocity conveniently set the stage for Turner's own theory of its extinction:

> With the agility and ferocity of the tiger; with the body of unequaled magnitude and strength, it is possible the Mammoth may have been at once the terror of the forest and of man! And may not the human race have made the extirpation of this terrific disturber a common cause?[49]

Both Jefferson's "Great Claw or Megalonyx" and Turner's "Terror of the Forest" added ominous new images of warring species to the American landscape, although neither article appeared in print for two more years. Nonetheless, when they did, there was clear evidence that Turner's new monster had acquired several distinctive traits of Jefferson's clawed creature. In addition to its voracious appetite and remarkable leaping powers, Turner now claimed that the mammoth was also a clawed creature, an opinion voiced unambiguously in a footnote referring directly to Jefferson's Megalonyx.

> I have often expressed a belief, that whenever the entire skeleton should be found, it would appear to have been armed with claws. I am now more confirmed in this opinion, for after this Memoir was written, the Society received a collection of bones here treated of, and among them the *os calcis*, or heel bone, of a *clawed* animal.[50]

Jefferson himself was forced at this time to publish a postscript to his own article on the Megalonyx acknowledging that he had erred in

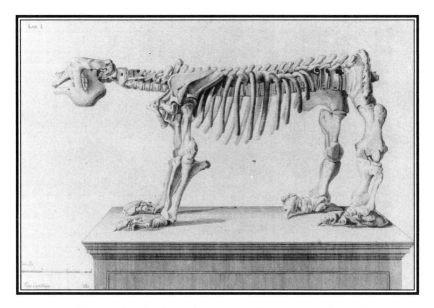

FIGURE 40. Drawing by the Spanish naturalist Juan-Bautista Bru of the reconstructed skeleton of an extinct clawed creature found in South America. Georges Cuvier's description of the Megatherium as a slothlike animal led Thomas Jefferson to retract his claims that the Megalonyx was a ferocious lionlike creature. Courtesy Bibliothèque centrale du Muséum national d'histoire naturelle, Paris.

identifying the unknown creature as a lionlike animal. In the interim between the reading of his paper and its publication two years later, Jefferson's young collaborator Caspar Wistar had called his attention to an account and drawing of the skeleton of a similar clawed animal dug up near the river La Plata in Paraguay, which had been mounted by the Spanish naturalist Juan-Bautista Bru in the Royal Cabinet of Natural History at Madrid. By coincidence, a French official visiting Madrid in 1796 had seen the skeleton and sent a set of Bru's unpublished drawings to Paris where Georges Cuvier presented the first scholarly paper on the animal (figure 40). Anglo-American naturalists had become aware of the Megatherium, as Cuvier called the creature, through the London-based *Monthly Magazine*, which had published a summary of Cuvier's paper and his copy of the Spanish engraving.

The twelve-foot-long skeletonized animal, which stood about six feet high, had very large claws but only a few molars in its pointed snout, characteristics which Cuvier recognized closely resembled the traits of sloths and anteaters among living animals. Like the elephant, the animal was herbivorous and fed on leaves, shrubs, and branches of trees. "It adds to the numerous facts that tell us that the animals of the ancient world all differ from those we see on earth today," Cuvier concluded. "For it is scarcely probable that, if this animal still existed, such a remarkable species could hitherto have escaped the researches of naturalists."[51]

In the heated debate over the Megalonyx, Jefferson's colleague Caspar Wistar offered the first truly technical paper on this animal's bones. Published at the same time as Jefferson's memoir, his detailed anatomical description of the specimens contributed strongly to the transmutation of the lionlike monster into a harmless animal in the sloth family. Adjunct professor of anatomy, surgery, and midwifery at the University of Pennsylvania, Dr. Wistar had recently been elected curator of the American Philosophical Society, where he had become the country's rising young authority on fossils.

Steering clear of the large cosmological questions raised by the existence of extinct species, Wistar compared the bones of the Megalonyx to Cuvier's Megatherium. In his scientific opinion, they were similar but distinct species, both of which belonged to the family of clawed creatures without cutting teeth, such as the sloths and anteaters. "We are naturally led to inquire whether these bones are similar to those of the great skeleton found lately at Paraguay, but for want of a good plate, or a full description we are unable at present to decide upon that subject."[52] Nonetheless, Cuvier's drawing suggested to him that the Megalonyx and the Megatherium were probably not the same species, although they shared some similarities. Wistar's own short memoir was illustrated by an engraving of the bones from the Virginia cave whose anatomical detail gave the large claws a menacing aspect that undoubtedly left an indelible impression of the beast's ferocity in the minds of many readers, despite his conclusions to the contrary (figure 41).

On Sunday evenings, Dr. Wistar often entertained members of the society and visiting naturalists, and during the summer of 1799, after the publication of these papers, speculation about the American *incognitum* was undoubtedly a common topic of conversation among his guests. Even though he was aware of Cuvier's growing list of extinct species, Dr. Wistar voiced no published opinion about them. He had

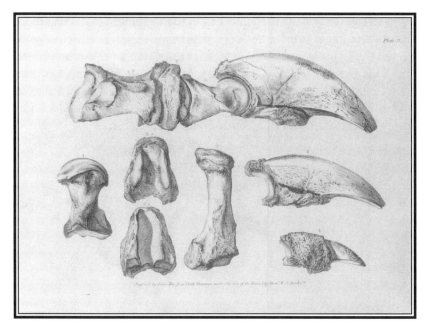

FIGURE 41. Drawing of the toe bones and claws of the Megalonyx from Thomas Jefferson's memoir on an unidentified creature found in a Virginia cave, 1799. Jefferson's article depicted the animal as a lionlike creature, prompting many American naturalists to imagine the *incognitum* as an elephant with claws. Courtesy American Philosophical Society, Philadelphia.

been a referee for George Turner's paper and was probably responsible for the judge's inclusion of the "Megolicks of Paraguay" among the five large animals considered likely to be unknown extinct creatures.[53] Dr. Wistar's clinical approach, however, did little to dampen speculation about the *incognitum*'s appetite, which was greatly magnified by Turner's clever theory and taken quite seriously by his colleagues at the Philosophical Society.

George Turner himself was a member of the committee appointed in 1798 by Thomas Jefferson, as president of the American Philosophical Society, that sent out a printed appeal the following year soliciting information about American antiquities both natural and archaeological. The letter stressed the importance of finding "one or more skeletons of the Mammoth, so called, and of other unknown animals as either have been, or hereafter may be discovered in America."[54] Signed by Jefferson, Wistar, Turner, and Peale, the letter designated Big Bone Lick as the likely site for finding a whole skeleton. But those who received the letter were not the ones to unearth such a skeleton, nor was Big Bone the site where it was found. Instead, the action shifted back to the Hudson River valley, where a farmer digging for marl, a claylike peat soil, in the bog marshes near Rev. Annan's farm, created a sensation with the discovery of a nearly complete skeleton.

13

Exhumation of the Monster

"Gracious God, what a jaw! How many animals have been crushed by it!" was the exclamation of all. A fresh supply of grog went round, and the hearty fellows covered with mud, continued the search with encreasing vigor.

—Rembrandt Peale, 1803

DIGGING HAD CONTINUED sporadically in the Hudson River valley ever since Rev. Annan's discovery of bones during the Revolutionary War, although the number of sites multiplied with the escalating interest in the *incognitum*. Orange and Ulster Counties, the area north of the Hudson River highlands at West Point, where Annan's old farm was located, proved to be an unexpectedly abundant source of fossil remains. The small settlement of Montgomery at Ward's Bridge, three miles north of Annan's farm, was the center of many of the discoveries. In 1792, Captain Joseph Barber called attention to the boglands there with the discovery of several enormous ribs on his farm near the Walkill River, which flowed through Orange County. The draining of these swampy areas began in earnest about the time Ezra Stiles passed through Newburgh, as farmers increasingly ditched the wet and miry marshes to remove the rich black marl to fertilize their fields.

Sylvanus Miller, an attorney from New York, recalled having seen some of these large bones as a child while attending grammar school near Ward's Bridge, where he grew up in the early 1790s.[1] In 1794, a number of bones were unearthed near Peter Millspaw's farm about five miles west of this settlement. Dr. James G. Graham, a local physician whose family owned a large estate in nearby Ulster County, sent several of these bones to his friend Dr. Richard Bayley, a professor of anatomy at Columbia College, who placed them in the institution's anatomical museum. From Shawangunk, several miles north of Ward's Bridge, Dr. Graham documented numerous discoveries in the area, including "a tooth (one of the grinders), and some hair, about three inches long, of a dark dun color," found by Mr. Alexander Colden about four feet below the surface. According to Dr. Graham—who was soon to play an integral role in Charles Willson Peale's excavation of the first complete skeleton from this area—"These large bones are uniformly found in deep wet swamps only, by farmers, in digging up black mold and *marl* for the purpose of manuring their lands."[2]

The neighborhood around Ward's Bridge was fairly quiet until the early fall of 1799 when workmen digging a marl pit on John Masten's farm four miles west of Newburgh found a huge thighbone, nearly eighteen inches around at its narrowest part. After news of the unusual discovery spread throughout the neighboring farms, a crowd of about a hundred people gathered at the site to engage in three days of digging, encouraged by a local minister and several physicians, including Dr. Graham himself, who apparently helped supervise the excavation.

Ladling water from the marl pit with milk pails, buckets, and bowls, the farmers and farmhands extracted a large number of bones until rising waters forced them to give up on the fourth day. They used oxen and chains to drag the largest specimens from the earth, breaking an immense tusk into three pieces in the process. Although many of the bones were broken by the carelessness of the crowd, when the specimens were laid out on John Masten's granary floor, they constituted the rudiments of a complete skeleton, which the old German-speaking farmer subsequently exhibited to "strangers" for a small fee.[3] Realizing that they would be more valuable once he had all the animal's bones, Masten refused to sell the strange specimens, although several offers were made.

Rembrandt Peale's account of his father's excavation of bones in Orange County two years later is the principal source for this story. Peale later remembered that Masten confessed to him his lack of interest in the fossil remains until "the learned physician, the reverend divine, to whom he had been accustomed to look upwards, gave importance to the objects which excited the vulgar stare of his more inquisitive neighbors."[4] With thinly veiled contempt for the crowds at the marl pit, Peale pictured them as ignorant country folk: "All were eager at the expense of some exertions, to gratify their curiosity in seeing the ruins of an animal so gigantic, of whose bones very few among them had ever heard, and over which they had so often unconsciously trod."[5]

The mysterious bones seem to have lain on Masten's granary floor for nearly a year until new discoveries the following fall revived interest among the local gentry. By then, the physicians and clergymen had been alerted to their significance by the American Philosophical Society's public appeal for such antiquities. On September 10, 1800, in the wake of the growing awareness of the new discoveries in Orange County, Dr. Graham wrote to the New York physician Dr. Samuel Latham Mitchill, a professor at Columbia College and the city's foremost scientist. Educated in the 1780s at the University of Edinburgh, Mitchill was editor of the monthly *Medical Repository*, the nation's first scientific journal, which he had helped establish in 1797. The journal's articles covered a wide range of topics in medicine and natural history, from the disappearance of the swallows in autumn to the mineralogical history of New York.[6]

Before telling Dr. Mitchill about the recent discovery of a nearly intact skeleton, Dr. Graham briefly reviewed the various discoveries of bones in Orange County during the past decade. Even though he failed to mention John Masten's farm by name or the frenzied scene there described by Rembrandt Peale, Dr. Graham did convey the escalating excitement of the new diggings at this site in early September. "Many of them have been raised, but some much broken, especially the bones of the head, which, I am persuaded, lie entire, and in their natural order."[7] The prospect of obtaining a complete skeleton led him to alert the New York scientific community to the exciting new discovery: "I have procured two bones of this last discovered skeleton, and sent them to New-York, by Edward W. Laight, Esq. for the purpose of having them examined by yourself, and other well-informed naturalists in the city." The influence of Jefferson's Megalonyx and George Turner's speculation about an elephant with claws were evident in his opinion that one of these bones was a metacarpal bone "which indicates the animal to have been claw-footed."

The large number of sites where bones had been discovered in the small area around Ward's Bridge convinced Dr. Graham that the unknown animals must have been quite numerous. While he clearly accepted the idea of extinction, his comments on the creature's disappearance demonstrate how George Turner's image of the "ferocious" carnivore eased the conscience of American Protestants concerned about the animal's disappearance: "And why Providence should have destroyed an animal or species it once thought proper to create, is a matter of curious inquiry and difficult solution. If, however, they were voracious, it must appear happy for the human race that they are extinct, by whatever means."

News of the Orange County diggings also brought the New York attorney Sylvanus Miller back to this neighborhood in early September to compare these bones with the specimens he had seen at grammar school there nearly a decade earlier. "On my arrival at Newburgh, I was informed, that about twelve miles to the westward of that place had lately been discovered the skeleton of an animal of uncommon magnitude, and decidedly larger than that of any which we have at this time any knowledge."[8] Ten days after Dr. Graham wrote to Dr. Mitchill, Miller himself wrote to him, emphasizing the good prospects for obtaining a whole skeleton from these recently unearthed bones. "There remains, however, no doubt, but that the residue of the bones are there, and nothing but want of exertions, or means to defray expense, will hinder the whole from being procured."[9] The urgent tone of this letter stemmed from the size of the "skeleton lately discovered" whose bones, Miller claimed, "afford a spectacle truly astonishing" owing to their lack of decay: "They are, however, not as yet entirely procured, though great exertions have been made, and are still making, to effect so desirable an object. The difficulty is made much greater by the influx of water, continually rushing in from the bottom and sides to the hollow already made." Like Dr. Graham, several bones of the foot suggested to Miller that the animal "once had claws."

These letters announcing the exciting new discovery were published in the October issue of Dr. Mitchill's *Medical Repository*. Along with an article about the bones by Dr. Elias Winfield published in the Newburgh newspaper the *Rights of Man*, they set in motion a chain of events that led first to an attempt by the newly elected President Thomas Jefferson to obtain the bones. In late November, shortly after these notices were published, Jefferson went to Washington, D.C., to await the outcome of the presidential race in which he and his running mate Aaron Burr had opposed the incumbent John Adams. Even though the election would be decided by the House of Representatives because his running mate, Aaron Burr, had received an equal number of electoral votes, Jefferson wrote to his friend Robert R. Livingston to offer him the position of secretary of the navy in his cabinet and, more important, to ask his help in acquiring bones from the new Hudson River site:

> I have heard of the discovery of some large bones, supposed to be of the mammoth, at about thirty or forty miles distance from you, and among the bones found, are said to be some of which we have never been able to procure. The bones I am most anxious to obtain are those of the head and feet, which are said to be among those found in your State, as also the ossa innominata, and the scapula.[10]

Promising to pay whatever expenses that might be incurred, Jefferson politely urged Livingston to use his influence in acquiring these specimens: "Could I so far venture to trouble you on this subject, as to engage some of your friends near the place, to procure for me the bones above mentioned?"

Writing to an influential New York politician whose estate was north of Orange County, Jefferson was off target with his request, since the bones he sought were in the hands of a farmer who apparently showed only a modicum of deference toward the local gentry. In his reply to Jefferson three weeks later, Livingston revealed the tense situation created by John Masten's possession of the bones, which rendered the powerful landlord and politician, not to mention the newly elected president, momentarily impotent. "When I first heard of the discovery," Livingston wrote,

> I made some attempts to possess myself of them, but found they were a kind of common property, the whole town having joined in digging for them till they were stopped by the autumnal rains. They entertain well-grounded hopes of discovering the whole skeleton, since these bones are not, like all those they have hitherto found in that County, placed within the vegetable world, but are covered with a stratum of clay,—that being sheltered from the air and water they are more perfectly preserved.[11]

Jefferson's efforts to obtain the bones from Shawangunk were in stark contrast to the political crisis caused by the election results. By early February, the outcome of the election was in the hands of the House of Representatives, where the New England Federalists threw their support to Aaron Burr in a desperate effort to keep Jefferson out of the White House. Barely a week before the matter was put to a formal vote, Jefferson wrote to Dr. Caspar Wistar, apprising him of Chancellor Livingston's unsuccessful efforts to acquire the bones. Jefferson had given up hope of obtaining a complete skeleton from the Orange County residents: "From this extract, and the circumstances that the bones belong to the town, you will be sensible of the difficulty of obtaining any considerable portion of them." Instead, he recommended that Livingston ask only for selected bones: "It is not unlikely they would with common consent yield a particular bone or bones, provided they may keep the mass for their own town."[12]

During the winter months, the excitement over the bones of the American *incognitum* grew. In April 1801, the controversy took a new turn when the *Medical Repository* published a short note entitled "Extinct Species of Animals," reporting that the list of extinct quadrupeds compiled by the Parisian anatomist Georges Cuvier now numbered twenty-three, including the mammoth, the long-headed rhinoceros, the great fossil tortoise, and "a sort of dragon."[13] Published as a separate booklet in Paris, Cuvier's latest list of extinct creatures had been widely reprinted in Europe and revealed the close contacts between the American naturalists and himself.[14]

The American mammoth and Jefferson's megalonyx figured prominently in Cuvier's survey of extinct creatures, which included an eloquent, if self-serving, appeal for international collaboration in the search for extinct quadrupeds. In Cuvier's acknowledgment of extinction, the earth's geological history began to materialize with new clarity in the fossil remains under his scrutiny. The editors of the *Medical Repository* added to Cuvier's long list of extinct creatures the observation that

> the State of New York is now the theatre of the latest discoveries that have been made of fossil bones. . . . But these are not all which the earth contains. There are *parts* of skeletons of which M. Cuvier cannot speak with equal assurance; but of which, however, enough is known to encourage hope that the list of zoological antiquities will be soon lengthened.[15]

The following month Chancellor Livingston's letter to Jefferson was read to the American Philosophical Society, alerting Philadelphians to the fruitful digging in Orange and Ulster counties.[16] In fact,

Charles Willson Peale, the proprietor of the city's foremost collection of curiosities, had already begun to make inquiries himself concerning the new discoveries. Peale had learned of the Shawangunk bones from a clipping about the discovery sent to him by his wife's family in New York City and the articles published in Dr. Mitchill's *Medical Repository*.

Frustrated in his efforts to acquire more information about the bones through his father-in-law's contacts in Newburgh, Peale decided to travel to Orange County himself to visit the site.[17] Peale traveled first to New York, where he got guarantees of financial backing from his wife's family and a letter of introduction to Dr. Graham from Dr. Mitchill, before sailing up the Hudson to Newburgh. Received graciously by Dr. Graham, Peale went to John Masten's farm the morning after his arrival, carrying a trunk with an abundant supply of drawing paper, charcoal, pens, and ink, to disguise the real purpose of his visit. At the farm, Peale found the better part of a complete skeleton already laid out on the granary floor where, according to his son Rembrandt Peale, the bones had been occasionally visited by the curious.

Peale had barely begun drawing the bones when Masten invited him to lunch. It was at this time that the farmer's eldest son suddenly inquired whether Peale might be interested in purchasing the bones, even though Peale had carefully avoided expressing any such intention. Forced by the farmer's refusal to set a price, Peale offered $200 for the bones already collected, plus another $100 for those he could dig up at a future date. The farmer's awareness of the value of such curiosities was evident, for Masten told Peale that a great profit could be made by a traveling show that exhibited the bones from town to town. As Peale later confided to his wife, he answered with his own bargaining ploy, warning the farmer of the unpredictable returns from tavern shows and the unreliable morals of itinerant showmen.[18]

After considering Peale's offer overnight, Masten sold the skeleton to him the next morning for the amount Peale offered, plus a double-barreled rifle for his son and gowns from New York for his daughters. Peale was anxious to conclude the deal, since on his way to Masten's farm that morning he had encountered an African American who told him that he had just met a man along the road asking directions to Masten's farm and expressing interest in buying the skeleton. The bones were hurriedly packed into wooden barrels and carried to Newburgh in Masten's own wagon where Peale loaded them onto a sailing vessel and departed the next morning for New York.

In less than four days, Peale was on his way back to Philadelphia, where he planned to determine what bones were missing from the skeleton and to prepare a more ambitious excavation at Masten's farm later in the summer. Returning to New York with his trophies, Peale briefly exhibited a giant thighbone and several drawings at his host's home and described in his diary the sensation they created among New York's polite society: "The Vice President of the United States [Aaron Burr], and a considerable number of Ladies and Gentlemen came to see the Bones. The news of them must have blew like wild fire, for upwards [of] 80 persons came to see them that evening."[19] From New York, Peale wrote to Thomas Jefferson informing him of his acquisition and explaining the arduous task that lay ahead of completing the skeleton: "The pits dug to get the bones I possess, are large, and now full of water, and one of them is 12 feet deep, and from the situation of the morass and the surrounding lands, it appears an Herculean task to explore the bottom where the remainder of the bones are supposed to lay."[20]

Even before Peale's final excavations began, news of his upcoming exhibit spread rapidly around the country through newspaper reports. On July 22, 1801, Kline's Carlisle Weekly Gazette noted that Mr. Peale now has "the bones of the great American animal commonly called the Mammoth," and "within the space of two or three months he expects to have it in his power to put together a complete skeleton for the Museum."[21] In Philadelphia, Peale had already begun to reconstruct the skeleton to determine what bones were missing from the collection he had bought from John Masten. "Very few Bones are wanting among my assemblage," he wrote to Robert Patterson.

> Yet those are so important, & the certainty so great of finding them in the Spot whence they were procured, that I am induced to suspend the Labour which I had begun of fastening them together, & take effectual Means to procure every thing that remains of this enormous animal.[22]

Among the missing bones were several vertebrae and ribs, a tusk and thighbone, and, most important, the lower jaw and the top of the skull.

Peale postponed his second trip to Masten's farm to retrieve the rest of the bones until after the summer harvest, to prevent Masten's crops from being trampled by the hordes of onlookers attracted by the diggings. In the interim, Peale tried to raise money to pay for the excavations and to devise a method for draining water from the marl pits, the principal obstacle to the success of his enterprise. "I have made drawings of the Elephant and other great Bones found in different parts of the world. And I have extracted from various Authors every thing I can find interesting on Bones," he wrote to Dr. Graham at Shawangunk, urging him to assure John Masten that his return was imminent.[23]

On July 17, 1801, Peale exhibited his drawings at a meeting of the American Philosophical Society and requested a loan of $500 to underwrite his excavations and reconstruction of the skeleton. A week later, the loan was granted at a special meeting attended by twenty-six members, including Dr. Caspar Wistar, Rev. Nicholas Collin, and the governor of Pennsylvania. Meanwhile, Peale wrote to Jefferson requesting his help in obtaining several large tents and a pump from the navy agent in New York. But before the president's authorization arrived, Peale left for New York with his museum assistant Jotham Fenton, Dr. James Woodhouse, a professor of chemistry at the University of Pennsylvania, and his young son Rembrandt, who was already an exceptionally good portrait artist.

Traditionally, the marl pits dug by Orange County farmers were generally about twelve feet long by five feet and only three feet deep, but according to Charles Willson Peale's own account, the pit dug by the farmers at John Masten's farm was considerably larger and was filled with twelve feet of water when Peale's party arrived back at the site in early August to finish excavating the missing bones. The first problem Peale faced was how to pump the water from the large pit so that his laborers could dig out the bones still buried in the layer of soft white shell marl at the bottom.

Peale had brought pumps, ropes, pulleys, and augers from New York, but at the site he devised his own method of draining the deep pit. Hiring a local millwright, he constructed a "crab," or large wooden tripod, with a block and tackle at its apex supporting a chain of buckets that scooped water from the pit. The apparatus was driven by a millwheel twenty feet in diameter, rotated by several persons treading inside the wheel, which set an endless chain of buckets in motion, lifting the water from the pit high up on the scaffolding into a long drainage trough. Peale's elaborate pumping machine, which required the labor of three men walking inside the wheel and removed an estimated 1,440 gallons of water per hour, soon emptied the hole of water and enabled a dozen laborers to begin shoveling the wet marl from the bottom of the pit (figure 42).

In many respects, the pumping machine itself became the principal attraction at the site, and the "highway" passing through Masten's farm was soon clogged with the coaches, wagons, carriages, and horses of the onlookers who gathered at the entrance to the field to witness the spectacle: "Rich and poor, men, women, and children, all flocked to see the operation," Rembrandt Peale later wrote, "and a swamp always noted as the solitary abode of snakes and frogs, became the active scene of curiosity and bustle."[24] The diggings took on a festive air with the watered-down liquor that Peale doled out and the squealing children who amused themselves by walking inside the mill wheel.

Despite the dedication of his workers and the ingenuity of his pumping device, Peale was forced to abandon the costly excavation at Masten's farm when the soft banks of the pit began to slide in on the workers, who had turned up remarkably few bones. In the end, John Masten had made a good deal for the digging, getting $100 for the few bones Peale could salvage from the marl pit, not to mention his share of the high wages paid the laborers.[25] Among the bones retrieved were a few grinders, a piece of the sternum, a hipbone, fragments of the head bone, and some bones of the feet. The lower jaw bone, the most sought-after specimen, had eluded Peale's grasp, and its absence led him and his colleagues to seek out other sites in the area.

Following the disappointing results at Masten's farm, Peale moved his operations eleven miles west to a bog marsh on Captain Joseph Barber's property, where four ribs had been found eight years earlier, the same bones that Barber had shown to Ezra Stiles when he visited Poughkeepsie in 1792. The idea of working the site on Barber's property came from a local physician, Dr. Gallatin, whom Peale met through Dr. Graham, his host at Shawangunk. Loading his wagon with bones and gear from Masten's farm, Peale walked several hours to the new site, where Captain Barber graciously granted him permission to excavate further. Here Peale's workers simply drained the marsh by digging a ditch.[26]

But the laborers still found few bones, only two rotten tusks, a few small grinders, toe bones and vertebrae, a broken scapula, and an almost entire set of ribs, none of which were missing from the former collection. Even though Captain Barber gave him two ribs dug up earlier, Peale was exceedingly frustrated and disappointed at not finding the

FIGURE 42. Charles Willson Peale's painting *Exhumation of the Mastodon*, 1806–8. Peale's emblematic painting commemorated the excavation of the skeleton of the American *incognitum* at John Masten's farm near Newburgh, New York. Maryland Historical Society, Baltimore.

sought-after lower jaw and skull of the great beast. "The Pit we had now made was 40 feet long & 36 feet wide & 12 feet below the level of the morass, with such an extent I thought it hopeless to expect to find any of the other relicks of this Animal by digging farther around," he noted in his diary. "Therefore I quit the search & [paid] off my labourers, who went away perfectly satisfied."[27]

Nearly a month's digging in the hot August sun had yielded few bones, but Peale's labors had mobilized considerable support from local physicians and clergymen, who continued to suggest new sites nearby. Besides Dr. Graham, at whose home the Peales were staying, Captain Barber proved to be the most helpful of his associates, personally accompanying the party in early September to Rev. Annan's old farm and to Alexander Colden's property, where a grinder and quantity of hair had been found several years earlier. Finally, at Dr. Gallatin's suggestion, Barber led the Peales about five miles west of Ward's Bridge, across the Walkill River, to the tenant farm of Peter Millspaw, located on an estate of which the doctor was an executor, where several bones had been found three years earlier.

Desperate to find the missing bones, Peale's party set out for Millspaw's farm at dawn in a wagon loaded down with the pump, block and tackle, and scaffolding used to support the pumping device. Crossing the Walkill at the falls, they climbed over a hill and descended into a sparsely settled woodland to Peter Millspaw's log hut. "Here we fastened our horses, and followed our guide to the center of the morass, or rather marshy forest, where every step was taken on rotten timber and the spreading roots of tall trees, the luxuriant growth of a few years, half of which were tottering over our heads," Rembrandt later wrote. "Breathless silence had here taken her reign amid unhealthy fogs, and nothing was heard but the fearful crash of some mouldering branch or towering beach."[28] Millspaw led Peale's party to a bog fenced off to protect his cattle, where he himself had found several bones in 1798, several of which Dr. Graham had sent to Dr. Bayley at Columbia a few years earlier.

The Peales used long iron rods with wooden cross handles to locate hard objects beneath the earth's surface. When the piercing rod struck some bones, Peale's crew dug a large twelve foot deep pit, measuring nearly forty feet square, where the pumping machinery was again erected, driven this time be a windlass instead of the millwheel. Finally, after several days of fruitless digging, when they were about to give up, Jotham Fenton's rod struck a large collection of bones nearby, about eighty feet from the marl pit. Beckoning to Peale's son Rembrandt, the two men thrust their spades into the soft earth and gave a cry when they struck the edges of a large bone. All hands quickly gathered around, energized by the prospect of a reward for their labors. Quickly clearing away the trees and brush and pulling up the sod, they shoveled away the black marl and the damp yellow clay where the bones lay. Under Peale's supervision, they carefully uncovered the animal's shoulder blade, then the ulna and radius, the bones of the upper foreleg, and finally, to the delight of everyone, the shape of the long-sought-after lower jaw emerged from the moist soil.

"After such a variety of labour and length of fruitless expectation," Rembrandt Peale later wrote, "this success was extremely grateful to all parties, and the unconscious woods echoed with repeated huzzas!" Then, in an ominous echo of George Turner's ferocious, claw-footed elephants, Peale evoked their joy and horror at the massive bone: "'Gracious God, what a jaw! how many animals have been crushed by it!' was the exclamation of all. A fresh supply of grog went round, and the hearty fellows covered with mud, continued the search with increasing vigour."[29] These bones found at Millspaw's bog were not so well preserved, but with Dr. Graham's return of the bones formerly sent to Columbia College, they rendered a nearly complete second skeleton. The Peales had two extra piercing rods fashioned by a local blacksmith to search for the animal's massive skull, but when they finally uncovered it, they found only a disintegrating heap of which only the pearly white grinders remained intact.

Packed into large wooden chests, the bones were driven in wagons to Newburgh where they were transferred to a sailing vessel bound for New York. Two days later, arriving in New York, Peale displayed a few bones at the home of his family friend and host, Major Stagg, and in his own words, "multitudes of the Citizens" came to see them. "Their magnitude surprised many and only served to excite their curiosity to see the intire Skeleton," he wrote in his diary.[30]

Back in Philadelphia, Peale spent three months meticulously reconstructing the skeletons with the assistance of his black servant Moses Williams, his sons Rembrandt and Raphaelle, and the anatomical expertise of Dr. Caspar Wistar, who had tried unsuccessfully to get these bones for Thomas Jefferson. In October, while at work on the reconstruction, Peale gave the president a complete account of his excavation in Orange County, along with an indication of the difficult task of mounting the skeletons. The enormous tusk retrieved from Masten's marl pit had been broken into three pieces, but when repaired, it measured nearly eleven feet, curving gently to a semicircle with a moderate spiral. "The form [is] beautiful as infinite varied circles & spirals can make it," Peale wrote to Jefferson.[31]

Using bones from all three sites as models, Rembrandt carved wooden duplicates of the missing pieces until he had formed two complete skeletons. "Nothing in either skeleton is imaginary," Rembrandt later wrote. "And what we have not unquestionable authority for we leave deficient, which happens in only two instances, the *summit* of the head, and the *end* of the tail."[32] Rembrandt's drawing of an elephant-like creature, with short, upturned tusks, was used as a guide in their reconstruction. Peale's son already envisioned taking the second skeleton to Europe where anatomists eagerly awaited resolution of the American *incognitum*'s identity.

On Christmas Eve, 1801, members of the American Philosophical Society were finally invited to Peale's Philadelphia Museum to view the great beast's skeleton, which stood eleven feet high at the shoulders and fifteen feet long from chin to rump. Immediately after this private showing, the museum's Mammoth Room, located in the southeast chamber of Philadelphia's historic Philosophical Hall, across the street from the State House, was opened to the public with considerable fanfare for a fee of fifty cents. In February 1802, the exhibition was publicized by a parade through the city led by Moses Williams, Peale's black servant, who wore an Indian headdress and rode on a white horse behind a trumpeter heralding the event.

Rembrandt Peale's younger brother Rubens called the mammoth their "pet," but from the very beginning, its mounted skeleton was cloaked in an aura of violence in the Peales' promotional literature. Filled with bloody images, the first broadside advertising the "Skeleton of the Mammoth" evoked a menacing image of the mammoth with a long excerpt from the romanticized version of Jefferson's Shawnee legend published more than a decade earlier in Mathew Carey's *American Museum* (figure 43). Once again, Peale's patrons heard about the race of animals "huge as the Precipice, cruel as the bloody panther, swift as the descending Eagle and terrible as the Angel of Night."[33]

Peale's own comments referred to the mammoth as the "Antique Wonder of North America" and called the Indian legend a "confused tradition among the natives of our country." But the huge skeleton itself was used to evoke the animal's all-powerful stature with words recalling Jefferson's rebuttal of Buffon: "whatever might have been the appearance of this ENORMOUS QUADRUPED when clothed with flesh, his massy bones can alone lead us to imagine; already convinced that he was the LARGEST of *Terrestrial Beings!*"[34] In the ensuing months, a kind of mammoth fever swept the nation, ranging from the "mammoth bread" sold by a Philadelphia baker to the "mammoth cheese" weighing 1,230 pounds sent to President Thomas Jefferson by John Leland, a Baptist minister in Cheshire, Massachusetts, on behalf of the town's

Skeleton of the Mammoth

IS NOW TO BE SEEN

At the Museum, in a separate Room.

FOR ADMITTANCE TO WHICH, 50 CENTS; TO THE MUSEUM,
AS USUAL, 25 CENTS.

---

*Of this Animal, it is said the following is a Tradition, as delivered in
the very terms of a Shawanee Indian:*

" TEN THOUSAND MOONS AGO, when nought but gloomy forests covered this land of the sleeping Sun, long before the pale men, with thunder and
fire at their command, rushed on the wings of the wind to ruin this garden of
nature----------when nought but the untamed wanderers of the woods, and men as
unrestrained as they, were the lords of the soil-----a race of animals were in being,
huge as the frowning Precipice, cruel as the bloody Panther, swift as the descending Eagle, and terrible as the Angel of Night. The Pines crashed beneath their
feet; and the Lake shrunk when they slaked their thirst; the forceful Javelin in
vain was hurled, and the barbed arrow fell harmless from their side. Forests were
laid waste at a meal, the groans of expiring Animals were every where heard ;
and whole Villages, inhabited by men, were destroyed in a moment. The cry of
universal distress extended even to the region of Peace in the West, and the Good
Spirit interposed to save the unhappy. The forked Lightning gleamed all around,
and loudest Thunder rocked the Globe. The Bolts of Heaven were hurled upon
the cruel Destroyers alone, and the mountains echoed with the bellowings of death.
All were killed except one male, the fiercest of the race, and him even the artillery
of the skies assailed in vain. He ascended the bluest summit which shades the
source of the Monongahela, and roaring aloud, bid defiance to every vengeance.
The red Lightning scorched the lofty firs, and rived the knotty oaks, but only
glanced upon the enraged Monster. At length, maddened with fury, he leaped over
the waves of the west at a bound, and this moment reigns the uncontrouled Monarch
of the Wilderness in despite of even Omnipotence itself."

[*Carey's Museum, December, 1790,—page 284.*]

Ninety years have elapsed since the first remains of this Animal were found
in this country----they were then thought to be the remains of a GIANT: Numerous have been the attempts of scientific characters of all nations, to procure a
satisfactory collection of bones ; at length the subscriber has accomplished this
great object, and now announces that he is in possession of a SKELETON of this
ANTIQUE WONDER of North America; after a long, laborious and uncertain enterprize.
They were dug up in Ulster county, (State of New York) where they must have
lain *certainly* many hundred years-------no other vestige remains of these animals ;
nothing but a confused tradition among the natives of our country, which states
their existence, *ten thousand Moons ago ;* but, whatever might have been the appearance of this ENORMOUS QUADRUPED when clothed with flesh, his massy bones
can alone lead us to imagine ; already convinced that he was the LARGEST of
Terrestrial Beings!   C. W. PEALE.

NB. *The Mammoth and Museum will be exhibited by lamp light, every evening,
(Sunday evenings excepted) until* 10 o'Clock.

[*Printed by John Ormrod.*]

FIGURE 43. Broadside advertising the exhibition of the American
incognitum's reconstructed skeleton at Peale's Philadelphia Museum,
ca. 1802. Popularly known as the "mammoth," this skeleton belonged
then to an unidentified creature until the French anatomist Georges
Cuvier formally named the animal the mastodon four years later.
Courtesy American Philosophical Society, Philadelphia.

residents. Federalist politicians, smarting from their recent electoral defeat, mocked Jefferson's preoccupation with the bones and the hoopla over the Peales' exhibition.

Rembrandt Peale responded with a "mammoth feast," a farewell dinner in mid-February for his European tour with the second skeleton. Thirteen guests dined at a banquet table under the skeleton's rib cage while a pianist played "Yankee Doodle" and the guests toasted the mammoth's success in Europe: "The American People: may they be as preeminent among the nations of the earth, as the *canopy* we sit beneath surpasses the fabric of the mouse," a reference to the skeleton of a mouse that Peale had placed next to the mammoth.[35]

Two days later, Samuel Ewing, a Philadelphia lawyer, published an unsigned, satirical poem about Peale's mammoth in *The Port Folio*, a Federalist journal launched the previous month by Jefferson's adversaries. The poem mocked Peale's banquet and the museum's proprietor, who sent his sons "wherever toe-nails of a flea are found" to expand his collection of curiosities. "Bones of a Mammoth found by some rude boor, / While, heedless of his luck, he dug manure."[36] Fellow Federalists, unnerved by the popularity of the mammoth among Jefferson's supporters, successfully blocked Peale's efforts to acquire public funding for his museum from federal and state governments. But at the same time this satirical poem appeared, the Pennsylvania legislature granted Peale the use of the newly vacated State House for his museum, although the skeleton of the mammoth remained in its own room across the street at Philosophical Hall.

Undeterred by the Federalist criticism, Rembrandt and his seventeen-year-old brother Rubens departed in late March for New York to exhibit the second skeleton before sailing for Europe. The Philadelphia newspapers had already called attention to their imminent trip, framing the European tour in terms reminiscent of Jefferson's rebuttal of Buffon's theory of American degeneracy. "Mr. Peale has procured the bones of another [skeleton], which, if this meets with encouragement, will be fitted up, and sent to Europe, to convince the Naturalists there of the superior growth of American animals over those of the old world."[37] In New York, Dr. Samuel Latham Mitchill, editor of the *Medical Repository*, expressed similar sentiments in the first official notice to the scientific community of Peale's reconstruction of the mammoth: "A complete skeleton of this enormous creature will be a grand addition to Mr. Peale's Museum, and tend to refute the opinions of some speculative philosophers, that the animals of the western continent are of a puny or diminutive growth."[38]

In New York, after the Peales had assembled the mammoth's skeleton, newspapers announced the opening of the exhibition of "a Skeleton of the Behemoth or Mammoth, an animal with teeth of the carnivorous kind."[39] Two days later, Rubens notified his father they had already received $340, although many of the visitors were skeptical of the parts carved out of wood, especially the tusks, of which only a small fragment of the tip was real ivory.[40] People also found fault with the animal's form, complaining that the neck was too short, the tusks were too long, and the hind legs were where the fore legs should be, but crowds of visitors continued to fill the gallery. Tired of repeating so frequently the skeleton's story, Rembrandt had a broadside printed in April, entitled "A short Account of the Behemoth or Mammoth," which relieved him of this chore.

Compared with the advertisement for the Philadelphia skeleton, Rembrandt's New York broadside was quite subdued, omitting entirely the romanticized "Indian" legend and relying instead on the dry language of a scientific memoir to sketch the skeleton's history. The skeletons discovered in Orange County, Peale pointed out, culminated nearly a century of speculation after the first bones were found near Albany, "and were supposed to be of a GIANT." Dismissing Matthew Carey's account of the mammoth as Indian tradition embellished by English poetic sentiments, Peale attempted to answer visitors who contended that the giant tusks were figments of his imagination: "There is a Tusk at Philadelphia, which I propose taking to Europe with me, found in the same neighborhood, which measures 10 feet 7 inches. From this I have correctly formed an artificial pair, differing in nothing but the length, which I have made 7 inches shorter."[41]

Despite its dry tone, traces of the romantic narrative were woven into the description of the "carnivorous" beast, including details from the Bible stories crucial to shaping American views of "wild" nature. The headline itself alluded to the "Behemoth," the largest of God's creatures described in the Book of Job. The epigraph "Earth sinks beneath him as he moves along" was borrowed from Edward Young's pre-romantic poem "A Paraphrase of the Book of Job," which pictured the Behemoth as a monster: "His ribs are as ribs of brass, and his backbone as molten iron."[42]

In the New York broadside, with the "Indian" legend gone, Peale also relied on subtle scientific "facts" to create an undercurrent of terror while continuing to maintain, despite evidence to the contrary, that the prongs on the mammoth's teeth were proof the animal was a carnivore. "This animal has teeth of the Carnivorous kind—would it not be ridiculous to say that it is the only exception to the rule by which all animals are distinguished? It is however probable, that he made use of flesh and herbage indiscriminately," Peale stated, slightly altering his earlier view of the beast's diet. For further effect, he called attention to other evidence of its ferocity: "The feet shew strong appearances of having been armed with small claws."[43]

Among the New Yorkers who came to see the skeleton was the physician and engraver Alexander Anderson, a connoisseur of such shows ever since his youthful association with the Tammany Society's American Museum. Now retired from medicine, he had become the new republic's most accomplished woodcut artist, specializing in images drawn from natural history. Indeed, his wood engraving of the "New York Mammoth," which later appeared in an American edition of Thomas Bewick's *A General History of Quadrupeds*, was probably made at Rembrandt's exhibition (figure 44). One of the earliest public images of Peale's mammoth, Anderson's drawing shows the tusks turned upward at this time, before Rembrandt's European tour, during which time he decided that the tusks should be reversed.[44]

In mid-May, when Rembrandt postponed their departure for Europe to continue the exhibition, his public notice made artful use of the public's conjecture about the mysterious animal's identity:

> Was it an Elephant, it would be an astonishing monument of some mighty revolution in our globe; for by no system or train of reasoning could it be proved more modern than the Mosaic Deluge. But as it is not an Elephant, having held among Carnivorous, the same rank which the Elephant holds among Graminivorous animals, its remains found only in a northern latitude, its existence no where known and almost obliterated from the annals of tradition—we are lost in conjecture, whether we enquire into its kind, its existence, or its use.[45]

Such publicity struck a responsive chord among Peale's New York audience and the exhibition turned out to be extremely rewarding financially, netting the Peale brothers more than $2,000, which they used to

THE MAMMOTH OF NEW-YORK.

FIGURE 44. Engraving by Alexander Anderson of the "mammoth" exhibited by Rembrandt Peale in New York en route to England in 1802. The illustration confirms that at this stage, the great beast's tusks were inserted pointing upward, although Rembrandt Peale later reversed them upon his return from London.

underwrite their trip to Europe.[46] And in September 1802, Rembrandt and his younger brother Rubens arrived in London, where the mammoth skeleton was exhibited in a building formerly used by the Royal Academy. The admittance fee of two shillings sixpence limited Peale's audience to "Ladies and Gentlemen of the first respectability."

Rembrandt produced a forty-six-page pamphlet for the exhibition, *Account of the Skeleton of the Mammoth, a Non-Descript Carnivorous Animal of Immense Size, Found in America*, which he dedicated to Sir Joseph Banks, the city's leading naturalist. The pamphlet briefly summarized the scientific debate over the bones, from Cotton Mather's letter to the Royal Society to Dr. William Hunter's famous article. But its principal focus was on the story of the excavations in Orange County and the recovery of the skeletons: "Every farmer with his wife and children, for twenty miles round in every direction, with waggons, carriages, and horses, flocked to see the operation. Some of the neighbors, with an eye to the certain prospect of profit, began to think of finding a similar treasure in their morasses."[47] For the first time, Peale provided an exciting narrative of the discovery, describing in detail the arduous task of recovering and reconstructing the skeletons, as well as offering fresh speculation about the unknown animal's character and identity.

In an effort to provide learned Londoners with a scientific description of the bones, Rembrandt also attempted to analyze the animal's anatomical structure. His main concern was differentiating the *incognitum* from the elephant, since several London anatomists had claimed that the bones belonged to an elephant rather than an extinct species. The tusks and teeth were the focus of his assertion that the American monster was a carnivore. Everything from the cone-shaped protuberances and enamel on the grinders to the shape of the tusks and motion of the jaw were introduced as evidence of its carnivorous nature.

Evidently at this stage the tusks had been mounted pointing upward like an elephant's, but Peale's commentary already revealed his own doubts about this arrangement: "It's the opinion of many, that these tusks might have been reversed in the living animal, with their points downwards; but as we know not the kind of enemy it had to fear, we judged only by analogy in giving them the direction of the elephant."[48] For the time being, Peale reluctantly accepted the upturned tusks, but his abiding belief in the animal's carnivorous nature soon led to their reversal, possibly while the skeleton was still being exhibited in England.

Sir Joseph Banks sent a copy of Peale's pamphlet to Johann Friedrich Blumenbach, the German anatomist who was still trying to solve the mystery of the Ohio *incognitum,* as he called the American monster. In February, Blumenbach thanked Banks for Peale's account of the mammoth, which he found highly interesting, "though none of his arguments could persuade me to believe that it has been a carnivorous animal."[49] Even with the assembled skeleton before them, the English anatomists still disagreed about the creature's identity, its possible extinction, and such mundane matters as whether the unknown animal had a trunk.

In addition to the advertisements inserted periodically in London newspapers, Rembrandt published a series of articles in the *Philosophi-*

cal Magazine to alert Britain's learned community to the exhibition. Two of these articles reveal the tenacity of Rembrandt's belief that the American *incognitum* was a carnivore, an assumption that finally led to a remarkable alteration in the mounting of the tusks. His first article, in early 1803, "A Short Account of the Mammoth," stressed even more heavily the anatomical evidence for the monster's carnivorous appetite:

> I am decidedly of the opinion, since it cannot be contradicted by a single proof or fact, that the mammoth was exclusively carnivorous, by which I mean, that he made no use of vegetable food, but either lived entirely on flesh or fish; and not improbably upon shell-fish, if, as there are many reasons to suppose, he was of an amphibious nature.[50]

Now convinced that the tusks of this amphibious creature should be turned upside down, Peale pointed out that the position of their sockets and their extraordinary curvature rendered the horns useless when upturned. "This position was evidently absurd: I therefore resolved on reversing them; in which position, in consequence of their twist or double curve, they appear infinitely more serviceable."[51] In visualizing the beast as an amphibious animal, Peale altered his perception of its diet, conjuring up images of the downturned tusks scrounging for shellfish, although the flesh-eating monster still lurked in the shadows: "But, whether amphibious or not, in the inverted position of the tusks he could have torn an animal to pieces held beneath his foot, and could have struck down an animal of common size, without having his sight obstructed, as it certainly would have been in the other position."[52]

In the following month's issue of the *Philosophical Magazine*, Peale provided English readers with a striking illustration comparing the head of the mammoth with that of an elephant. This addition to his earlier essay contrasted the elephant's short, upwardly inclined tusks with the downturned curvature of the mammoth's tusks (figure 45). The change in direction was warranted, Peale claimed, because the mammoth was carnivorous and amphibious and would have used the tusks "in striking down small animals, or in detaching shell-fish from the bottom of rivers, or even in ascending the banks."[53]

In Philadelphia, Rembrandt's father Charles Willson Peale questioned the wisdom of this alteration of the mammoth's skeleton when

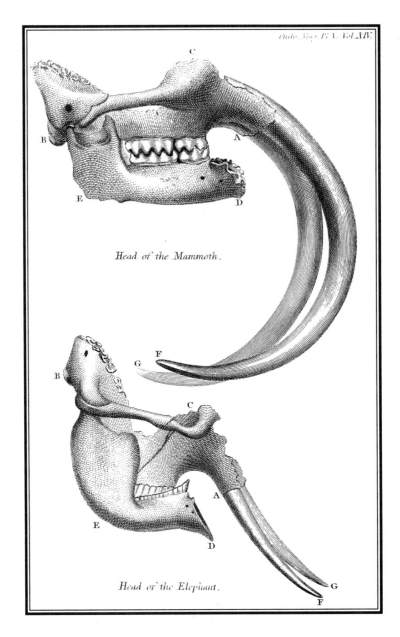

Head of the Mammoth.

Head of the Elephant.

FIGURE 45. Heads of the elephant and mammoth drawn by Rembrandt Peale, 1803. Published in the *Philosophical Magazine*, this drawing illustrated Peale's theory the *incognitum* was a carnivore whose downturned tusks were used to tear its prey to pieces and to dig up shellfish along the shores of lakes. Courtesy American Philosophical Society, Philadelphia.

he first saw his son's drawing. "I have seen your sketch of the comparisson [*sic*] of the head of the Elephant and Mammoth in the Philosophical Magazine, and I am anxious to know your particular reasons for changing the tusks of the Mammoth."[54] The elder Peale felt his son should not have attempted a scientific description of the skeleton but would have preferred to have it written by Dr. Thomas Pole, a Philadelphia physician living in London.

Unaware of his father's misgivings, Rembrandt was already at work on an expanded version of his earlier pamphlet which appeared in July 1803 under the cumbersome title *An Historical Disquisition on the Mammoth, or Great American Incognitum, an Extinct, Immense, Carnivorous Animal, whose Fossil Remains have been found in North America*. This polished essay contrasts sharply with the hastily executed pamphlet he had used the previous fall to promote his London exhibit. The narrative of the recovery and reconstruction of the bones was fleshed out to provide an engaging account of his father's excavation and mounting of the skeletons. In addition, Peale compiled the most serious scientific description to date of the bones, although the memoir's title, like the text, revealed his lingering taste for showmanship and steadfast belief the animal was carnivorous. Reversing his earlier opinion that the tusks of the mammoth curved upward like an elephant's, he now placed them curving downward, giving the American *incognitum* menacing, walrus-like fangs.

In his anatomical description of the teeth, Peale still maintained that the mammoth was "exclusively carnivorous," but now, under the influence of European anatomists, he took pains to qualify this argument, stating that he did mean not to imply the animal was "a *beast of prey*, like the tiger, wolf, &c." but, rather, that it probably fed on turtles, shellfish, and fish, using the inverted tusks instead for "rooting up shellfish, or in climbing the banks of rivers and lakes."[55] Abandoning the idea of an elephant with claws, Peale now imagined the *incognitum* as a amphibious creature inhabiting the great lakes of America, feeding on "such animals as could not well escape him and would not require much artifice or speed to be caught."[56]

For the English museum audience, Peale repositioned the Shawnee Indian legend at the end of his revised pamphlet, with a kind of disclaimer that reflected his own ambivalence about the fable. "The language of this Tradition is certainly English and perhaps a little too highly dressed; but the ideas are truly Indian: it is given in another form in Jefferson's notes on Virginia."[57] In fact, these ideas were more English than Indian, for as Peale himself revealed, their true literary origin lay in the era's romantic poetry and novels.

Of course, extinction and geological time remained controversial ideas even after the Peales' exhumation of the monster, as clergymen and congregations realized that its discovery undermined the story told by Moses about the earth's history. Perhaps the most striking new element in Rembrandt Peale's *Disquisition on the Mammoth, or Great American Incognitum* was the prominence of Georges Cuvier's theories about fossils, what was coming gradually to be seen in Europe as scientific proof for the existence of extinct creatures and prehistoric nature. Instead of beginning his essay with Cotton Mather's letter to the Royal Society, Peale now launched immediately into several long, laudatory excerpts from Cuvier's scholarly article appealing for international collaboration in the pursuit of extinct species, which he now numbered at twenty-three. "It is now universally known that the globe which we inhabit, on every side presents irresistible proofs of the greatest revolutions," Cuvier maintained, overstating the acceptance of his catastrophic view of the earth's history. "The varied productions of living nature, which embellish the surface, is but a garment covering the ruins of an antecedent state of nature."[58]

Peale's *Disquisition* was later displayed in gilt frames in the Mammoth Room at his father's museum, where it brought Cuvier's disconcerting theories about the catastrophic changes responsible for the earth's geological history to the attention of the museum's American audience.[59] "Immense collections of shells lie buried far from any sea, and at heights inaccessible to its waves; fishes are found in veins of slate, and vegetable impressions at heights and depths equally astonishing," Cuvier informed the public, alluding to the specter of a prehuman past haunting everyone's imagination. "But what is most surprising, is the disorder which reigns in their relative positions; here, a stratum of shells covers another of vegetables; there, fishes are found over terrestrial animals, which in their turn are placed over plants or shells."[60]

No doubt many Americans viewed with horror this vision of the earth's prehuman past, because it not only offended their religious beliefs but also undermined their sense of dominance over the natural world, a view deeply embedded in both their religious doctrine and scientific thought. But Rembrandt Peale embraced the logic of the bones, choosing to give the idea of extinction the authority of religious truth:

"We are forced to submit to concurring facts as the voice of God—the bones exist, the animals do not!"[61] In this fashion, the *incognitum's* bones could be viewed as symbols of the immense power of the nation's newly discovered natural antiquity rather than the blasphemous logic of a heretical scientific doctrine.

In publicizing Cuvier's theories, Peale struggled to retain a benevolent view of God's nature and the antediluvian world even while he envisioned cataclysmic events in the earth's natural history. Admitting the incomprehensible character of extinction, he viewed the animal's bones as incontrovertible evidence of its reality: "Formerly it was as unphilosophical and impious to say that any thing ceased to exist which had been created, as it is now to say the reverse, because innumerable concurring facts prove that the race of many animals have become extinct," he observed, with an adroit turn of phrase.[62] "These great facts speak an universal language and compel us to believe that a time has been when numbers of animals, and what is more extraordinary, larger animals than now remain, existed, had their day, and have perished."[63]

By the time Rembrandt's *Disquisition* appeared, the London exhibition was languishing, and the Peales owed $350 in back rent for the exhibition room. Lowering the price of admission helped, but they still did not have enough money to cover their debts. In an apologetic letter to Peale's father, Sir Joseph Banks put his finger on their underlying problem—the small size of London's polite society: "Every body of Real Curiosity I beleive [sic] went once at Least to see it but Sir in the best peopled Quarters people of this description are not so numerous as we would wish them to be."[64]

After a long delay, Rembrandt finally wrote to his father of their misfortune, complaining that the enthusiasm of the London literati was waning. "Wars and rumors of wars, have lately much alarmed the good folk here," he observed of Napoleon's rise to power and the deteriorating relation between England and France.[65] In April 1803, Peale still envisioned a triumphal visit to Paris to meet France's renowned anatomist Georges Cuvier and the anticipated windfall to be gained by selling the skeleton to the National Museum of Natural History. However, England's declaration of war against France a month later ended these hopes, and the Peales had to turn their thoughts toward other, more mundane, pursuits.

Discouraged by its lack of success, Rembrandt closed the London exhibition in the early summer and took the skeleton on a tour through the countryside, hopeful of recouping their losses. But with Napoleon threatening to invade England, Peale could drum up little interest. In the early fall, greatly demoralized by the show's meager returns, the Peales packed up their bones and returned to Philadelphia, accompanied by their principal creditor, a London bookseller and immigrant, whom their disappointed father paid off upon their arrival.

Economically, the London tour was disappointing, not to mention the Peales' failure to reach Paris, where Cuvier eagerly awaited the skeleton. Nonetheless, the excursion was a significant cultural event, especially back in Philadelphia. Rembrandt Peale's *Disquisition* brought new celebrity to Peale's skeleton in Europe and America and greatly aided Cuvier in his efforts to identify the American *incognitum*. More important, Peale's London pamphlet had even wider repercussions in America, framing for the first time the perceptions of the mythical beast as a carnivore. Very likely, the beast returned home with its tusks downturned, an even more imposing emblem of the new republic's conquering spirit. The final step in the monster's birth came a few years later, with the naming of the creature and its consecration in the artistic world by Charles Willson Peale, whose painting *The Exhumation of the Mastodon* depicted the marl pit at John Masten's farm as the womb of American ingenuity and industry, as well as the mastodon's birthplace.

14

The Mastodon of Nations

Although the putting these Skeletons together was a long and arduous work, yet the novelty of the subject, the producing the form and,
as it would seem a *second creation*, was delightful and every day's work
brought its pleasures.

—Charles Willson Peale

THE NAPOLEONIC WARS between England and France slowed the
European anatomists' efforts to discover the identity of the American
incognitum, but at home, the pursuit of the creature continued apace as
the mining of salt licks and boglands turned up more bones. For many
enterprising Americans, the fossil remains were a valuable commodity
to be exported to Europe, although this often had to be done surrepti-
tiously, since the creature had become a symbol of American nationalism. The manifestation of this symbolism took many forms, but the
cultural events that first fixed the massive jaws in American national
consciousness were the publication of Rembrandt Peale's London pamphlet and the large historical painting created by his father several years
later to commemorate the monster's birth. Both of these artworks,
which were displayed at Peale's Philadelphia Museum alongside the
skeleton, helped shape both the symbolic meaning of the mastodon and
the nation's first view of prehistoric nature.

In his son's absence, the exhibition of the American *incognitum*
at Peale's Philadelphia Museum had been quite successful, netting its
owner nearly $2,000 during the first year of its exhibition.[1] Having
lobbied successfully with the Pennsylvania legislature for use of the
recently vacated State House, Peale had moved the bulk of his natural history collection into spacious new quarters, across the street,

although the Mammoth Room remained behind as a separate attraction at the Philosophical Hall.

The elder Peale had kept up a lively correspondence with President Jefferson concerning the American *incognitum*, particularly the
bones still missing from his skeleton—the upper part of the head and
the toes. In early 1802, shortly before Rembrandt's departure for London, Peale enlisted the president's assistance in obtaining an enormous skull found in a Kentucky creek bed near Big Bone Lick. Dr.
John Sillman, who lived near the salt lick, visited Peale's museum
and informed him about the head bone, which he promised to send
upon his return to the Ohio valley. In April, Major John Brown of
Boone County, where the lick was located, informed the president
that the fossil skull had been sent to the American Philosophical Society. Unfortunately, this specimen turned out to be the skull of a fossil ox or buffalo, still quite large and definitely an unidentified creature, but a great disappointment to Peale.

In July 1803, after his sons sailed for England, Peale sent Jefferson
news of another discovery of bones at Big Bone Lick by Dr. William Goforth, a physician who had settled in Cincinnati a few years earlier.
Hand delivered to Peale's museum by his old friend Thomas Proctor,
Dr. Goforth's letter described an enormous cache of newly excavated
bones, including the upper skull, the lower jaws with many teeth, and
a tusk twenty-one inches around at its base and weighing a hundred
pounds. The demand for the bones in Europe, probably sparked by news
of Rembrandt's tour, spurred Dr. Goforth's efforts to retrieve a complete
skeleton. According to Peale, his letter had inquired "whether he could
make money by bringing [the skeleton] across the Mountains to exhibit
it in the Atlantic Ports or whether he might not get something handsome by carrying it to Europe."[2] In early August, detailed descriptions
of these new specimens were made public in the *Gazette of the United
States*, adding to the urgency with which Peale sought to acquire the
collection. "I shall endeavor to get these bones, or at least a knowledge
of the head as soon as I can," he wrote to his sons in England, telling
them about his letter to the president and Dr. Wistar's offer to help finance the purchase.[3]

Even before Napoleon broached the subject of selling the Louisiana Territory, Jefferson had secured a small appropriation from Congress to finance a secret expedition to find a land route to the Pacific
and to explore the vast western territory (figure 46). To lead this expe-

FIGURE 46. Portrait of Thomas Jefferson by Rembrandt Peale, 1805. Collection of New York Historical Society.

dition, he appointed his private secretary Meriwether Lewis, who selected his friend Captain William Clark, brother of George Rogers Clark, to share the command. Born in Albemarle County, the young Lewis had served as a militiaman in the suppression of the Whiskey Rebellion and fought Indians in the Ohio valley before becoming the president's secretary. During the campaigns against the Indians, Lewis had served under Captain Clark, and the two young soldiers formed a friendship that led to their subsequent collaboration.

In February, with plans for the expedition under way, Jefferson wrote to his friend Bernard Lapécède in Paris that Lewis and Clark might find not only the bones of the fossil elephant but also those of a living mammoth and a megatherium, the clawed creature similar to Jefferson's megalonyx that Georges Cuvier had identified.

> It is not improbable that this voyage of discovery will procure us further information of the Mammoth, & of the Megatherium. For you have possibly seen in our Philosophical transactions, that, before we had seen the account of that animal by Mr. Cuvier, we had found here some remains of an enormous animal incognitum, whom, from the disproportionate length of h[is] claw, we had denominated Megalonyx, and which is probably the same animal.[4]

In July 1803, while the Peale brothers were touring England's provincial towns, Lewis left Washington, D.C., to meet with Clark and his slave York on the Ohio River at Louisville, before the party headed west to St. Louis, the expedition's point of departure. Traveling down the Ohio from Pittsburgh, he stopped in Cincinnati in late September to inspect Dr. Goforth's collection of bones, as the president had asked him to do. Before making a side trip to Big Bone Lick, he wrote to Jefferson describing in detail the bones and the circumstances under which the doctor had collected them.

Most of the bones collected were still at the Lick, but Lewis was able to view some of them at the doctor's home, including the upper part of a skull, a large tusk weighing one hundred pounds, and several grinders. "The Elephants teeth which I saw in the possession of Dr. Goforth," Lewis wrote, "weigh from four to eleven pounds, and appear to me precisely to resemble a specimen of these teeth which I saw in the possession of Dr. Wistar of Philadelphia."[5] The frontal bone of the skull was so badly decayed Lewis could offer little information about its shape, although he provided an extensive description of the form and composition of the tusks. Having received permission from Dr. Goforth to take a large tusk still at the Lick, Lewis promised to send it to the president, along with two grinders. No record of the specimens has survived, since the crates containing the bones were lost when the boat carrying them sank at the Natchez landing on the lower Mississippi River.

In the following year, Dr. Goforth apparently shipped his entire collection to Pittsburgh with the intention of transporting the bones to Philadelphia to sell them to Peale or the American Philosophical Society. However, in 1806, Thomas Ashe, an Irish traveler and writer, passed through the Ohio valley looking for natural curiosities. Living a carefree, opportunistic life, Ashe had come to America partly to escape debts and an unsavory reputation in his homeland. Introducing himself at Pittsburgh as a schoolteacher, he learned of Dr. Goforth's valuable collection of bones and descended the Ohio to Cincinnati where after ingratiating himself with the doctor, he was hired to act as an agent to sell the bones in New Orleans. Returning to Pittsburgh with authorization from the doctor, he retrieved the crates of bones, which had been deposited with a local physician, and shipped several tons down the Mississippi to New Orleans.

To Dr. Goforth's dismay, Ashe then sent the bones to London, after rejecting an offer of $7,000 in New Orleans, which he claimed was only one-tenth their true value. In England, he exhibited the unassembled bones at the Liverpool museum and elsewhere before selling the entire collection and absconding with the money, without compensating Dr. Goforth. To publicize the Liverpool exhibition, Ashe published two brief memoirs containing an inventory of the contents of the ten crates and an eclectic commentary on the *incognitum* pirated from other authors, including Thomas Jefferson's *Notes*, Rembrandt Peale's *Disquisition*, and George Turner's essay.[6] Among the items in the crates was a well-preserved skull with the jaws and grinders still intact, the head bone so coveted by Charles Willson Peale.

Not long after his return from England, Rembrandt and his older brother Raphaelle took their skeleton of the *incognitum* on a tour through the southern states. In March 1804, they were in Charleston, South Carolina, where advertisements announced the exhibition of "The Great Aborigine of America," whose thighbone weighed seventy-eight pounds:

> It is presumed that very few of the inhabitants will neglect the only opportunity that perhaps will ever occur of beholding the largest and most extraordinary Remains of the *antediluvian* world; so *interesting*

346 THE MASTODON OF NATIONS

from the facts which it proves, so *venerable* from its *antiquity*, and so *remarkable* in its construction.[7]

In May, the elder Peale wrote to James Calhoun, the mayor of Baltimore, to solicit his aid in ensuring "the success of my Son Rembrandt's Exhibition of the Skeleton of the great American incognitum, commonly called the Mammoth, in the City over which you preside as chief Magistrate."[8] There the skeleton was exhibited in the city's elegant assembly room, constructed for the balls of Baltimore Dancing Assembly. "This stupendous production of the Antediluvian world is more interesting to Americans than it even was in England, where it attracted the attention of all classes, particularly the learned, who regarded it as the most extraordinary natural curiosity the world has ever beheld," Rembrandt's advertisement declared.[9]

Back in Philadelphia, the death of Charles Willson Peale's second wife Betsy in February had distracted the museum proprietor from his pursuit of the *incognitum's* skull and toe bones. His wife died in childbirth, leaving the sixty-three-year-old father with a large family to look after in his old age. Nonetheless, the indefatigable Peale redoubled his efforts to make the Philadelphia Museum a national institution, pouring his energy into classifying his specimens according to the Linnaean system, with the Latin, English, and French names placed over each case. On May 12, 1804, while Philadelphia celebrated the Louisiana Purchase, a European traveler arrived at Peale's doorstep with high praise for the museum collection. Baron Alexander von Humboldt was a young Prussian scholar and naturalist returning from five years of exploration in South America, where, to Rembrandt Peale's delight, he had found mammoth bones "perfectly distinguishable by the great carniverous teeth."[10]

Humboldt began his tour of the museum with the Mammoth Room, located in Philosophical Hall, where he entered the exhibition through a door framed with the thirteen-foot-long whale jawbones. The *incognitum's* skeleton was displayed behind a protective railing, dwarfing the smaller skeletons of a monkey, grayhound, parrot, groundhog, and mouse exhibited in the same room. On the walls were the pages of Rembrandt's *Disquisition*, hung in ninety-two gilt frames, along with engravings of the mammoth bones and Cuvier's drawing of the Megatherium, the clawed creature from South America. Inside the railing were similar bones found in Virginia, including an eight-inch-long claw of Jefferson's Megalonyx, a reminder of the violence of the ante-diluvian world. Although Humboldt left no detailed record of his view-ing of the skeleton, the tusks of the *incognitum* may already have been turned downward. At some point, after Rembrandt's return from Eng-land, the tusks on the mammoth skeleton at the Philadelphia Museum were reversed and remained so for at least a decade.

Despite his inability to obtain public funding for his museum, Peale's career was at its peak, his reputation enhanced by the recovery and reconstruction of the mammoth's skeleton and the steady growth of his museum. Traveling to Washington with Humboldt, he intro-duced him to President Jefferson, who invited them to dine with him several times at the White House, where the gracious naturalist enter-tained his host with gossip from European courts and news from South America.

The patronage of President Jefferson added to Peale's prestige when the first shipments of Indian artifacts and natural history specimens began to arrive from Lewis and Clark's expedition the following year. On President Jefferson's order, the explorers deposited many skins and skeletons collected on the expedition in Peale's museum, since no one else was prepared to mount them. In 1805, they sent him the badly damaged skin of an unknown species of the antelope, which Peale suc-cessfully mounted, calling the creature a "forked horned antelope." Nu-merous bird specimens donated to Peale's museum by Lewis and Clark were used by Alexander Wilson, a young Scottish émigré artist, to cre-ate the lush drawings for his book *American Ornithology*, the first hand-colored images of American flora and fauna since Mark Catesby's books nearly a century earlier.

Upon the expedition's triumphant return to the capitol, Peale's museum became the repository of an extraordinary collection of Indian artifacts, including a feathered peace pipe and an ermine-skin mantle presented to Meriwether Lewis by a friendly Shoshoni chief who had been instrumental in the expedition's success. After exhibiting these artifacts as symbols of peace between nations, Peale later placed the mantle on a wax figure of Lewis at the museum. The peace pipe in his hand was an expression of Peale's own pacifism, along with a label con-taining a speech allegedly made by Lewis requesting that the Indians "bury the hatchet deep in the ground never to be taken up again—that henceforward you may smoke the *Calumet* of Peace and live in perpet-ual harmony, not only with each other but with the white men, your

brothers, who teach you many useful arts."[11] Peale's idealistic sentiments were subverted, however, by the artist who painted Lewis's likeness holding a rifle instead of the calumet, perhaps a more truthful depiction of American conquest and continental expansion (figure 47).

To President Jefferson's dismay, Lewis and Clark failed to find any
fossil elephants living in the western wilderness, although they did
bring back a few bones and skins belonging to unidentified creatures.
Disappointed by his own inability to acquire specimens from the Hudson River valley and the loss of Clark's meager harvest of bones at Big
Bone Lick, Jefferson intensified his efforts to acquire the cache of bones
reportedly in the hands of the Cincinnati physician Dr. William Goforth. In early December 1806, unaware the bones were already out of
the country, Dr. Caspar Wistar wrote to the doctor on behalf of the
president asking how the American Philosophical Society might obtain some of the bones, especially the long-sought-after skull.

Embarrassed by the loss of his collection, Dr. Goforth replied
promptly, writing directly to Jefferson to inform him that the bones had
disappeared down the Mississippi River and were probably on their way
to Europe. Having made no detailed inventory of the specimens, he
apologized for being able to supply only "a general description as I can
give from memory" of his collection. Although he had failed to weigh
or measure the monstrous thighbones, he remembered that the largest
of several tusks was nearly eleven feet long and weighed one hundred
pounds. There were as many teeth or grinders, each weighing from
twelve to twenty pounds, as a wagon with four horses could draw. The
bones of one paw, which had four claws, nearly filled a flour barrel and
were similar to those of a bear's foot, which were abundant at the same
site. Laid out in a single line, the vertebrae measured some sixty feet, although the doctor doubted that they all belonged to a single animal.

Dr. Goforth also provided the president with a short account of
his own excavations and called attention to the likelihood of finding
new bones at the site, provided permission could be obtained from
David Ross, the owner of Big Bone Lick, who resided in Virginia.
The doctor had obviously given up any hope of retrieving the ten
crates of bones carried away by Thomas Ashe to England, although
now, with the president's interest, he had high hopes of leading another excavation at the site.

Jefferson had known David Ross, the owner of Big Bone Lick, for a
number of years, and the burdens of his office did not prevent him from

FIGURE 47. Watercolor portrait of Meriwether Lewis by C. B. J. F. de Saint-Memin, 1807. Painted from a wax figure in Peale's Philadelphia Museum, the artist substituted a long rifle for the Indian peace pipe that Peale had placed in Lewis's hand. Collection of New York Historical Society.

immediately writing to Virginia to ask for permission to make further excavations at the salt lick. But instead of employing the hapless Dr. Goforth to undertake the excavation, the president hired Captain William Clark, who was about to embark on a trip to St. Louis after being appointed superintendent of Indian affairs in the Louisiana Territory by the president. In February 1807, while Clark was still in Washington, Jefferson wrote to Dr. Wistar, informing him of Clark's imminent departure and requesting a list of the bones desired to complete the American Philosophical Society's fossil collection. "Captain Clarke, companion of Captain Lewis, who is now here, agrees, as he passes through the country, to stop at the Lick, employ laborers, and superintend the search at my expense, not that of the society, and to send me the specific bones wanted." Jefferson also reserved for himself an instrumental role in the disposal of the bones through his generous offer to underwrite the excavation.[12]

At Big Bone Lick, Captain Clark worked for several weeks with ten hired laborers to mine yet another batch of bones from the seemingly inexhaustible site. Chagrined by the paltry results of his early diggings, in late September he sent discouraging news back to the president: "The Lick has been pillaged so frequently that but few valuable bones are to [be] found entire."[13] Several badly decayed skulls dug out of the mire by his men crumbled into pieces when the soft mud was removed. Vapors from the lick, located in a cold, damp valley, aggravated Clark's rheumatism, and several of his laborers came down with chills and fever. But his perseverance finally paid off, eventually turning up a sizable collection which he dispatched to Washington.

In early November, Jefferson received an eleven-page report describing the operation, which clearly had gone far beyond the original mandate simply for specimens to fill the gaps in the American Philosophical Society's collection. In addition to a jawbone, tusks, teeth, and ribs of an animal identified as the "Elephant," Clark listed the skulls, jawbones, tusks, teeth, ribs, a thighbone and leg, and bones of the paw from the "mammoth," or *incognitum*, not to mention miscellaneous bones from the buffalo, goat, horse, cow, and several unknown creatures. Crated in three large boxes, the bones were shipped down the Ohio to New Orleans where they were loaded onto schooners headed for the East Coast, to be delivered directly to the president at the White House.

Emboldened by the success of his bone hunting, Clark volunteered his own commentary on the eclectic array of specimens, often with accurate insights surprising for his untrained eye. "Haveing no treatis on Comparritive Anatomy, I am compelled to Make use of the Most Common terms."[14] Among the bones collected, he recognized the jawbones and teeth of both the "Mammoth" and the "Elephant," the latter a common term for the fossil elephant found in Siberia, whose distinctive flat-faced, striated grinders had earlier been described in detail by George Turner and numerous other anatomists, attempting to differentiate them from the American *incognitum*. Even though Clark correctly concluded that the mixture of these bones at the lick was evidence that both animals had once existed there, he was puzzled by the larger question of when this might have occurred: "I cannot Collect from any source of Probable conjecture the Period of existence of those tremendous Animals."

Like George Turner, Clark felt the remains of smaller animals found in the mire suggested these creatures had been the prey of ferocious carnivores: "At a depth of from *five* to *Eight* feet, we struck upon Several small Collections of half Masticated willow, which was evidently the Contents of the Stomachs of some of those smaller animals, on which the Mammoth Most probably preyed." Judge Turner's elephant with claws still exerted considerable influence over Clark's muddled interpretation of the bones: "As it is evident from the head teeth and Paw of the Mammoth it must have been a Carnivorous, is it not most probable that those Licks were the Places to which they frequented for the purpose of preying on the smaller animals."

Rembrandt Peale's opinions also shaped Clark's speculation about the animal's appetite, for a few sentences later he qualified this initial statement:

> However, I do not think it improbable that the Mammoth may have fed upon herbage as well as flesh. The Tongue which from every appearance was the great conductor of every species of food into the Mouth, may have been constructed as well to Collect the *twigs* and boughs as to assist the Claws in separating the flesh.

To Jefferson's surprise, Clark's inventory of bones indicated that the great mass of the collection consisted of duplicates of those possessed by the society, which meant there would be extra bones for his own cabinet at Monticello and still others to donate to the national museum in Paris. In December, while still awaiting their arrival, the president wrote to Dr. Wistar, asking for his help in determining which bones the society needed: "But how to make the selection without the danger of sending away something which might be useful to our own society? Indeed, my friend, you must give a week to this object."[15]

News of this windfall only whetted the president's appetite for the entire collection of bones that Clark had dug up at the Kentucky salt lick. Jefferson immediately asked Clark to retrieve the large cache of bones he had stored at his brother's home at Clarkesville, on the Ohio side of the river across from Louisville:

> I find myself obliged to ask the addition of those which you say you have deposited with your brother at Clarkesville, such as ribs, backbones, leg bones, thigh bones, ham hips, shoulder blades, parts of the upper and under jaw, teeth of the Mammoth and Elephant, and parts of the Mammoth tusks.[16]

In his letter to Clark, drafted the same day he had written to Dr. Wistar, the president also mentioned that the large quantity of bones already shipped to him had given him the idea of making a gift of some of the duplicates to France's national museum. To make sure that the extra bones were forwarded, Jefferson then wrote to George Rogers Clark, asking him to ship the collection should his brother have already departed for St. Louis.

During the Napoleonic Wars, both England and France seized American ships that had stopped at enemy ports, and the impressment of American seamen into service by the British navy threatened to drag the United States into the conflict. In December 1807, shortly before he sent his letters to Dr. Wistar and William Clark, Jefferson signed into law the Embargo Act, forbidding all American ships from sailing to foreign ports. The embargo had relatively little effect on England, but the results were disastrous for American shipping, with the New England ports the hardest hit by the collapse of trade. During his last year in office, the Federalists therefore launched a bitter campaign against Jefferson's policy, hoping to embarrass him and undermine his party's effectiveness in the upcoming presidential election.

Ever since Samuel Ewing's satire of Peale's mammoth, the president had been the butt of many Federalist jokes about his obsession with the *incognitum's* bones. In 1807, these attacks were taken up by a schoolboy poet, William Cullen Bryant, the precocious thirteen-year-old son of a Massachusetts physician, whose rhyming couplets ridiculed Jefferson's bone hunting with explicit references to the Lewis and Clark expedition.

> *Go, wretch, resign thy presidential chair,*
> *Disclose thy secret measures, foul or fair,*
> *Go search with curious eyes for horned frogs,*
> *'Mid the wild wastes of Louisianan bogs;*
> *Or Where the Ohio rolls his turbid stream*
> *Dig for huge bones, thy glory and thy theme.*[17]

Bryant's poem was typical of the Federalist political invective in the *Port Folio*, the magazine that had published Ewing's poem. But contrary to what some historians and literary critics have claimed, the poem hardly reflects a disavowal of natural history by New Englanders. New England scholars from Cotton Mather to Ezra Stiles had played integral roles in the search for the *incognitum's* identity. Indeed, Joseph Dennie, editor of *The Port Folio*, later retracted his criticism of Peale's museum and published the museum's guide with praise for the owner's endeavors. Thus the link between natural history and nationalism went much deeper than partisan politics, being anchored in the bedrock beliefs of Puritan clergymen in the providential character of American expansion. None of this criticism seems to have deterred the president in his pursuit of the bones, for when the crates sent by Captain Clark arrived in Washington in early March, he had more than three hundred specimens unpacked and arranged in a large, unused room in the White House.

Two weeks later, while waiting for Congress to reconvene, Jefferson again invited Dr. Caspar Wistar to the White House to help him sort the bones:

I would propose, therefore, that you should come a few days before Congress rises, so as to satisfy that article of your curiosity. The bones are spread in a large room, where you can work at your leisure, undisturbed by any mortal, from morning till night, taking your breakfast and dinner with us.[18]

Jefferson could hardly contain his glee at the enormity of the precious collection, which included four pieces of the head, one distinctly showing the whole face of the animal: "The height of the forehead is most remarkable," he told Dr. Wistar before enumerating the contents of the collection. The president's handwritten inventory grouped the bones according to species, to ascertain the significance of the collection.[19] There were four jawbones of the mammoth, with several teeth in them, and three tusks, the largest nearly ten feet long, together with numerous grinders and some two hundred small bones, chiefly from the foot: "This is probably the most valuable part of the collection, for General Clarke, aware that we had specimens of the larger bones, has gathered up everything of the small kind."[20]

With the assistance of Dr. Wistar, who finally came to Washington in late June during Jefferson's last year in office, the bones were divided into three groups. Those missing from the American Philosophical Society's collection went to Philadelphia to fill the gaps in Peale's skeletons. Anticipating the arrival of a second shipment of bones from William Clark, Jefferson kept only a few bones for himself from this initial collection, most notably the upper and lower jawbones. The bulk of the duplicates, as he had already envisioned, were sent to the National Institute in France for its natural history museum, including the enormous tusk.

By this time, the American *incognitum* was no longer an unknown creature, for as Jefferson later pointed out in a letter to William Clark, the bones sent to Paris led anatomists there finally to identify the animal: "These have enabled them to decide that the animal was neither a mammoth nor an elephant, but of a distinct kind, to which they have given the name of Mastodon, from the protuberance of its teeth."[21] Then, with surprising ease, Jefferson offered his own reconsidered opinion on the controversy over the animal's diet: "These, from their forms, and the immense mass of their jaws, satisfy me this animal must have been arboriverous," he concluded, employing his own awkward term to indicate the animal was a herbivore. This change of heart did not diminish the monster's gargantuan stature, however: "Nature seems not to have provided other food sufficient for him, and the limb of a tree would be no more to him than a bough of a cotton tree to a horse."

Jefferson gave Clark the mistaken impression that the shipment of bones he had sent to Paris in July had led to the naming of the mastodon. This mistake was the result of a curious sequence of events illustrating how disjointed transatlantic communications were during the Napoleonic Wars. In April, Charles Willson Peale informed Jefferson that he himself had learned of the naming of the mastodon from Cuvier's report to the National Institute on the shipment of bones from the president. "In the report by Mr. Cuvier on the fossil bones which you presented to the National Institute, I find the committee have given the name *Mastodonte* to the animal which we commonly call Mammoth."[22] Still convinced that his own specimen was a carnivore, Peale was satisfied that the American *incognitum* was now differentiated from the grass-eating Siberian mammoth: "It is pleasant however to have a name by which we may know it from the Siberian Animal, which evidently must be a Graminivorous animal if the Grinders correspond with the flat surfaced teeth found here."

Unsure of the appropriateness of the *incognitum's* new name, Peale was wrestling with the problem of renaming his own skeleton, and he asked Jefferson's opinion about the rechristening. Peale considered announcing the new name at a banquet beneath the great beast's rib cage, reminiscent of Rembrandt's "Mammoth Feast." Jefferson gave his approval to the name change and offered his own explanation of the logic behind Cuvier's naming of the creature:

> I have no doubt that the marked differences between the elephant & our colossal animal entitle him to a distinct appellation. One of these differences & a striking one, is in the protuberances on the grinding surface of the teeth, somewhat in the shape of the mamma, mastos, or breast of a woman, which has induced Cuvier to call it the Mastodonte, or bubby-toothed.[23]

Neither Jefferson nor Peale apparently was aware that the extinct species had actually been identified nearly three years earlier, in Georges Cuvier's memoir "Sur le grande mastodonte," which provided the first systematic analysis of the animal's anatomy and formally named the mastodon. The lapse is curious, since both men were usually alert to new ideas emanating from the Parisian naturalists. In Peale's case, the lack of communication can be attributed to the French anatomists' failure to respond to his letters, which had accompanied the natural history specimens sent from America. In April 1808, when Rembrandt traveled to Paris, Peale had given him a letter to be hand delivered to Cuvier, complaining about his failure to acknowledge the receipt of the plaster casts that Peale had sent of bones from Jefferson's Megalonyx and the skull of an unknown ox-like creature. Nine months later, after Rembrandt returned from Paris, his father wrote again to Cuvier to thank him for sitting for a portrait by his son, but this letter still made no mention of Cuvier's naming of the mastodon: "We are finding from time to time many fossil remains in different parts of American that excite admiration on what kind of Animals has in a for- mer period inhabited this Country," Peale explained, unaware of Cu- vier's extensive analysis of extinct American species.[24]

In any case, the elder Peale did become aware of Cuvier's report during the first months of 1809 and passed along the information in his April query to Jefferson. Evidently, Jefferson himself had not seen the memoir, although Cuvier had used the term *mastodonte* in his formal letter thanking Jefferson for the gift, which the president received barely a week after James Madison's inauguration and his own retire- ment from the presidency. Jefferson may well have overlooked this de- tail in his move to Monticello until he received the news of the mastodon's naming from Peale a few weeks later.

From a scientific point of view, the mystery of the beast's identity was finally solved in 1806 when Cuvier, aided by the drawings Peale had made for Dr. Michaelis and his son Rembrandt's *Disquisition*, for- mally declared the mastodon an extinct species, separate from both the Siberian Mammoth and the living elephants. The new name, inspired by the conical protuberances on the tooth's crown, combined the Greek words for breast and tooth, although his view of the animal's diet differed drastically from that popularized by the Peales in America.

In Cuvier's authoritative scientific memoir, which described, named, and classified all the elephant-like creatures that had so puzzled everyone since the early eighteenth century, he clearly designated the extinct American animal as a herbivore that fed on roots, herbs, and aquatic plants, not shellfish or small game. Nevertheless, the name he chose was derived from the distinctive shape of its molars, and in American eyes, the enduring image of the legendary animal would be the awesome power of its jaws and grinders. Cuvier's essay "Sur le grande mastodonte" contained an elegant drawing of the reconstructed skeleton based on Rembrandt Peale's renderings in his *Disquisition* and set the stage for a general review of the geological implications of the existence of the extinct fossil elephants.

Shortly after Cuvier's naming of the American *incognitum*, Charles Willson Peale began work on a monumental painting to commemorate his historic excavation of the first complete skeletons of the American *incognitum*(figure 42). The view of the marl pit at John Masten's farm depicts the huge pumping machine towering over the farmers lifting bones from the watery mine while well-dressed onlookers stand around the edges. In the distance, lightning streaks through the darkened sky; startled horses gallop after a thunderclap; and black clouds threaten to envelop the whole scene.

Painted by the sixty-five-year-old Peale, the work was first conceived as a "historical, emblematical Picture" in the tradition of Benjamin West's history paintings, and its purpose was to create a monumental image of Peale's triumph. From the very beginning, Peale envisioned making the painting a family picture by introducing portraits of his wives and children. Eventually, when he finally stopped modifying the monumental work in 1808, the painting contained seventy-five figures and twenty individual portraits. When completed, the large canvas was hung in the Mammoth Room, along with Rembrandt's *Disquisition*, as a major symbolic statement about not only his family's role in the recovery and reconstruction of the skeletons but also the birth of monster itself.

The painting has often been identified as a genre painting valuable mainly for the descriptive details of the setting of the excavations: "The whole scene, painted after the manner of other scientific portraits of the day," observed paleontologist Henry Fairfield Osborn in the 1920s, "is a delightful reminiscence of the country life along the Hudson one hundred twenty years ago."[25] However, more probing interpretations since then have provided better insights into the subconscious and symbolic meaning of Peale's imagery. Beneath the painting's sentimentality lie many clues to the appeal of the mastodon to American nationalists in the early industrial era, not to mention its significance for modern lovers of prehistoric monsters in the age of Darwin and the dinosaurs.

In contrast to Osborn's view, art historian Lillian B. Miller highlighted the neoclassical aesthetics underlying the picture's composition. The stiff posture of the figures, who resemble immobile statues, reflect the plaster casts of neoclassical sculptures that Peale employed as models, including the Apollo Belvedere that he used for his own pose.[26] By the same token, Peale's own natural history, like Jefferson's, was influenced by the eighteenth-century idea of the Great Chain of Being. Both men still saw nature as "eternal" and "unaltered," although their views were less hierarchical than those of the church fathers who defended the perfection of God's nature and the accuracy of Moses' account of the earth's history.

The thunderstorm that Peale incorporated in the painting was an artistic convention allowing him to make his heroic drama a "sublime" scene and to introduce an element that had been a characteristic feature of the Romantic landscape ever since Thomas Burnet's turbulent vision of the earth's surface as a natural ruin. Together with the metaphorical view of fossils as the monuments of natural antiquity—the coins and medals of nature's antiquity, in Robert Hooke's famous analogy—this Romantic view enabled the founding fathers to substitute natural history for the new republic's missing ancient history, joining the glory of classical antiquity, which they so admired, with their natural law doctrine and religious beliefs.

Although this analogy had a long history, contemporary critics have tended to identify the view largely with nineteenth-century American landscape painting, placing its primary expression among painters of the Hudson River school and the American West, from Thomas Cole to Albert Bierstadt. "A matter of national pride, the mastodon also suggested the great western wilderness that constituted the American landscape at the beginning of the nineteenth century," according to Lillian B. Miller, using a familiar euphemism for the area inhabited by Indian peoples.

> Two decades hence, that wilderness would become a positive cultural value, the theme of artists and writers, who, seeking an American past in which they could root their art, found it not in the ruins of civilization as in Europe, but in the promise of prosperity embodied in the pristine forests and unsettled plains of the American West.[27]

The American dream of an empire in the West, like the "errand in the wilderness" of the first Puritan settlers, was actually less idealistic than this, being based on a brutal conquest of the Indian peoples and the alleged savagery of the wild nature, a violence implied in the term *wilderness* itself. In reality, the forests were not pristine, nor were the plains unsettled; they were, in the eyes of white settlers, areas inhabited by savages, both animal and human. The prosperity that the wilderness promised came from "free" lands that had to be seized by force of arms in the name of piety and progress. The discovery of prehistoric nature in America simply added a new dimension to this ambiguous view of the American wilderness, creating in the process an antediluvian world inhabited by monstrous carnivores whose extinction became God's blessing on the promised land.

Despite his belief in the benevolence of God's nature, when he reflected on its significance years later in his autobiography, Peale saw his own excavation and reconstruction of the American *incognitum* as a "second creation": "Although the putting these Skeletons together was a long and ardious [sic] work, yet the novelty of the subject, the producing the form and, as it would seem a *second creation*, was delightful, and every day's work brought its pleasures."[28] As literary historian Bryan J. Wolf pointed out, there is a deeper meaning to Peale's thunderstorm and the symbolism attached to his painting of *The Exhumation*:: "Peale's figures seek to penetrate the silence of the natural world; their drama lies in their effort to drag knowledge out of a nature not only recalcitrant but at moments ominous and threatening, as the surge of thunder clouds and peal of lightning suggests."[29]

Without fully developing its implications, Wolf's probing of the imagery's subconscious significance exposes the underlying meaning of this fusion of natural history and nationalism: "Natural history substitutes in the New World for the lack of human history. The power of Peale's painting turns on the ability of his figures to subdue nature through persistence and ingenuity."[30] In this perspective, the approaching thunderstorm represents to Wolf the retributive power of a nature at once violated and vengeful, responding to the intrusive machinery of industrial society, mining the earth's fossil treasures.

More recently, iconologist Laura Rigal's deconstruction of Peale's *Exhumation* offered a complex semiotic interpretation of the painting's imagery, inspired by the late Michel Foucault's methodology.[31] Her reading of the painting links Peale's portrayal of the social world around Masten's marl pit to the Jeffersonian ideal of an agrarian republic which was, as she points out, imperialistic despite its democratic rhetoric and opposition to industrialism. Being a land-based philosophy, this agrarianism was necessarily expansionist, and as a result, natural history itself served as a vehicle of empire, becoming an ideology of conquest and commerce in the American West. But the dynamism of this new mythology remains somewhat obscured by the detachment of her insights into the coded significance of Peale's painting and Jefferson's political economy, which she calls "a discursive mechanism for the creation and preservation of a natural national culture."[32]

The most useful product of such an analysis is its emphasis on the ambivalence of Peale's own views of the politics of the natural world. After the Revolution, he rejected radical republicanism, claiming that his museum collecting and the pursuit of natural history were above both politics and religion. "Facts not theories, are the foundation on which the whole superstructure is built," Peale declared even while he sought to infuse natural history with national purpose.[33] As Rigal herself reveals, the language of science was riddled with religious assumptions and an implicit acceptance of the expansionist rhetoric of Jeffersonian America.

Peale took great pride in the classical arrangement of his stuffed animals, which he felt emphasized the harmony of the natural world. "I love the study of Nature, for it teacheth benevolence."[34] Yet despite his belief in the "Peaceable Kingdom," Peale's museum included several tableaux depicting the brutality of nature, most notably a snarling wolf with blood dripping from its fangs that is standing over the entrails of a lamb. The key to understanding these images of terror associated with the idea of extinction and the emerging concept of evolution in the early nineteenth century lies in the casual acceptance by scientifically minded scholars of all ages of a "Romantic" view of nature. Whether it was the catastrophic destruction of Noah's Flood or the carnivorous prehistoric monsters who were the forerunners of Darwin's survival of the fittest—the taste for violence in industrial America reflected a hostile world in which self-interest and competition had become the keys to survival in an expanding market society. Peale's *Exhumation of the Mastodon*, oddly enough, stands as a curious monument to this hostile view of nature, disguised in the idealistic rhetoric of Enlightenment philosophy and the self-serving moralism of Protestant religious beliefs.

Without probing too deeply into the paradox of Peale's mentality, art historians have called attention to the way that his *Exhumation* portrays the invasion of nature's secrets by the ingenuity of American machinery, despite his belief in the benevolence of God's nature. In the final analysis, the huge mechanical apparatus erected to drain John

Masten's marl pit descends directly from Francis Bacon's early-seventeenth-century philosophy of natural history, which combined the missionary zeal of British colonialism with the practical application of scientific knowledge to the mine the earth's wealth, to build canals, and to quarry rock—an aggressive penetration of the earth's crust that led in the seventeenth century to the discovery of many fossils and the first "scientific" theories of the earth's history.

With the exception of a few drawings of its leg bones, the mastodon has virtually no presence in Peale's painting. The centerpiece of the painting is the marl pit and the scaffolding containing the buckets on the conveyor belt, a mechanized digging device whose "teeth" scoop up water from the pit while the laborers' axes and shovels bite into the trees and earth nearby. Science critic Carolyn Merchant's critique of Bacon's natural philosophy in *The Death of Nature* gives us a more appropriate framework for interpreting the picture's underlying symbolism: Bacon's s scientific method used mechanical devices to wrench nature's secrets from the earth in a manner that he himself compared to the Inquisition: "For like as a man's disposition is never well known or proved till he be crossed, nor Proteus ever changed shapes till he was straitened and held fast, so nature exhibits herself more clearly under the trials and vexations of art [mechanical devices] than when left to herself."[35] In Bacon's metaphor for scientific inquiry, natural philosophy becomes the province of miners and blacksmiths: "Why should we not divide natural philosophy into two parts, the mine and the furnace?" In the new Baconian world, as Merchant observes, "miners and blacksmiths became the model for the new class of natural philosophers who would interrogate and alter nature."[36] Two hundred years later, Peale worked these principles of inquiry into his *Exhumation*, and behind his belief in the harmony of nature lay a naïve faith in the machinery of industrial America.

The roots of Peale's view, if not all scientific culture itself, reach deep into the soil of Christianity to the catastrophic destruction of the "first earth" by the Great Deluge and the errand in the wilderness, or "wild nature," by the descendants of Noah's Ark. Even though the mastodon later became a dismal figure in a museum world dominated by Darwinism and the dinosaurs, at the beginning of the century the American *incognitum* stood as an emblem of not only the white man's dominion over nature but also the discovery and conquest of prehistoric nature.

15

The Mastodon in the Age of Dinosaurs

It is impossible to reflect on the changed state of the American continent without astonishment. Formerly it must have swarmed with
great monsters, like the southern parts of Africa; but now we find only
the tapir, guanaco, armadillo, and capybara; mere pygmies compared
with the antecedent, allied races.

—Charles Darwin, 1836

THE SKELETON OF Peale's mastodon, with its tusks turned downward,
stood for more than a decade at the Philadelphia Museum, a symbol of
American nationalism and the savagery of prehistoric nature. For many
Americans, the extinct monster had become a metaphor for dominance rather than evidence of a heretical evolutionary doctrine threatening to subvert the divinely ordained natural order. Briefly, before the
discovery of dinosaurs, the mastodon ruled supreme in an as yet ill-de-
fined antediluvian world. While the Peales no longer believed that the
animal consumed deer and elk, the great beast was still the largest of all
terrestrial creatures, a ruling species that was the model for the prehistoric monsters to follow in the age of Darwin and the dinosaurs.

Not until midcentury when Darwin's *Origin of Species* finally
burst the bubble of divine design in God's nature did the dinosaurs
emerge to dethrone the mastodon. By then, many scientists and others had made prehistoric monsters the surrogate rulers of a prehuman
past whose foreboding landscape resembled the American wilderness. In these two places, the "struggle for existence" pitted superior
species against inferior life-forms, both animal and human. Filtered
through a century of intellectual debate and romantic reveries, the
curious mixture of Indian legend, evangelical zeal, scientific method,

and nationalistic fervor led to the belief that ruling species existed even in prehistoric nature.

Surprisingly, the discovery of an extinct species had little religious significance for Deists like Jefferson and Peale, who continued to believe in the perfection of God's nature despite the mastodon's contribution to the new science of paleontology. Neither showed much interest in the controversies regarding the age of the earth and geological time. For them, the exhumation of the mastodon was an archaeological event, the excavation of a monument to the nation's natural antiquity and future glory, the equivalent of Greek and Roman ruins, rather than evidence of a prehuman past and geological time. In effect, the prehistoric monster connected the new nation with a mythic past worthy of the empire builders of the American West.

After Jefferson retired from the presidency, visitors to Monticello found him engaged in mundane pursuits like gardening and the cataloging his cabinet of curiosities. Entering the spacious room housing his collections, guests encountered walls covered with the heads and horns of elk, deer, and buffalo, together with Indian artifacts brought back by Lewis and Clark. In February 1815, George Ticknor wrote an account of the mastodon's presence at Monticello: "On the third [wall], among the other striking matters, was the head of a mammoth, or as Cuvier calls it, a mastodon, containing the only *os frontis*, Mr. Jefferson tells me, that has yet been found."[1] Jefferson renewed his correspondence with Charles Willson Peale shortly after Peale's own retirement, at age sixty-eight, to his newly purchased farm outside Philadelphia. Handing over management of the Philadelphia Museum to his son Rubens, in exchange for a generous annuity to finance his farming, the older Peale took little part in the mastodon's public life. In 1811, when nearly all of the museum's collection had been consolidated at the State House, the mastodon was moved from Philosophical Hall into the Mammoth Room, where it was displayed alongside the "Aboriginal Costumes, [and] Implements."

In December 1816, Édouard de Montulé, a French traveler, visited Peale's Philadelphia Museum and made a drawing of the "mammoth," preserving for posterity an image of the skeleton with its tusks still turned downward, which was published in his *Voyage en Amérique* five years later (figure 48). Tired of family politics, Peale's son Rembrandt opened his own museum in Baltimore, where the second skeleton was displayed, presumably with its tusks downturned as

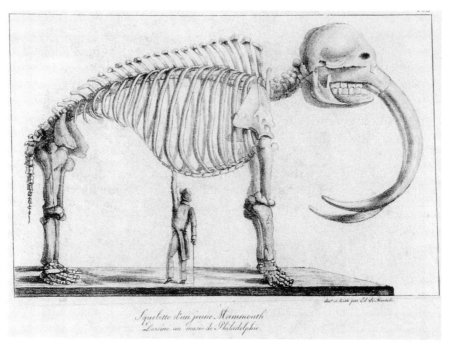

Squelette d'un jeune Mammouth
Dessine au musee de Philadelphie

FIGURE 48. Drawing of the "mammoth" skeleton at Peale's Philadelphia Museum from the French traveler Édouard de Montulé's *Voyage en Amérique*, 1821. The great beast's tusks remained downturned for more than a decade, owing to Rembrandt Peale's belief that the animal was a ferocious carnivore. Photograph by permission of the Rare Book Room, Buffalo & Erie County Public Library.

well. For the time being, these skeletons offered visitors an oddly skewed view of the prehistoric creature, but one that few people questioned until Georges Cuvier's scholarly analysis of the fossil elephants became more widely known.[2]

In the English-speaking world, Christians were absorbing the idea of extinction in novel ways by making the disappearance of various species part of God's design for humanity. Among the new architects of this providential view of the earth's prehuman past was Dr. James Parkinson, a London surgeon and collector of fossils. Beginning in 1804, his three-volume work entitled *Organic Remains of a Former World* presented the successive creation and destruction of species as phases in the progress of God's nature toward a more perfect form—that of the human species.[3] Rather than denying the existence of a prehuman past, Parkinson advocated acceptance of the fossil record, but he framed the reality of extinct species as part of a series of divine reconstructions of God's nature, events testifying to the wisdom of the Creator and conforming to the popular nineteenth-century belief in the progress of society from savagery to civilization.

By the first decades of the nineteenth century, acceptance of a prehuman past and geological time was commonplace among the leading European anatomists. In Germany, Johann Friedrich Blumenbach included the "Ohio *incognitum*" in his early description of the "fossil monsters from the pre-Adamite world," first published in 1797. Reissued in 1810 in a new edition, the volume included his drawing of the giant grinder of the American *incognitum* that he had obtained from the British Museum during his visit to London. Like Parkinson, he accepted the mutability of God's creation without rejecting the religious truth of Christian doctrine: "Every paving-stone in Göttingen is a proof that species, or rather whole genera of creatures, have disappeared."[4] For Blumenbach, this catastrophe did not signify the disappearance of the guiding hand of the Creator from the earth's history. On the contrary, he maintained that such events actually augmented the grandeur of the divine design, creating a new cosmology for Christianity compatible with the fossil record.

Ruth Elson's study of nineteenth-century American schoolbooks, *Guardians of Tradition*, reveals how rapidly the idea of extinction was adapted to doctrines of white supremacy long before social Darwinism made these ideas fashionable in the late nineteenth century. In Joseph Richardson's *The American Reader*, published in 1813, children were taught that the extinction of the American Indian was ordained by nature's God: "The religion of nature, the light of revelation, and the pages of history, are combined in the proof, that God has ordered that nations shall become extinct, and that others shall take their place."[5] Such beliefs were not yet anchored in geological science or the fossil record, but they lent themselves easily to similar interpretations when theories of scientific racialism were later used to substantiate beliefs in racial superiority and the doctrine of Manifest Destiny. In fact, European theories of race, like the Dutch craniologist Petrus Camper's concept of the facial angle, were already becoming popular in America.

The connection between extinct species and craniology was quite explicit among American anatomists, who were introducing scientific racialism into the mainstream of higher education. At Harvard University, the lecture notes of William Dandridge Peck, the nation's leading authority on zoology, indicate that he used paired drawings of the skulls of a "Negro" and an orangutan to illustrate Camper's theory of the facial angle[6] (figure 49). In this theory, innate human intelligence was correlated with the degree of slant in the human skull. Peck used similar drawings of the skulls of a Greenlander, an Eskimo, a Tahitian, a Georgian, and an African as the basis for his detailed comparison of their facial angles and his remarks about race. Like many promoters of craniology, Peck was not an overt advocate of white supremacy but a scientist whose devotion to the observation and description of all flora and fauna, including human craniums, was conceived as a scientific endeavor celebrating the beauty of God's nature.

In 1822, Peck's successor, John C. Warren, a professor of anatomy and surgery at Harvard Medical School, published his *Comparative View of the Sensorial and Nervous Systems in Men and Animals*, the nation's first treatise on comparative anatomy and craniology. His pioneering work demonstrates the popularity of theories of scientific racialism in the highest circles of American education. Even though he sought to discredit the idea that brain size determined intelligence, Warren's treatise was distinguished by its systematic technical descriptions of human skulls and represented the first empirical craniometric study by an American. Faith in the emerging field of craniology put the authority of the natural sciences and medicine behind the scientific theories of race that had been an essential part of comparative anatomy throughout the controversy over the American monster's identity.

Elsewhere, European craniological theories were entering the American national culture with the more explicit purpose of proving the biological superiority of the white race. In November 1808, John Augustine Smith, a professor of anatomy and surgery at New York's College of Physicians and Surgeons, based his introductory lecture in anatomical instruction on the theories of scientific racialism popular in Europe. "I shall endeavour to prove that the anatomical structure of the Europeans, whatsoever may be the cause, is superior to that of the Asiatic, the aboriginal American, and the African, or, at least, that it is farther removed from the brute creation."[7] To fortify his argument about the inferiority of the Africans, he drew on the theories of Dr. Charles White, who had charted the gradation of the facial angle in the natural world from the snipe to the Apollo Belvedere to prove the races of

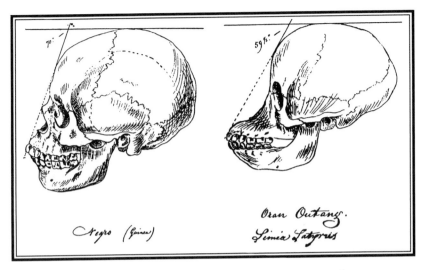

FIGURE 49. Drawings of the skulls of an African American and an orang-utan from the manuscript lectures of William Dandridge Peck, professor of natural history at Harvard College, ca. 1820. These profiles were used to illustrate Petrus Camper's theory of the facial angle, which correlated innate human intelligence with the shape of the skull. Courtesy of the Harvard University Archives.

humankind other than European were actually distinct, naturally inferior species.

Cuvier's *Comparative Anatomy* formed the contemporary authority for many of Dr. Smith's anatomical measurements, although the French naturalist had not participated in the debate among craniologists about the superiority of the white race. Nonetheless, Cuvier had encouraged French explorers to collect human skulls on their expeditions, and he issued specific instructions on how to undertake such activities.[8] In 1800, Cuvier prepared a short memoir for a French explorer's expedition to the South Seas, emphasizing the importance of obtaining human skulls for anatomical research on the various human races. His "Instructions on Research relative to the Anatomical Differences of the Diverse Human Races" recommended that naturalists "visit the places where the dead are deposited" whenever voyagers witnessed or took part in battles involving savages. "To boil the bones in a solution of soda or of caustic potash and rid them of their flesh is a matter of several hours," he declared, matter-of-factly.[9] "The sailors may oppose these operations taking place on their ship, which appear to them barbarous," he warned, "but in an expedition which has as its end the advancement of science, it is necessary for the leaders to allow themselves to be governed only by reason."[10]

With a steady flow of new specimens arriving in Paris thanks to Napoleon's military campaigns, Cuvier had become the world's leading authority in the field of comparative anatomy. His principal interest remained the extinct fossil quadrupeds, which were now the subject of heated debate in the French academy since his colleague Lamarck presented his controversial theory of the organic evolution of life-forms from simple to complex species. In 1812, Cuvier tried to refute this theory by publishing a four-volume collection of essays on extinct quadrupeds, *Recherches sur les ossemens fossiles de quadrupèdes*, including his famous article naming the mastodon.

Written for a popular audience, Cuvier's introductory essay, or "Preliminary Discourse," offered a general theory of the earth's history, taking into account the fossil record. In his opinion, the bones of extinct quadrupeds bore little resemblance to any living animals, and for that reason, the latter could not have ascended from earlier species in the gradual process of transformation outlined by Lamarck. Instead, Cuvier envisioned extinction as the result of a series of violent upheavals or catastrophes involving the extermination of entire species and, equally important, the creation of new geological epochs, each with their own flora and fauna.

Even though Cuvier withheld comment on the causes of these violent revolutions and the question of the earth's age, his theory introduced the notion of a succession of creations before the appearance of human life, culminating in a relatively recent catastrophe that gave birth to human history. Occasionally, Cuvier spoke of the earth's history in terms of "thousands of centuries," but for the most part, his essay expanded the magnitude of geological time without disturbing the traditional Christian notion that *human* history went back only a few thousand years. Moreover, for many Christians, the violent geological upheavals that Cuvier described could be interpreted as divinely appointed events designed to prepare the earth for new forms of life, leading to the highest form—humans.

Immediately translated into English by the British naturalist Robert Kerr, Cuvier's "Essay on the Theory of the Earth" was immensely popular among Anglo-Americans, where his ideas lent authoritative scientific support to the catastrophists of the Christian world. In his preface to this popular translation, Robert Jameson of Edinburgh praised Cuvier for refuting Lamarck's theory that extinct quadrupeds were the antecedents of living species: "The structure of the earth, and the mode of distribution of extraneous fossils or petrifactions, are so many direct evidences of the truth of the scriptural account of the formation of the earth."[11]

In 1812, when Cuvier's *Recherches sur les ossemens fossiles* appeared, his list of extinct quadrupeds had grown considerably since his earlier projections. As Martin J. S. Rudwick pointed out, Cuvier seems to have assembled a virtual zoo of extinct quadrupeds in his anatomical museum.[12] However, among the extinct species in his collection, the American mastodon and Siberian mammoths still reigned supreme, the largest of all terrestrial beings, even though they were harmless herbivores in the French anatomist's eyes. Perhaps only the Mosasaurus, or "Maastricht Crocodile," whose massive skull and jaws had been brought to Paris by Napoleon's troops in the 1790s, was a likely contender for the new ruling species in the antediluvian world. In 1808, when Cuvier finally named this creature Mosasaurus, he concluded that the animal had been a giant marine lizard, whose monstrous size was no more strange than that of the Megatherium and the Megalonyx.

Paleontology and geology in America were still in their infancy at this time, although Peale's skeleton had popularized the idea of extinction and accelerated the search for other extinct species. In the spring of 1817, the New York physician Dr. Samuel Latham Miller participated in unearthing a mammoth skeleton from a peat bog not far from John Masten's farm. Recently retired from the Senate, Dr. Mitchill published his *Sketches of the Mineralogical History of New York* in installments in his journal the *Medical Repository*, in which the first announcements of Cuvier's list of extinct species had appeared. In 1818, encouraged by Thomas Jefferson, Mitchill then published an American edition of Cuvier's *Theory of the Earth*. Meanwhile, other American naturalists like the young Philadelphia physician Richard Harlan, who had succeeded Caspar Wistar as the main authority on fossil vertebrates, began to expand the search for fossils into the new realm of extinct reptilian species.

In Philadelphia, where the mastodon was still an archaeological treasure as well as a paleontological specimen, Charles Willson Peale ended his retirement and returned from his farm, at age eighty-one, to take over management of the museum again from his son Rubens. Among the first projects he undertook to revive the museum's declining status was painting a full-length self-portrait commissioned by the trustees of the newly incorporated Philadelphia Museum. Begun in August 1822, *The Artist in His Museum* was conceived as an emblematic painting and offered yet another monumental image of the mastodon bones as symbols of the nation's natural antiquity.

Nearly nine feet high, the painting depicts Peale raising a red damask curtain to reveal the interior of his museum (figure 50). The rows of portraits of American patriots and the cases of stuffed birds form a deep perspective effect drawing viewers into the picture. In the shadows, the mounted skeleton of the mastodon is barely visible, although its giant thighbone and jaw loom large in the foreground at Peale's feet, the conical protuberances on the grinders highlighted. In the left foreground, the limp feathered carcass of an American turkey lies on top of a taxidermist's chest, with the open drawer revealing the scalpels and pincers used to mount the bird. The wild turkey was already a national emblem, like the bald eagle pictured in the bird cases above, and gives symbolic meaning to the mastodon skeleton and bones as relics of the nation's natural antiquity.

Not long after Peale completed this painting, John Godman, a young Philadelphia doctor, published the first truly scientific description of the mastodon's bones by an American. Godman had received his medical education in Baltimore before moving to Philadelphia in 1821, where he briefly served on the faculty of professors who lectured at Peale's museum and later married Rembrandt Peale's daughter Angelica. A restless, energetic figure with a delicately handsome face, he contracted tuberculosis while writing his treatise and so retired from medicine to complete his book.

Borrowing heavily from Rembrandt Peale's *Disquisition* and Cuvier's *Ossemens fossiles*, Godman discusses not only the anatomical configuration of the bones but also the most recent discoveries and the sites where the bones had been found in greatest abundance. Despite including long excerpts from Rembrandt's narrative of the recovery of the mastodon bones in Orange County, Godman corrected his father-in-law's erroneous mounting of the tusks. "This position is certainly unnatural, as Cuvier has clearly shown. Nothing therefore can justify us in placing these tusks otherwise than in the elephant, unless we find a skull which has them actually implanted in a different manner."[13]

FIGURE 50. Charles Willson Peale's famous self-portrait *The Artist in His Museum*, 1822. The thighbone and lower jaw of the mastodon figure prominently in the foreground while the extinct animal's reconstructed skeleton lurks in the shadows of Peale's emblematic painting. Courtesy Pennsylvania Academy of the Fine Arts, Philadelphia, gift of Mrs. Sarah Harrison (Joseph Harrison Jr. Collection).

Like Thomas Jefferson's dramatic descriptions of the Potomac River water gap and the Natural Bridge, the mastodon stirred romantic sentiments in the otherwise clinical tone of Godman's treatise:

> The emotions experienced, when for the first time we behold the giant relics of this great animal, are those of unmingled awe. We cannot avoid reflecting on the time when this huge frame was clothed with its peculiar integuments, and moved by appropriate muscles; when the mighty heart dashed forth its torrents of blood through vessels of enormous caliber, and the mastodon strode along in supreme dominion over every other tenant of the wilderness.[14]

Even though the mastodon's jaws and grinders were evidence of a herbivorous animal, they still evoked an image of power. "Looking at its ponderous jaws, armed with teeth peculiarly formed for the most effectual crushing of the firmest substances, we are assured that its life could only be supported by the destruction of vast quantities of food."[15]

No sooner had Dr. Godman finished praising the mastodon's supreme power, than the saber-shaped tooth of another extinct species was discovered in England, thereby announcing the existence of a new race of monsters, which soon challenged the mastodon's supremacy in prehistoric nature. In 1822, James Parkinson, the English physician who had popularized the idea that geological epochs were part of God's design for humanity, published a small book on organic fossil remains in British strata, in which he mentioned the jaws and teeth of an unidentified reptilian creature found in a slate quarry north of Oxford, to which he gave the name Megalosaurus, or "giant lizard."

Five years earlier, when Georges Cuvier paid his first visit to England, William Buckland, an Anglican clergymen and the first professor of geology at Oxford University, showed him this same specimen, a large jawbone with sharp, bladelike teeth. Cuvier believed that the specimen belonged to a giant, unknown reptile and was similar to remains from Normandy that he had identified as fossil crocodiles. In fact, the jaws and teeth of the Megalosaurus were quite different from Cuvier's Mosasaurus, and in 1824, when Buckland finally published a description of the jawbone, with its fine saw-toothed edges and single, large saber-like tooth jutting out, he suggested the creature was an elephant-size predatory lizard, a terrestrial rather than a marine monster.

In his report to the Geological Society of London, Buckland referred to similar bones discovered a few years earlier by Dr. Gideon
Algernon Mantell, a physician from the south coast of England, who
had published a book entitled *The Fossils of South Downs*. Shortly before his book appeared in 1822, Dr. Mantell's wife Mary Ann found
several large fossilized teeth along a country road near Lewes, where
her husband was attending a patient. Recognizing the teeth as belonging to an unknown herbivore, Dr. Mantell added at the last
minute some drawings of the teeth in his book on the region's fossils.
Even though the teeth resembled an elephant's incisors, they had
been found in an older geological stratum usually associated with
reptiles, where the remains of mammals were never found. "As no
known existing reptiles are capable of masticating their food, I could
not venture to assign the tooth in question to a saurian," he concluded, unable to classify the creature.[16]

Dr. Mantell took the tooth to a meeting of the Geological Society
of London, where he was disappointed by the lack of interest among his
fellow members, including Dr. Buckland, who claimed the specimens
were the front teeth of a large fish related to the *Anarchicas lupus*, or
wolffish. In June 1824, Dr. Mantell asked his friend Charles Lyell, a
young British geologist and secretary of the Geological Society, to take
the tooth to Paris and show it to Cuvier. Initially, Cuvier pronounced
the tooth to be the upper incisor of a rhinoceros, but in the new edition
of his *Ossemens fossiles*, published later the same year, he dismissed the
similarity as superficial and concluded instead that the curious specimen belonged to an extraordinary unidentified reptilian creature.

Frustrated by his colleagues' confusion, Dr. Mantell compared his
specimens with the fossil remains in the Hunterian Museum of the
Royal College of Surgeons, which housed some of the late John
Hunter's immense anatomical collection. By chance, he encountered
another researcher there, who recognized the similarity between the
fossil teeth and those of a Central American iguana lizard which he
himself was studying. In February 1825, when Dr. Mantell finally presented his report on the fossils to the Royal Society of London, he
called the extinct reptile the Iguanodon, a name suggested to him by
his colleague Rev. William Conybeare, who had also coined the
names Megalosaurus and Mosasaurus. Using Cuvier's technique of
extrapolating the size of an animal from small bone fragments, Dr.

Mantell estimated the Iguanodon to have been a sixty-foot-long reptilian monster, the largest of the new saurian species.

The discovery of this as yet unclassified group of extinct reptiles was accelerated by the stunning geological treatise published by Dr. Mantell's friend Charles Lyell, whose *Principles of Geology,* published in 1830, dealt a devastating blow to the catastrophist school of geologists. In this seminal work, Lyell revived James Hutton's uniformitarian doctrines, arguing with new authority that the earth's geological history was the result of existing natural forces operating over long periods of time rather than in periodic catastrophes. The book's subtitle summarized his argument: "Being an attempt to explain the former changes of the earth's surface, by reference to causes now in action." Unlike Hutton, who had made virtually no use of the fossil record, Lyell defined geology to include organic as well as inorganic change and employed fossil evidence to show that the extinction of species was part of the ordinary processes of nature, operating over millions of years.

Rejecting Lamarck's idea of a progression from simple to complex forms of life, Lyell saw the disappearance of species in terms of a struggle for survival occasioned by the migration of animals and the geographic dispersion of species. His view of this process was cyclical rather than progressive, which led him in a whimsical passage to imagine the reappearance of the extinct saurian species on the earth: "The huge iguanodon might reappear in the woods, and the ichthyosaur in the sea, while the pterodactyl might flit again through umbragious groves of tree-ferns."[17]

The second volume of Lyell's *Principles of Geology,* published in 1832, took up the species question and explicitly rejected Lamarck's thesis of organic transformation, focusing instead on the geographic dispersion of species and the effects of migration by animals. According to Donald Worster, Lyell made violence virtually a universal law of nature and therefore a fully acceptable natural phenomenon: "The most insignificant and diminutive species, whether in the animal or vegetable kingdom, have each slaughtered their thousands, as they disseminated themselves over the globe," Lyell claimed, reviving the metaphor of warring species.[18] In his view, the competition of species for territory and food was part of the regular and constant order of nature, and the extinction of species was the result of everyday processes, not cataclysmic events, as the catastrophists claimed.

Lyell's scientific theory challenged the traditional Linnaean view of the nature, in which the only struggle for existence was between predator and prey. This older concept was now replaced by the idea of entire animal species competing for the limited natural resources of a geographic region. "So long as all species lived in fixed, permanent, eternally assigned stations, there was no reason for violent competition," Donald Worster said of Lyell's theory. "But introduce natural forces that pushed creatures out of their settled places and sent them in search of new homes in far corners of the earth, and no end of conflict was possible."[19]

Sales of Lyell's book were remarkable from the outset, but its popularity did not derive solely from the soundness of its geological theory or the rigorous scientific methodology he recommended for future study of the earth's history. Woven into Lyell's narrative were the threads of scientific racialism that had been a large part of the field of comparative anatomy for generations. Extinction once again was applied with scientific authority not only to the disappearance of animal species but to the disappearance of human races as well, more particularly to the extermination of the so-called savage peoples: "A faint image of the certain doom of a species less fitted to struggle with some new condition in a region which it previously inhabited, and where it has to contend with a more vigorous species, is presented by the extirpation of savage tribes by the advancing colony of some civilizing nation."[20]

Using words whose harshness would be called genocidal today, Lyell left little doubt who the victims of this naturalistic process were to be: "Yet few future events are more certain than the speedy extermination of the Indians of North America and the savages of New Holland in the course of a few centuries, when these tribes will be remembered only in poetry and tradition."[21] Extinction of the Indians was taken for granted in the era of Andrew Jackson's presidency, and geological theories like Lyell's helped legitimize the idea by making their slaughter part of natural history.

In 1832, when the twenty-three-year-old Charles Darwin boarded the HMS *Beagle* for his historic voyage to the Galapagos Islands, he carried in his luggage the first volume of Lyell's *Principles of Geology*. Nearly two years later, while in the harbor at Montevideo, shortly before he set sail for Patagonia and the southern coast of Argentina, Darwin received the second volume in the mail. Earlier, while on an excursion up the Parana River north of Buenos Aires, he himself had dug up bones of the *Megatherium* and a mastodon molar from the red clay of the pampas, which he described as "one wide sepulchre for these extinct quadrupeds."[22]

Guided by Lyell's *Principles of Geology*, Darwin described the geology of the Patagonian coast as the *Beagle* sailed south toward Tierra del Fuego. The level plains of Patagonia were cut off all along the coastline by perpendicular cliffs, exposing fossil remains that confirmed Lyell's theory that the form of extinct species was closely related to that of existing animals. However, as Darwin himself observed, the living species were much smaller than their extinct ancestors, and this led him to embrace in an offhand manner an updated version of Buffon's theory of American degeneracy: "If Buffon had known of these gigantic armadillos, llamas, great rodents, and lost pachydermata, he would have said with a greater semblance of truth, that the creative force in America had lost its vigour, rather than that it had never possessed such powers."[23]

Long after Thomas Jefferson had repudiated Buffon's theory, the idea was still alive in Darwin's mind, reinforced now by Lyell's geological view of extinction: "It is impossible to reflect without the deepest astonishment, on the changed state of this continent. Formerly it must have swarmed with great monsters, like the southern parts of Africa, but now we find only the tapir, guanaco, armadillo, and capybara; mere pigmies compared to the antecedent races."[24] In Patagonia, before reaching the Galapagos Islands, Darwin was puzzled by the circumstances that had caused the disappearance of these monstrous races: "What then has exterminated so many living creatures?"

Stopping briefly at Tierra del Fuego, Darwin went ashore with a party to meet the inhabitants of this desolate promontory at the tip of South America: "Their country is a broken mass of wild rock, lofty hills, and useless forests: and these are viewed through mists and endless storms," he wrote in his journal.[25] His harsh view of the landscape paralleled an equally hostile description of the people there whom he called "savages," who painted their faces black except for a white band across the eyes and made "hideous grimaces" while mimicking the gestures and utterances of their unwelcome visitors. "Viewing such men, one can hardly make oneself believe they are fellow-creatures, and inhabitants of the same world," Darwin noted, echoing the sentiments of the polygenesists who argued that non-European races were actually separate, naturally inferior species.[26]

By the time that Darwin returned to England to write *Origin of Species*, the new saurian monsters discovered in the previous decade were making their presence felt in the prehistoric world. In his absence, several gigantic marine lizards had achieved new notoriety in the scientific literature and popular magazines. Before Darwin's departure, his colleague at the Geological Society, Rev. William Conybeare, had reconstructed two extinct seagoing reptiles, *Ichthyosaurus* and *Plesiosaurus*. Based on complete skeletons unearthed in southern England, these aquatic creatures were portrayed as fierce predators, cold-blooded reptiles which inhabited a prehuman landscape where *Pterodactyls*, or flying reptiles, wheeled ominously overhead.

Illustrations of this new prehistoric landscape were already appearing in popular magazines as the beasts escaped from the scientific literature into the realm of public culture. In 1833, London's *Penny Magazine* used a wood engraving entitled *Organic Remains Restored*, replete with fossil reptiles, to illustrate several anonymous articles on geology. As Martin J. S. Rudwick showed in his *Scenes from Deep Time*, the first visual images of these saurian monsters often portrayed them as smiling creatures, basking on beaches in tropical climates resembling Eden-like pastoral scenes.[27]

The best-known fossil reptile was Dr. Gideon Mantell's *Iguanodon*, whose bones were a central attraction at the Mantellian Museum in the seaside resort of Brighton on England's south coast. Publication of Mantell's short article "The Geological Age of Reptiles" in 1831 had already popularized the notion of a distinct epoch dominated by reptilian monsters preceding the era of mammals and human history. However, the true turning point in the emergence of these monstrous creatures came in 1838 when Mantell's own book *Wonders of Geology* appeared, with vivid depictions of their habitat. Based on lectures at his Brighton museum, he pictured "The Country of the Iguanodon" as a lush tropical landscape inhabited by fierce saurian creatures: "Arborescent ferns, palms, and yuccas, constituted its groves and forests, delicate ferns and grasses, the vegetable clothing of its soil. It was peopled by enormous reptiles, among which the colossal Iguanodon and the Megalosaurus were the chief."[28]

What gave this new prehistoric world its menacing character was the book's frontispiece, which showed several dragon-like *Iguanodons* preying on one another, their jaws and teeth ripping into the flesh with a fury reminiscent of George Stubbs's lion attacking a horse. The engraving was from a painting by John Martin, a successful English landscape artist of the Romantic era, whose dark, tumultuous paintings of the Deluge had earned him a reputation as the era's foremost painter of biblical scenes. In his violent image of prehistoric nature, "the peaceful, pastoral tone of so many earlier scenes has been abruptly replaced by the nightmarish 'Gothick' melodrama of the Martinesque style," observed Martin J. S. Rudwick of the turbulent new view of the "Age of Reptiles."[29] After this, prehistoric nature was increasingly portrayed as a violent place ruled by carnivores, similar in spirit to the early views of the American *incognitum's* dominance of the wilderness landscape and the antediluvian world.

In America, the saurian monsters were less well known than the mastodon, although an American author of children's books, "Peter Parley," the pseudonym of Samuel Griswold Goodrich, included lively images of *Ichthyosaurus* and *Plesiosaurus* in his *Wonders of Earth Sea and Sky*, published in 1837. His illustrations portrayed these saurian sea lizards basking in a tidal pool, but his text hinted at their new role as the rulers of prehistoric nature: "The Icthyosaurus was a great tyrant, and used to prey on every creature that came within his reach; this is known by the fossil remains found inside of his body."[30]

Goodrich's image of the *Ichthyosaurus* as a tyrant of the prehistoric world was borrowed directly from the landscape of terror previously associated with the American *incognitum*. In 1831, he reproduced Charles Willson Peale's broadside advertising the exhibition of the "mammoth" in his *Child's First Book of History*, introducing his young readers to the American monster as the "uncontrouled Monarch of the Wilderness" and the "largest of all Terrestrial Beings!" The mastodon clearly served as the model for the metaphor of dominance which Goodrich later applied to the new reptilian rulers of prehistoric nature. To Americans, the mastodon still ruled supreme in the antediluvian world largely because they were not yet fully aware of the saurian monsters looming on the horizon.

In the 1830s, the second mastodon skeleton was finally on display at Rembrandt Peale's museum in Baltimore, with its elegant, curved tusks turned upward, as Alfred Jacob Miller's lithograph reveals (figure 51). In 1831, New Yorkers could see a brand-new collection of bones recently excavated at Big Bone Lick by Captain Ben-

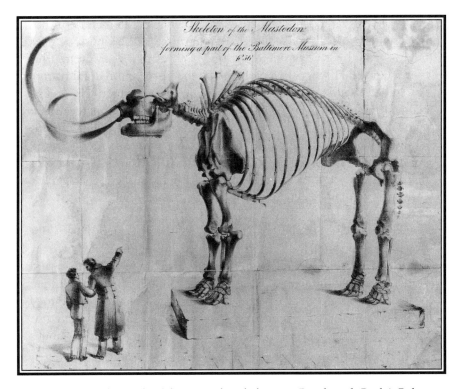

FIGURE 51. Lithograph of the mastodon skeleton at Rembrandt Peale's Baltimore Museum by Alfred J. Miller, 1836. By this time, the animal's tusks had been reversed to their correct upturned position, although many Americans continued to see the mastodon as a ferocious monster that dominated the natural world. Courtesy Maryland Historical Society, Baltimore.

jamin Finnell, who lived near the site. The enormous collection thrilled Benjamin Silliman, a professor of geology at Yale College and editor of the nation's leading scientific magazine, the *American Journal of Science and Arts*. In his report from New York on Finnell's collection, which included some twenty-two tusks, up to eleven feet long and weighing more than five hundred pounds, Silliman conveyed their awesome effect: "They produce in the beholder the strongest conviction that races of animals formerly existed on this continent, not only of vast magnitude, but which must also have been very numerous; and the Mastodon, at least, ranged in herds, over probably the entire American continent."[31]

Four years later, Dr. James Deane of Greenfield, Massachusetts, noticed some strange, birdlike foot marks imprinted in the sandstone slabs
used to pave his town's sidewalks. In March of that year, he told his
friend Edward Hitchcock, a professor of chemistry and natural history
at Amherst College, about the tracks in stone, which Dr. Deane
claimed resembled a large turkey's foot. Trained as a Congregational
clergyman at Yale College, Hitchcock had studied geology under Benjamin Silliman, with whom he became close friends before going to
Amherst in 1825. Several months later, after receiving casts of the foot
marks, Hitchcock traveled to Greenfield where he spent the summer
collecting similar specimens at the quarries from which the flagstones
had come.

The following year Hitchcock published the first scientific description of these puzzling footprints in Silliman's prestigious *American Journal of Science and Art*, under the title "Ornithichnology," a new word
coined to signify the science of bird tracks. Found in the red sandstone
beds of the Connecticut River valley, the largest of these three-toed
foot marks measured seventeen inches, with toes that terminated in
claws and a stride of four to six feet—all indications of an enormous
creature:

> Indeed, I hesitate not to say, that the impression made on the mud ap-
> pears to have been almost as deep, indicating a pressure almost as
> great, as if an Elephant had passed over it. I could not persuade my-
> self, until the evidence became perfectly irresistible, that I was exam-
> ining merely the track of a bird.[32]

Extrapolating the size of the animal from the largest-known species of
bird, the African ostrich, whose foot was only ten inches long, Hitchcock estimated the extinct creature had been from twelve to fifteen feet
tall and had weighed nearly two hundred pounds.

The mysterious foot marks were actually quite well known in the
Connecticut River valley, whose inhabitants often referred to them
as the tracks of "Noah's Ravens." Hitchcock found similar impressions on the sidewalks in front of the court house at Northampton
and in the flagstones of Deerfield and South Hadley. The first specimen, containing a row of five tracks, had been dug up near South
Hadley in 1802 by a farmer named Pliny Moody, but not until 1836,

when Hitchcock's monograph was published, was any attempt made to describe them scientifically.

Like Benjamin Silliman, Hitchcock was adept at integrating the latest geological knowledge into the biblical narrative. Many members of the new generation of European and American scientists criticized any attempts to use geological evidence to prove the literal truth of the Bible, but natural theology prevailed in America as the dominant belief among both the general public and the country's schoolteachers, college professors, and clergymen. Edward Hitchcock's *Elementary Geology*, published in 1840, went through thirty editions in twenty years and was typical of the textbooks that used Lyell's theories to demonstrate the "Doctrine of Design," the idea that all natural history, including prehistoric nature, was further evidence of God's power and the truth of revealed religion.

In 1841, Charles Lyell himself made the first of several trips to the United States, where he lectured before immense crowds in cities along the Atlantic coast. At Boston, he delivered a series of lectures at the Lowell Institute before an overflow audience of three thousand. In the winter, Lyell delivered an equally well attended course of lectures in New York. His *Lectures on Geology* were published by Horace Greeley, editor of the *New York Tribune*, who noted that Lyell had spoken before "large and respectable audiences in the principal Cities of the Union."[33] Despite his emphasis on the natural processes at work on the earth's surface, Lyell assured his audiences that the succession of geological epochs had been called into existence by the Creator: "Geology shows that all things are the works of one Intelligence—one Mind—all links in one chain: that the Earth must have been admirably fitted for successive states which were to endure for ages."[34]

During his American travels, Lyell also visited Big Bone Lick, "a place of great geological celebrity." Traveling with two naturalists from Cincinnati, he found the marshes much reduced in size, owing to the leveling of the surrounding forest: "The removal of tall trees allowed the sun's rays to penetrate freely to the soil, and dry up part of the morass." The remarkable buffalo paths leading to springs, which sixty years ago had been "bare, hard and well trodden as a high road," were still visible through the surrounding countryside, overgrown with grass, but the buffalo themselves were gone. "Within the memory of persons now living, the wild bisons or buffaloes crowded to these springs, but they have retreated for many years, and are now as unknown to the inhabitants as the mastodon itself."[35]

Even as Lyell sounded the death knell for Big Bone Lick, a new monster was being erected from mastodon bones found near the Missouri River in the American West. In early 1840, after laboring for five months, Albert Koch, a German immigrant and proprietor of the St. Louis Museum, unearthed a large cache of mastodon bones nearby on the shore of the Pomme de Terre River, in Benton County, Missouri.[36] Koch made geological records of the soil where his new discovery lay, noting the large quantities of cypress burrs, tropical cane, and swamp moss embedded near the bones. When mounting the skeleton, however, Koch used the bones of several mastodons, adding extra ribs and vertebrae, to create an oversized monstrosity whose skeleton stood fifteen feet high and thirty feet long, with its tusks jutting upward like horns. Dubbed the Missourium theristrocaulodon, the creature was first exhibited in St. Louis and then brought to Louisville in the summer of 1841, shortly before Lyell's arrival in Boston.

In October, Koch's Missourium went on display in Philadelphia at the Masonic Hall, where the city's naturalists flocked to see the mastodon's latest reincarnation. At a meeting of the American Philosophical Society, Dr. Richard Harlan, one of the country's leading authorities on fossils, gave it his stamp of approval, calling the exhibition "one of the most remarkable collections of fossil bones of extinct animals which have hitherto been brought to light in this country."[37] Even though he pointed out several ill-conceived constructions in Koch's mounting of the skeleton, Harlan assured the society's members that Koch's subsequent research "would enable him to rectify these errors."[38]

By the time Charles Lyell reached Philadelphia, Koch was already on his way to England to exhibit his Missourium in London's famous Egyptian Hall. In what may well have been the mastodon's first encounter with the saurian species, Koch's broadsides advertising the exhibition claimed that the new American monster dwarfed this fossil reptile: "This unparalleled Gigantic remains, when its huge frame was clad with its peculiar fibrous integuments, and when moved by its appropriate muscles, was Monarch over all the Animal Creation; the Mammoth, and even the mighty Iguanodon may easily have crept between his legs"[39] (figure 52). Crowds flocked to see the American monster, and the exhibition was so successful it remained on display in London for nearly eighteen months.

Missourium Theristrocaulodon,
OR LEVIATHAN MISSOURIENSIS
OPEN FOR EXHIBITION, IN THE
Saloon at the rere of Tommey's Hotel,
ENTRANCE IN GREAT BRITAIN-STREET,
(*Opposite the Lying-in-Hospital.*)
PARTICULAR DESCRIPTION and EXPLANATIONS GIVEN EVERY DAY AT 3 o'C. BY Mr. A. KOCH.

This unparalled Gigantic remains, when its huge frame was clad with its peculiar fibrous integuments, and when moved by its appropriate muscles, was Monarch over all the Animal Creation ; the Mammoth, and even the mighty Iguanodon may easily have crept between his legs, and now is universally acknowledged by all the European and American Men of Science, to be the greatest Phenomenon ever discovered in natural h story. On viewing this vast relic, which after lying prostrate in the bosom of the Earth for Thousands of Years, now standing erect in all its grandeur, the beholder will be lost in wonder and astonishment, at its immensity and perfect preservation.

The MISSOURIUM was disinterred in 1840, after Five Months labour, in N. lat. 40., W. long. 95.

ITS LENGTH IS THIRTY FEET, ITS HEIGHT NEAR FIFTEEN FEET.
From Point to Point of the Tusks 21 Feet.

There will also be exhibited Specimens of THREE SPECIES OF GENUS TETRACAULODON, With Microscopical Sections of their Tusks, also Three species of the Genus MASTODON,

From the great applause this Unique Collection has already received in London and other large Cities in England, during the last 18 Months, and the Attraction it has already created being so well known the Proprietor considers further remarks unnecessary.

Mr. A. KOCH, the discoverer of this Collection is present to give explanations of the specimens, and will also show, and make statements, which bear indisputable evidence, that the human race existed cooval or contemporary with the above animals.

ADMISSION, - - - - ONE SHILLING.

Pamphlets containing a description of the Missourium, with its supposed habits, Indian tradition concerning it &c., &c., can be had at the Door or Saloon.

Doors open from Half-past 9 in the Morning, 'til 10 in the Evening.

C. CROOKES, PRINTER 87, CAPEL-STREET, DUBLIN.

FIGURE 52. Broadside advertising the exhibition of Albert Koch's "*Missourium theristrocaulodon*" in Dublin, Ireland, ca. 1843. Constructed from the bones of several mastodons, Koch's skeleton was reputedly larger than the mammoth and the *Iguanodon*, an early dinosaur described by Dr. Gideon Mantell. Courtesy American Philosophical Society, Philadelphia.

Koch's Missourium arrived in England at a significant moment in the history of prehistoric monsters, when an entirely new group of creatures had been identified that were destined to displace the mastodon as the ruling species in the antediluvian world. Only a few months earlier, on Friday, July 30, 1841, Richard Owen, England's foremost expert on the saurian species, presented a historic paper to the British Association for the Advancement of Science formally classifying for the first time a new group of fossil reptiles—the dinosaurs, or "terrible lizards."[40] A professor of comparative anatomy at the Royal College of Surgeons, Dr. Owen had traveled around the country for three years under the association's sponsorship, gathering information about all known fossil reptiles in Britain. The new group he designated as Dinosauria contained only three species: William Buckland's Megalosaurus and Gideon Mantell's *Iguanodon* and *Hylaeosaurus*, all known only from a few bones and teeth.

Dr. Owen's new grouping of these saurian species grew out of his desire to refute the evolutionist ideas of Lamarck's followers, who argued that living organisms had progressively evolved from simple to complex life-forms over millions of years. In Owen's opinion, which echoed Buffon's theory of degeneracy, living reptiles were degenerate creatures when compared with their ancestors, the elephant-size dinosaurs of the Mesozoic era. Published the following year in the association's *Proceedings*, Dr. Owen's paper quietly launched a new era in prehistoric nature.

Initially, some of London's leading geologists were quite impressed with Koch's Missourium, applauding the discovery of an even larger species of the fossil elephants. Dr. Gideon Mantell, discoverer of the *Iguanodon*, welcomed the new challenger into the ranks of extinct monsters: "It is the largest of all hitherto known fossil mammals—thirty feet long and fifteen feet in height."[41] But when Dr. Owen disclosed the fraudulent mounting of Koch's skeleton, London anatomists began to denounce the exhibition. Removal of the extra ribs and vertebrae, together with a correct arrangement of the other bones, Dr. Owen declared, would reduce the animal to its proper form of an ordinary mastodon.[42]

Even though Koch himself addressed the Geological Society in early April, defending the authenticity of his skeleton, he closed the London show the following summer and took the Missourium on tour to Ireland and Germany. In May 1844, after exhausting his welcome elsewhere, Koch returned to London on his way home. Here he ensured the financial success of his tour by selling his entire collection of fossils to the British Museum for a down payment of $2,000 plus $1,000 a year for the rest of his life.

Inspired by the financial success of his Missourium, Koch immediately launched a new exhibition upon his return home which signaled the arrival in America of the first sea monsters identified with the saurian species. In March 1845, Koch assembled from several different sites in Alabama a collection of bones belonging to a "gigantic fossil reptile," to which he gave the name Hydrarchos, or "water king." In the summer, he took his new creation, a giant sea serpent with tiny paddle-like flippers, to New York, where the 114-foot-long skeleton was exhibited at the Apollo Rooms on Broadway, not far from P. T. Barnum's new American Museum.

In October, before leaving for Europe, Dr. Koch's Hydrarchos was on display in Boston, but educated Bostonians quickly exposed the sea serpent as a hybrid creature constructed out of the bones of many different animals. Zoologist Jeffries Wyman debunked Koch's exhibition in a paper he read to the Boston Society of Natural History, pointing out that its flippers were made of fossilized mollusk shells and the vertebrae were assembled from at least five *Zeuglodons*, a giant seagoing mammal that Richard Owen had identified a decade earlier as a whale-like mammal rather than a reptile.

To advertise his exhibition, Koch plastered posters on Boston's city walls with headlines that read "Sea Serpent Alive" but whose fine print informed citizens they could see the skeleton of "that colossal and terrible reptile the *sea serpent,* which *when alive,* measured thirty feet in circumference."[43] The British geologist Charles Lyell happened to be in Boston again to deliver another series of lectures at the Lowell Institute, and the placards caught his eye: "The public were also informed that his hydrarchos, or water king, was the Leviathan of the Book of Job."[44] Each day during his lectures, Lyell had to answer the question whether the great fossil skeleton from Alabama was of the sea serpent formerly seen on the coast near Boston. During his subsequent travels through Alabama, Lyell visited the exact spot where Koch had allegedly dug up the bones of his Hydrarchos, only to discover that portions of the animal's vertebral column had been obtained fifteen miles away from its skull.[45]

By the time Lyell's letter to Benjamin Silliman warning him of the hoax reached New England, Koch was again on his way to London hoping to repeat the success of his earlier tour with the Missourium. British anatomists were immediately suspicious of Koch's new American monster and quickly publicized the hoax. Dr. Gideon Mantell sent a letter to the *Illustrated London News* reminding readers of Koch's previous show: "Mr. Koch is the person who, a few years ago, had a fine collection of fossil bones of elephants and mastodons, out of which he made up an enormous skeleton, and exhibited it in the Egyptian Hall, Piccadilly, under the name of 'Missourium.'"[46] Forced out of England by disclosures of his fraud, Koch took the sea monster to Dresden, where an important German anatomist made a special study of the creature, which was published in 1847. Impressed by the authenticity of Koch's skeleton, Frederick Wilhelm IV, the king of Prussia, purchased the monstrosity for the Royal Museum in Berlin, but once again, scientists there revealed the skeleton as a forgery.

In the 1840s during his second tour of North America, Charles Lyell himself saw evidence of the mastodon's continuing preeminence in American eyes. In Boston, only a week before he sailed for England, he was shown three different skeletons, including one found on a farm in New Jersey where five other skeletons reportedly lay buried together. But the largest and most complete skeleton was one unearthed the previous year in the Hudson River valley not far from John Masten's farm.

The summer of 1845 had been unusually dry in Orange County, and the ponds had dried up on Nathaniel Brewster's farm, leaving beds of peat exposed in a shallow pool of water on his property. Late one afternoon, the spades of workmen digging marl from the wet, spongy soil struck something hard, which turned out to be skull of a mastodon. News of the discovery spread quickly, attracting a large group of neighbors and travelers who watched as the bones of an entire mastodon were uncovered almost perfectly preserved. The nearly intact skeleton was deposited in Brewster's barn, where the bones were cleaned and then wired up by Dr. A. J. Prime, a physician from nearby Newburgh.

In October, Brewster's son and son-in-law exhibited the skeleton in New York at the Minerva Room on Broadway, a few doors from where Dr. Koch's Hydrarchos had been on display the previous summer. While the mastodon was being exhibited, the *American Journal of Agriculture and Science* published an article entitled "The Great American Mastodon" by Dr. A. J. Prime and Ebenezer Emmons, a lecturer in geology at the Williams College Lyceum of Natural History. Even though the authors took great pride in how carefully they had reconstructed the skeleton, the figure illustrating their article shows a rather crudely mounted specimen, whose ramrod-stiff backbone gives it an oddly rigid stance. Besides the detailed narrative of its excavation, their article even divulges the contents of the great beast's stomach, which reportedly contained from four to six bushels of twigs, leaves, and other vegetable matter. "This opinion was confirmed on removing the pelvis, underneath which, in the direction of the last of the intestines, was a train of the same material, about three feet in length and four inches in diameter."[47]

From New York, Brewster's son and son-in-law toured several New England towns for three or four months before finally selling the twenty-five-foot-long skeleton in early 1846 for $5,000 to Dr. John Collins Warren, a professor of anatomy at Harvard Medical School. After transporting the bones to Boston in the boxes constructed for their tour, Warren had the skeleton reassembled under the direction of a local physician before exhibiting the extraordinary new mastodon for several days. Proud of his new acquisition, the Harvard professor arranged for a private viewing by Charles Lyell and gave him an excellent daguerreotype of the newly mounted skeleton, probably the first photograph ever made of the American monster.

Returning one evening through the city's streets, Lyell encountered a noisy group of poor Bostonians protesting President James K. Polk's declaration of war against Mexico by mocking the Texans who had precipitated the fight.[48] Even though New Englanders opposed the war, they had been instrumental in nurturing the millennial beliefs and nativist spirit underpinning the doctrine of Manifest Destiny, the newly coined term being used by the Democrats to justify the invasion of Mexico.

Many northerners like Ralph Waldo Emerson publicly denounced the war because they feared the annexation of Mexican territory would bring racially inferior people into American society: "The United States will conquer Mexico, but it will be as the man swallows arsenic, which brings him down in turn." But privately Emerson expressed a harsher belief in the inevitability of American expansion, couched in unequivocal racial terms: "It is very certain that the strong British race which have now overrun so much of this continent, must also overrun [Texas], and Mexico and Oregon also, and it will in the course of ages be a small import by what particular occasions and methods it was done."[49]

By the 1840s, the missionary zeal of the Puritan conquest was joined by the scientific racialism of the craniologists to form a potent new rationale for the settlement of western lands and the extermination of the Indian peoples. As Reginald Horsman showed, white supremacy achieved a kind of religious as well as scientific meaning in the doctrine of Manifest Destiny during the Romantic era.

> The growth and acceptance of the Romantic movement in American literature parallels in time the growth and acceptance of the new scientific racialism. . . . Science provided a solid basis for the new assumptions, but the creative writers often gave dramatic expression to the new beliefs of racial superiority and destiny even before the scientists provided specific proofs for what had been assumed.[50]

Like the mastodon during this period, the race myth became part of the new republic's natural antiquity, in effect creating a mythic past for American society out of the scientific study of human skulls. Just as geological strata recorded the extinction of inferior species by the superior life-forms, comparative anatomy confirmed the superiority of the white race over non-European peoples. In America, craniology, or the science of human skulls, made a decisive contribution to the merging of natural history and nationalism in the new doctrines of racial superiority.

In 1845, when Lyell visited Philadelphia, the world's leading authority in the field of craniology was Samuel George Morton, a Quaker physician who had begun to collect human skulls in 1830 to illustrate his anatomy lecture "The Different Forms of the Skull As Exhibited in the Five Races of Man." Nine years later, he published his *Crania Americana*, based on the meticulous measurement of the cranial capacity of 486 human skulls gathered from around the world[51] (figure 53), and Benjamin Silliman's journal praised this work as "the most extensive and valuable contribution to the natural history of man" that had appeared on the American continent."[52]

Morton's theory did not overtly promote white supremacy, largely for fear of criticism by the clergy, but his highly praised research provided what appeared to be scientific proof of the superior cranial capacity of the Caucasian race. More important from the point of view of race theory, he concluded that "the physical characteristics which distinguish the different races, are independent of external causes." In

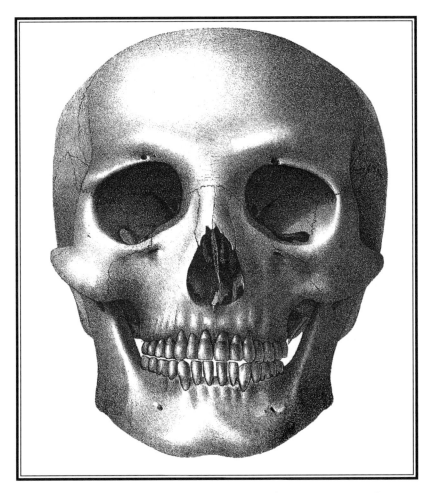

FIGURE 53. Lithograph by John Collins for Samuel George Morton's *Crania americana*, 1839. This skull of a Muskogee Indian was among the many specimens collected by American doctors from battlefields during the Jackson era. Morton's master work was used by supporters of polygenesis to defend the idea that non-European races were separate, naturally inferior species.

other words, the unity of the human species did not exist, and the inferiority of the non-European races was a permanent trait inherited from what he called the "primeval diversities among men." This was a veiled reference to the popular theory of polygenesis, which held that non-European races were separate, naturally inferior species. Perhaps the most disturbing aspect of Morton's research, like Thomas Jefferson's views of race, was that it came from a dedicated scientist, not an apologist for slavery, although advocates of the innate inferiority of African Americans quickly used Crania Americana to defend white supremacy.

American craniologists were applying the doctrines of extinction and the struggle for existence to racial groups long before Darwin's Origin of Species appeared. In New York, Dr. John Augustine Smith was still using Camper's facial angle to prove the superiority of the Caucasian race. "The intellect of a race is always in proportion to the obtuseness of that angle," he explained in a lecture to the Lyceum of Natural History, "The Different Races of Men," in December 1842.[53] Smith also applied the doctrines of extinction and the struggle for existence to African American slaves, assuring his audience that they would surely be exterminated if they were freed: "This upon the principle that as society advances there must inevitably, in the course of time, be a struggle for the means of subsistence; and whenever and wherever that struggle comes, the weaker party—as the Negroes certainly are—must be driven to the wall."[54] In America, scientific racialism went hand in hand with geology since Dr. Smith's lecture was published in 1843 as an appendix in Horace Greeley's New York edition of Charles Lyell's Lectures on Geology.

Nearly every American comparative anatomist combined craniology with an interest in the study of extinct species in the geological past. Samuel George Morton's specialty in geology was the Cretaceous, the final period of the Mesozoic era, whose fossil evidence revealed the first flowering plants as well as the remains of the saurian species, who were just beginning to make their presence known in America. His Synopsis of the Organic Remains of the Cretaceous Group of the United States, published in 1834, summarized the few known vertebrates from this period, including the saurians.

Like the racial superiority of the Caucasians, the mastodon's dominance was now anchored in a mythic past, the primordial beginnings of life on earth, where religious beliefs and scientific truths converged to celebrate the ruling species, both animal and human. This amalgam of ideas was expressed in many forms, from the clergymen who gave authority to the doctrine of Manifest Destiny to the early historians of westward expansion. In The Oregon Trail, Francis Parkman pictured the harshness of frontier life in terms auguring Darwinism: "From minnows to men, life is an incessant war."[55]

Only a year after the discovery of Warren's mastodon, Samuel W. Eager published a history of Orange County, New York, that testified to the enduring symbolic character of the American monster, when the dinosaurs first appeared on the scene. In his own lifetime, the author as a young boy had witnessed Charles Willson Peale's excavations at John Masten's farm and, nearly a half-century later, the unearthing of the Warren mastodon on Nathaniel Brewster's farm. For him, the mastodon was still a gargantuan beast and a ruling species:

> Contemplating the remains as exhumed from their resting place for unknown ages, we instinctively think of his great and lordly mastery over the beasts—of his majestic tread as he strode these valleys and hill tops—of his anger when excited to fury—stamping the earth till trembling beneath his feet, sniffing the wind with disdain, and uttering his wrath in tones of thunder. The mind quails beneath the oppressive grandeur of the thought, and we feel as if driven along by the violence of a tornado.[56]

Like many Americans of the Jacksonian era, Eager felt a certain bewilderment at the cosmological issues raised by the existence of a vast prehuman past that neither science nor the Scriptures could fully explain. Two key questions remained unanswered in his mind: what had caused the death of these "terrestrial monarchs," and when did they perish? Were they pre-Adamites destroyed by a catastrophe? Or were they carried to a common grave by the Deluge of the Scriptures? "Upon these subjects, wrapt in the deep mystery of many ages, we have no fixed or well-considered theory," Eager confessed, although he was obviously familiar with the latest opinions of the geologists.[57] In many respects, the deepening sense of geological time and the succession of creations only enhanced the majesty of God's power, strengthening the belief in the messianic purpose of the American nation and its conquest of wild nature, including the savage peoples barely removed from brute creation.

Afterword
The Myth of Wild Nature

What men see in Nature is a result of what they have been taught to
see—lessons in school, doctrines they have heard in church, books
they have read. They are conditioned most of all by what they mean
by *Nature*, a word that has gathered around itself paradox and ambi-
guity ever since the fifth century B.C.
                    —Marjorie Hope Nicolson, *Mountain Gloom*
                    and Mountain Glory

IN EARLY AMERICA, the founding fathers combined patriotism and
prehistoric nature to create an American monster—a symbol of overwhelming power in a psychologically insecure society. The doctrine
that gave birth to this ferocious prehistoric creature was the common
belief in the savagery of the natural world, including the human inhabitants of the lands that the European settlers termed an uninhabited
wilderness. In many respects, the master metaphor of early American
culture was this idea of the wilderness, or what might be more appropriately called the myth of wild nature, since this was a figure of speech
used by Europeans to define the character of the natural world, not
something inherent in nature itself. The idea of the wilderness, or wild
nature, was a human construct—a fantasy world of cruelty and violence—created to justify the violent conquest and colonization of the
New World by Christian conquerors, in whose eyes the so-called savage peoples were pagan infidels barely removed from brute creation.
With the discovery of extinct species and geological time, this idea of
the savagery of nature was applied to the prehuman past in which fero-

cious carnivores became the surrogate rulers of a new wilderness world in which no humans existed.

Unfortunately, for many people today, wild nature still signifies violence, competition, and the paradigm of dominance—the notion that the prehistoric world was actually *ruled* by vicious carnivores. Now that we have seen how this idea gave birth to the American monster, we will explore briefly its relevance to the prehistoric monsters in our own lives. What can the American monster teach us about *Tyrannosaurus rex* and the robotic raptors of *Jurassic Park* that have replaced the mastodon as symbols of dominance in prehistoric nature?

In the nineteenth century, the dinosaurs were slow to dethrone the mastodon as the ruling species in the newly discovered realm of prehistoric nature. Not until the construction of the first life-size models of the fossil reptiles in England in the 1850s did the saurian species begin to challenge the American monster. Even after the publication of Charles Darwin's *Origin of Species*, the widespread belief in the doctrine of divine design in the natural world remained strong in American society as geological truths continued to be incorporated into religious beliefs and national consciousness after the Civil War. Published in 1859, Darwin's masterwork actually intensified the evangelical spirit in America while at the same time undermining the idea that science served to confirm the truth of revealed religion. In the increasingly urban nation, this hostility toward Darwin's theory of natural selection was paralleled by the acceptance of many elements of his argument, most notably the notion of a violent struggle for existence.

After the Civil War, social Darwinism became a powerful ally of white supremacy among a wide spectrum of influential Americans, from museum curators and Yale professors to Congregational ministers and evangelical Christians. Inspired by the English philosopher Herbert Spencer, who coined the phrase "survival of the fittest," American scientists and industrialists further developed the analogy between the extinction of prehistoric animals and the extermination of the so-called inferior races in the age of corporations and overseas expansion. By the beginning of the twentieth century, scientific racialism had acquired new respectability in America, as paleontologists, financed by wealthy magnates like J. P. Morgan and Andrew Carnegie, made the dinosaurs symbols of dominance for the white race and the new ruling species of prehistoric nature. Despite the uproar over Darwin's materialistic assumptions, his theory of natural selection actually gave new scientific authority to the myth of wild nature—the doctrine that had given birth to the American monster.

The dinosaurs made their first public appearance in England in 1854 at the famous Crystal Palace Park, where Queen Victoria's scientifically minded husband Prince Albert decided to place models of prehistoric animals in the public gardens surrounding the palace. Under the supervision of Richard Owen, the country's leading paleontologist, the British sculptor and artist Benjamin Waterhouse Hawkins was hired to construct the life-size models of the dinosaurs out of bricks, iron columns and hoops, tiles, and concrete, all painted in colors to simulate the living creatures. Derived from pictorial representations of the saurian species, Gideon Mantell's *Iguanodon* and *Hylaeosaurus* were among the giant lizards appearing on islands in artificial tidal pools amidst the fountains and waterfalls of the Italian gardens (figure 54). To inaugurate the exhibition, Waterhouse Hawkins invited London's leading scientists to dine with him on New Year's Eve 1853, inside the huge model of the *Iguanodon*, an idea inspired by Charles Willson Peale's much publicized "Mammoth Feast" fifty years earlier.

Paleontologists today often view the Crystal Palace Park exhibition as the exclusive realm of the dinosaurs, a kind of coronation for the new ruling species in prehistoric nature. In fact, when he first began work on the project, the mastodon was uppermost in Waterhouse Hawkins's mind: "In the first week of September, 1852, I entered upon my engagement to make [a] mastodon, or any other models of the extinct animals that I might find most practicable," he later told an audience at London's Society of the Arts.[1] A bird's-eye view of the Crystal Palace Park grounds in a contemporary painting shows the mastodon and mammoths as far larger in size than the dinosaurs located on a nearby island.[2] Even though the map in Richard Owen's guidebook for the Crystal Palace exhibition shows several extinct mammals standing on the separate island, his text mentions only the fossil reptiles. Evidently, the mastodon and mammoth models were never actually constructed, although an "Irish elk" and a few other mammals eventually appeared on the island with the saurians.

In London, the dinosaurs' triumph over the mastodon was complete when the prehistoric landscape at Crystal Palace enshrined a new ruling species. Forty thousand people attended Queen Victoria's opening of the grounds in June 1854, celebrating not only Britain's aspirations to empire, but also the domestication of these wild creatures from

FIGURE 54. Engraving from the *Illustrated London News* (1853) of the first life-size dinosaur models in the studio of the artist Benjamin Waterhouse Hawkins, 1853. Created for the grounds around London's Crystal Palace Park, these sculptures helped popularize the notion that prehistoric nature was dominated by monstrous carnivores.

the pre-Adamite world: "In the context of the imperial celebration that characterized the Crystal Palace exhibits as a whole," according to Martin J. S. Rudwick, "the scientific reconstruction of that alien realm was as much an expression of successful *conquest* as the caging of fierce exotic beasts in the zoo in Regent's Park."[3]

The publication of Charles Darwin's *Origin of Species* five years later opened the modern era of conflict between scientific truth and revealed religion by pitting his doctrine of natural selection against the traditional Christian idea of God's creation of all nature. From the point of view of the American monster and the paradigm of dominance, Darwin's theory of evolution gave new life to the violent view of prehistoric nature by providing scientific authority for the metaphor of warring species: "From the war of nature, from famine and death, the most exalted object which we are capable of conceiving, namely, the production of the higher animals, directly follows."[4] Even though he used the term sparingly, Darwin employed a brutal metaphor that had underpinned the notion of the "struggle for existence" in political philosophy ever since Thomas Hobbes first popularized the idea in seventeenth-century England.

In the late eighteenth century, England's Industrial Revolution witnessed the incorporation of similar ideas in Adam Smith's theory of economic competition and Thomas Robert Malthus's *Essay on Population*, which argued that population growth must eventually outrun the supply of food and lead to an intense competition for natural resources. Darwin himself claimed that Malthus's essay had first given him the idea of natural selection as an evolutionary factor. In *Origin of Species*, he warned that the struggle for existence should be understood only in a "metaphorical sense," but this was precisely the realm in which its influence was most pernicious. In effect, the doctrine of warring species greatly reinforced the myth of wild nature in scientific thought and popular culture.[5]

The dinosaurs did not appear in America until shortly before the Civil War, when Joseph Leidy, a professor of anatomy at the University of Pennsylvania, obtained the nearly complete skeleton of an enormous fossil reptile found during the summer of 1858 on a New Jersey farm. At age thirty-five, Leidy was already the nation's leading comparative anatomist, having published descriptions of several unusual teeth found in Cretaceous rocks near the Missouri River, which he considered to be "lizard-like." In December 1858, when his description of the New Jersey skeleton was published, Leidy named the creature *Hadrosaurus*, or duck-billed dinosaur, which he felt was related in a general way to the *Iguanodon*. However, working with the first dinosaur anywhere to be described from a nearly complete skeleton, Leidy gave the creature an entirely different posture than that of the clumsy, elephant-like fossil reptiles imagined by British anatomists: "The great disproportion of size between the fore and back parts of the skeleton of *Hadrosaurus*, leads me to suspect that this great extinct herbivorous animal may have been in the habit of browsing, sustaining itself, kangaroo-like, in an erect position on its back extremities and tail."[6]

In 1858, Edward Hitchcock, now the president of Amherst College, finally published his *Ichnology of New England*, on the fossil foot marks of the Connecticut River valley, which some naturalists now suspected belonged to the saurian species. The frontispiece of his detailed monograph showed a New England couple in a carriage blithely passing by the "Moody Foot Mark Quarry" in South Hadley, Massachusetts, where the first tracks had been found by Pliny Moody more than a half-century earlier (figure 55). Even though he now considered a wide range of extinct creatures as candidates for the foot marks, including several saurians whose remains were found in the red sandstone elsewhere, Hitchcock was still convinced that the giant footprints belonged to large birds. The remoteness of dinosaurs from his thoughts was evident in his conclusions about the religious significance of the tracks:

> We are apt to speak of these ancient races as monstrous, so unlike existing organisms as to belong to another and quite different system of life. But they were only wise and benevolent adaptations to the changing conditions of our globe. One common type runs through all the present and past systems of life, modified only to meet exigencies, and identifying the same infinitely wise and benevolent Being as the Author of all.[7]

In his *Travels in America*, Charles Lyell, a devout Christian himself, remarked on the way that religious beliefs in America inhibited discussion of his new geological theories. Under the heading "Prejudices Opposed to the Reception of Geological Truths," he lamented, the lack of free expression in Pennsylvania, which nonetheless did have a free press, widely extended suffrage, and religious toleration:

FIGURE 55. The "Moody Foot Mark Quarry, South Hadley, Massachusetts," from Edward Hitchcock's *Ichnology of New England*, 1855. Originally discovered by a farmer a half-century earlier, these footprints were believed to be the tracks of large birds referred to as "Noah's Ravens" by local inhabitants.

"Yet all this machinery is not capable, as we have seen, of securing even so much of intellectual freedom as shall enable a student of nature to discuss freely the philosophical questions which the progress of science brings naturally before him."[8] The publication of Darwin's *Origin of Species* further underscored this current of hostility toward the geological sciences, rupturing definitively the bond between scientific truths and revealed religion in the eyes of many Americans. Among many evangelical Christians, extinct species now came to symbolize the atheistic ideas of modern science threatening the doctrine of divine design in God's nature.

Immediately after the Civil War, Nathaniel Southgate Shaler, a native of Newport, Kentucky, and a newly appointed professor of paleontology at Harvard, came to Big Bone Lick to undertake excavations aimed at determining more precisely the order of succession of the extinct species found there. Evidently, the lick was not quite exhausted, for in addition to his own collecting, a wagon load of mammoth bones was discovered during excavations by workmen improving the facilities for barreling the saline waters. Unlike the past, when the American monster's bones were highly prized trophies, these discoveries were now looked at skeptically by local inhabitants. Later, when Shaler became dean of the Lawrence Scientific School at Harvard University, he told the story of an old man who sat on the periphery of his excavations every day until the workmen finally uncovered the bones of a fossil elephant. At that moment, the old man stood up and exclaimed with disgust, "That knocks Moses!" and walked away, never to be seen again at the site.[9]

Similar sentiments surfaced about this time in a strange incident in New York City, where plans for the erection of a Paleozoic museum in Central Park were disrupted by thugs hired by "Boss" Tweed's political machine.[10] Shortly after the Civil War, Benjamin Waterhouse Hawkins, the British sculptor responsible for the first life-size models of the dinosaurs at Crystal Palace Park, moved to New York to pursue his artistic career. In early May 1868, he was asked by the commissioners of Central Park to create a pavilion to exhibit the "original forms of life inhabiting the great Continent of America." Hawkins immediately accepted the project, revealing in his letter of acceptance the popular appeal of such exhibitions in England: "The interest in the remains of ancient animal life which Geology has revealed in the last century is world wide, and almost romantic in its influence upon the imagination," he wrote, unaware that his prehistoric monsters would be unwelcome in America.[11]

In their annual report outlining the proposed Paleozoic museum, the commissioners confirmed Hawkins's opinion about the romantic vistas opened up by the discovery of prehistoric nature:

> Only in very recent times, which men still remember, was the discovery made that the earth has had a vast antiquity; that it has teemed with life for countless ages, and that generations of the most gigantic and extraordinary creatures lived through long geological periods, and were succeeded by other kinds of creatures equally colossal and equally strange.[12]

Without naming the new generation of monsters, the commissioners clearly had in mind passing the torch from the mastodon and the mammoth to the saurians: "Huge fishes, enormous birds, monstrous reptiles, and ponderous uncouth mammals had possession of a world, in which man, if there, had not yet established a record of his preeminence."[13]

Sketches for the proposed museum indicate that the tableau of prehistoric life was to be located in a large interior space constructed of cast-iron arches covered by an immense Victorian arbor, with gallery walks at two levels along each side of a rocky island where the restorations of prehistoric animals were displayed (figure 56). At one end of the tableau were the dinosaurs—dominated by the huge, upright figure of Joseph Leidy's *Hadrosaurus* fending off a smaller saurian reptile whose long snout and menacing teeth introduced into the scene the drama of warring species. Behind the *Hadrosaurus* were two *Laelaps*, newly discovered carnivorous dinosaurs, which Leidy's student Edward Drinker Cope had recently discovered in the Cretaceous beds of nearby New Jersey. Near the *Laelaps*, which were devouring another victim, appears the long neck of *Elasmosaurus*, a forty-foot-long marine reptile sent to the Philadelphia Academy of Sciences from Kansas.

Hawkins's drawing of his tableau depicts the eclipsing of the mastodon by the dinosaurs. The American monster, with its trunk uplifted, appears forlornly in the background, upstaged by the immense, kangaroo-like figure of *Hadrosaurus*, turning its hind side to the former rulers of the antediluvian world. Among the other mammals are two giant sloths, the Megatherium and the Megalonyx, and a pair of *Gliptodonts*, armadillo-like creatures, scuttle toward an unidentified Ice

FIGURE 56. Sketch by Benjamin Waterhouse Hawkins of the proposed Paleozoic museum in New York's Central Park, 1868. Pictured in the foreground
are several *Hadrosaurus*, or duck-billed dinosaurs, and *Laelaps*, forerunners of
the carnivorous monsters that were to replace the mastodon as the rulers of
prehistoric nature in the twentieth century. Detail from photograph, courtesy
Department of Library Services, American Museum of Natural History.

Age carnivore near the railing in the foreground. Drawn to scale, the
lithograph shows the intimidating size of the new saurian monsters,
which tower over the spectators viewing the prehistoric scene from behind a railing.

For nearly two years, while ground was being broken for the museum's foundation in the southwest corner of Central Park opposite
63rd Street, Hawkins worked in a makeshift studio creating life-size
models of these prehistoric monsters. In the spring of 1870, goaded by
Tammany Hall politicians, the New York State legislature approved a
new city charter and established a department of public works that took
over the functions of the old park commission. For several years,
William Marcy Tweed, better known as "Boss" Tweed, had been ma-
neuvering to take control of the city government, and he finally succeeded in putting his right-hand man Peter "Brains" Sweeny in control

of the park. In the first report of the Tweed commissioners, Sweeny referred to the prehistoric creatures as "specimens of animals alleged to be of the pre-Adamite period," hinting at the undercurrent of antipathy toward the geological sciences. Estimating the final cost of the Paleozoic museum at $300,000, the commissioners declared this was "too great a sum to expend upon a building devoted to paleontology—a science which, however interesting, is yet so imperfectly known as not to justify so great a public expense for illustrating it."[14]

Waterhouse Hawkins continued to work on his models until December when the Tweed commissioners informed him his services would no longer be needed. In the spring of 1871, Commissioner Henry Hilton, a former New York judge and loyal Tweed supporter, arrived at the artist's temporary studio in Central Park with a gang of laborers who proceeded to destroy with sledgehammers the artist's life-size restorations, sketch models, and molds. Under orders from Tweed to cart away the broken fragments for burial at an undisclosed site, Hilton told Hawkins that "he should not bother himself about dead animals, when there were so many living ones to care for."[15]

As Ruth Elson's survey of nineteenth-century American schoolbooks shows, Darwin's *Origin of Species* came as a shock to many Americans accustomed to the biblical story that God created the natural world for the dominion of man. "Schoolbooks before the Civil War accept without question the biblical history of the world and the creation of man. The Garden of Eden and its inhabitants are as real as the Appalachians."[16] However, the fundamental assumption inhibiting acceptance of Darwinian evolution was the common belief that man was the central object of God's creation and that the natural world existed solely to serve his needs. Contradictions between the new science and literal interpretations of the Bible, like the age of the earth or the existence of extinct species, were incidental problems compared with the threat posed by Darwinism to the idea of man's dominion over the natural world.

With the rising hostility toward Darwin's ideas and the emergence of the dinosaurs, the mastodon drifted into obscurity, becoming a neglected scientific specimen rather than a national symbol. In the summer of 1848, with Peale's Philadelphia Museum on the brink of bankruptcy, the mastodon skeleton was sent to Europe by speculators to be auctioned off to the highest bidders. King Louis Philippe of France tried to buy the skeleton for the Jardin des plantes but was thwarted when he

FIGURE 57. Peale's mastodon skeleton. Hessisches Landesmuseum, Darmstadt, Germany.

was forced to flee the country after his monarchy was overthrown by
revolutionaries. A few years later, the skeleton was acquired by a museum in Darmstadt, Germany, where an archival report of the acquisition referred to the monster's carnivorous past: "In the Grand-ducal
Museum there is set up the skeleton of a prehistoric animal, known
under the name of Ohio-animal or flesh eating elephant, and named
the *Mastodon* by naturalists."[17] In 1852, when John Warren published
his monograph *The Mastodon Giganteus of North America*, he simply
noted that the Peale skeleton had disappeared several years earlier
without any authentic account of its whereabouts. Meanwhile, Warren's own magnificent mastodon skeleton had retreated into the shadows of the scientific world, being kept as a prize anatomical specimen
in a small exhibition room at Harvard until its sale to J. P. Morgan more
than a half-century later.

After the Civil War, construction of the transcontinental railroads
led to several discoveries of dinosaur bones in the foothills of the Rocky

Mountains. The dinosaur rush there triggered a widely publicized rivalry between the country's two leading paleontologists, Edward Drinker Cope of Philadelphia and Othniel Charles Marsh of Yale's Peabody Museum of Natural History. As a young boy, Cope's interest in prehistoric creatures had been kindled by Dr. Albert Koch's infamous sea serpent Hydrarchos. In the ensuing rivalry, Marsh pictured his enormous new dinosaurs as sluggish, small-brained swamp dwellers, whereas Cope represented the smaller *Laelaps* as nimble, bipedal creatures, portrayed in illustrations as sprightly kangaroo-like carnivores. Publicity surrounding these new discoveries and the all-out war between these two paleontologists filled the newspapers, creating a new public awareness of these prehistoric monsters.

In the age of the robber barons, the excavation of dinosaur bones became a largely western enterprise financed by wealthy tycoons while rival paleontologists competed to see who could excavate the largest skeleton. Initially, Marsh's *Brontosaurus* reigned supreme in the American public's newly awakened awareness of prehistoric monsters, but by the end of the century, the Pittsburgh steel magnate Andrew Carnegie's team of paleontologists had excavated the world's largest skeleton, the *Diplodocus*, which became widely known worldwide thanks to the paintings and plaster replicas that he commissioned of the gigantic creature. In 1905, an immense replica of Carnegie's long-necked herbivore was unveiled at the Natural History Museum in London, marking the triumph of America's prehistoric life over England's paleontological specimens.

Not until the 1890s, when the young paleontologist Henry Fairfield Osborn brought the dinosaurs back to life at the American Museum of Natural History with his mountings of the great saurian skeletons from the Far West were these prehistoric monsters truly resurrected in America as symbols of dominance. In 1906, the financier J. P. Morgan paid $30,000 for the famous "Warren Mastodon," which he donated to the American Museum, but by then the American monster was no longer the ruling species in prehistoric nature. In this same year, with financing from J. P. Morgan, Osborn put the skeleton of *Tyrannosaurus rex* on display at the museum, inaugurating the reign of a new race of monstrous carnivores whose massive jaws were destined to symbolize the savagery of prehistoric nature and the paradigm of dominance in corporate America.

Even though the mastodon had slipped into the shadows of the museum world, the symbolism of the savagery of prehistoric nature and its concomitant belief in the racial superiority of white America was reborn with a new virulence in the early twentieth century. Once again the concept of extinct species was applied to human societies as it had been in the heyday of the American monster. In 1923, when Osborn coauthored an article, "The Dawn Man," dealing with prehistoric humans, he pictured the continual warfare between the humanoid Cro-Magnons and the primitive Neanderthals in terms reminiscent of the early-nineteenth-century American views of the Indians' extinction: "It was a case always of the complete extermination of the weak by the strong. The law of the survival of the fittest is not a theory, but a fact."[18]

In the early twentieth century, scientific racialism gained new respectability in mainstream American culture as the idea of extinction came to signify again the natural superiority of the white race and the extermination of so-called weaker races. Like many of his colleagues at the American Museum, Osborn was an enthusiastic advocate of craniology and continued to use Petrus Camper's facial angle to explain the superior cranial capacity of the white race. He also used the savagery of prehistoric nature to buttress the social Darwinist idea that the so-called racially inferior people would disappear as inexorably as the Cro-Magnons had exterminated the Neanderthals. His colleague William King Gregory equated the projected disappearance of the Australian aborigines, whose cranial capacity was allegedly smaller than that of the white race, with the extinction of the Neanderthals: "The fate of such inferior peoples is sealed. They will be wiped out just as surely, though perhaps in a more humane and less primitive fashion, as the Cro-Magnon exterminated the Neanderthal."[19]

The modern pictorial stereotypes of the dinosaurs as monstrous predators who ruled a violent prehistoric world were created by Osborn's protégé, Charles R. Knight, a young illustrator at the American Museum of Natural History. His classic images of *Tyrannosaurus rex*, with its menacing jaws and daggerlike teeth, which were widely reproduced in museum murals and magazine illustrations, represented the archetypal image of the savagery of prehistoric nature for millions of Americans in the twentieth century.

Like the founding fathers, Knight also depicted the mammoth as a ferocious adversary of primitive man. In his children's book *Before the*

FIGURE 58. Illustration by Charles R. Knight from his children's book *Before the Dawn of History*, 1935, showing Neanderthal men attacking a mammoth. Knight's illustration originally appeared in Henry Fairfield Osborn's article "The Dawn Man," which used the savagery of prehistoric nature to support social Darwinist ideas about the racial superiority of the white race. Courtesy McGraw-Hill Companies.

Dawn of History, his illustration of the Neanderthals showed them attacking a woolly mammoth with stones, spears, and clubs (figure 58).

> Man, even in his primitive forms, seems always to have been a killer—perforce, it may be but certainly a destroyer of life whenever and wherever he could find it. The flesh of animals appealed to an always ravenous appetite, and to assuage these hunger pangs he even risked his life in encounters with huge creatures many times his own bulk.[20]

Knight's image originally appeared in the article by his mentor Henry Fairfield Osborn, "The Dawn Man," in which he used the savagery of prehistoric nature to confirm the social Darwinist ideas of racial superiority and survival of the fittest.

The popularity of *Jurassic Park* dinosaurs today demonstrates that the paradigm of dominance—the idea that prehistoric nature was ruled by ferocious carnivores—continues to have great currency in contemporary scientific literature and consumer culture. Thanks to a new generation of vicious robotic raptors and digital monsters spawned in Hollywood, nearly everyone believes the dinosaurs actually *ruled* the earth for 150 million years, even though this belief has no scientific basis. Moreover, television broadcasters, novelists, and paleontologists alike routinely describe the new breed of dinosaurs as the "ultimate killing machines," with undisguised admiration for their lethal jaws and teeth.[21] While no one can deny *Tyrannosaurus rex* was a ferocious carnivore, the mastodon's story demonstrates why we need to question the common assumption that monstrous predators ruled prehistoric nature.

Paleontologist Bob Bakker's controversial theories about the sleek, smart, warm-blooded killers like *Velociraptor* transformed dinosaurs into the nimble, fast-moving villains of Stephen Spielberg's slasher movies (figure 59). But Bakker's book *Dinosaur Heresies* employs the same metaphor of dominance associated earlier with the American masto-

FIGURE 59. Drawing by paleontologist Robert Bakker of the new breed of dinosaurs, nimble, warm-blooded carnivores like this *Deinonychus*, which emerged as a new icon of terror and dominance in the film *Jurassic Park*. Paleontologists today use the same metaphor of dominance first applied to prehistoric creatures by American naturalists who saw the mastodon as a ferocious carnivore that ruled the antediluvian world. Courtesy Peabody Museum of Natural History, Yale University.

don. In Bakker's own words, appropriately updated for consumers in the global market, "Dinosaurs spread their ecological hegemony across a worldwide empire, devoid of geographical limits. No corner of the Mesozoic world withstood colonization by the dinosaurs."[22]

Even for the less glamorous paleontologists who study unthreatening creatures like the Ice Age mammoths, the paradigm of dominance still forms a fundamental part of the prehistoric landscape, a sort of naturalistic element that is simply taken for granted. Paleontologist Peter Ward's provocative study of the mass extinction of the Ice Age mammals, *The Call of Distant Mammoths*, pictures the early mammals, who lived with the dinosaurs in the late Cretaceous period, as ratlike, nocturnal creatures that hid from the carnivores during the day: "And who could blame them, given the absolute dominance of the larger, more ferocious, and perhaps smarter dinosaurs?" he exclaims, turning dinosaurs into dictators with a single turn of phrase.[23] Although Ward himself is skeptical of the notion that mammals became the dominant land animals because they were superior life-forms, his summary of this older argument for the extinction of the dinosaurs reveals how thoroughly the old rhetoric still permeates the language of science: "The early mammals did not immediately take over the earth but had to serve rather lengthy apprenticeship to the then-incumbent terrestrial overlords, the dinosaurs. Eventually, however, quality prevailed, and the dinosaurs became obsolete."[24]

In today's global marketplace, "Empire and Extinction" still go hand in hand as American scientists and media personalities continue to popularize the paradigm of dominance in their portrayal of the dinosaurs as a ruling species. Yet when we look at the current dinosaur cult in historical perspective, the roots of this belief in a violent prehistoric nature clearly seem to lie in the fertile soil of European colonialism and American nationalism, specifically in the founding fathers' early efforts to create the nation's first prehistoric monster, the mastodon: "The American obsession with bones, especially with *big* fossil bones left by gigantic creatures, has a history going back to the founding fathers, and is woven inextricably into an emergent sense of national destiny from the beginning," declared W. J. T. Mitchell in his deconstruction of the dinosaurs.[25]

Beyond the political problem of maintaining American hegemony in an era of global markets lies a more disturbing scenario for advocates of the free enterprise system—the possible extinction of the myth of wild nature itself. As the mastodon's story reveals, this idea was an insidious concept originally promulgated to justify the European colonization of America. In the hands of the founding fathers, the myth of a wilderness frontier became an integral part of American nationalism, helping justify the violent conquest of the western territories and the extermination of the Indian peoples. Nineteenth-century apologists for corporate expansion used social Darwinist ideas to perpetuate the belief in the savagery of prehistoric nature and the extermination of so-called inferior races. Now the ecological crisis spawned by the globalization of commercial society threatens to destroy not only the wilderness but also the metaphor validating such unbridled exploitation of the natural world.

In many ways, the savagery of prehistoric nature today may be replacing the wild west as the symbol of violent nature in American culture. But whatever the logic behind the new mythology, the prospect of further destruction of the environment by industrial society poses a serious dilemma for the metaphor underpinning the American dream of individual freedom. How will the myth of wild nature, of warring species and violent competition, be perpetuated when the idea of nature itself has ceased to exist, when we can no longer contrast our affluent lifestyle with the savagery of the natural world?

Biologists today agree that we are experiencing an extinction event of unprecedented scale, analogous in many ways to what happened when the dinosaurs died out. Furthermore, mass extinction has become a real threat to industrial civilization, through either nuclear war or environmental degradation. For this reason, we are faced with the formidable task of creating new symbols of the natural world, of exorcising from the language of natural history the metaphor of war, which no activity in nature, not even the most frightening events in the food chain, remotely resembles. Even famine and disease, which provided the foundation for Darwin's evolutionary principle, do not create armies and weapons of mass destruction; only humans have acquired this capability. In fact, there is considerable evidence that war as conducted by humans is a profoundly artificial enterprise, an *unnatural* act, although numerous efforts are made every day to convince us that such aggressive behavior is part of human nature.

Living as we do in a society in which militaristic metaphors, from the "war on drugs" to the "war on poverty," are applied to all social problems, altering the paradigm of dominance will not be easy. In his remarkable study of violence in America, *On Killing*, Lieutenant Colonel David Grossman, a professional soldier and an expert on the psychology of war, shows that killing is so *unnatural* an act that American soldiers need to be subjected to sophisticated psychological conditioning to become killers.[26] Among the techniques the army uses to achieve this state of mind is desensitizing soldiers' innate inhibitions against killing—by getting them to laugh at violence and to praise aggressive behavior. In Grossman's opinion, American children are subjected to a similar process of conditioning by their exposure to violence in the media. The rage of *Tyrannosaurus rex* may seem remote from such training techniques, but the name of this American monster, "King of the Tyrant Lizards," should be warning enough of the subconscious symbolism at the heart of such fantasies of absolute power and brutality.

In our own vexing age of biotechnology and genetic engineering, our views of prehistoric nature are undergoing serious revision. Indeed, the manipulation of DNA means the concept of nature itself may be an endangered species as it becomes more difficult, if not impossible, to draw the line between so-called wild nature and human culture. Looked at positively, we are in the process of redefining what the word *nature* means to us.

Myth and metaphor are essential elements in any redefinition of our view of the natural world and social life—they are the mental constructs that need to be reinvented if we are to give cultural life to other values besides those of violent conquest. No amount of scientific truth can rectify a problem that lies mainly in the realm of mythology. Darwin's theory of natural selection gave powerful new meaning to the myth of wild nature, but its application in this sense depended on the widespread belief in the progress of nations from savagery to civilization—which entailed the dehumanization of the so-called primitive peoples and ancient cultures, if not of the past itself.

From the vantage point of cultures that still respect their ancestors, the natural world looks quite different: "It is absolutely impossible to conceive such a view of nature coming from, say, a Hopi in the American southwest," points out Donald Worster of Darwin's emphasis on the violent struggle for survival. "Nor could a Hindu, though living in a land that has known Malthusian conditions of scarcity for a very long time, have devised such a theory, not merely because he lacks the scientific training but because nothing in his religious, social, or personal values could lead him to such an outlook on nature."[27] Even the paintings of Cro-Magnon artists, a prehistoric people who might have feared being eaten by predators, portrayed the Ice Age elephants with reverence, drawing them on the walls of their caves illuminated by oil lamps, leaving us poignant evidence that the paradigm can be changed.

In the end, the most difficult challenge may be incorporating Darwin's ecological view of natural history—the interdependence of all forms of life—in a philosophy of nature purged of the ubiquitous metaphor of warring species. Living in a society in which violence is a way of life, in which so many citizens feel the need to arm themselves against unseen enemies, this will be difficult. The alternative is to become an extinct species ourselves, exterminated by either our exhaustion of the earth's resources or our incessant wars.

Imagine for a moment that nature is not wild—that the original state of all living beings consists of a natural system characterized by interdependence, in which conflict and competition exist but no species is dominant and war is a profoundly unnatural act. Look at *Tyrannosaurus rex* as a minority species, an isolated meat eater living precariously at the top of a pyramidal food chain inhabited by millions of other life-forms that are not subordinate species but living creatures, many of whom will outlive the so-called ruling species. In this spirit, perhaps we can now imagine the massive jaws of the mastodon eating twigs, branches, and leaves instead of deer and elk—and let the metaphorical monsters serve other purposes. The monster's maw can become a symbol of nature's omnipotence, not a fantasy creature symbolizing man's absolute power and dominion over nature. The myth of wild nature can be transformed into a metaphor of communality rather than the symbol of a savage natural realm separate from human history. In many ways, Darwin himself provided such a perspective by viewing humankind as part of a sublimely complex natural world. In other words, enjoy being part of nature, for a change, and look into the monster's jaws without fear. Enjoy being free from the human predators who prey on the anxiety and insecurity of individuals living in a society whose arrogance and egotism are an insult to the integrity of the natural world.

Notes

NOTES TO INTRODUCTION

1. Rembrandt Peale, *Disquisition on the Mammoth* (London: E. Lawrence, 1803), reprinted in Keir B. Sterling, ed., *Selected Works in Nineteenth-Century North American Paleontology* (New York: Arno Press, 1974), 222.

2. [Charles Willson Peale], "Skeleton of the Mammoth," broadside, Philadelphia [1801]. The original literary account of this Indian myth appeared in Mathew Carey's journal *American Museum* 8 (1790): 284.

3. "Squelette d'un jeune mammouth," plate VI, in Édouard de Montulé, *Travels in America, 1816–1817* (Bloomington: Indiana University Publications, 1950; orig. Paris, 1821), 28.

4. George Louis Leclerc, comte de Buffon, *A Natural History. General and Particular* . . . , trans. William Smellie, 3rd ed., London, 1790, 5:129, cited by John C. Greene, *The Death of Adam* (Ames: Iowa State University Press, 1959), 150.

5. [American Museum], "Museum & Wax-Work, at the Exchange, New York," broadside, New York, 1793.

6. John Filson, *The Discovery, Settlement and present State of Kentucke* (New York: Corinth Books, 1962; orig. 1784), 36.

7. Thomas Jefferson to General George Rogers Clark, December 19, 1781, reprinted in Henry Fairfield Osborn, *Cope: Master Naturalist* (Princeton, NJ: Princeton University Press, 1931), 13.

8. Edward Taylor, "The Description of the Great Bones dug up at Claverack on the Banks of Hudson's River, A.D. 1705," reprinted in Donald E. Stanford, "The Giant Bones of Claverack, New York, 1705," *New York History* 40 (1959): 59–60.

9. Martin J. S. Rudwick, *Scenes from Deep Time* (Chicago: University of Chicago Press, 1992), 14.

NOTES TO CHAPTER 1

1. Lord Cornbury to the Royal Society, November 30, 1705, reprinted in C. R. Weld, *History of the Royal Society* (London: John W. Parker, 1848), 1:421.

See also Donald E. Stanford, "The Giant Bones of Claverack, New York, 1705," *New York History* 40 (1959): 48.

2. Weld, *Royal Society*, 421.

3. The text of Johannis Abeel's letter that Lord Cornbury enclosed to the Royal Society is reprinted in Weld, *Royal Society*, 422.

4. Ibid.

5. *Boston News-Letter*, July 30, 1705, reprinted in Stanford, "Bones of Claverack," 47.

6. Ibid.

7. Details from Robert Livingston's career are from Cynthia A. Kierner, *Traders and Gentlefolk* (Ithaca, NY: Cornell University Press, 1992); and Lawrence H. Leder, *Robert Livingston* (Chapel Hill: University of North Carolina Press, 1961).

8. Rev. Benjamin Wadsworth, "Wadsworth's Journal," *Massachusetts Historical Society Collections*, 4th ser., 31 (1852): 104.

9. Stanford, "Bones of Claverack," 52.

10. Diary entry dated June 1706, copied in 1760 by Edward Taylor's grandson Ezra Stiles. See Franklin B. Dexter, ed., *Extracts from the Itineraries and Other Miscellanies of Ezra Stiles* (New Haven, CT: Yale University Press, 1916), 82.

11. Details of Edward Taylor's life are from Karl Keller, *The Example of Edward Taylor* (Amherst: University of Massachusetts Press, 1975); and Norman Grabo, *Edward Taylor* (New York: Twayne, 1961).

12. William S. Simmons, *Spirit of the New England Tribes* (Hanover, NH: University Press of New England, 1986).

13. The full text of Taylor's poem is reprinted in Stanford, "Bones of Claverack," 56–61.

14. Ibid., 58.

15. Cotton Mather, *Magnalia Christi Americana*, 2:500–2, cited by Richard Slotkin, *Regeneration through Violence* (Middletown, CT: Wesleyan University Press, 1973), 155. For an analysis of Mather's literature of exorcism and the symbolism of Og, see Slotkin, *Regeneration*, 154–55.

16. Stanford, "Bones of Claverack," 59.

17. Ibid.

18. Dexter, *Extracts*, 82.

19. Ezra Stiles, Edward Taylor's grandson, heard the details of these Indian stories from his Uncle Eldad Taylor many years later and made note of them in 1760. See Dexter, *Extracts*, 82; and Stanford, "Bones of Claverack," 53.

20. Stanford, "Bones of Claverack," 60.

21. Keller, *Edward Taylor*, 87.

22. Richard Ruland and Malcolm Bradbury, *From Puritanism to Postmodernism* (New York: Penguin Books, 1991), 26.

23. Joseph Dudley to Cotton Mather, July 10, 1706, reprinted in Stanford, "Bones of Claverack," 49–50.

24. Details of Mather's relations with Governor Joseph Dudley are from Kenneth Silverman, *The Life and Times of Cotton Mather* (New York: Harper & Row, 1984), 193–226.

25. See Otho T. Beall Jr., "Cotton Mather's Early 'Curiosa Americana' and the Boston Philosophical Society of 1683," *William and Mary Quarterly*, 3rd ser., 18 (1961): 360–72.

26. Thomas Sprat, *History of the Royal Society* (St. Louis: Washington University Studies, 1958), xix.

27. Ibid., 394.

28. See James R. Jacob, "Newtonian Theology and the Defense of the Glorious Revolution," in Robert P. Maccubbin and Martha Hamilton-Phillips, eds., *The Age of William III & Mary II* (Williamsburg, VA: College of William and Mary, 1989): 161–64.

29. Silverman, *Life and Times*, 243.

30. Ibid., 168.

31. The full text of Mather's letter to the Royal Society is reprinted in David Levin, "Giants in the Earth: Science and the Occult in Cotton Mather's Letters to the Royal Society," *William and Mary Quarterly* 3rd ser., 45 (1988): 762.

32. Ibid., 767.

33. Ibid.

34. Ibid., 768.

35. Ibid., 762.

36. Ibid., 767.

37. Had Mather read Bernal Diaz del Castillo's account of Cortez's conquest of the Aztecs, he would surely have mentioned the gigantic bones shown to the Spaniards in September 1519 by the chiefs of the high mountain city-state of Tlaxcala, en route to the Aztec capital of Tenochtitlan. "And in order that we might judge the bulk of these people, they brought us a bone which had belonged to one of them, so large, that when they placed it upright it was as high as a middling sized man," Diaz wrote. "It was the bone between the knee and the hip; I stood by it, and was of my height, though I am as tall as the generality of men." Bernal Diaz del Castillo, *The True History of the Conquest of Mexico* (New York: Robert M. McBride & Co., 1927 [orig. 1568]), 143.

38. Levin, "Giants in the Earth," 768.

39. Ibid., 764.

40. Cotton Mather to Dr. John Woodward, July 3, 1716, cited by Otho T Beall Jr. and Richard H. Shryock, *Cotton Mather: The First Significant Figure in American Medicine* (Baltimore: Johns Hopkins University Press, 1954), 48.

41. Levin, "Giants in the Earth," 769.

42. Silverman, *Life and Times*, 210.

43. Quotation from Cotton Mather's diary, July 1711, cited by Josephine K. Piercy, ed., introduction to *The Christian Philosopher*, by Cotton Mather (Gainesville, FL: Scholar's Facsimiles & Reprints, 1988 [orig. 1721]), v.

44. Ibid.

45. Levin, "Giants in the Earth," 761.

46. Ibid., 765–66.

47. Ibid., 755.

48. Pershing Vartanian, "Cotton Mather and the Puritan Transition into the Enlightenment," *Early American Literature* 7 (1973): 222.

NOTES TO CHAPTER 2

1. John C. Greene, *The Death of Adam* (Ames: Iowa State University Press), 128.

2. Nehemiah Grew's drawing of the grinder is reproduced in W. N. Edwards, *The Early History of Palaeontology* (London: British Museum of Natural History, 1967), 50.

3. William Somner, *Chartham News*, in *The Antiquities of Canterbury* (Wakefield, England: EP Publishing, 1977 [orig. 1703]), 186. Somner's pamphlet was originally published in 1669.

4. Ibid., 187.

5. Richard Waller, *The Posthumous Works of Robert Hooke* (London: Sam Smith and Benj. Walford, 1705; facsimile reprint, New York: Johnson Reprint, 1969), 439.

6. John Luffkin, "Part of a Letter from Mr. John Luffkin to the Publisher, concerning some large Bones lately found in a Gravel-pit near Colchester," *Philosophical Transactions* 22 (1701): 924–25.

7. Waller, *Posthumous Works*, 290.

8. Ibid., 291.

9. Ibid., 450.

10. Carolyn Merchant, *The Death of Nature* (San Francisco: Harper & Row, 1980), 170–71.

11. Waller, *Posthumous Works*, 335.

12. Thomas Burnet, *The [Sacred] Theory of the Earth* (London: R. Norton, 1684), 1:140.

13. Ibid., 1:196.

14. Ibid., 1:140.

15. From the 1726 edition of Burnet's *Sacred Theory*, cited by Marjorie Hope Nicolson, *Mountain Gloom and Mountain Glory* (Ithaca, NY: Cornell University Press, 1959), 198.

16. Ibid., 197.

17. Burnet, *Sacred Theory*, I:dedication, n.p.
18. Ibid., 96.
19. Ibid., 110.
20. This point is developed in M. C. Jacob and W. A. Lockwood's "Political Millenarianism and Burnet's *Sacred Theory*," *Science Studies* 2 (1972): 265–79; see also Martin J. S. Rudwick, *The Meaning of Fossils* (New York: Science History Publications, 1976), 77–81; and Nicolson, *Mountain Gloom*.
21. Jacob and Lockwood, "Political Millenarianism," 274.
22. Burnet, *Sacred Theory*, 5.
23. See B. Sprague Allen, *Tides in English Taste* (Cambridge, MA: Harvard University Press, 1937), 1:161.
24. Basil Willey, *The Eighteenth Century Background* (Boston: Beacon Press, 1961), 232.
25. See Cotton Mather, *The Diary of Cotton Mather, D.D., F.R.S. for the Year 1712*, ed. William R. Manierre II (Charlottesville: University Press of Virginia, 1964), 93.
26. John Woodward, *An Essay toward a Natural History of the Earth: And Terrestrial Bodies, Especially Minerals* (London: R. Wilkin, 1695), 1.
27. Ibid., 6.
28. Ibid., 258.
29. Ibid., 15, 17.
30. Ibid., foreword, n.p.
31. Ibid., 83.
32. Ibid., 147.
33. Ibid., 248.
34. From the 1723 edition of Woodward's *Essay*, 49, cited by Greene, *Death of Adam*, 53.
35. Woodward, *Essay*, 95.
36. Ibid., 30.
37. For an interesting discussion of this equation of fossils with archaeological remains, see Martin J. S. Rudwick, "The Shape and Meaning of Earth History," in David C. Lindberg and Ronald L. Numbers, eds., *God and Nature* (Berkeley and Los Angeles: University of California Press, 1986): 296–321.
38. See Rudwick, *Meaning of Fossils*, 87.
39. Cited by Martin J. S. Rudwick, *Scenes from Deep Time* (Chicago: University of Chicago Press, 1992), 14.
40. Ibid., 6.
41. Ibid., 14–16.
42. Rudwick, *Meaning of Fossils*, 69.
43. Bernard McGrane, *Beyond Anthropology* (New York: Columbia University Press, 1989), 62.

44. Ernest Lee Tuveson, *The Redeemer Nation: The Idea of America's Millennial Role* (Chicago: University of Chicago Press, 1968), 17.

NOTES TO CHAPTER 3

1. "An extract of several letters from Cotton Mather, D.D., to John Woodward, M.D., and Richard Waller, Esq., "*Philosophical Transactions* 29 (1714): 63.

2. Ibid.

3. Francis Nevile, "A Letter of Mr. Francis Nevile to the Right Reverend St. George Lord Bishop of Clogher, R.S.S.," *Philosophical Transactions* 29 (1715): 369.

4. Thomas Molyneux, "Remarks upon aforesaid Letter and Teeth, by Thomas Molyneux, M.D. and R.S.S. Physician to the State in Ireland: Addres'd to his Grace the Lord Archbishop of Dublin," *Philosophical Transactions* 29 (1715): 371.

5. Ibid., 374.

6. Ibid., 377.

7. Ibid., 378.

8. Ibid., 382.

9. Thomas Molyneux, "An Essay concerning Giants," *Philosophical Transactions* 22 (1700–1): 489.

10. Molyneux, "Remarks," 380.

11. Ibid.

12. Henry H. Howorth, *The Mammoth and the Flood* (London: Sampson, Low, Marston, Searle and Rivington, 1887), 78.

13. Robert Silverberg, *Mammoths, Mastodons and Man* (New York: McGraw-Hill, 1970), 27.

14. Howorth, *Mammoth*, 2.

15. Richard Waller, *The Posthumous Works of Robert Hooke* (London: Sam Smith and Benj. Walford, 1705; facsimile reprint, New York: Johnson Reprint Corp., 1969), 439.

16. In 1697, Ides's personal secretary Adam Brand published an account of Ides's travels that was translated into English the following year. English translations of Ides's own *Travels* first appeared in 1706 and subsequently became quite popular in Europe during the first half of the eighteenth century.

17. Howorth, *Mammoth*, 73.

18. Ibid., 74.

19. Johann Bernard Müller, "The Manners and Customs of the Ostiacks," in [Friedrich Christian Weber], *The Present State of Russia*, 2 vols. (London: W. Taylor, 1722–23; facsimile reprint, London, 1968), 2:50.

20. Ibid., 2:51.
21. Ibid.
22. Ibid., 2:52.
23. Ibid.
24. Ibid., 2:50.
25. Ibid., 2:51.
26. Laurence Lange, "Journal of Laurence Lange's Travels to China," in [Weber], *Present State of Russia*, 2:15.
27. Lange, "Travels to China," 2:16.
28. Howorth, *Mammoth*, 50; see Bell's *Travels*, 1783 ed., 2:195.
29. Sir Hans Sloane, "An Account of Elephants Teeth and Bones Found under Ground," *Philosophical Transactions* 35 (1728): 464.
30. For details, see Sir Hans Sloane, "Of Fossil Teeth and Bones of Elephants, Part the Second," *Philosophical Transactions* 35 (1728): 505.
31. George Lyman Kittredge, "Cotton Mather's Scientific Communications to the Royal Society," *Proceedings of the American Antiquarian Society* 26 (1916): 22–23.
32. Sloane, "Fossil Teeth," 512.
33. Ibid., 497.
34. Ibid., 498.
35. John P. Breyne, "A Letter from John Phil. Breyne, M.D.F.R.S. to Sir Hans Sloane, Bart. Pres. R.S. with Observations and a Description of some Mammoth's Bones dug up in Siberia, proving them to have belonged to Elephants," *Philosophical Transactions* 40 (1737): 127.
36. Ibid., 128.
37. Ibid., 129.
38. Ibid.
39. Ibid.
40. Ibid., 138.
41. Ibid., 137.

NOTES TO CHAPTER 4

1. Mark Catesby, *The Natural History of Carolina, Florida, and the Bahamas Islands* (London, 1743), vol. 2, preface, vi–vii, cited by William Martin Smallwood, *Natural History and the American Mind* (New York: Columbia University Press, 1941), 26.
2. Catesby, *Natural History*, app., vii; cited by George Gaylord Simpson, "The Beginnings of Vertebrate Paleontology in North America," *Proceedings of the American Philosophical Society* 86 (1942): 134.
3. Ibid.
4. For details on the natural history circle, see Brooke Hindle, *The Pursuit*

of Science in Revolutionary America, 1735–1789 (Chapel Hill: University of North Carolina Press, 1956), 20 ff.

5. Peter Kalm, *Travels in North America,* 2d ed. (London: T. Lowndes, 1772), 75.

6. John Bartram to Peter Collinson, September 20, 1751, in Edmund Berkeley and Dorothy Smith Berkeley, eds., *The Correspondence of John Bartram, 1734–1777* (Gainesville: University Press of Florida, 1992), 335.

7. Ibid., 334.

8. Ronald W. Clark, *Benjamin Franklin: A Biography* (New York: Random House, 1983), 93.

9. Ibid., 93–94.

10. William M. Darlington, ed., *Christopher Gist's Journals* (Pittsburgh: J. R. Weldin & Co., 1893), 56.

11. Ibid., 57.

12. Michael N. McConnell, *A Country Between: The Upper Ohio Valley and Its Peoples, 1724–1774* (Lincoln: University of Nebraska Press, 1992), 90.

13. Darlington, *Gist's Journal,* 58.

14. Gist's journal of 1750 was not made public until 1776, when Governor [Thomas] Pownall published it in London as an appendix to his "Topographical Description of North America," and even then, few copies of that work seem to have found their way to America.

15. Ezra Stiles to Thomas Jefferson, Yale College, June 21, 1784, in Julian Boyd, ed., *The Papers of Thomas Jefferson* (Princeton, NJ: Princeton University Press, 1953), 7:314–15.

16. Roberta Ingles Steele and Andrew Lewis Ingles, eds., *Escape from Indian Captivity: The Story of Mary Draper Ingles and Her Son Thomas Ingles* (Radford, VA: Steele and Ingles, 1969), 12.

17. Henry Bouquet to Bartram, July 15, 1762, in Berkeley and Berkeley, *Correspondence,* 564.

18. James Wright to Bartram, August 22, 1762, in Berkeley and Berkeley, *Correspondence,* 568.

19. Ibid.

20. Ibid.

21. Ibid., 569.

22. Collinson to Bartram, June 11, 1762, in Berkeley and Berkeley, *Correspondence,* 563.

23. Collinson to Bartram, July 25, 1762, in Berkeley and Berkeley, *Correspondence,* 566.

24. Collinson to Bartram, December 10, 1762, in Berkeley and Berkeley, *Correspondence,* 581.

25. Bartram to Collinson, May 1, 1763, in Berkeley and Berkeley, *Correspondence*, 590.

26. Bartram to Collinson, May 10, 1764, in Berkeley and Berkeley, *Correspondence*, 629.

27. Nicholas B. Wainwright, *George Croghan: Wilderness Diplomat* (Chapel Hill: University of North Carolina Press, 1959), 206.

28. Ibid., 213.

29. [George Croghan], "Croghan's Journal; May 15–September 26, 1765," in Reuben Gold Thwaites, ed., *Early Western Travels, 1748–1846* (Cleveland: Arthur H. Clark, 1904), 132.

30. Wainwright, *Wilderness Diplomat*, 226.

31. Whitfield J. Bell Jr., "A Box of Old Bones: A Note on the Identification of the Mastodon, 1766–1806," *Proceedings of the American Philosophical Society* 93 (1949): 171.

32. Captain Harry Gordon, "Journey Down the Ohio in 1766," in Newton D. Mereness, ed., *Travels in the American Colonies* (New York: Macmillan, 1916), 466.

33. Bell, "A Box of Old Bones," 177.

34. Wainwright, *Wilderness Diplomat*, 239.

35. Croghan to Lord Shelburne, January 16, 1767, in Edward M. Kindle, "The Story of the Discovery of Big Bone Lick," *Kentucky Geological Survey*, ser. 6, no. 41 (1931): 201.

36. *Pennsylvania Chronicle*, October 19–26, 1767.

37. Ibid., October 26–November 2, 1767.

NOTES TO CHAPTER 5

1. Marguerite Duval, *The King's Garden*, trans. Annette Tomarken and Claudine Cowen (Charlottesville: University Press of Virginia, 1982), 67.

2. "Evolution," *Encyclopedia of the Social Sciences*, ed. Edwin R. A. Seligman (New York: Macmillan, 1931), 3:649.

3. Henry Fairfield Osborn, *Proboscidea* (New York: American Museum Press, 1936), 6.

4. Herbert Levanthal, *In the Shadow of the Enlightenment* (New York: New York University Press, 1976), 220.

5. Ibid., 221.

6. George Louis Leclerc de Buffon, *Histoire naturelle, générale et particulière* (Paris: Imprimerie royale, 1749), 1:12.

7. Ibid., 1:99.

8. Ibid., 1:612.

9. Jean Étienne Guettard, "Memoire dans lequel on compare le Canada à

la Suisse par rapport à ses minéraux," *Memoire de l'Academie royal des sciences,* Paris, 1752, 189–220; cited by George Gaylord Simpson, "The Beginnings of Vertebrate Paleontology in North America," *Proceedings of the American Philosophical Society* 86 (1942): 144.

10. Buffon, *Histoire naturelle*, 4:170.

11. Ibid., 6:61.

12. Ibid., 7:3–4.

13. This point is developed extensively by Jacques Roger in *Buffon: A Life in Natural History* (Ithaca, NY: Cornell University Press, 1997).

14. Buffon, *Histoire naturelle*, 7:5.

15. Ibid., 7:3.

16. Roger, *Buffon*, 337.

17. Arthur O. Lovejoy, *The Great Chain of Being* (Cambridge, MA: Harvard University Press, 1950), 220.

18. Ibid., 219.

19. Buffon, *Histoire naturelle*, 9:87.

20. Gilbert Chinard, "Eighteenth Century Theories of America As a Human Habitat," *Proceedings of the American Philosophical Society* 91 (February 1947): 31.

21. Buffon, *Histoire naturelle*, 9:104.

22. Ibid., 9:110–11.

23. Ibid., 9:110.

24. Chinard, "America As a Human Habitat," 32.

25. Buffon, *Histoire naturelle*, 9:126.

26. Ibid.

27. Ibid., 9:127.

28. Ibid., 9:126.

29. Ibid.

30. Buffon, *Histoire naturelle*, 11:10.

31. Ibid., 11:63.

32. Ibid., 11:86.

33. Ibid., 11:170.

34. Antonello Gerbi, *The Dispute of the New World* (Pittsburgh: University of Pittsburgh Press, 1973), 7.

35. Buffon, *Histoire naturelle*, 12:xiii.

36. Ibid.

37. Ibid.

38. S. Peter Dance, *The Art of Natural History* (Woodstock, NY: Overlook Press, 1978), 59.

39. Buffon, *Histoire naturelle*, 14:374.

40. Ibid.

41. John Lyon and Phillip R. Sloan, eds., *From Natural History to the*

History of Nature (Notre Dame, IN: University of Notre Dame Press, 1981), 3.

42. Collinson's letter to Buffon has not survived, but Buffon himself included a French translation of its text in *Histoire naturelle, supplement V,* "Des époques de la nature" (Paris: Imprimerie royale, 1778), 5:506.

NOTES TO CHAPTER 6

1. Benjamin Franklin to George Croghan, August 5, 1767, in Albert Henry Smythe, ed., *The Writings of Benjamin Franklin* (New York: Macmillan, 1905–7), 5:39.

2. Ibid., 5:40.

3. Peter Collinson to John Bartram, September 19, 1767, in Edmund Berkeley and Dorothy Smith Berkeley, eds., *The Correspondence of John Bartram* (Gainesville: University Press of Florida, 1992), 689.

4. Benjamin Franklin to William Franklin, August 28, 1767, in Leonard W. Labaree, ed., *The Papers of Benjamin Franklin* (New Haven, CT: Yale University Press, 1970), 14:242–43.

5. Peter Collinson, "An Account of some very large Fossil Teeth found in North America," *Philosophical Transactions* 57 (1767): 465.

6. Ibid., 466.

7. Peter Collinson, "Sequel to the foregoing Account of the large Fossil Teeth," *Philosophical Transactions* 57 (1767): 468.

8. Ibid., 469.

9. Ibid.

10. Benjamin Franklin to Abbé Chappe, January 31, 1768, in Smythe, *Writings*, 92–93.

11. William Hunter, "Observations on the Bones commonly supposed to be Elephants Bones, which have been found near the River Ohio in America," *Philosophical Transactions* 58 (1769): 36.

12. Ibid., 37.

13. Ibid.

14. Ibid.

15. Ibid., 38.

16. Ibid.

17. Ibid., 42.

18. Ibid.

19. Ibid., 37.

20. Ibid., 36.

21. Ibid., 45.

22. John Kobler, *The Reluctant Surgeon: A Biography of John Hunter* (Garden City, NY: Doubleday, 1960), 149.

23. Peter Collinson to John Bartram, May 17, 1768, in Berkeley and Berkeley, *Correspondence of John Bartram*, 701–2.

24. Details of George Stubbs's career are from Peter Fuller, "Variations on a Theme," *New Society* 70 (1984): 139–40.

25. W. D. Ian Rolfe, "William and John Hunter: Breaking the Great Chain of Being," in W. F. Bynum and Roy Porter, eds., *William Hunter and the Eighteenth-Century Medical World* (Cambridge: Cambridge University Press, 1985), 313–14.

26. Donald Worster, *Nature's Economy: A History of Ecological Ideas* (Cambridge: Cambridge University Press, 1977), 48.

27. Ibid.

28. Thomas Pennant, *Synopsis of Quadrupeds* (Chester, England: J. Monk, 1771), 91.

29. Ibid., 91–92.

30. Ibid., 92.

31. Ibid.

32. Oliver Goldsmith, introduction to *A New and Accurate System of Natural History*, by R. Brookes (London: Newberry, 1763–64), in Arthur Friedman, ed., *Collected Works of Oliver Goldsmith* (Oxford: Oxford University Press, 1966), 5:238.

33. Ibid., 5:246–47.

34. Ibid., 5:238.

35. Ibid., 5:238, 243.

36. Arthur O. Lovejoy, *The Great Chain of Being* (Cambridge, MA: Harvard University Press, 1950), 231.

37. Winifred Lynskey, "Goldsmith and the Chain of Being," *Journal of the History of Ideas* 6 (1945): 370.

38. Oliver Goldsmith, *An History of the Earth and Animated Nature* (London: J. Nourse, 1774), 4:283–84.

39. Ibid.

NOTES TO CHAPTER 7

1. Whitfield J. Bell Jr., *John Morgan: Continental Doctor* (Philadelphia: University of Pennsylvania Press, 1965), 178.

2. Willard Rouse Jillson, *Big Bone Lick* (Louisville: Standard Printing, 1936), 20–21.

3. Reuben Gold Thwaites and Louise Phelps Kellogg, *Documentary History of Dunmore's War: Thomas Hanson's Journal* (Madison: Wisconsin Historical Society, 1905), 121.

4. Jillson, *Big Bone Lick*, 77–78.

5. Nicholas Cresswell, *The Journal of Nicholas Cresswell, 1774–1777*, ed. Lincoln MacVeagh (New York: Dial Press, 1924), 44.

6. Ibid., 88.

7. Ibid.

8. Ibid., 88–89.

9. Ibid., 93.

10. Joseph J. Ellis, *After the Revolution* (New York: Norton, 1979), 19.

11. Ibid., 9.

12. Ibid., 12; see also Gilbert Chinard, "Eighteenth Century Theories of America as a Human Habitat," *Proceedings of the American Philosophical Society* 91 (1947): 37.

13. Ellis, *After the Revolution*, 12.

14. John Adams, Diary, October 14, p. 177, in *The Works of John Adams*, ed. Charles Francis Adams (Boston: Little Brown, 1850–66), 2:397; cited by Whitfield J. Bell Jr., "A Box of Old Bones: A Note on the Identification of the Mastodon," *Proceedings of the American Philosophical Society* 93 (1949): 171.

15. William Snow Miller, "Abraham Chovet: An Early Teacher of Anatomy in Philadelphia," *Anatomical Record* 5 (1911): 162.

16. John Adams to Abigail Adams, August 14, 1776, in L. H. Butterfield, ed., *Adams Family Correspondence* (Cambridge, MA: Harvard University Press, 1963), 2:96.

17. *Pierre Eugène Du Simitière: His American Museum 200 Years After*, catalog for an exhibition at the Library Company of Philadelphia, July–October 1985, item 10:8.

18. Ezra Stiles, Diary, August 25, 1777, in *The Literary Diary of Ezra Stiles*, ed. Franklin Bowditch Dexter (New York: Scribner, 1901), 2:201.

19. Ibid.

20. For details of Annan's excavation, see Robert Annan, "Account of a Skeleton of a large animal, found near Hudson's river," *Memoirs of the American Academy of Arts and Sciences* (Boston: Isaiah Thomas, 1793), 2:160–64.

21. George Washington to Lafayette, New Windsor, December 14, 1780, cited in Marquis de Chastellux, *Travels in North America* (Chapel Hill: University of North Carolina Press, 1963; orig. Paris, 1786), 1:339.

22. Chastellux, *Travels*, 1:189.

23. Ibid., 1:192.

24. Annan, "Account of a Skeleton," 2:164.

25. Stiles, Diary, February 17, 1781, in Dexter, *Literary Diary*, 2:511.

26. Ibid., 511–12.

27. Jillson, *Big Bone Lick*, 79–81.

28. Thomas Jefferson, *Notes on the State of Virginia* (New York: Norton, 1972; orig. 1787), 44.

29. Ibid., 45.
30. Ibid., 46–47.
31. Ibid., 47.
32. Ibid., 53.
33. Ibid., 53–54.
34. Ibid., 43.
35. Ibid., 54.
36. Ibid., 44.
37. Ibid.
38. Ibid., 45–46.
39. Samuel W. Thomas and Eugene H. Conner, "George Rogers Clark (1752–1818): Natural Scientist and Historian," *Filson Club History Quarterly* 41 (1967): 214. I am grateful to Donald Janzen for calling my attention to this indispensable article on Clark's role as a naturalist.
40. George Rogers Clark to Thomas Jefferson, February 20, 1782, cited in Thomas and Conner, "George Rogers Clark," 215.
41. Thomas Jefferson to George Rogers Clark, November 26, 1782, ibid., 215.

NOTES TO CHAPTER 8

1. François-Jean, marquis de Chastellux, *Travels in North America in the Years 1780, 1781, and 1782* (Chapel Hill: University of North Carolina Press, 1963), 145.
2. Joel J. Orosz, *Curators and Culture: The Museum Movement in America, 1740–1870* (Tuscaloosa: University of Alabama Press, 1990), 36.
3. Pierre Eugène Du Simitière to William Deming, October 8, 1781, cited by Paul Ginsberg Sifton, "Pierre Eugène Du Simitière (1737–1784): Collector in Revolutionary America" (Ph.D. diss., University of Pennsylvania, 1960), 277.
4. Hans Huth, "Pierre Eugène Du Simitière and the Beginnings of the American Historical Museum," *Pennsylvania Magazine of History and Biography* 69 (1945): 318.
5. Johann David Schoepf, *Travels in the Confederation [1783–1784]* (New York: Bergman Publishers, 1968; orig. German ed., 1788), 86.
6. Ibid., 268.
7. Ibid., 269.
8. Ibid.
9. Du Simitière to Stephen Payne Adye, May 28, 1783, cited by Sifton, "Du Simitière," 279.
10. Charles Coleman Sellers, *Charles Willson Peale* (New York: Scribner, 1969), 460.

11. Arthur Campbell to Thomas Jefferson, November 7, 1782, in Julian P. Boyd, ed., *The Papers of Thomas Jefferson* (Princeton, NJ: Princeton University Press, 1952), 6:201.

12. Arthur Campbell to Thomas Jefferson, November 29, 1782, in Boyd, *Papers*, 6:208.

13. Ibid.

14. Du Simitière to Isaac Melcher, January 17, 1784, cited by Sifton, "Du Simitière," 280.

15. Thomas Jefferson to Thomas Walker, September 25, 1783, in Boyd, *Papers*, 6:339–40.

16. Archibald Cary to Thomas Jefferson, October 12, 1783, in Boyd, *Papers*, 6:342–46.

17. Sellers, *Charles Willson Peale*, 204.

18. Samuel W. Thomas and Eugene H. Conner, "George Rogers Clark (1752–1818): Natural Scientist and Historian," *Filson Club Quarterly* 41 (1967): 217.

19. George Rogers Clark to Thomas Jefferson, February 8, 1783, cited by Thomas and Conner, "Clark," 218.

20. John Walton, *John Filson of Kentucke* (Lexington: University of Kentucky Press, 1956), 13–14.

21. John Filson, *The Discovery, Settlement and present State of Kentucke* (New York: Corinth Books, 1962; orig., 1784), 32.

22. Ibid., 34.

23. Ibid., 35–36.

24. Ibid., 36.

25. Ibid.

26. Ibid., 51–52.

27. Richard Slotkin, *Regeneration through Violence* (Middletown, CT: Wesleyan University Press, 1973), 279.

28. Ibid., 281.

29. William Carlos Williams, *In the American Grain* (New York: Albert & Charles Boni, 1925), 137.

30. Filson, *Kentucke*, 57–58.

31. Thomas Jefferson, *Notes on the State of Virginia* (New York: Norton, 1954; orig. 1784), 19.

32. Ibid.

33. Ezra Stiles, Diary, June 8, 1784, in *The Literary Diary of Ezra Stiles*, ed. Franklin Bowditch Dexter (New York: Scribner, 1901), 3:125.

34. Ibid., 126.

35. Franklin B. Dexter, ed., *Extracts from the Itineraries and Other Miscellanies of Ezra Stiles* (New Haven, CT: Yale University Press, 1916), 83.

36. Dexter, *Itineraries*, 83.

37. Ezra Stiles, Diary, February 17, 1781, in Dexter, *Literary Diary,* 2:511–12.

38. Thomas Jefferson to Ezra Stiles, Hartford, June 10, 1784, in Boyd, *Papers,* 7:304–5.

39. Ezra Stiles to Thomas Jefferson, June 21, 1784, in Boyd, *Papers,* 7:312.

40. Ezra Stiles, Diary, August 24, 1784, in Dexter, *Literary Diary,* 3:134.

41. Stiles, Diary, September 8, 1785, in Dexter, *Literary Diary,* 3:183.

42. Robert Annan, "Account of a Skeleton of a large animal, found near Hudson's river," *Memoirs of the American Academy of Arts & Sciences* 2 (1793): 162–63.

43. Ibid., 163.

44. Thomas Jefferson to Ezra Stiles, Paris, July 17, 1785, in Boyd, *Papers,* 8:299–300.

45. Ezra Stiles, Diary, April 26, 1786, in Dexter, *Literary Diary,* 3:214–16; see also Samuel Holden Parsons to Stiles, Middletown, Connecticut, April 27, 1786, an enclosure in Stiles letter to Jefferson, May 8, 1786, in Boyd, *Papers,* 9:477–78.

46. Samuel H. Parsons to Ezra Stiles, in Boyd, *Papers,* 9:477.

47. Ibid.

48. Stiles Diary, April 26, 1786, in Dexter, *Literary Diary,* 3:214–15.

49. Ibid., 215.

50. Parsons to Stiles, in Boyd, *Papers,* 9:477.

51. Ezra Stiles to Thomas Jefferson, May 8, 1786, in Boyd, *Papers,* 9:476.

52. Stiles, Diary, September 26, 1786, in Dexter, *Literary Diary,* 3:240.

NOTES TO CHAPTER 9

1. Thomas Jefferson, *Notes on the State of Virginia,* ed. William Peden (New York: Norton, 1954), 162.

2. Ibid., 163.3. Thomas Jefferson to James Madison, May 11, 1785, in Julian P. Boyd, ed., *The Papers of Thomas Jefferson* (Princeton, NJ: Princeton University Press, 1953), 8:147.

4. Thomas Jefferson to James Monroe, June 17, 1785, ibid., 8:229.

5. Thomas Jefferson to Chastellux, June 7, 1785, ibid., 8:184.

6. Jefferson, *Notes,* 63.

7. Ibid.

8. Ibid., 138.

9. Ibid., 143.

10. Ibid.

11. Ibid.

12. Ibid.

13. Ibid., 138.

14. Ibid.

15. Ibid.

16. In the fourteenth volume of his *Histoire naturelle*, published in 1766, Buffon turned his attention to the apes, including the orangutan, which he described as "an ape as tall and strong as a man, and equally ardent for woman as for its own females." See John C. Greene, *The Death of Adam* (Ames: Iowa State University Press, 1959), 181.

17. A. A. Lipscomb and A. E. Bergh, *The Writings of Thomas Jefferson* (Washington, DC: Thomas Jefferson Memorial Association, 1903), 4:449.

18. Thomas Jefferson to Hogendorp, October 13, 1785, in Boyd, *Papers*, 8:632.

19. Jefferson's own recollections of his days in Paris were noted by Daniel Webster during a visit to Monticello in 1824; see Paul Leicester Ford, *The Works of Thomas Jefferson* (New York: Putnam, 1905), 12:393.

20. Ibid.

21. For Jefferson's recollection of the anecdote, see *The Life and Selected Writings of Thomas Jefferson*, ed. Adrienne Koch and William Peden (New York: Modern Library, 1944), 176–80. Another version of the incident can be found in a letter from William Carmichael to Thomas Jefferson, October 15, 1787, in Boyd, *Papers*, 12:240–41.

22. Ford, *Works*, 12:393.

23. Thomas Jefferson to Archibald Cary, January 7, 1786, in Boyd, *Papers*, 9:158.

24. Thomas Jefferson to John Sullivan, January 7, 1786, in ibid., 9:160.

25. James Madison to Thomas Jefferson, November 15, 1785, in ibid., 9:38, received by Jefferson on January 16, 1786.

26. For details, see Thomas Jefferson to C. W. F. Dumas, February 2, 1786, in ibid., 9:243–44.

27. Rev. James Madison to Thomas Jefferson, March 27, 1786, in ibid., 9:357.

28. David Ramsay to Thomas Jefferson, in ibid., 9:441.

29. Ibid.

30. Rev. James Madison to Thomas Jefferson, December 28, 1786, in ibid., 10:644.

31. Thomas Jefferson to Buffon, October 1, 1787, in ibid., 12:194–95.

32. Lapécède to Thomas Jefferson, October 25, 1787, in ibid., 12:287–88.

33. Ford, *Works*, 12:394.

34. In the margin of his manuscript, with regard to his estimate of 30,000 or 35,000 years for the first formation of bodies of water, Buffon noted: "À la date de 25 or 26 mille ans (correction): de 700 mille ans; second correction: d'un million d'annés de la formation"; see [Georges-Louis de

Leclerc de] Buffon, *Des époques de la nature*, ed. Gabriel Gohau (Paris: Editions rationalistes, 1971), 83.

35. Ibid., 141.

36. Ibid., 140–41.

37. Ibid., 3.

38. George Louis Leclerc de Buffon, *Histoire naturelle, supplement v* (Paris: Imprimerie royale, 1778), 511.

39. See William Peden's footnotes in Jefferson, *Notes*, 261–62.

40. Thomas Jefferson to James Madison, January 1, 1784, in Boyd, *Papers*, 6:437.

41. Ford, *Works*, 3:392. This edition of Jefferson's *Notes* contains the controversial passages that were later revised in the Stockdale edition.

42. Buffon, *Époques*, 158.

43. George Louis Leclerc de Buffon, *Histoire naturelle, générale et particulière, supplement iv*, (Paris: Imprimerie royale, 1777), 4:531.

44. Ronald W. Clark, *Benjamin Franklin: A Biography* (New York: Random House, 1983), 160.

45. Benjamin Franklin, "Observations concerning the Increase of Mankind, Peopling of Countries, &c," in *The Papers of Benjamin Franklin*, ed. Leonard W. Labaree (New Haven, CT: Yale University Press, 1961), 4:234.

46. Buffon, *Histoire naturelle*, 3:502.

47. Ibid., 528. For a discussion of Buffon's role in early scientific racialism, see Richard H. Popkin, "The Philosophical Bases of Modern Racism," in Craig Walton, ed., *Philosophy and the Civilizing Arts* (Athens: Ohio University Press, 1974), 135–36.

48. Buffon, *Histoire naturelle*, 3:528.

49. John Lyon and Phillip R. Sloan, introduction to *From Natural History to the History of Nature*, by John Lyon and Phillip R. Sloan (Notre Dame: University of Notre Dame Press, 1981), 27.

NOTES TO CHAPTER 10

1. Details of Dr. Michaelis's career are from Whitfield J. Bell Jr., "A Box of Old Bones: A Note on the Identification of the Mastodon, 1766–1806," *Proceedings of the American Philosophical Society* 93 (1949).

2. Ibid., 174.

3. Ibid., 175.

4. John C. Greene, *The Death of Adam* (Ames: Iowa State University Press, 1959), 30.

5. See Immanuel Kant, "On the Distinctiveness of the Races in General," in Earl W. Count, ed., *This Is Race* (New York: Henry Schuman, 1950).

6. Johann Friedrich Blumenbach, "On the Natural Variety of Mankind,"

in Thomas Bendyshe, ed., *The Anthropological Treatises of Johann Friedrich Blumenbach* (London: Longman, Green, Longman, Roberts, & Green, 1865), 98.

7. Ibid., 1795 ed., 190.

8. Ibid.

9. Ibid., 190–91.

10. Ibid., 269.

11. George Mosse, *Toward the Final Solution: A History of European Racism* (Madison: University of Wisconsin Press, 1985), 21.

12. John C. Greene, *American Science in the Age of Jefferson* (Ames: Iowa State University Press, 1984), 324.

13. Ibid.

14. Ibid., 324–25.

15. Ibid.

16. Mosse, *Final Solution*, 31.

17. Blumenbach, *Anthropological Treatises*, 1795 ed., 234.

18. Blumenbach, "Skulls of Different Nations," 1795 ed., 155–58.

19. John Kobler, *The Reluctant Surgeon: A Biography of John Hunter* (Garden City, NY: Doubleday, 1960), 234.

20. W. D. Ian Rolfe, "William and John Hunter: Breaking the Great Chain of Being," in W. F. Bynum and Roy Porter, eds., *William Hunter and the Eighteenth-Century Medical World* (Cambridge: Cambridge University Press, 1985), 317.

21. Stephen Jay Gould, "Bound by the Great Chain," *Natural History*, November 1983, p. 24.

22. John Hunter, "Observations on the fossil Bones presented to the Royal Society by His most Serene Highness the Margave of Anspach," *Philosophical Transactions* 84 (1794): 409.

23. Kobler, *Reluctant Surgeon*, 298.

24. Ibid.

25. For a study of Hutton's cyclical view of time, see Stephen Jay Gould, *Time's Arrow, Time's Cycle: Myth and Metaphor in the Discovery of Geological Time* (Cambridge, MA: Harvard University Press, 1987).

26. James Hutton, "Theory of the Earth; or an investigation of the laws observable in the composition, dissolution, and restoration of land upon the globe," *Transactions of the Royal Society of Edinburgh* 1 (1788): 215.

27. Ibid., 304.

28. Ibid., 217.

29. Greene, *Death of Adam*, 167.

30. Kobler, *Reluctant Surgeon*, 299.

31. Rolfe, "Breaking the Chain," 316.

32. Judy Egerton, *George Stubbs, Anatomist and Animal Painter* (London: Tate Gallery, 1976), 34.

33. Peter Fuller, "Variations on a Theme," *New Society*, October 25, 1984, p. 140.

NOTES TO CHAPTER 11

1. Antonello Gerbi, *The Dispute of the New World* (Pittsburgh: University of Pittsburgh Press, 1973), 249.

2. William J. Free, *The* Columbian Magazine *and American Literary Nationalism* (The Hague: Mouton, 1968), 12.

3. Gerbi, *Dispute*, 247. Instead of "abuse," Gerbi's text reads "all of the European Thersiteses," a reference to a foul-mouthed and grossly abusive character in Homer's *Iliad*.

4. David Rittenhouse, "Some Observations on the Structure of the Earth in Pennsylvania and the Adjoining Countries," *Columbian Magazine* 1 (October 1786): 49.

5. Ibid., 50.

6. Ibid., 52.

7. Ibid., 53.

8. David Rittenhouse to Thomas Jefferson, September 28, 1785, in Julian P. Boyd, ed., *The Papers of Thomas Jefferson* (Princeton, NJ: Princeton University Press, 1953), 8:566.

9. Rittenhouse, "Observations," 53.

10. Ibid.

11. "Description of a remarkable Tooth, in the possession of Mr. Peale," *Columbian Magazine* 1 (September 1787): 655.

12. Anonymous, "A great tooth of some unknown animal found at Tioga, on the Susquehannah, handed over to Mr. Peale to have a drawing made of it," *Proceedings of the American Philosophical Society* 22 (1786): 146.

13. "A Description of Bones, &c Found near the Ohio River," *Columbian Magazine* 1 (November 1786): 103–7.

14. [Lewis] Nicola, "Observations on petrified bones found near the Ohio; thigh-bone, tusk and grinder, brought to the city by Maj. Craig," *Early Proceedings of the American Philosophical Society* (Philadelphia: McCalla & Stavely, 1884), 22, part 3: app. Read on March 5, 1784.

15. "A Description of Bones," *Columbian Magazine*, 105.

16. Ibid., 106.

17. Ibid., 107.

18. Francis Hopkinson to Thomas Jefferson, April 14, 1787, in Boyd, *Papers*, 11:289–90.

19. *Columbian Magazine* 1 (March 1787): 206–8.

20. John Stockdale to Thomas Jefferson, August 3, 1787, in Boyd, *Papers*, 11:677.

21. Joel Barlow to Thomas Jefferson, June 15, 1787, in ibid., 11:473.

22. *Columbian Magazine* 1 (August 1787): 573–74.

23. Ibid., 574.

24. Ibid., 575.

25. Thomas Jefferson, *Notes on the State of Virginia* (New York: Norton, 1972), 25.

26. *Columbian Magazine* 1 (September 1787): xx.

27. [Alexander Hamilton], "Federalist Paper no. 11," in *The Federalist*, ed. Edward Mead Earle (New York: Modern Library, 1941), 69. This article originally appeared in the *Independent Journal*, November 23, 1787.

28. For a discussion of Hamilton's passage, see Gerbi, *Dispute of the New World*, 250–51, and of De Pauw's voiceless dogs, 56–57.

29. Charles Thomson, "An investigation of the justice of Mons. Buffon's opinion respecting the Man of America," *Columbian Magazine* 2 (March 1788): 135.

30. Ibid., 136.

31. Free, *American Literary Nationalism*, 126.

32. Ezra Stiles to Thomas Jefferson, May 8, 1786, in Boyd, *Papers*, 9:478.

33. Jefferson, *Notes*, 97.

34. Ibid., 98–99.

35. Ibid., 100.

36. Ibid., 281–82.

37. The full text of Clark's unpublished letter is reprinted in Samuel W. Thomas and Eugene H. Conner, "George Rogers Clark (1752–1818): Natural Scientist and Historian," *Filson Club History Quarterly* 41 (1967): 208–11.

38. Dr. Nicholas Collin, "An Essay on those inquiries in Natural Philosophy, which at present are most beneficial to the United States of North America," *Transactions of the American Philosophical Society* 3 (1793): xv.

39. Ibid., iii.

40. Ibid., xxiii.

41. Ibid.

42. *Kentucky Gazette*, March 8, 1788, cited in John Walton, *John Filson of Kentucke* (Lexington: University of Kentucky Press, 1956), 100.

43. *Kentucky Gazette*, October 3, 1789.

44. "Of the enormous bones found in America," *American Museum, or Universal Magazine* 8 (1790): 284.

NOTES TO CHAPTER 12

1. Ezra Stiles, Diary, February 25, 1792, in *The Literary Diaries of Ezra Stiles*, ed. Franklin Bowditch Dexter (New York: Scribner, 1901), 3:443.

2. Stiles, Diary, October 3, 1792, in ibid., 3:476.

3. Stiles, Diary, October 12, 1792, in ibid., 3:477.

4. Ibid.

5. Ibid.

6. T[imothy] Matlack, "A large tusk found in the back country," *Proceedings of the American Philosophical Society* 22 (1791): 193.

7. [Timothy] Matlack and [Caspar] Wistar, "A Large Thigh bone found near Woodbury Creek in Gloucester County, N.J." *Proceedings of the American Philosophical Society* 22 (1791): 154.

8. Francis Hopkinson, "An Address to the American Philosophical Society," *Miscellaneous Essays and Occasional Writings* (Philadelphia, 1792), 1:362, cited by Brooke Hindle, *The Pursuit of Science in Revolutionary America, 1735–1789* (Chapel Hill: University of North Carolina Press, 1956), 269.

9. Robert Annan, "Account of a Skeleton of a Large Animal, found near Hudson's River," *Memoirs of the American Academy of Arts and Sciences* (Boston: Isaiah Thomas, 1793), 2:1, 162–63.

10. Ibid.

11. Ibid., 163.

12. Samuel H. Parsons, "Discoveries Made in the Western Country, by General Parsons," *Memoirs of the American Academy of Arts and Sciences* 2, no. 1 (1793): 122.

13. Ibid., 122.

14. Ibid., 123.

15. Tammany Society, *American Museum: Under the Patronage of the Tammany Society*, broadside, June 1, 1791, New York: Thomas & James Swords, New York Historical Society. For a history of the museum, see Paul Semonin, "Citizens and Strangers: The American Museum before Barnum" (Ph.D. diss., University of Oregon, 1994).

16. [Gardiner Baker], *Museum & Wax-Work at the Exchange, New York*, broadside, November 25, 1793, n.p., New York Historical Society. This broadside is reproduced in Robert and Gale S. McClung, "Tammany's Remarkable Gardiner Baker," *New York Historical Society Quarterly* 43 (April 1958): 143.

17. Alexander Anderson, M.D., *Diarum commentarium vitae* (New York: 1793–1798, microfilm of original manuscript in the Columbiana Collection, Manuscript Room, Columbia University), January 3, 1793.

18. Samuel Latham Mitchill, *The Life, Exploits, and Precepts of Tammany; the Famous Indian Chief* (New York: J. Buel, 1795), 7.

19. Ibid., 8.

20. Ibid., 122.

21. Willard Rouse Jillson, *Big Bone Lick: An Outline of Its history, Geology and Paleontology to Which Is Added an Annotated Bibliography of 207 Titles* (Louisville: Big Bone Lick Association, 1936), 36.

22. Anderson, M.D., *Diarum*, May 12, 1795.

23. Ibid., April 21, 1796.

24. *The Elephant*, broadside, Newburyport, 1797, New York Historical Society.

25. Edmund Burke, *Reflections on the Revolution in France* (New York: Penguin Books, 1981), 333.

26. Henry Wansey, *The Journal of an Excursion to the United States of North America in the Summer of 1794*, in Lillian B. Miller, ed., *The Selected Papers of Charles Willson Peale* (New Haven, CT: Yale University Press, 1988), 2, part 1:99.

27. Charles Willson Peale, broadside, "My design in forming this Museum," Philadelphia, 1792, in Miller, *Peale Papers*, 2, part 1:15.

28. Ibid., 15–16.

29. Étienne Geoffroy Saint-Hilaire and Jean-Baptiste Lamarck to Charles Willson Peale, January 30, 1796, in Miller, *Peale Papers*, 2, part 1:142.

30. Details of Cuvier's early career are from Martin J. S. Rudwick, ed., *Georges Cuvier, Fossil Bones, and Geological Catastrophes* (Chicago: University of Chicago Press, 1997).

31. Georges Cuvier, "Memoir on the Species of Elephants, Both Living and Fossil," in Rudwick, *Cuvier*, 22. Read on April 4, 1796.

32. Ibid., 21.

33. Ibid., 22.

34. Ibid., 24.

35. Thomas Jefferson, "A Memoir on the Discovery of certain Bones of a Quadruped of the Clawed Kind in the Western Parts of Virginia," *Transactions of the American Philosophical Society* 4 (1799): 251, reproduced in Keir B. Sterling, ed., *Selected Works in Nineteenth-Century North American Paleontology* (New York: Arno Press, 1974).

36. Ibid., 252.

37. Ibid., 253.

38. Ibid., 255–56.

39. Charles Willson Peale to Étienne Geoffroy Saint-Hilaire, April 30, 1797, in Miller, *Peale Papers*, 2, part 1:201.

40. Ibid.

41. George Turner, "Memoir on the extraneous fossils denominated mammoth bones; principally designed to show that they are the remains of more than one species of non-descript animal," *Transactions of the American Philosophical Society* 4 (1799): 513.

42. Ibid., 514.

43. Ibid., 515.

44. Ibid., 516.

45. Ibid.

46. Ibid., 517.

47. Ibid., 517–18.
48. Ibid., 518.
49. Ibid.
50. Ibid., 515.
51. Georges Cuvier, "Note on the skeleton of a very large species of quadruped, hitherto unknown, found in Paraguay and deposited in the Cabinet of Natural History in Madrid," in Rudwick, *Cuvier*, 32. Read shortly before his memoir on the fossil elephants of April 4, 1796.
52. C[aspar] Wistar, "A Description of the Bones deposited, by the President, in the Museum of the Society, and represented by the annexed plates," *Transactions of the American Philosophical Society* 4 (1799), 531, reproduced in Keir B. Sterling, ed., *Selected Works in Nineteenth-Century North American Paleontology* (New York: Arno Press, 1974).
53. Turner, "Memoir," 516.
54. John C. Greene, *The Death of Adam* (Ames: Iowa State University Press, 1959), 109.

NOTES TO CHAPTER 13

1. Sylvanus Miller, "Account of Large Bones dug up in Orange and Ulster Counties (State of New York): in a Letter from Sylvanus Miller to Dr. Mitchill; dated New-York, September 20, 1800," *Medical Repository* 4 (October 1800): 212.
2. Dr. James G. Graham, "Further Account of the Fossil Bones in Orange and Ulster Counties," *Medical Repository* 4, no. 2 (October 1800): 214.
3. Charles Coleman Sellers, *Mr. Peale's Museum* (New York: Norton, 1980), 127; Charles Willson Peale listed the following bones in Masten's original collection: fragments of the skull, five feet of one tusk, the neck and vertebrae, part of the tail, the breastbone and ribs, the pelvis, both shoulder blades, both forelegs complete, a femur, tibia, and fibula from the hind legs.
4. Rembrandt Peale, *Historical Disquisition on the Mammoth, or, Great American Incognitum, an Extinct, Immense, Carnivorous Animals, whose Fossil Remains have been found in America*, reprinted in Keir B. Sterling, ed., *Selected Works in Nineteenth-Century North American Paleontology* (New York: Arno Press, 1974; orig. London, 1803), 22.
5. Ibid., 19.
6. Details of Mitchill's life are from Courtney Robert Hall, *A Scientist in the Early Republic* (New York: Russell & Russell, 1962); and William Smallwood, *Natural History and the American Mind* (New York: Columbia University Press, 1941).
7. Graham, "Further Account of the Fossil Bones," 213.
8. Miller, "Account of Large Bones," 211.

9. Ibid.

10. Thomas Jefferson to Robert R. Livingston, Washington, December 14, 1800, in Paul Leceister Ford, ed., *The Writings of Thomas Jefferson* (New York: Putnam, 1905), 9:151.

11. Long extracts from Livingston's letter to Jefferson, January 7, 1801, were included in Jefferson's letter to Dr. Caspar Wistar, Washington, February 3, 1801, which is reprinted in Henry Fairfield Osborn, "Thomas Jefferson as a Paleontologist," *Science* 82 (December 6, 1935): 535.

12. Ibid.

13. "Extinct Species of Animals," *Medical Repository* 4 (April 1801): 419.

14. The full text of Cuvier's paper is reprinted in Martin J. S. Rudwick, ed., *Georges Cuvier, Fossil Bones, and Geological Catastrophes* (Chicago: University of Chicago Press, 1997), 45–58.

15. "Extinct Species of Animals," *Medical Repository* 4 (April 1801): 419, 420.

16. [R. R.] Livingston, "Teeth of some extinct animal found in New York, with a description in a letter to Jefferson," in *Early Proceedings of the American Philosophical Society* 22 (date?): 312. Read on May 22, 1801.

17. Charles Willson Peale to Andrew Ellicott, July 12, 1801, in Lillian B. Miller, ed., *The Selected Papers of Charles Willson Peale* (New Haven, CT: Yale University Press, 1988), 2, part 1:342.

18. Charles Willson Peale to Elizabeth DePeyster Peale, June 28, 1801, in Miller, *Peale Papers*, 2, part 1:336.

19. Sellers, *Mr. Peale's Museum*, 129; see also Charles Willson Peale, Diary, June 29, 1801, in Miller, *Peale Papers*, 2, part 1: 334.

20. Charles Willson Peale to Thomas Jefferson, June 29, 1801, in Miller, *Peale Papers*, 2, part 1:338.

21. Sellers, *Mr. Peale's Museum*, 130.

22. Charles Willson Peale to Robert Patterson, July 24, 1801, in Miller, *Peale Papers*, 2, part 1:348.

23. Charles Willson Peale to Dr. James G. Graham, July 20, 1801, in ibid., 1:346.

24. Rembrandt Peale, *Disquisition*, 25.

25. Sellers, *Mr. Peale's Museum*, 138; in Peale's report to Jefferson, October 11, 1801, he listed the following bones found during the excavation at Masten's pit: part of the breastbone and the sacrum, a tibia and fibula, the missing vertebrae, fragments of the underjaw, and a second tusk.

26. Rembrandt Peale, *Disquisition*, 28.

27. Peale, Diary, in Miller, *Peale Papers*, 2, part 1:363.

28. Rembrandt Peale, *Disquisition*, 30–31.

29. Ibid., 32–33.

30. Ibid., 2, pt. 1:369.

31. Charles Willson Peale to Thomas Jefferson, October 11, 1801, in Miller, *Peale Papers*, 2, part 1:372.

32. Rembrandt Peale, *Disquisition*, 36.

33. Charles Willson Peale, "Skeleton of the Mammoth," broadside [ca. 1801], American Philosophical Society; reprinted in Seller's *Mr. Peale's Museum*, 146.

34. Ibid.

35. Charles Coleman Sellers, *Charles Willson Peale* (New York: Scribner, 1969), 302. The guests at Peale's dinner party were his three sons, several close friends of the family, members of Philadelphia's manufacturing community, and William Rush, the sculptor who had helped assemble the skeleton.

36. The full text of Samuel Ewing's "Satire on the Mammoth," appears in Miller, *Peale Papers*, 2, part 1:401–9.

37. *Aurora*, January 9, 1802, in Miller, *Peale Papers*, 2, part 1:377.

38. *Medical Repository* 5 (1802): 83.

39. *New York Evening Post*, April 3, 1802, in Rita Susswein Gottesman, *The Arts and Crafts in New York* (New York: New York Historical Society, 1965): 3:438.

40. Rubens Peale to Charles Willson Peale, April 7, 1802, in Miller, *Peale Papers*, 2, part 1:425.

41. Rembrandt Peale, "A Short Account of the Behemoth or Mammoth," broadside [New York, 1802], American Philosophical Society.

42. Ibid.

43. Ibid.

44. Alexander Anderson's wood engraving is reproduced in Ann Shelby Blum, *Picturing Nature: American Nineteenth-Century Zoological Illustration* (Princeton, NJ: Princeton University Press, 1993), 19.

45. *The American Citizen and General Advertiser*, May 18, 1802, in Gottesman, *Arts and Crafts*, 3:440.

46. Sellers, *Mr. Peale's Museum*, 156.

47. Rembrandt Peale, *Account of the Skeleton of the Mammoth, a Non-Descript Carnivorous Animal of Immense Size, found in America* (London: E. Lawrence, 1802), 18–21.

48. Ibid., 26.

49. Johann Friedrich Blumenbach to Sir Joseph Banks, February 2, 1803, in Lillian B. Miller, ed., *The Collected Papers of Charles Willson Peale and His Family, 1735–1885* (Millwood, NY: Kraus Microform, 1980, microfiche), Series IIA/card 27, line B, spaces 10–13.

50. Rembrandt Peale, "A Short Account of the Mammoth," *Philosophical Magazine* 14 (1803): 166.

51. Ibid., 167.

52. Ibid., 168.

53. Rembrandt Peale, "On the Differences which exist between the Heads of the Mammoth and Elephant," *Philosophical Magazine* 14 (1803): 229.

54. Charles Willson Peale to Rembrandt and Rubens Peale, April 1, 1803, in Miller, *Peale Papers*, 2, part 1:517.

55. Rembrandt Peale, *Disquisition*, 75, 53.

56. Ibid., 80.

57. Ibid., 88–89.

58. Ibid., 2.

59. Charles Willson Peale, *Guide to the Philadelphia Museum* (Philadelphia, 1804): 6.

60. Rembrandt Peale, *Disquisition*, 3.

61. Ibid., 9.

62. Ibid., 75.

63. Ibid., 74.

64. Sir Joseph Banks to Charles Willson Peale, February 2, 1804, in Miller, *Peale Papers*, 2, part 1:634.

65. Excerpts from Rembrandt's letter are included in Charles Willson Peale to Thomas Jefferson, June 2, 1803, in ibid., 1:533.

NOTES TO CHAPTER 14

1. Receipts for the year 1802 indicate that the Mammoth earned $1,831.48 in the first full year of its exhibition and $5059.49 in the five years from 1802 to 1807; see Charles Coleman Sellers, *Charles Willson Peale* (New York: Scribner, 1969), 348.

2. Charles Willson Peale to Raphaelle Peale, July 19, 1803, in Lillian B. Miller, ed., *The Selected Papers of Charles Willson Peale and His Family* (New Haven, CT: Yale University Press, 1988), 2, part 1:583.

3. Charles Willson Peale to Rembrandt and Raphaelle Peale, August 7, 1803, in Miller, *Peale Papers*, 2, part 1:593.

4. Thomas Jefferson to Bernard Lacépède, February 24, 1803, in Donald Jackson, ed., *Letters of the Lewis and Clark Expedition* (Urbana-Champaign: University of Illinois Press, 1962), 15–16.

5. Meriwether Lewis to Thomas Jefferson, October 3, 1803, in ibid., 130.

6. See Th[omas] Ashe, *Memoirs of Mammoth, and various other extraordinary and stupendous Bones* (Liverpool: G. F. Harris, 1806).

7. *Charleston Times*, March 19, 1804, in Miller, *Peale Papers*, 2, part 1: 653–54.

8. Charles Willson Peale to James Calhoun, May 12, 1804, in Miller, *Peale Papers*, 2, part 1: 671.

9. *Federal Gazette and Baltimore Daily Advertiser*, May 26, 1804, in Miller, *Peale Papers*, 2, part 1:677.

10. *New York Herald*, June 9, 1804, in Charles Coleman Sellers, *Mr. Peale's Museum* (New York: Norton, 1980), 161.

11. Ibid., 240.

12. Thomas Jefferson to Dr. Caspar Wistar, February 25, 1807, in Willard Rouse Jillson, *Big Bone Lick: An Outline of Its History, Geology and Paleontology* (Louisville: Big Bone Lick Association Publications, no. 1, 1936), 48.

13. William Clark to Thomas Jefferson, September 20, 1807, in Howard C. Rice, "Jefferson's Gift of Fossils to the Museum of Natural History in Paris," *Proceedings of the American Philosophical Society* 95 (1951): 600.

14. William Clark to Thomas Jefferson, November 10, 1807, in ibid., 601.

15. Thomas Jefferson to Dr. Caspar Wistar, December 19, 1807, in Jillson, *Big Bone*, 51.

16. Thomas Jefferson to William Clark, December 19, 1807, in ibid., 49.

17. George Gaylord Simpson, "The Beginnings of Vertebrate Paleontology in North America," *Proceedings of the American Philosophical Society* 86 (1942): 155–56.

18. Thomas Jefferson to Dr. Caspar Wistar, March 20, 1808, in Jillson, *Big Bone*, 53.

19. Jefferson's handwritten list is reproduced in Rice, "Jefferson's Gift," 606–7.

20. Jillson, *Big Bone*, 54.

21. Thomas Jefferson to William Clark, September 10, 1809, in Jillson, *Big Bone*, 55.

22. Charles Willson Peale to Thomas Jefferson, April 3, 1809, in Miller, *Peale Papers*, 2, part 2:1189.

23. Thomas Jefferson to Charles Willson Peale, May 5, 1809, in ibid., 1201.

24. Charles Willson Peale to Georges Cuvier, January 20, 1809, in ibid., 1170.

25. Henry Fairfield Osborn, "Mastodons of the Hudson Highlands," *Natural History* 23 (1923): 4.

26. Lillian B. Miller, "Charles Willson Peale as History Painter: *The Exhumation of the Mastodon*," *American Art Journal* 13 (1981): 62–63.

27. Ibid., 51.

28. Charles Coleman Sellers, *Charles Willson Peale* (New York: Scribner, 1969), 299.

29. Bryan J. Wolf, *Romantic Re-vision: Culture and Consciousness in Nineteenth-Century American Painting and Literature* (Chicago: University of Chicago Press, 1982), 125.

30. Ibid.

31. Laura Rigal, "Peale's Mammoth," in David C. Miller, ed., *American Iconology* (New Haven, CT: Yale University Press, 1993), 18–38.

32. Ibid., 21.

33. Ibid., 23. "Discourse Introductory to a Course of Lectures on the Science of Nature; with original music, composed for and sung on the occasion," November 8, 1800, delivered in the Hall of the University of Pennsylvania (Philadelphia: Zachariah Poulson Jr., n.d.), 41.

34. Sellers, *Charles Willson Peale*, 307.

35. Carolyn Merchant, *The Death of Nature* (San Francisco: Harper & Row, 1980), 169.

36. Ibid., 171.

NOTES TO CHAPTER 15

1. George Ticknor to Thomas Jefferson, February 7, 1815, excerpted in Howard C. Rice Jr., "Jefferson's Gift of Fossils to the Museum of Natural History in Paris," *Proceedings of the American Philosophical Association* 95 (1951): 610.

2. Édouard de Montulé, *Voyage en Amérique, en Italie, en Sicile et en Egypte, pendant les annés 1816, 1817, 1818 et 1819* (Paris: Chez Dalanay, 1821). The illustrations were published in a separate and now rare quarto volume entitled *Recuil des cartes et des vues du voyage en Amérique, en Italie,* [etc.] (Paris, 1821). See also Édouard de Montulé, *Travels in America, 1816–1817* (Bloomington: Indiana University Press, 1950).

3. For details of Parkinson's illustrations and concept of the earth's antiquity, see John C. Greene, *The Death of Adam: Evolution and Its Impact on Western Thought* (Ames: Iowa State University Press, 1959), 120–23; and Martin J. S. Rudwick, *Scenes from Deep Time* (Chicago: University of Chicago Press, 1992), 17–20.

4. Johann Friedrich Blumenbach, "Contributions to Natural History," in Thomas Bendyshe, ed., *The Anthropological Treatises of Johann Friedrich Blumenbach* (London: Longman, Green, Longman, Roberts, & Green, 1865), 283.

5. Ruth Miller Elson, *Guardians of Tradition: American Schoolbooks of the Nineteenth Century* (Lincoln: University of Nebraska Press, 1964), 79.

6. See William Martin Smallwood, *Natural History and the American Mind* (New York: Columbia University Press, 1941), 302–5. Peck was appointed as a professor of natural history at Harvard in 1805 and continued to teach there until his death in 1822.

7. J[ohn] Augustine Smith, "A Lecture introductory to the second Course of Anatomical Instruction in the College of Physicians and Surgeons for the State of New-York," *New-York Medical and Philosophical Journal and Review* 1 (1809): 33.

8. For discussions of Cuvier's anthropological instructions, see Georges Hervé, "Les instructions anthropologiques de G. Cuvier," *Revue de l'école*

d'anthropologie de Paris 20 (1910): 289–302; and George W. Stocking Jr., "French Anthropology in 1800," in George W. Stocking Jr., ed., *Race, Culture and Evolution* (Chicago: University of Chicago Press, 1982), 29–31.

9. Ibid.

10. Ibid.

11. Robert Jameson, preface to *Essay on the Theory of the Earth*, by [Georges] Cuvier, trans. Robert Kerr (Edinburgh: William Blackwood, John Murray, and Robert Baldwin, 1813), *v*.

12. Rudwick, *Deep Time*, 30–36.

13. John D. Godman, *American Natural History* (Philadelphia: Carey & Lea, 1826; facsimile reprint; New York: Arno Press, 1974), 230.

14. Ibid., 208.

15. Ibid.

16. Sidney Spokes, *Gideon Algernon Mantell: Surgeon and Geologist* (London: J. Bale, Sons, and Danielson, 1927), 20–21. See also Edwin H. Colbert, *Dinosaurs: An Illustrated History* (Maplewood, NJ: Hammond, 1983), 12.

17. Rudwick, *Deep Time*, 48.

18. See Donald Worster, *Nature's Economy: A History of Ecological Ideas* (Cambridge: Cambridge University Press, 1977), 142.

19. Ibid., 144.

20. Greene, *Death of Adam*, 255.

21. Ibid.

22. Charles Darwin, *Journal of Researches into the Geology and Natural History of the various countries visited by H.M.S. Beagle* (London: Henry Colburn, 1839), in *The Works of Charles Darwin* (New York: New York University Press, 1987), 2:121.

23. Ibid., 2:164–65.

24. Ibid., 2:165.

25. Ibid., 2:185.

26. Ibid., 2:184.

27. Rudwick, *Deep Time*, 59–78.

28. Ibid., 78.

29. Ibid., 80.

30. Ibid., 73.

31. "Report of Messrs. Cooper, J. A. Smith, and DeKay to the Lyceum of Natural History, on a collection of Fossil bones, disinterred at Big Bone Lick, Kentucky, in September, 1830, and recently brought to New York," *American Journal of Science* 20 (1831): 371.

32. Edward Hitchcock, "Ornithichnology.—Description of the Foot marks of Birds, (Ornithichnites) on new Red Sandstone in Massachusetts," *American Journal of Science* 29 (1836): 319.

33. Charles Lyell, *Lectures on Geology, delivered at the Broadway Taberna-*

cle, in the city of New York (New York: Greeley & McElrath, 1843), reprinted in Hubert C. Skinner, ed., *Charles Lyell on North American Geology* (New York: Arno Press, 1978), vi, 25.

34. Charles Lyell, *Travels in North America, 1841–42* (New York, 1845), cited by Willard Rouse Jillson, *Big Bone Lick: An Outline of Its History, Geology and Paleontology* (Louisville: Big Bone Lick Association, 1936), 106.

35. Ibid.

36. Details of Koch's career are from Robert Silverberg, "The Sea Serpent of Dr. Koch," *Scientists and Scoundrels* (New York: Crowell, 1965), 51–70; and Richard Altick, *The Shows of London* (Cambridge, MA: Harvard University Press, 1978), 289.

37. Cited by Silverberg, "Sea Serpent," 57–58.

38. Ibid., 58.

39. *Missourium Theristrocaulodon,"* broadside, Dublin: C. Crookes, n.d., American Philosophical Society, Philadelphia.

40. Details on the early discovery of the dinosaurs are from David Norman, *Dinosaur!* (New York: Prentice-Hall, 1991); and Edwin C. Colbert, *Dinosaurs: An Illustrated History* (Maplewood, NJ: Hammond, 1983). See also Paul Semonin, "Empire and Extinction: The Dinosaur As a Metaphor for Dominance in Prehistoric Nature, *Leonardo* 30 (1997): 171–82.

41. Cited by Herbert Wendt, *Before the Deluge* (Garden City, NY: Doubleday, 1968), 264.

42. In February 1843, more than a year after the arrival of Koch's monster at Egyptian Hall, Dr. Owen read a paper before the Geological Society of London, pointing out numerous errors in Koch's mounting of the skeleton.

43. Charles Lyell, *A Second Visit to the United States of North America* (New York: Harper & Brothers, 1849), 2:107.

44. Ibid.

45. Ibid., 1:65–66.

46. Cited by Silverberg, "Sea Serpent," 63.

47. Prime and Emmons's article is quoted in Henry Fairfield Osborn, "Mastodons of the Hudson Highlands," *Natural History* 23 (1923): 13.

48. Lyell, *Second Visit,* 2:271.

49. Quoted in Reginald Horsman, *Race and Manifest Destiny: The Origins of American Racial Anglo-Saxonism* (Cambridge, MA: Harvard University Press, 1981), 177.

50. Ibid., 159.

51. Samuel George Morton, *Crania Americana* (Philadelphia: John Pennington, 1839). In 1851, at the time of his death, Morton's collection included some 1,050 skulls from 150 nations and filled sixteen glass cases in the gallery of the Academy of Sciences in Philadelphia.

52. Horsman, *"Race and Manifest Destiny,* 127.

53. J[ohn] Augustine Smith, "Sketch of a Lecture: Different Races of Men," in Charles Lyell, *Lectures on Geology* (New York: Greeley & McElrath, 1843), 54.

54. Ibid.

55. Worster, *Nature's Economy*, 126.

56. A long extract from Samuel Eager's *An Outline History of Orange County* (1846–47) appears in Henry Fairfield Osborn, "Hudson Highlands," 3–8.

57. Osborn, "Hudson Highlands," 5.

NOTES TO AFTERWORD

1. Benjamin Waterhouse Hawkins, lecture to the Society of Arts, London, 1854, quoted in Martin J. S. Rudwick, *Scenes from Deep Time* (Chicago: University of Chicago Press, 1992), 140.

2. This unidentified period painting is reproduced in David Norman, *Dinosaur!* (New York: Prentice-Hall, 1991), 11.

3. Rudwick, *Deep Time*, 244.

4. Charles Darwin, *The Origin of Species* (London: Penguin Books, 1968; orig. 1859), 459.

5. Ibid., 116.

6. Joseph Leidy, *Proceedings of the Academy of Natural Sciences* 10 (1858): 217, quoted in Edwin H. Colbert, *Dinosaurs: An Illustrated History* (Maplewood, NJ: Hammond, 1983), 22.

7. Edward Hitchcock, *Ichnology of New England* (Boston: William White, 1858), 190.

8. Charles Lyell, *A Second Visit to the United States of North America* (New York: Harper Bros., 1849), 237.

9. Willard Rouse Jillson, *Big Bone Lick: An Outline of Its History, Geology and Paleontology* (Louisville: Big Bone Lick Association, 1936), 65.

10. Details of the aborted plans for the Paleozoic museum in New York are from Adrian J. Desmond, "Central Park's Fragile Dinosaurs," *Natural History* 83 (1974): 65–71; and Edwin H. Colbert and Katherine Beneker, "The Paleozoic Museum in Central Park, or the Museum That Never Was," *Curator* 2 (1959): 137–150.

11. Colbert and Beneker, "Paleozoic Museum," 140.

12. Ibid., 141.

13. Ibid.

14. Desmond, "Fragile Dinosaurs," 71.

15. Ibid.

16. Ruth Miller Elson, *Guardians of Tradition: American Schoolbooks of the Nineteenth Century* (Lincoln: University of Nebraska Press, 1964), 17.

17. George Gaylord Simpson and H. Tobien, "The Rediscovery of Peale's Mastodon," *Proceedings of the American Philosophical Society* 98 (1954): 279.

18. Henry Fairfield Osborn and William King Gregory, "The Dawn Man," *McClure's* 55 (1923): 27.

19. Ibid., 28.

20. Charles R. Knight, *Before the Dawn of History* (New York: McGraw-Hill, 1935), 110.

21. See for example Norman, *Dinosaur!*, 73; and Michael Crichton, *Lost World* (New York: Knopf, 1995), 193. For a discussion of contemporary views of the dinosaurs, see Paul Semonin, "Empire and Extinction: The Dinosaur As a Metaphor for Dominance in Prehistoric Nature," *Leonardo* 30 (1997): 171–82.

22. Robert T. Bakker, *The Dinosaur Heresies* (New York: Morrow, 1986), 33.

23. Peter D. Ward, *The Call of Distant Mammoths: Why the Ice Age Mammals Disappeared* (New York: Springer-Verlag, 1997), 56.

24. Ibid., 97.

25. W. J. T. Mitchell, *The Last Dinosaur Book* (Chicago: University of Chicago Press, 1998), 111.

26. See Lieutenant Colonel Dave Grossman, *On Killing* (Boston: Little, Brown, 1995); and David Grossman, "Trained to Kill," *Christianity Today*, August 10, 1998, pp. 1–8.

27. Donald Worster, *Nature's Economy: A History of Ecological Ideas* (Cambridge: Cambridge University Press, 1985), 169.

Bibliography

Acomb, Evelyn M., ed. "The Journal of Baron Von Closen." *William and Mary Quarterly*, 3rd. ser., 10 (1953): 196–236.

Adams, William Howard, ed. *The Eye of Thomas Jefferson.* Washington, DC: National Gallery of Art, 1976.

Alderson, William T. *Mermaids, Mummies, and Mastodons: The Emergence of the American Museum.* Washington, DC: American Association of Museums, 1992.

Allen, B. Sprague. *Tides in English Taste.* 2 vols. Cambridge, MA: Harvard University Press, 1937.

Altick, Richard D. *The Shows of London.* Cambridge, MA: Harvard University Press, 1978.

Anderson, Alexander. *Diarum commentarium vitae.* New York, 1793–98. Columbiana Collection, Manuscript Room, Columbia University Library.

Anderson, Benedict. *Imagined Communities: Reflections on the Origin and Spread of Nationalism.* London: Verso, 1983.

Annan, Robert. "Account of a Skeleton of a large animal, found near Hudson's river." *Memoirs of the American Academy of Arts and Sciences* 2, part 1 (1793): 160–64.

Anonymous. "Of the enormous bones found in America." *American Museum, or Universal Magazine* 8 (1790): 284–85.

Ashe, Th[omas]. *Memoirs of Mammoths.* Liverpool: G. F. Harris, 1806.

Aubin, Robert A. "Grottoes, Geology, and the Gothic Revival." *Studies in Philology* 31 (1934): 408–16.

Augusta, Dr. Josef. *A Book of Mammoths.* London: Paul Hamilyn, 1962.

Bailey, Kenneth P. *The Ohio Company of Virginia and the Westward Movement, 1748–1792.* Glendale, CA: Arthur H. Clark, 1939.

Bakker, Robert T. *The Dinosaur Heresies.* New York: Morrow, 1986.

Beall, Otho T. Jr. "Cotton Mather's Early 'Curiosa Americana' and the Boston Philosophical Society of 1683." *William and Mary Quarterly*, 3rd ser., 18 (1961): 360–72.

Beall, Otho T. Jr., and Richard Shryock. *Cotton Mather: First Significant Figure in American Medicine.* Baltimore: Johns Hopkins University Press, 1954.

Bell, John. *A Journey from St. Petersburg to Pekin, 1719–22.* New York: Barnes & Noble, 1966.

Bell, Whitfield J. Jr. "A Box of Old Bones: A Note on the Identification of the Mastodon." *Proceedings of the American Philosophical Society* 93 (1949): 169–77.

———. *John Morgan: Continental Doctor.* Philadelphia: University of Pennsylvania Press, 1965.

Berkeley, Edmund, and Dorothy Smith Berkeley, eds. *The Correspondence of John Bartram, 1734–1777.* Gainesville: University Press of Florida, 1992.

———. *The Life and Travels of John Bartram: From Lake Ontario to the River St. John.* Tallahassee: University Presses of Florida, 1982.

Blum, Ann Shelby. *Picturing Nature: American Nineteenth-Century Zoological Illustration.* Princeton, NJ: Princeton University Press, 1993.

Blumenbach, Johann Friedrich. *The Anthropological Treatises of Johann Friedrich Blumenbach,* ed. Thomas Bendyshe. London: Longman, Green, Longman, Roberts, & Green, 1865.

Boeh, Dwight, and Edward Schwartz. "Jefferson and the Theory of Degeneracy." *American Quarterly* 9 (1957): 448–53.

Breyne, John P. "A Letter from John Phil. Breyne, M.D. F.R.S. to Sir Hans Sloane, Bart. Pres. R.S. with Observations, and a Description of some Mammoth Bones Dug up in Siberia, Proving them to have belonged to Elephants." *Philosophical Transactions* 40 (1737): 124–38.

Brooke, James Hadley, ed. *Science and Religion: Some Historical Perspectives.* Cambridge: Cambridge University Press, 1991.

Buffon, Georges Louis Leclerc de. *Des époques de la nature.* Paris: Éditions rationalistes, 1971; org. 1778.

———. *Histoire naturelle, générale et particulière.* 44 vols. Paris: Imprimeries royale, 1749–88.

Burnet, Thomas. *The [Sacred] Theory of the Earth.* London: R. Norton, 1684.

Bush, Alfred L. *The Life Portraits of Thomas Jefferson.* Charlottesville, VA: Thomas Jefferson Memorial Foundation, 1987.

Bynum, W. F., and Roy Porter, eds. *William Hunter and the Eighteenth-Century Medical World.* Cambridge: Cambridge University Press, 1985.

Chastellux, François-Jean, Marquis de. *Travels in America in the Years 1780, 1781 and 1782.* 2 vols. Chapel Hill: University of North Carolina Press, 1963.

Chinard, Gilbert. "Eighteenth-Century Theories on America as a Human Habitat." *Proceedings of the American Philosophical Society* 91 (1947): 27–57.

Clark, Ronald W. *Benjamin Franklin: A Biography.* New York: Random House, 1983.

Colbert, Edwin H. *Dinosaurs: An Illustrated History*. Maplewood, NJ: Hammond, 1983.

Colbert, Edwin H., and Katherine Beneker. "The Paleozoic Museum in Central Park, or the Museum That Never Was." *Curator* 2 (1959): 137–50.

Collin, Dr. Nicholas. "An Essay on those inquiries in Natural Philosophy, which at present are most beneficial to the United States of North America." *Transactions of the American Philosophical Society* 3 (1793): iii–xxvii.

Collins, Richard. *History of Kentucky*. 2 vols. Covington, KY: Collins and Co., 1882.

Collinson, Peter. "An Account of Some Very Large Fossil Teeth Found in North America." *Philosophical Transactions* 57 (1767): 464–69.

Cooper, William. "Notices of Big Bone Lick." *American Journal of Geology* 1 (1831): 158–74.

Count, Earl W., ed. *This Is Race*. New York: Henry Schuman, 1950.

Craven, Wayne. "The American and British Portraits of Benjamin Franklin." In *Reappraising Benjamin Franklin: A Bicentennial Perspective*, ed. Wayne Craven. Newark: University of Delaware Press, 1993. 247–71.

Cresswell, Nicholas. *The Journal of Nicholas Cresswell, 1774–77*. New York: Dial Press, 1924.

Crichton, Michael. *Lost World*. New York: Knopf, 1995.

Croghan, George. "Croghan's Journal; May 15–September 26, 1765." In *Early Western Travels, 1748–1846*, ed. Reuben Gold Thwaites. Cleveland: Arthur H. Clark, 1904.

Cross, Stephen J. "John Hunter, the Animal Oeconomy and Late Eighteenth-Century Physiological Discourse." *Studies in History of Biology* 5 (1981): 1–110.

Cutler, William Parker, and Julia Cutler, eds. *Life, Journals and Correspondence of Rev. Manasseh Cutler*. Cincinnati: Robert Clarke and Co., 1888.

Czerkas, Sylvia Massey, and Donald F. Glut. *Dinosaurs, Mammoths and Cavemen: The Art of Charles R. Knight*. New York: Dutton, 1982.

Daniels, George H. *Science in American Society*. New York: Knopf, 1971.

Darwin, Charles. *Journal of Researches into the Geology and Natural History of the various countries visited by H.M.S. Beagle*. London, 1839. In *The Works of Charles Darwin*. New York: New York University Press, 1987.

———. *The Origin of Species*. London: Penguin Books, 1968; orig. 1859.

Daubenton, Louis Jean Marie. "Mémoire sur des os et des dents remarquables par leur grandeur." *Mémoires de l'Académie royale des sciences, Paris* (1764): 206–29.

Desmond, Adrian J. "Central Park's Fragile Dinosaurs." *Natural History* 83 (1974): 65–71.

Dexter, Franklin B., ed. *Extracts from the Itinerary and Other Miscellanies of Ezra Stiles*. New Haven, CT: Yale University Press, 1916.

Dexter, Franklin B., ed. *The Literary Diary of Ezra Stiles.* 3 vols. New York: Scribner, 1901.

Dickason, Olive Patricia. *The Myth of the Savage and the Beginnings of French Colonialism in the Americas.* Edmonton: University of Alberta Press, 1984.

Dunwell, Frances F. *The Hudson River Highlands.* New York: Columbia University Press, 1991.

Durant, G. P., and W. D. Ian Rolfe. "William Hunter (1718–1783) As Natural Historian: His 'Geological' Interests." *Earth Sciences Histories* 3 (1984): 9–24.

Duval, Marguerite. *The King's Garden.* Charlottesville: University Press of Virginia, 1982.

Earnest, Ernest. *John and William Bartram: Botanists and Explorers.* Philadelphia: University of Pennsylvania Press, 1940.

Edwards, W. N. *The Early History of Palaeontology.* London: British Museum, 1967.

Egerton, Judy. *George Stubbs, Anatomist and Animal Painter.* London: Tate Gallery, 1976.

Ehrenreich, Barbara. *Blood Rites: Origins and History of the Passions of War.* New York: Henry Holt, 1997.

Ellis, Joseph J. *After the Revolution.* New York: Norton, 1979.

Elson, Ruth Miller. *Guardians of Tradition: American Schoolbooks of the Nineteenth Century.* Lincoln: University of Nebraska Press, 1964.

Emerson, Ralph Waldo. *Nature.* In *Ralph Waldo Emerson: Essays and Lectures.* New York: Library of America, 1983; orig. 1836.

Emmons, Ebenezer, and A. J. Prime. "The Great American Mastodon." *American Journal of Agriculture and Science* 2 (1845): 203–12.

Evernden, Neil. *The Social Creation of Nature.* Baltimore: Johns Hopkins University Press, 1992.

Ewers, John C. "William Clark's Indian Museum in St. Louis, 1816–1838." In *A Cabinet of Curiosities,* ed. Whitfield J. Bell Jr. et al. Charlottesville: University Press of Virginia, 1967.

Fagin, W. Bryllion. *William Bartram, Interpreter of the American Landscape.* Baltimore: Johns Hopkins University Press, 1933.

Farber, Paul. "Buffon and Daubenton: Divergent Traditions within the *Histoire naturelle.*" *Isis* 66 (1975): 63–74.

Feduccia, Alan, ed. *Catesby's Birds of Colonial America.* Chapel Hill: University of North Carolina Press, 1985.

Fender, Stephen. "Franklin and Emigration: The Trajectory of Use." In *Reappraising Benjamin Franklin: A Bicentennial Perspective.* Newark: University of Delaware Press, 1993.

Filson, John. *The Discovery, Settlement and Present State of Kentucke.* New York: Corinth Books, 1962; orig. 1784.

Fleming, Thomas, ed. *Benjamin Franklin: A Biography in His Own Words*. New York: Harper & Row, 1972.

Franklin, Benjamin. *The Papers of Benjamin Franklin*, ed. Leonard W. Larabee and Whitfield J. Bell. New Haven, CT: Yale University Press, 1959–70.

———. *The Writings of Benjamin Franklin*, ed. Albert Henry Smyth. New York: Macmillan, 1906.

Free, William J. *The Columbian Magazine and American Literary Nationalism*. The Hague: Mouton, 1968.

Freeman, Douglas Southall. *George Washington: A Biography*. Vol. 5. New York: Scribner, 1952.

Fuller, Peter. "Variations on a Theme." *New Society* 70 (1984): 139–40.

Gerbi, Antonello. *The Dispute of the New World: The History of a Polemic, 1750–1900*. Pittsburgh: University of Pittsburgh Press, 1973.

———. *Nature in the New World*. Pittsburgh: University of Pittsburgh Press, 1985.

Gipson, Lawrence Henry. *Lewis Evans*. Philadelphia: Historical Society of Pennsylvania, 1939.

Gist, Christopher. *Christopher Gist's Journals*, ed. William M. Darlington. Pittsburgh: J. R. Weldin and Co., 1893.

Godman, John D. *American Natural History*. Philadelphia: Carey and Lea, 1826. Reprint, New York: Arno Press, 1974.

Goldsmith, Oliver. *A History of the Earth and Animated Nature*. 8 vols. London: J. Nourse, 1774.

Goode, George Brown. "The Beginnings of Natural History in America." In *Contributions to the History of American Natural History*, ed. Keir B. Sterling. New York: Arno Press, 1974.

Gordon, Harry. "Journey Down the Ohio in 1766." In *Travels in the American Colonies*, ed. N. D. Mereness. New York: Macmillan, 1916.

Gossett, Thomas F. *Race: The History of an Idea in America*. Dallas: Southern Methodist University Press, 1963.

Gould, Stephen Jay. "Bound by the Great Chain." *Natural History* 11 (November 1983): 20–24.

———. *Time's Arrow, Time's Cycle: Myth and Metaphor in the Discovery of Geological Time*. Cambridge, MA: Harvard University Press, 1987.

Grabo, Norman S. *Edward Taylor*. New York: Twayne, 1961.

Graham, Dr. James G. "Further Account of the Fossil Bones in Orange and Ulster Counties." *Medical Repository* 4, no. 2 (1800): 213–14.

Greene, John C. *American Science in the Age of Jefferson*. Ames: Iowa State University Press, 1984.

———. *The Death of Adam: Evolution and Its Impact on Western Thought*. Ames: Iowa State University Press, 1959.

Greene, John C. "Science and the Public in the Age of Jefferson." *Isis* 49 (1958): 13–25.

Grossman, Lt. Col. Dave. *On Killing*. Boston: Little, Brown, 1995.

Guettard, Jean-Étienne. "Mémoire dans lequel on compare le Canada à la Suisse, par rapport à ses minéraux." *Mémoires de l'Académie royale des sciences, Paris* (1756): 189–220.

Hall, Courtney Robert. *A Scientist in the Early Republic*. New York: Russell and Russell, 1962.

Harris, Neil. *The Artist in American Society: The Formative Years, 1790–1860*. New York: George Braziller, 1966.

Hartnagel, C. A., and Sherman C. Bishop. *The Mastodons, Mammoths and Other Pleistocene Mammals of New York State*. Albany: University of the State of New York, 1922.

Hepworth, Brian. *Edward Young (1683–1765)*. Cheshire, England: Carcanet Press, 1975.

Hinderaker, Eric. *Elusive Empires: Constructing Colonialism in the Ohio Valley, 1673–1800*. Cambridge: Cambridge University Press, 1997.

Hindle, Brooke. *David Rittenhouse*. Princeton, NJ: Princeton University Press, 1964.

———. *The Pursuit of Science in Revolutionary America, 1735–1789*. Chapel Hill: University of North Carolina Press, 1956.

Hitchcock, Edward. *Ichnology of New England*. Boston: W. White, 1858. Reprint, New York: Arno Press, 1974.

———. "Ornithichnology." *American Journal of Science* 29 (1836): 307–40.

Hooke, Robert. *The Posthumous Works of Robert Hooke*, ed. Richard Waller. New York: Johnson Reprint Corp., 1969; facsimile ed. London: Sam Smith and Benj. Walford, 1705.

Horsman, Reginald. *Race and Manifest Destiny: The Origins of American Racial Anglo-Saxonism*. Cambridge, MA: Harvard University Press, 1981.

Howorth, Henry H. *The Mammoth and the Flood*. London: Sampson, Low, Marston, Searle, and Rivington, 1887.

Hulbert, Archer Butler. *The Ohio River: A Course of Empire*. New York: Putnam, 1906.

Hunter, John. *Essays and Observations on Natural History, Anatomy, Physiology, Psychology, and Geology*, ed. Richard Owne. 2 vols. London: John Van Voorst, 1837.

———. "Observations on the fossil Bones presented to the Royal Society by his most Serene Highness the Margave of Anspach." *Philosophical Transactions* 84 (1794): 407–17.

Hunter, William. "Observations on the Bones Commonly Supposed to Be Elephant Bones, Which Have Been Found near the River Ohio in

America." *Philosophical Transactions of the Royal Society of London* 58 (1769): 34–45.

Huth, Hans. "Pierre Eugène Du Simitière and the Beginnings of the American Historical Museum." *Pennsylvania Magazine of History and Biography* 69 (1945): 315–25.

Ides, Evert Ysbrandszoon. *Three Years Travel from Moscow overland to China.* London: W. Freeman, 1706.

Ingles, John, Sr. *Escape from Indian Captivity: The Story of Mary Draper Ingles and her son Thomas Ingles*, ed. Roberta Ingles Steele and Andrew Lewis Ingles. Radford, VA: Steele and Ingles, 1969.

Irmscher, Christoph. *The Poetics of Natural History: From John Bartram to William James.* New Brunswick, NJ: Rutgers University Press, 1999.

Jackson, Donald, ed. *Letters of the Lewis and Clark Expedition.* Urbana-Champaign: University of Illinois Press, 1962.

Jacob, James R. "Newtonian Theology and the Defense of the Glorious Revolution." In *The Age of William III and Mary II*, ed. Robert P. Maccubbin and Martha Hamilton-Phillips. Williamsburg, VA: College of William and Mary Press, 1989.

Jacob, Margaret C., and Wilfred A. Lockwood. "Political Millenarianism and Burnet's *Sacred Theory.*" *Science Studies* 2 (1972): 265–79.

James, Alfred P. *The Ohio Company: Its Inner History.* Pittsburgh: University of Pittsburgh Press, 1959.

Jefferson, Thomas. "A memoir on the discovery of certain bones of the quadruped of the clawed kind in the western parts of Virginia." *Transactions of the American Philosophical Society* 4 (1797): 246–60. Reprinted in *Selected Works in Nineteenth-Century North American Paleontology*, ed. Keir B. Sterling. New York: Arno Press, 1974.

———. *Notes on the State of Virginia*, ed. William Peden. New York: Norton, 1972; orig. 1785.

———. *The Papers of Thomas Jefferson*, ed. Julian P. Boyd. Princeton, NJ: Princeton University Press, 1950–82.

———. *The Works of Thomas Jefferson*, ed. Paul Leicester Ford. New York: Putnam, 1904–5.

Jillson, Willard Rouse. *Big Bone Lick: An Outline of its History, Geology and Paleontology to which is added an annotated bibliography of 207 titles.* Louisville: Big Bone Lick Association, publication no. 1, 1936.

Johnston, J. Stoddard, ed. *First Explorations of Kentucky.* Louisville: John P. Morton Co., 1898.

Jones, H. Mumford. *O Strange New World: American Culture, the Formative Years.* New York: Viking Press, 1964.

Jordan, William. *Divorce among the Gulls.* San Francisco: North Point Press, 1991.

Kalm, Peter. *Travels in North America*. 2 vols. London: T. Lowndes, 1772.

Kant, Immanuel. "On the Distinctiveness of the Races in General." In *This Is Race*, ed. Earl W. Count. New York: Henry Schuman, 1950.

Keller, Karl. *The Example of Edward Taylor*. Amherst: University of Massachusetts Press, 1975.

Kemp, Martin. *Dr. William Hunter at the Royal Academy of Arts*. Glasgow: University of Glasgow Press, 1975.

Kennedy, Roger C. *Hidden Cities: The Discovery and Loss of Ancient North American Civilization*. New York: Free Press, 1994.

Kierner, Cynthia A. *Traders and Gentlefolk: The Livingstons of New York, 1675–1790*. Ithaca, NY: Cornell University Press, 1992.

Kimball, Marie. *Jefferson: War and Peace*. New York: Coward-McCann, 1947.

Kindle, Edward M. "The Story of the Discovery of Big Bone Lick." *Kentucky Geological Survey*, 6th ser., 41 (1931): 195–212.

King, William. *An Essay on the Origin of Evil*. London: J. Stephen, 1732.

Kircher, Anthanasius. *Mundus subterraneus*. 2 vols. Amsterdam, 1665.

Kittredge, George Lyman. "Cotton Mather's Scientific Communications to the Royal Society." *Proceedings of the American Antiquarian Society* 26 (1916): 18–57.

Knight, Charles R. *Before the Dawn of History*. New York: McGraw-Hill, 1935.

Knight, David M. *Natural Science Books in English, 1600–1900*. New York: Praeger, 1972.

Kobler, John. *The Reluctant Surgeon: A Biography of John Hunter*. Garden City, NY: Dolphin Books, 1960.

Leder, Lawrence H. *Robert Livingston, 1654–1728, and the Politics of Colonial New York*. Chapel Hill: University of North Carolina Press, 1961.

Levanthal, Herbert. *In the Shadow of the Enlightenment: Occultism and Renaissance Science in Eighteenth-Century America*. New York: New York University Press, 1976.

Levin, David. "Giants in the Earth: Science and the Occult in Cotton Mather's Letters to the Royal Society." *William and Mary Quarterly*, 3rd ser., 45 (1988): 751–70.

Lindberg, David C., and Ronald L. Numbers, eds. *God and Nature: Historical Essays on the Encounter between Christianity and Science*. Berkeley and Los Angeles: University of California Press, 1986.

Lister, Adrian, and Paul Baln. *Mammoths*. New York: Macmillan, 1994.

Looby, Christopher. "The Constitution of Nature: Taxonomy and Politics in Jefferson, Peale, and Bartram." *Early American Literature* 22 (1987): 252–73.

Lovejoy, Arthur O. *The Great Chain of Being: A Study of the History of an Idea*. Cambridge, MA: Harvard University Press, 1950.

Lowenthal, David. *The Past Is a Foreign Country.* Cambridge: Cambridge University Press, 1985.

Luther, Frederic N. "Jefferson As a Naturalist." *Magazine of American History* 13 (1885): 379–90.

Lyell, Charles. *Lectures on Geology, delivered at the Broadway Tabernacle, in the city of New York.* New York: Greeley and McElrath, 1843. Reprinted in *Charles Lyell on North American Geology,* ed. Hubert C. Skinner. New York: Arno Press, 1978.

———. *A Second Visit to the United States of North America.* New York: Harper Bros., 1849.

Lynskey, Winifred. "Goldsmith and the Chain of Being." *Journal of the History of Ideas* 6 (1945): 363–74.

———. "The Scientific Sources of Goldsmith's Animated Nature." *Studies in Philology* 40 (1943): 33–57.

Lyon, John, and Phillip Sloan, eds. *From Natural History to a History of Nature: Readings from Buffon and His Critics.* Notre Dame, IN: University of Notre Dame Press, 1981.

Maccubbin, Robert P., and Martha Hamilton-Phillips, eds. *The Age of William III and Mary II: Power, Politics, and Patronage, 1688–1702.* Williamsburg, VA: College of William and Mary Press, 1989.

Malone, Dumas. *Jefferson and His Time: Jefferson the Virginian.* Boston: Little, Brown, 1948.

Marx, Leo. *The Machine in the Garden: Technology and the Pastoral Ideal in America.* Oxford: Oxford University Press, 1964.

Mather, Cotton. *The Christian Philosopher.* Gainesville, FL: Scholar's Facsimiles and Reprints, 1968; orig. 1721.

———. *The Diary of Cotton Mather, D.D., F.R.S. for the Year 1712,* ed. William R. Manierre II. Charlottesville: University Press of Virginia, 1964.

Matthew, William D., *Dinosaurs.* New York: American Museum of Natural History, 1915.

McCleland, Hugh, ed. *George Washington in the Ohio Valley.* Pittsburgh: University of Pittsburgh Press, 1955.

McClung, Robert, and Gale S. McClung. "Tammany's Remarkable Gardiner Baker." *New York Historical Society Quarterly* 43 (April 1958): 143–69.

McConnell, Michael N. *A Country Between: The Upper Ohio Valley and Its Peoples, 1724–1774.* Lincoln: University of Nebraska Press, 1992.

McGrane, Bernard. *Beyond Anthropology: Society and the Other.* New York: Columbia University Press, 1989.

Meinig, D. W. "The Colonial Period." In *Geography of New York State,* ed. John H. Thompson. Syracuse, NY: Syracuse University Press, 1966.

Merchant, Carolyn. *The Death of Nature.* San Francisco: Harper & Row, 1980.

Miller, Charles A. *Jefferson and Nature*. Baltimore: Johns Hopkins University Press, 1988.

Miller, Lillian B. "Charles Willson Peale As History Painter: *The Exhumation of the Mastodon.*" *American Art Journal* 13 (1981): 47–68.

———. *The Collected Papers of Charles Wilson Peale and His Family, 1735–1885*. Millwood, NY: Kraus Microform, 1980.

———. *Patrons and Patriotism: The Encouragement of the Fine Arts in the United States, 1790–1860*. Chicago: University of Chicago Press, 1966.

———. *The Selected Papers of Charles Willson Peale and His Family.* 4 vols. New Haven, CT: Yale University Press, 1983–96.

Miller, Perry. "The Romantic Dilemma in American Nationalism and the Concept of Nature." In *Errand in the Wilderness*, by Perry Miller. Cambridge, MA: Harvard University Press, 1956.

Miller, Sylvanus. "Account of Large Bones dug up in Orange and Ulster Counties (state of New-York): in a Letter from Sylvanus Miller to Dr. Mitchill; dated New-York, September 20, 1800." *Medical Repository* 4, no. 2 (1800): 211–12.

Miller, William Snow. "Abraham Chovet: An Early Teacher of Anatomy in Philadelphia." *Anatomical Record* 5 (1911): 147–72.

Mitchell, W. J. T. *The Last Dinosaur Book*. Chicago: University of Chicago Press, 1998.

Mitchill, Samuel Latham. *The Life, Exploits, and Precepts of Tammany; the Famous Indian Chief*. New York: J. Buel, 1795.

Molyneux, Thomas. "Remarks upon aforesaid Letter and Teeth, by Thomas Molyneux, M.D. and R.S.S. Physician to the State in Ireland: Address'd to his Grace the Lord Archbishop of Dublin." *Philosophical Transactions* 29 (1715): 370–84.

Montulé, Édouard de. *Travels in America, 1816–1817*. Bloomington: Indiana University Publications, 1950; orig. Paris, 1821.

Morgan, Edmund. *The Gentle Puritan: A Life of Ezra Stiles, 1727–1795*. New Haven, CT: Yale University Press, 1962.

Morton, Samuel George. *Crania Americana*. Philadelphia: John Pennington, 1839.

Mosse, George. *Toward the Final Solution: A History of European Racism*. Madison: University of Wisconsin Press, 1985.

Nash, Roderick. *Wilderness and the American Mind*. New Haven, CT: Yale University Press, 1967.

Nevile, Francis. "A Letter of Mr. Francis Nevile to the Right Reverend St. George Lord Bishop of Clogher, R.S.S. Giving an Account of some large Teeth lately dugg up in the North of Ireland, and by his Lordship communicated to the Royal-Society." *Philosophical Transactions* 29 (1715): 367–70.

Nicholson, Marjorie Hope. *Mountain Gloom, Mountain Glory: The Development of the Aesthetics of the Infinite*. New York: Norton, 1959.

Norman, David. *Dinosaur!* New York: Prentice-Hall, 1991.

Novak, Barbara. *Nature and Culture: American Landscape Painting, 1825–1875*. New York: Oxford University Press, 1980.

O'Brien, Raymond J. *American Sublime: Landscape and Scenery of the Lower Hudson Valley*. New York: Columbia University Press, 1981.

Oelschlaeger, Max. *The Idea of Wilderness: From Prehistory to the Age of Ecology*. New Haven, CT: Yale University Press, 1991.

Orosz, Joel. J. *Curators and Culture: The Museum Movement in America, 1740–1870*. Tuscaloosa: University of Alabama Press, 1990.

Osborn, Henry Fairfield. *Cope: Master Naturalist*. Princeton, NJ: Princeton University Press, 1931.

———. "Mastodons of the Hudson Highlands." *Natural History* 23 (1923): 3–24.

———. *Proboscidea: A Monograph of the Discovery, Evolution, Migration and Extinction of the Mastodonts and Elephants of the World*. New York: American Museum Press, 1936.

———. "Thomas Jefferson as a Paleontologist." *Science*, December 6, 1935, pp. 533–38.

Osborn, Henry Fairfield, and William King Gregory. "The Dawn Man." *McClure's Magazine* 55 (1923): 19–28.

Ostrom, John H. "Mr. Peale's Missing Mastodon." *Discovery* 17 (1983): 3–9.

Parsons, Samuel H. "Discoveries Made in the Western Country, by General Parsons." *Memoirs of the American Academy of Arts and Sciences* 2, part 1 (1793): 119–27.

Patterson, John S. "Thomas Jefferson's Contributions to Natural History." *Natural History* 19 (1919): 405–10.

Paulin, Charles O., and John K. Wright. *Atlas of the Historical Geography of the United States*. Washington, DC: Carnegie Institution of Washington and American Geographical Society of New York, 1932.

Peale, Rembrandt. *Account of the Skeleton of the Mammoth, a Non-Descript Carnivorous Animal of Immense Size, Found in America*. London: E. Lawrence, 1802.

———. *Disquisition on the Mammoth, or, Great American Incognitum, an Extinct, Immense, Carnivorous Animal whose Fossil Remains have been found in North America*. New York: Arno Press, 1974; orig. London, 1803.

———. "On the Differences which exist between the Heads of the Mammoth and Elephant." *Philosophical Magazine* 14 (1803): 228–29.

———. "A Short Account of the Behemoth or Mammoth." Broadside. New York, April 1802. American Philosophical Society.

Peale, Rembrandt. "A Short Account of the Mammoth." *Philosophical Magazine* 14 (1803): 162–69.

Pearce, Roy Harvey. *Savagism and Civilization*. Berkeley and Los Angeles: University of California Press, 1988.

Pennant, Thomas. *A Synopsis of Quadrupeds*. Chester: J. Monk, 1771.

Peterson, Merrill D. *Thomas Jefferson: A Reference Biography*. New York: Scribner, 1986.

Popkin, Richard. "The Philosophical Bases of Modern Racism." In *Philosophy and the Civilizing Arts*, ed. Craig Walton and J. P. Anton. Athens: Ohio University Press, 1974.

Porter, Charlotte M. *The Eagle's Nest: Natural History and American Ideas, 1812–1842*. Tuscaloosa: University of Alabama Press, 1986.

Pownall, Thomas. *A Topographical Description of the Dominions of the United States of America*. Pittsburgh: University of Pittsburgh Press, 1949. Reprint of 1784 ed.

Randall, Willard Sterne. *Thomas Jefferson: A Life*. New York: Henry Holt, 1993.

Regis, Pamela. *Describing Early America: Bartram, Jefferson, Crèvecoeur, and the Rhetoric of Natural History*. De Kalb: Northern Illinois University Press, 1992.

Rice, Howard C. Jr. "Jefferson's Gift of Fossils to the Museum of Natural History in Paris." *Proceedings of the American Philosophical Society* 95 (1951): 599–610.

———. *Thomas Jefferson's Paris*. Princeton, NJ: Princeton University Press, 1976.

Richardson, Edgar P., Brooke Hindle, and Lillian B. Miller. *Charles Willson Peale and His World*. New York: Harry N. Abrams, 1983.

Rigal, Laura. "Peale's Mammoth." In *American Iconology*, ed. David C. Miller. New Haven, CT: Yale University Press, 1993.

Rittenhouse, David. "Some Observations on the Structure of the Surface of the Earth in Pennsylvania and the Adjoining Countries." *Columbian Magazine* 1 (October 1786): 49–53.

Roger, Jacques. *Buffon: A Life in Natural History*. Ithaca, NY: Cornell University Press, 1997.

Rolfe, W. D. Ian. "William and John Hunter: Breaking the Great Chain of Being." In *William Hunter and the Eighteenth-Century Medical World*, ed. W. F. Bynum and Roy Porter. Cambridge: Cambridge University Press, 1985.

———. "William Hunter (1718–1783) on the Irish 'Elk' and Stubbs's Moose." *Archives of Natural History* 11 (1983): 263–90.

Rudwick, Martin J. S., ed. "Encounters with Adam, or at Least the Hyenas: Nineteenth-Century Visual Representations of the Deep Past." In *His-*

tory, *Humanity and Evolution*, ed. James R. Moore. Cambridge: Cambridge University Press, 1989.

———. *Georges Cuvier, Fossil Bones, and Geological Catastrophes*. Chicago: University of Chicago Press, 1997.

———. *The Meaning of Fossils: Epistles in the History of Paleontology*. New York: Science History Publications, 1976.

———. *Scenes from Deep Time: Early Pictorial Representations of the Prehistoric World*. Chicago: University of Chicago Press, 1992.

———. "The Shape and Meaning of Earth History." In *God and Nature*, ed. David C. Lindberg and Ronald L. Numbers. Berkeley and Los Angeles: University of California Press, 1986.

Ruland, Richard, and Malcolm Bradbury. *From Puritanism to Postmodernism*. New York: Penguin Books, 1991.

Schoepf, Johann David. *Travels in the Confederation (1783–1784)*. New York: Bergman, 1968.

Sellers, Charles Coleman. *Charles Willson Peale*. New York: Scribner, 1969.

———. *Mr. Peale's Museum*. New York: Norton, 1980.

Semonin, Paul. "Citizens and Strangers: The American Museum before Barnum." Ph.D. diss., University of Oregon. 1994.

———. "Empire and Extinction: The Dinosaur As a Metaphor for Dominance in Prehistoric Nature." *Leonardo* 30 (1997): 171–82.

———. "Monsters in the Marketplace: The Exhibition of Human Oddities in Early Modern England." In *Freakery: Cultural Spectacles of the Extraordinary Body*, ed. Rosemarie Garland Thomson. New York: New York University Press, 1996.

———. "'Nature's Nation': Natural History as Nationalism in the New Republic." *Northwest Review* 30 (1992): 6–41.

Sifton, Paul Ginsberg. "Pierre Eugène Du Simitière (1737–1784): Collector in Revolutionary America." Ph.D. diss., University of Pennsylvania, 1960.

Silverberg, Robert. *Mammoths, Mastodons and Man*. New York: McGraw-Hill, 1970.

———. *Scientists and Scoundrels*. New York: Crowell, 1965.

Silverman, Kenneth. *The Life and Times of Cotton Mather*. New York: Harper & Row, 1984.

Simmons, William S. *Spirit of the New England Tribes*. Hanover, NH: University Press of New England, 1986.

Simpson, George Gaylord. "The Beginnings of Vertebrate Paleontology in North America." *Proceedings of the American Philosophical Society* 86 (1942): 130–88.

———. "The Discovery of Fossil Vertebrates in North America." *Journal of Paleontology* 17 (1943): 26–38.

Simpson, George Gaylord, and H. Tobien. "The Rediscovery of Peale's

Mastodon." *Proceedings of the American Philosophical Association* 98 (1954): 279–81.

Sloane, Sir Hans. "An Account of Elephants Teeth and Bones Found Under Ground." *Philosophical Transactions* 35 (1727–28): 457–71.

———. "Of Fossil Teeth and Bones of Elephants, Part the Second." *Philosophical Transactions* 35 (1727–28): 497–514.

Slotkin, Richard. *Regeneration through Violence: The Mythology of the American Frontier, 1600–1860*. Middletown, CT: Wesleyan University Press, 1973.

Sluder, Lawrence Lan. "God in the Background: Edward Taylor As Naturalist." *Early American Literature* 7 (1973): 265–71.

Smallwood, William Martin, and Mabel Sarah Coon Smallwood. *Natural History and the American Mind*. New York: Columbia University Press, 1941.

Smith, Margaret Bayard. *The First Forty Years of Washington Society*. New York: Scribner, 1906.

Somner, William. *The Antiquities of Canterbury*. Wakefield, England: E. P. Publishing, 1977; orig. London: R. Knaplock, 1703.

Stanford, Donald E. "The Giant Bones of Claverack, New York, 1705, Described by the Colonial Poet, Reverend Edward Taylor (ca. 1642–1729) in a Manuscript Owned by Yale University Library." *New York History* 40 (1959): 47–61.

Stein, Roger. "Charles Willson Peale's Expressive Design: The Artist in His Museum." *Prospects* 6 (1981): 139–85.

Stocking, George W. Jr. "French Anthropology in 1800." In *Race, Culture and Evolution*, by George W. Stocking Jr. Chicago: University of Chicago Press, 1982.

Stone, Richard. "Cloning the Wooly Mammoth." *Discover*, April 1999, pp. 56–63.

Stubbs, George. *The Anatomy of the Horse*, ed. Eleanor M. Garvey. New York: Dover, 1976.

Taylor, Basil. "George Stubbs: 'The Lion and Horse Theme.'" *Burlington Magazine* 107 (1965): 81–86.

Thomas, Samuel W., and Eugene H. Conner. "George Rogers Clark (1752–1818): Natural Scientist and Historian." *Filson Club Quarterly* 41 (1967): 202–26.

Thomson, Charles. "Investigations of the Justice of Buffon's Opinions of Man in America." *Columbian Magazine* 2 (March 1788): 135–37.

Thwaites, Reuben Gold, ed. *Early Western Travels, 1748–1846*. Cleveland: Arthur H. Clark, 1904.

Thwaites, Reuben Gold, and Louise Phelps Kellogg, eds. *Documentary History of Dunsmore's War*. Madison: Wisconsin Historical Society, 1905.

Tolmaqchoff, L. P. "The Carcasses of the Mammoth and the Rhinoceros Found in the Frozen Ground of Siberia." *Transactions of the American Philosophical Society* 23, part 1 (1929): 5–74.

Tooley, R. V., and Charles Bricker. *Landmarks of Mapmaking*. New York: Crowell, 1976.

Tuchman, Barbara W. *Practicing History: Selected Essays*. New York: Ballantine Books, 1982.

Tucker, Louis Lenoard. "'Ohio Show-Shop': The Western Museum of Cincinnati, 1820–1867." In *A Cabinet of Curiosities*, ed. Whitfield J. Bell Jr. et al. Charlottesville: University Press of Virginia, 1967.

Turner, George. "Memoir on the extravenous fossils denominated mammoth bones; principally designed to show that they are the remains of more than one species of non-descript animal." *Transactions of the American Philosophical Society* 4 (1799): 510–18.

Tuveson, Ernest Lee. *The Redeemer Nation: The Idea of America's Millennial Role*. Chicago: University of Chicago Press, 1968.

Van Riper, A. Bowdoin. *Men among the Mammoths: Victorian Science and the Discovery of Human Prehistory*. Chicago: University of Chicago Press, 1993.

Vartanian, Pershing. "Cotton Mather and the Puritan Transition into the Enlightenment." *Early American Literature* 7 (1973): 213–24.

Wade, William. *Panorama of the Hudson River from New York to Albany*. New York: William Wade, 1845.

Wainwright, Nicholas B. *George Croghan: Wilderness Diplomat*. Chapel Hill: University of North Carolina Press, 1959.

Walton, John. *John Filson of Kentucke*. Lexington: University of Kentucky Press, 1956.

Ward, Peter D. *The Call of Distant Mammoths: Why the Ice Age Mammals Disappeared*. New York: Springer-Verlag, 1997.

Warren, John C. *The Mastodon giganteus of North America*. Boston: J. Wilson, 1852.

Washington, George. *The Diaries of George Washington*, ed. Donald Jackson. 5 vols. Charlottesville: University Press of Virginia, 1987.

———. *The Journal of Major George Washington*. London: T. Jeffreys, 1754.

Weber, Friedrich Christian, ed. *The Present State of Russia*. London: W. Taylor, 1722–23.

Weeks, Lyman Horace, and Edwin M. Beacon, eds. *An Historical Digest of the Provincial Press*. Boston: Society for Americana, 1911.

Weld, C. R. *A History of the Royal Society*. London: John W. Parker, 1848.

Wendt, Herbert. *Before the Deluge*. Garden City, NY: Doubleday, 1968.

Willey, Basil. *The Eighteenth Century Background: Studies on the Idea of Nature in the Thought of the Period*. Boston: Beacon Press, 1961; orig. 1940.

Williams, William Carlos. *In the American Grain*. New York: Albert and Charles Boni, 1925.

Winthrop, John. *Winthrop's Journal*, ed. James Kendall Hosmer. New York: Scribner, 1908.

Wistar, Caspar. "A description of the bones deposited by the President [Jefferson] in the museum of the Society." *Transactions of the American Philosophical Society* 4 (1799): 526–31. Reprinted in *Selected Works in Nineteenth-Century North American Paleontology*, ed. Keir B. Sterling. New York: Arno Press, 1974.

Wolf, Bryan J. *Romantic Re-vision: Culture and Consciousness in Nineteenth-Century American Painting and Literature*. Chicago: University of Chicago Press, 1982.

Woodward, John. *An Essay toward a Natural History of the Earth*. London: R. Wilkin, 1695.

Worster, Donald. *Nature's Economy: A History of Ecological Ideas*. Cambridge: Cambridge University Press, 1977.

Index

dinosaurs *(continued)*
species, 393–94, 407–8; *Tyrannosaurus rex* and, 393, 404–5, 410–11
Dinwiddie, Gov. Robert, 94–96
Disquisition on the Mammoth. See Peale, Rembrandt
"Doctrine of Monsters," 62; Molyneux's rejection of, 65–66; rebirth of, 187, 212; Sloane's refutation of, 76–78; Stiles and, 207–8, 210, 212
Douglas, James: surveying in Ohio valley, 167–68
Ducoyne, Jean Baptiste: George Rogers Clark and, 280
Dudley, Gov. Joseph: Claverack bones and, 25–27
Dunmore, John Murray, Earl of: 166–67
Du Simitière, Pierre Eugène, 173; American *incognitum* and, 174, 187–90; American Revolution and, 173–74; Rev. Annan's bones and, 187–89; Continental Congress and, 173–74, 187; Jefferson and, 192, 194; Missouri bones and, 194; portrait of Washington, 174

Eager, Samuel: Warren mastodon and, 391
ecological crisis: wild nature and, 409
"Elephant, The,": broadside for exhibit of, 296–97
Ellicott, Andrew: and giant tooth at Tioga, 268
Elson, Ruth: on American schoolbooks, 365, 402
Emerson, Ralph Waldo: on Mexican-American War, 387
Emmons, Ebenezer: Warren mastodon and, 386–87
empire, American, 3, 13, 358–59; Sam Adams vision of, 170–71; Brackenridge and, 171; Continental Congress and, 170–71; Jefferson and, 179–80; Ramsay's evangelical view of, 265
Enlightenment, American: Mather and, 38; religious beliefs and, 12, 38
Époques de la Nature. See Buffon, George Louis Leclerc de
Eustache de Seve, Jacques: engravings of, 132–33
Evans, Lewis: "Map of the Middle British Colonies," 97

evolution: Cuvier opposes idea of, 368–69; Charles Darwin and, 231; Erasmus Darwin and, 258; Lamarck's theory of, 300; Lyell's opposition to, 374; Owen's opposition to, 384
Ewing, Samuel: on Peale's mammoth, 330
Exhumation of the Mastodon (Peale), 357–61, Bacon and, 360–61; Jeffersonian ideals and, 359–60; neoclassical aesthetics of, 357–58; Osborn's view of, 357; as Romantic landscape, 358–59; violation of nature and, 359
extermination: of American Indians, 409; of inferior races, 393
extinction, 3, 8, 14; American Indians and, 264, 365; of African-Americans, 390; Annan on, 209–10; Bartram on, 103–4; Blumenbach on, 365; Buffon's views of, 112, 126, 128–30; craniology and, 365–66; Cuvier's extinct species, 320; Daubenton rejects, 129–30; God's design and, 364–65; Goldsmith's resistance to, 160; Hooke's speculation about, 45; Dr. Hunter and, 152; of *incognitum*, 52, 112, 209–10, 264, 283, 308–10, 365; of inferior races, 393; Irish elk and, 154–55; Jefferson rejects, 182, 230, 304–5; Lyell's view of, 374; opposition to idea of, 32, 41–42, 45–46, 72, 269; in Peale's *Disquisition*, 338–39; savagery of nature and, 392–93; scientific racialism and, 236, 393, 405; Stiles on, 208

facial angle: Camper's theory of, 239–40
Fenton, Jotham, 323, 326
Federalist Papers: on American degeneracy, 263, 274
Federalist Party: and Peale's mammoth, 330
Filson, John, 8, 9, 186, 197–98, 210; Big Bone Lick and, 198–200, Boone story and, 197–98, 201, 284; Burnet's Gothic landscape and, 199, 202–3; death of, 284; *incognitum* as a carnivore, 200; *incognitum* as "tyrant of the forest," 9, 200; map of Kentucky, 198–99; wild nature and, 201; William Hunter and, 199–200, 284
Finley, John: Boone and, 196–97
Finnell, Capt. Benjamin: and bones from Big Bone Lick, 378–79

polygenesis *(continued)*
support of, 388–89; Smith's opposition
to, 245; White's *Gradation in Man* and,
252
Polyphemus: Homeric giant, 32
Pope, Alexander: *De Origine Mali* and, 123;
"Great Chain of Being" and, 115, 136,
158, 305; Jefferson cites, 181, 308
Port Folio, The: Federalist criticism of Jefferson, 353
preformation, theory of: Mather's belief
in, 34
prehistoric nature: discovery of, 4, 14; Darwinian view of, 12; prehistoric monsters
as surrogate rulers in, 362–63; ruling
species in, 393; savagery of, 13–14, 236,
405, 409; scientific racialism and, 405;
violence in, 3–4, 14, 152, 154, 286,
374–75, 377–78, 396, 408–9; as a wilderness, 264, 359
prehuman past: Buffon's conception of, 226;
Cuvier and, 338; John Hunter and, 254;
Hutton's view of, 257; scientific racialism
and, 232; surrogate rulers of, 392–93
Preston, Col. William: views giant tooth,
192
Prime, Dr. A. J.: "Warren Mastodon" and,
386–87
Proctor, Thomas, 342
progress, idea of: Lord Kames and, 245; millenarianism and, 60–61; from savagery to
civilization, 57, 61, 170–71, 410
Puritanism, 3; American nationalism and,
24, 37; and Claverack bones, 21–24, 39;
Filson's Boone myth and, 201; frontier
and, 24; natural history and, 27–28,
38–39

Queen Anne, 26, 35, 39, 41; Lord Cornbury and, 17; resurgence of Anglicanism
under, 29; Royal Society and, 16

Ramsay, Dr. David: on Buffon's theory of
degeneracy, 224; evangelism and empire,
265; Jefferson's *Notes* and, 224
Ramsay, Nathaniel: founding of Peale's
Museum and, 195, 282; views bones of
incognitum, 195
rattlesnake: and bones of the *incognitum*,
269–71

Ray, John: doctrine of plenitude and,
41–42; *The Wisdom of God Manifested in
the Works of Creation*, 28
Raynal, Abbé: American degeneracy and,
171; Franklin's rebuke of, 221
Rennell, Major James: and John Hunter's
geology, 254
reproduction: Buffon's emphasis upon,
118–19; Mather's view of, 34. *See also*
preformation, theory of
Republicanism: American empire and,
170–71; natural history and messianic
purpose in, 265; rejection of Indian antiquity, 171
Restoration of William and Mary: Burnet
and, 48; Puritan society and, 39; religious
revival and, 26, 28, 39, 52
Revolutionary War. *See* American Revolution
Reynolds, Joshua: portrait of John Hunter,
250–51; Dr. William Hunter and, 146,
153
Richardson, Joseph: *The American Reader*
on extinction, 365
Rigal, Laura: analysis of Peale's *Exhumation*,
359–60
Rittenhouse, David: criticism of Jefferson,
267–68; discovery of giant tooth at
Tioga, 268; on fossils, 267; geological
view of landscape, 266–67
Rochambeau, Count de: Washington
meets, 175
Roman ruins, 4, 12; Burnet's use of
metaphor, 49, 52; elephants in England,
44,65
Romanticism, 9, 13, 442; Buffon and,
132–33; Burnet's *Sacred Theory* and, 49,
204; Carey's *American Museum* and, 286;
Filson's *Kentucke* and, 197, 201–4, 286;
English novels and, 285; French Revolution and, 298; Gothic view of landscape
and, 42, 286; in Jefferson's *Notes*, 203–4;
Jefferson's view of Natural Bridge and,
273–74, 372; landscape of fear, 298; scientific racialism and, 388; Shawnee legend and, 286; violence in nature and,
360
Ross, David: Big Bone Lick and, 348–49
Royal Society (London): Bacon's natural
philosophy and, 27–28; Collinson and,

Tyrannosaurus rex: Knight's images of, 405; as minority species, 411; J. P. Morgan and, 404; paradigm of dominance and, 404, 407; symbolism of, 393, 404, 410

unicorns: European belief in, 74; Guericke's fossil skeleton and, 74–75; Leibniz's drawing of, 74–75; Siberian mammoth and, 74; in Sloane's "Account of Elephants Teeth," 76; Strahlenberg's drawing and, 73–74
Ussher, Archbishop James: dating of God's creation, 16

Van Bruggen, Peter: giant tooth of Claverack and, 15
Van Rensselaer, Kiliaen, 18–19
Velociraptor: new breed of dinosaurs and, 407
violence in nature: Buffon's natural history and, 112, 116, 121–23; Bruckner's view of, 156–57; English prelates acceptance of, 123–24; Filson's *Kentucke* and, 201–2; Goldsmith's view of, 159; Lyell's *Principles of Geology* and, 374–75; Stubbs's images of, 259–61, 286; wilderness and, 358–59, 392. *See also* warring species
vis plastica: Aristotle's theory of, 31, 32
Voltaire: polygenesis and, 242
"vulcanism," 44

Wadsworth, Rev. Benjamin, 19
Walker, Thomas: Jefferson's rebuttal of Buffon and, 194–95
Waller, Richard: Mather's *Curiosa americana* and, 35; *Posthumous Works of Robert Hooke* and, 44; Royal Society and, 35, 44
Ward, Peter: extinction of Ice Age mammals, 408; paradigm of dominance and, 408
Warren, Dr. John Collins: acquires mastodon skeleton, 386–87; on disappearance of Peale's mastodon, 403; *The Mastodon Giganteus of North America,* 403; J. P. Morgan and "Warren Mastodon," 404; treatise on craniology, 366
warring species: Bruckner's view of, 156–57; Buffon and, 116, 122–23, 126–27; Carey's Shawnee legend and,

286; Darwin and, 286, 396, 409, 411; English prelates acceptance of, 123–24; extinction and, 236; King's *De origine mali* and, 123–24; as "Law of Nature," 156; Lyell's *Principles of Geology* and, 374–75; in Martin's "The Country of the Iguanodon," 377–78; myth of wild nature and, 396, 409, 378; Stubbs's images of, 259–62, 286; Turner's view of, 310
Washington, George, 2, 6–7, 162; at age twenty-one, 96; Arnold's betrayal, 6, 175; Chastellux visits, 176–77; Continental Army at West Point, 175–76; Croghan and, 164; Dunmore and, 96, 167, 170; Du Simitière's portrait of, 174; gift to Peale's Museum, 292; Gist as guide, 95; journal published in London, 96; land claims in Ohio valley, 167, 170; Ohio grinder and, 165–66, 178; Peale's portrait of, 165; trips to Ohio valley, 94–96, 99, 164–66; views bones at Annan's farm, 6–7, 176–78
Weber, Friedrich Christian: accounts of Dutch travelers to Siberia, 74
Webster, Noah: Carey's *American Museum,* and, 279; Clark's criticism of, 279–80; on Indian mounds, 279–80; letters to Stiles, 279
Webster, Pelatiah: brings Ohio bones to Stiles, 208–9
West, Benjamin, 357; Peale studies with, 281; on physiognomy of Jewish face, 247
Wharton, Samuel: Croghan and, 104
Whiston, William: *New Theory of the Earth,* 25
White, Charles, 250–51; Camper's facial angle and, 252; "Great Chain of Being" and, 250, 252; John Hunter's influence on, 250, 252; polygenesis and, 250, 252–53; *Regular Gradation in Man,* 252–53; skull series, 252–53
white supremacy: craniology and, 234, 236; Jefferson's view of, 217–19; social Darwinism as ally of, 393
wilderness, 3, 9; American nationalism and, 409; Boone and symbolism of, 201–2; Filson's view of, 201–2; as master metaphor, 392; mastodon and, 358; prehistoric nature as, 264, 359; Puritans and, 24, 39; as source of American

About the Author

PAUL SEMONIN worked professionally as a graphic artist for fifteen years before receiving his Ph.D. in history from the University of Oregon. His articles on natural history culture have appeared in *Leonardo* and the *Northwest Review*. He lives in Eugene, Oregon, and occasionally teaches history at nearby colleges and universities.